For
Earth's
Sake

The Commission on Developing Countries and Global Change

Anil Agarwal *(India)*

Julia Carabias *(Mexico)*

Martin Khor Kok Peng *(Malaysia)*

Adolfo Mascarenhas *(Tanzania)*

Thandika Mkandawire *(Senegal)*

Alvaro Soto *(Colombia)*

Erna Witoelar *(Indonesia)*

Executive Secretary:
Alvaro Soto *(Colombia)*

For Earth's Sake

A Report from the Commission on
Developing Countries and
Global Change

INTERNATIONAL DEVELOPMENT RESEARCH CENTRE
Ottawa • Cairo • Dakar • Montevideo • Nairobi • New Delhi • Singapore

Commission on Developing Countries and Global Change XZ

For Earth's sake : a report from the Commission on Developing Countries and Global Change. Ottawa, Ont., IDRC, 1992. vii + 145 p.

/Sustainable development/, /environment/, /environmental degradation/, /responsibility/, /social research/, /developing countries/ — /social implications/, /research needs/, /research capacity/, /technological dependence/, /development potential/, /international cooperation/, /trends/, /national level/.

UDC: 364.464   ISBN: 0-88936-622-5

Contents

List of Boxes

Foreword

The decision to support and fund the Commission on Developing Countries and Global Change originated from a proposal developed in a series of meetings at the International Development Research Centre (IDRC) in Ottawa, Canada. The meetings had been convened to consider options for supporting developing countries in the Human Dimensions of Global Change Programme. Both this Programme and the International Geosphere Biosphere Programme (IGBP) were conceived in recognition of the implications of global warming and other environmental problems and of the need to study those problems and related responses on a global scale.

The initial efforts in IGBP made it largely a First and Second World "show." Little or no attention was given to the Third World. In the social studies, such an omission is totally unacceptable. Social sciences are inherently value-laden; both objectives and methods of research can vary widely among different cultures and societies. Fortunately, it has become increasingly recognized that Third World social scientists must not only participate in the growing volume of work related to global change but must also play a significant role in determining what that work should be.

The establishment of the Commission on Developing Countries and Global Change, with support from IDRC and the Swedish Agency for Research Cooperation with Developing Countries (SAREC), was based on three key propositions:

- Global environmental problems have potentially catastrophic implications for many developing countries;
- Support for the participation by developing countries in dealing with these problems is lagging behind recognition of the need for their participation; and
- The biggest gap in both understanding and participation, and thus the greatest need for research support, lies in the field of applied (both policy- and program-related) social sciences.

The work of the Commission was to emphasize social studies; however, by no means are all of the Commissioners strictly social scientists. Neither social nor natural sciences have a monopoly on wisdom, and the Commissioners have brought to this book an interesting balance between the two cultures. The Commission, as well as IDRC and SAREC, recognizes that it is essential to

1

invoke both the social and natural sciences and, while recognizing their profound differences, to help bring them together in a collaborative way.

The first meeting of the Commission took place on Earth Day 1991. This overlap was coincidental; however, it could be regarded as symbolic in at least two ways. First, the work of the Commission of course involves the issue that is implicit in Earth Day: the environmental well-being of our planet. Second, and less evident, is the fact that Earth Day is a Northern idea, a Northern product, that is being exported to the rest of the world — not to imply that Earth Day is inappropriate; however, it must also be viewed from an alternative Southern perspective.

This book offers such a perspective and proposes a uniquely Southern agenda for research into global environmental change. It rejects the idea that we can resolve our ecological problems by simple adjustments of the economic system — or, as an economist would say, "internalizing the externalities." Rather, it asserts that sustainable development requires more fundamental changes. The authors have dared to envision a different future. Even more importantly, they have proposed ways to reach this future that can simultaneously satisfy the demands of equity, economy, and ecology.

We congratulate the Commissioners: this report will both focus and stimulate debate on strategies and priorities for mitigating the effects of global change. Around the issues of environment and development, free and open communication between scientists and policymakers is essential. Both IDRC and SAREC look forward to, and will continue to participate in and stimulate, such dialogue, for the sake of the Earth.

Keith Bezanson   **Anders Wijkman**

President   *Director General*
IDRC   *SAREC*

Acknowledgments

The Commission on Developing Countries and Global Change was established with the support of IDRC and SAREC and is composed of seven social scientists and practioners representing Central and South America, East and West Africa, and South and Southeast Asia:

- Anil Agarwal *(India)*,
- Julia Carabias *(Mexico)*,
- Martin Khor Kok Peng *(Malaysia)*,
- Adolfo Mascarenhas *(Tanzania)*,
- Thandika Mkandawire *(Senegal)*,
- Alvaro Soto *(Colombia)*, and
- Erna Witoelar *(Indonesia)*.

Coordination and intellectual support for the Commission was provided by a Secretariat located at, and generously supported by, the Royal Society of Canada in Ottawa, Canada. The Secretariat was headed by Alvaro Soto, as Executive Secretary to the Commission.

Rebecca Aird synthesized the written input and discussions of the Commissioners, and prepared the initial and final drafts of the report. To her, the Commission, and its sponsors, extend their deepest thanks.

The Commission worked together for almost a full year. It met for the first time in Ottawa, Canada, and subsequently in New Delhi, India, and Jakarta, Indonesia. The report is also the result of a wider consultative process carried out by the Commissioners in their respective regions. As such, it reflects the wide range of disciplines and viewpoints among social and natural scientists of the Third World.

The following participants attended the meeting on *Global Environmental Change: An Agenda for South Asian Social Scientists,* organized by the Centre for Science and Environment, New Delhi, India: from Bangladesh, Azizul Hoq Bhuiya; from India, Praful Bidwai, B.K. Roy Burman, Kamla Chowdhry, Ramchandra Guha, Sumit Guha, N.S. Jodha, Kailash Malhotra, Kuldip Mathur, Sudipto Mundle, Rajni Pairiwala, V.R. Panchmukhi, Vijay Pande, Jyoti Parikh, Shereen Ratnagar, Kalpana Sharma, Kumud Sharma, Chhatrapati Singh, K.S. Singh, and A. Vaidyanathan; from Nepal, Deepak Bajracharya, Girish Chandra Regmi, and Jyoti Tuladhar; and from Pakistan, Pervaiz Hasan and Arif Hassan.

Held in Mexico City, and encompassing the region of Central America and the Caribbean, the *Taller Mexico, Centroamerica y el Caribe, Cambios Ambientales Globales, Elementos para la Elaboración de una Agenda de Investigación para las Ciencias Sociales* was attended by the following participants: from Costa Rica, Pascal O. Girot; from the Dominican Republic, Victor Hugo de Lancer; from Mexico, Lourdes Arizpe, Raul Garcia Barrios, Ana Iramis Batis, Rolando Garcia, Carlos Johnson, Omar Massera, Estela Martinez, Betsabe Miramontes, Maria de Jesus Ordoñez, Enrique Provencio, Gabriel Quadri, Fernando Tudela, and Araceli Vargas; from Panama, Salvador Arias Peñate; and from Puerto Rico, Ariel Lugo. The organizers of this workshop and the Commissioners extend special recognition to Enrique Provencio for his contribution to the discussion and elaboration of the written material.

In South America, the *Consulting Meeting of the Commission on Developing Countries and Global Change* was held in Montevideo, Uruguay, with the participation of Jorge F. Sábato (Argentina), Julián M. Chacel (Brazil), Joaquin Vial (Chile), Maria Clara Rueda (Colombia), Rodolfo Rendón B. (Ecuador), Efrain Gonzáles de Olarte (Peru), Roberto Bissio (Uruguay), Roberto Fernández (Uruguay), and Edi W. Juri (Uruguay).

Extensive consultation took place in Indonesia. The following people provided their expertise: Mr Alfian (Jakarta Selatan), Alwi Dahlan (Jakarta Pusat), Daniel Dhakidae (Jakarta Selatan), Ismid Hadad (Jakarta Selatan), Mr Kismadi (Jakarta Pusat), Emil Salim (Jakarta Pusat), Adi Sasono (Jakarta Selatan), and V.T. Palan (London, UK). The following people acted as coresearchers and provided resource and secretarial support: Risa Bhinekawati (Jakarta), Claudia D'Andrea (Jakarta Selatan), Agus Purnomo (Jakarta), Retno Soetarjono (Jakarta Pusat), Ch'ng Kim See (Singapore), and Prof. Kernial Sandhu (Singapore). In addition, a questionnaire was sent to eminent environmentalists and scientists throughout Southeast Asia. For this, the Indonesian group would like to thank Mr Emil Salim and Prof. Kernial Sandhu.

Prof. Salau, a Nigerian scholar and coordinator of the CODESRIA (Council for the Development of Economic and Social Research in Africa) network on the environment, prepared an annotated bibliography of key environmental literature from Anglophone West African countries. For this, the Commission is grateful.

The Secretariat to the Commission was supported by Celina and Ian Campbell, who prepared an extensive annotated bibliography; Jane Halpin and Paula Hurtubise, who prepared a report on the global commons *(The Question of the Global Commons);* and Lissa Bjerkelund, who provided coordination and editorial support.

Finally, the Commission must acknowledge the contribution of the Human Dimensions of Global Change Programme. The reports from the two Programme workshops, held in Caracas, Venezuela, in 1989, and Dakar, Senegal, in 1990, and organized by the International Federation of Institutes for Advanced Study, greatly contributed to the discussions of the Commission.

Introduction

The work of the Commission on Developing Countries and Global Change was based on the acceptance by the Commissioners and the sponsoring organizations (IDRC and SAREC) of three key propositions:

1. Global environmental problems have potentially catastrophic implications for many developing countries;

2. Third World perspectives must be integrated into the international agenda on global environmental change; and

3. The social dimensions of these issues must be understood and resolved.

The Commission was to suggest options for increasing the understanding of social dimensions of global change. It was to examine what could be done to enhance the relevance of research on global change in relation to the needs and interests of Third World countries. The particular aims of the Commission were

- To present an alternative Southern perspective on global environmental and social issues;

- To propose elements of a more sustainable and equitable world order;

- To identify the most important social dimensions of environmental change in Third World countries;

- To present a research agenda that will reflect these priority issues;

- To recommend ways that existing research capacity in the Third World can be brought to bear on the problems of global environmental change; and

- To identify ways to strengthen research capacity in relation to these issues.

Broadly, the principal goal of the Commission was to raise the profile of Southern environment/development perspectives and concerns within the research community worldwide.

The intended audience for this book is not limited to social scientists. It is hoped that the work will contribute to an interest in, and commitment to, the social studies among a wide range of researchers and activists in environmental and developmental issues. There is need not only for social science research on environmental issues but also for the integration of social dimensions within environmental research. For this reason, in dealing with questions of research, reference to social scientists is generally avoided. Instead, the discussion focuses on the subject matter — social science research on environment/development issues — and the investigators are referred to as researchers on social issues.

The Process

This report was produced over a 10-month period through an iterative and consensual process of group discussions and debate, synthesis of written input, and collective review. The seven Commissioners met for the first time in Ottawa, Canada, in April of 1991. At this first meeting, the Commission established a preliminary outline of the report and a work plan. The Commissioners then returned to their home regions to consult with other environment/development researchers and decision-makers. Thus, the thinking of each Commissioner was informed by generous contributions from colleagues in each region. Written input from individual Commissioners was then synthesized. At the second meeting — held from 26 October to 8 November 1991 in New Delhi, India — key issues were reviewed and discussed in detail. These issues arose partly from the written material and partly from the spontaneous creativity of open debate. Based on this meeting, a draft report was prepared. The third meeting was held from 11 to 15 January 1992, in Jakarta, Indonesia. At this last meeting of the Commission, the report was finalized.

Central America and the Caribbean

For consultation in Mexico, Central America, and the Caribbean, a 3-day workshop was organized. Workshop participants included researchers from Costa Rica, the Dominican Republic, Mexico, Panama, and Puerto Rico. Many of the participants had also worked in other Central American countries, including El Salvador and Guatemala. The participants were organized into three working groups. The first group discussed global environmental change in general. They worked on understanding the differing perspectives and their effect on problem definition, and defined an analytical framework. The second group worked on a methodology for analyzing environmental problems. The third group identified broad research themes, intending to define those themes that encourage an integrative approach to investigation and understanding.

South America

The South American input evolved from a meeting in Montevideo, Uruguay. Participants included environmental and social researchers from Argentina, Brazil, Chile, Colombia, Ecuador, Peru, and Uruguay, as well as representatives of two key economic and policy institutes in Chile and Colombia.

Africa

The two Commissioners from Africa divided their responsibilities between West Africa, and Eastern and Southern Africa. For West Africa, several existing projects of CODESRIA were sources of relevant input. These included two recent CODESRIA conferences: one on environmental research capacity in Francophone Africa and another on gendering social science research in Africa, in which environment was a specific subtheme. Also used were materials from a conference jointly organized by CODESRIA and the Social Science Research Council in New York: *Whose Knowledge Counts: Relations Between Formal and Informal Institutions and Research Users.* An annotated bibliography on key environmental literature from Anglophone West African countries was commissioned; the CODESRIA document unit did an extensive bibliographic search on environmental issues and activities; and personal interviews were conducted with researchers working on environmental issues.

In Eastern and Southern Africa, insights into the regional problems and opportunities were garnered through personal experience in a variety of organizations and projects. These included an environmental research organization; an international nongovernmental organization (NGO); various research efforts organized by the United Nations Research Institute for Social Development (UNRISD), especially on the social dynamics of deforestation; and an overview for the United Nations Development Programme (UNDP) of NGOs involved in environment and development in Tanzania, Uganda, and Zambia. In addition, regional colleagues from a range of institutions shared information and perspectives, as did officials from various countries.

South Asia

A 1-day workshop on global environmental change was organized with social scientists and activists invited from Bangladesh, India, Nepal, and Pakistan. The seminar dealt with environmental issues cutting across the disciplines of economics, sociology and anthropology, history, women's studies, and political and legal sciences. An extensive annotated bibliography of South Asian social science research was also prepared, and the overall directions of social science research with respect to the environment were analyzed.

Southeast Asia

In Southeast Asia, a combination of general questionnaires (sent to 140 organizations) and in-depth personal interviews were used to solicit input from environmental and developmental NGOs, research institutes, independent researchers, and community workers. The region's two Commissioners and their research assistants participated in many regional workshops on the environment/development theme of the Commission. These workshops primarily involved researchers and community NGO leaders. They were asked to explain the social issues associated with environmental change that they considered most important. The Commissioners also participated in preparatory meetings for UNCED, the United Nations Conference on Environment and Development. These meetings provided an opportunity to gather opinions from a cross-section of Third World participants on global environment/development issues.

Outline of the Report

The Commission's final report, presented in this book, consists of three major parts. Part I provides a Southern perspective on the global environment/development crisis and on the global and national-level causes of this crisis. The elements of an equitable approach to sustainability are proposed, forming the foundation of a research agenda. Part II looks at the roles, problems, and potential of social research in relation to environment/development issues, including challenges specific to the South. Part III presents the research agenda itself, addressing the basic principles to guide environment/development research, the specific research topics, and the institutional and training requirements that would emerge from the identified research needs.

Terminology

North/South

A key language question is how to divide the nations of the world into two categories. The exercise is by definition unreasonable: no two categories could possibly offer an informative or sensitive method of defining such a complex collection. Nonetheless, some such distinction is not only valid but also crucial; this is clear from the history of attempts to make it.

The complex, loaded, and often ambiguous set of differences on which the distinction has historically been based relates in part to material wealth, degree of industrial and technological development, political history, culture, and location! Thus, variously used pairs include rich/poor, developed/developing, industrialized/nonindustrialized, First World/Third World, and North/South. Although far from completely satisfactory, the Commission favours the final two pairs, in particular, North/South. The alternatives are to varying degrees inappropriate, obsolete, or pejorative. For example, the rich/poor distinction does focus on one valid difference; however, because this terminology can neither reflect the nature of inequitable relations between South and North, nor the structural differences between countries, it leaves the impression that these differences are the result of random chance. Moreover, the classification tends to be based strictly on per-capita income, not accounting for other aspects of wealth.

The developed/developing terminology is also unacceptable. This pair implicitly assumes that "development" is strictly a function of income levels and technoindustrial complexity. Surely, considerations such as cultural richness and ethical maturity should rate at least as highly in determining whether a nation is "developed." A focus strictly on the level of industrialization overlooks more critical determinants of quality of life, not to mention the economic, cultural, and environmental implications of industrialization. Moreover, as many countries of the South are now heavily industrialized, categorization based on this factor is no longer relevant. In any case, the complexity of international relations in an increasingly globalized economy, and the development of regional trading blocs, have made obsolete classifications that are based on dependency models and centre–periphery relations.

Despite the fact that the North/South terminology also has its limitations, among which is the fact that some countries with high income levels are situated in the South, it is adequate for our purposes. The perspectives on the causes and consequences of global change presented in this report correspond to that of most countries in the South, and the environmental and developmental conditions of these countries are clearly distinct from those of the North. In addition, the problems of development, in terms of the most critical features, are shared by virtually all countries of the South.

The term Third World is also used in this report. This term developed from the felt need of nonaligned countries to distance themselves from the prevailing division of the world into capitalistic (First World) and socialistic (Second World) blocs. The classification has now lost some of its original context, and it has been some time since the terms have been interpreted on the basis of political nonalignment. Rather, the distinction implies a similar set of characteristics as "developing," but is not as biased.

"Global" Change

The report, in Chapter 1, offers an alternative perspective on the use of "global" as an adjective to qualify environmental issues. However, because of the prevailing connotations it now possesses, we have consciously minimized use of the world "global" in the context of environmental change. The Northern-based division of environmental problems into two categories — global and local — has left the South holding exclusive responsibility for "local" problems. Many in the South believe that this division is artificial; it denies and hides the international dimensions of many so-called local problems.

Environment/Development

Finally, in using the term "environment" we refer to the biophysical environment, including human relationships with, and dependencies on, this environment. Humans, like other species, participate in determining the biophysical environment. Past distinctions between the natural and human environments reflect the conceptual dissociation from nature that has contributed to the current crisis. Many traditional cultures, such as those of the Amazon, see the environment as a lived reality, a habitat, which has to used on a sustainable basis. For the outsider, the Amazon is a "wilderness" that must be exploited or transformed for profit or, at best, conserved in its natural state.

The concept of "development" encompasses a broad set of economic, social, cultural, and political conditions and relations, reflecting human–nature and human–human interactions. Our primary focus in this book is on the dimensions of the development crisis that both shape and reflect the environmental crisis. In addressing this subject, we have used the term "environment/development" crisis.

Perspectives of the Commission

Within the last decade, the linking of environment and development issues, and the acknowledgement of this linkage on the world stage, has been encouraging. At the same time, however, this apparent progress has been undermined by an evolving world order increasingly dominated by market economics. Noneconomic values and moral concerns (in particular, equity and ecology) are seen as extraneous or, at least, too impractical to address. Now, as the world environmental agenda is being developed, the Commission believes that it is essential that the linkage between environment, development, and equity be made fully meaningful. Profound changes are needed in development models, lifestyles, and economic and political relationships. We hope that the analysis and perspectives presented here contribute to this goal.

An enhanced understanding about the particular perspectives and concerns of the South in relation to environmental change is essential. Indeed, Southern thinking must be clearly integrated into the global agenda on environment/development issues — an agenda that is now dominated by the North. Similarly, partly as a function of financial clout, Northern perspectives also dominate the research of both development and the environment. Southern scholars and scientists have not adequately considered their research directions or priorities. Indeed, many in the South are unaware of the degree to which the perspectives and approaches that dominate environment/development research and debate are not of their own making. Research efforts are therefore strongly influenced by a distorted, unilateral image of

Southern problems. Such research has often helped to entrench inaccurate, detrimental stereotypes and has done little to alleviate basic problems such as poverty, lack of democracy, and resource degradation.

The global environmental issues considered in the North to be most pressing are not necessarily priorities for the South. Likewise, Southern environmental priorities, which tend to centre on immediate problems related to basic human needs, are under-represented on the global environmental agenda. Issues such as global warming and the loss of biological diversity have little meaning for people suffering the day-to-day consequences of starvation, malnutrition, or lack of basic health care.

Clearly, there are not only two opposing visions of environment/development issues: South versus North. Rather there are many views within both South and North; indeed, many peoples of the South and North hold similar views. For example, many public interest groups in both the South and the North believe that the inequities, high consumption, and wasteful production systems that benefit a minority of humanity are neither sustainable nor socially justifiable. At the heart of these issues, however, there are clear differences between South and North, and it is crucial that Southern interests be recognized and acknowledged as a basis for understanding and action.

PART I

Reframing the Debate:
A Southern Perspective on the Global
Environmental Crisis

Chapter 1

Understanding the Environment/Development Crisis: Back to Basics

The world today is characterized by unacceptably sharp differences between the poor and the opulent, the hungry and the overfed, the powerful and the powerless. The 20th century saw an unprecedented increase in overall economic output: however, simultaneously, it also saw extreme social and economic human inequality. The world's population has more than tripled since 1900. At the same time, the gross world product has increased 21 times, the consumption of fossil fuels 30 times, and industrial production 50 times. This enormous increase in wealth has not benefited all people equitably. The average income of the richest one billion people is 20 times larger than that of the poorest billion.

Most parts of the Third World are facing a severe economic and social crisis. Notwithstanding the apparent promise of development, throughout the 1980s, the increasing severity of socio-economic conditions was undeniable. Not only did existing development problems continue, but also the poor countries faced declining rates of expansion in production (see Box 1). Asymmetries between the South and the North have become even more pronounced. In some regions and countries, per-capita incomes have declined to the level of 20 or 30 years ago. Poverty, along with its social, environmental, and human implications, has increased.

At the same time, the environment worldwide is in crisis. At local, regional, and global levels, key features and processes of the natural world are being damaged or obliterated. Even though human societies have, since their earliest origins, affected many kinds of environmental transformation in the course of development, nothing compares to the changes that have been wrought in recent decades. Consequent awareness of critical environmental issues — atmospheric change, water pollution, unsustainable exploitation of renewable resources, deforestation, erosion, degraded carrying capacity, loss of biological diversity — has now extended well beyond academic circles into the central arena of public debate.

16

Box 1

Failing Hopes:
Examples of Reduced Growth and Increased Dependency in the South

In sub-Saharan Africa, per-capita income declined by 12 percent from 1980 to 1989. However, this average conceals even greater declines in many countries. In Uganda for instance, per-capita income declined 28 percent; in Niger, 24 percent; and in Zambia, 20 percent. Some of the most adversely affected countries are also among the poorest countries.

In Latin America and the Caribbean, per-capita gross national product (GNP) declined by 9.6 percent from 1981 to 1990. In Central America, the decline in per-capita GNP reached 17.2 percent. In this period, Latin America and the Caribbean sent net transfers of 212 billion United States dollars to creditors. The fact that the payments were to creditors from the First World eloqently expresses a critical dimension of the relationships of deepening dependency. Meanwhile, the number of poor in Latin America increased by 40 million, representing 43 percent of the population in 1986; in 1980, this figure was 41 percent. More integral measurements indicate that by 1990, poverty affected 62 percent of the population of Latin America and the Caribbean.

In many cases, the socioeconomic crisis is the result of development styles that destroy both human potentials and the environment. In fact, the two phenomena — the global environmental crisis and socioeconomic decline in the South — are the result of unsustainable systems of production and consumption in the North, inappropriate development models in the South, and a fundamentally inequitable world order. South–North relations are based on gross overexploitation of, and underpayment for, Southern resources and human labour. The competitive forces that make economic growth a necessity, operating within this imbalanced global political economy, have led to uneven, distorted development and levels of resource and environmental degradation that threaten life and the future of humanity itself. Within many countries of the South, these same kinds of relationships between environmental degradation and extreme poverty hold. In sum, through inappropriate production processes and technologies, the Earth's resources are being exhausted and polluted at an accelerating rate. An ever-increasing volume of goods and services are being produced, the majority of which are channeled toward filling the consumption demands of a minority, leaving the basic human needs of the poorer majority unmet.

From a Third World perspective, the development crisis and the environmental crisis in fact constitute a single social–ecological crisis — the most pressing challenge of our times. If current trends are not reversed, there will be ever scarcer resources to meet the demands of current and future generations of humanity, productive capacities will diminish, and the poverty levels of the peoples of the South will worsen.

An Evolutionary Overview

The state of the biophysical environment and the natural resource base in any particular region is the result of complex interactions between local ecosystems and human activities. The latter is conditioned by economic systems and conditions, social and cultural processes, the political order, legal and administrative systems, and the kinds of technologies in use.

No society's relationship with nature is static. Interactions change over time, and major shifts mark new historical phases. But historically, through an ongoing and gradual process of learning and adjustment, many cultures have adopted modes of self-reproduction and ways of interacting with nature that were sustainable. Over generations, new practices were selected and adopted; those that could not be sustained were abandoned. Such cultures coded the "dos" and "don'ts" into patterns of everyday life, forming a powerful body of indigenous knowledge that was evident in many forms of ecologically sound production in agriculture, fisheries, water management, and other sectors. These indigenous mechanisms were often disrupted by unforeseen natural catastrophes and invasions by foreign cultures. In some cases, populations moved to unfamiliar natural environments, disrupting systems of social organization that had evolved to a particular natural environment. In general, however, lifestyles, values, demographic pressures, and levels of technology were such that environmental burdens were minimized.

It was not until modern-day colonialism that there were ruptures on a global scale to the sociocultural mechanisms behind sustainable livelihoods. Traditional knowledge and resource-management systems were disregarded by the new rulers. The colonial powers wanted to acquire the wealth generated by the careful management of local environments or appropriate the land for production of goods for European markets. They did not, however, understand these environments or the rationale for, and systems of, traditional management (see Box 2).

The natural resources of the colonized territories were exploited and exported as raw materials, while imported products began to flood their markets. The local populations, steadily losing control over their resource base, became increasingly alienated. What were once community-managed commons steadily turned into state resources, whose purpose was mainly to benefit commercial interests.

As a general trend, environmental degradation became widespread with increasingly intense commercialization of the economy. As forests disappeared in parts of Africa and India, for example, firewood became scarce. As the availability of fodder declined, grasslands were severely overstocked and their productivity began to collapse. As erosion increased, once fertile land became wasteland. The scarcity of biomass engendered an acute human crisis. Women suffered the most, as the daily tasks of collecting fodder, wood, and water became more and more onerous. Children, especially girls, were increasingly required to work alongside their mothers to support the family.

In Africa and Asia, where independence was achieved in relatively recent history, a class of peoples educated by the colonizers, and no longer understanding or appreciating traditional ways, became leaders of the nations of the Third World. The result has been a deepening of the Westernization process. In the end, the colonization of the resource base appears easier to reverse than the colonization of the mind.

Similarly, in Latin America, where independence was won earlier than in Africa and Asia, the end of colonialism did not at first involve major changes. Production processes remained much the same as those that existed during the colonial period. The production of raw materials for export continued, with control now concentrated in a new elite who had become owners of the land. However, important changes in modes of production did occur with the agrarian reform — the result of armed revolution in

Box 2

The Economic–Ecological System of Traditional India

Farmers living in India's semi-arid lands, recognizing the risks of settled agriculture in an area with heavy weather fluctuations, traditionally adopted sustainable and risk-minimizing techniques. Indian villagers transformed their environment into a complex ecosystem of croplands, grasslands, and forests — an interactive, multipurpose biological system that responded to the seasonal rhythms of the area and minimized the social and economic impact of rainfall variation. Farmlands produced grains to feed people, and the crop residues fed farm animals; livestock provided not only milk but also manure and draught power; grasslands provided green fodder during the wet season; forests and trees provided firewood and leaf fodder during the dry season. Because the land was parched for most of the year, many water-storage devices were developed across the country. Indians thus became some of the world's greatest water harvesters — when the British landed, there were already hundreds of thousands of water tanks across India.

This system of production was supported by an elaborate arrangement of property rights and religious practices. Not only the cow but also the grazing lands were sacred. Many forests were also set aside as sacred groves, while the ponds themselves and their catchments also had religious significance.

The wealth generated in villages, through self-reliance and careful management of the local natural resource base, supported a range of skilled artisans producing a great variety of renowned and widely traded goods. Major cities sprang up along the Ganges River and elsewhere. Even the desert supported wealthy cities. Thus, before the British came, India was one of the wealthiest and most urbanized countries in the world, nearly totally literate. But the British failed to understand the Indian concept of community property management. As the community lands yielded to the state, the colonizing British disregarded their functions within the local village ecosystems and considered them wastelands. They became state property managed by a bureaucracy; the ensuing process was tantamount to systematic, state-sponsored destruction.

The entire economic–ecological system of India was turned on its head to produce goods for the metropolitan markets in the colonizing nation. Old Indian cities along the Ganges and elsewhere, dependent on the evolved urban–rural links, were pauperized; cities became steadily deurbanized; artisans went bankrupt and were pushed into the countryside; and the incidence of illiteracy, poverty, and famine grew greatly. Even today, most of the old Indian cities remain extremely poor. Within the hierarchy of urban systems, their place of primacy has been usurped by coastal metropolises like Bombay, Calcutta, and Madras, which did not even exist two centuries ago. These cities emerged and prospered as the Indian hinterland and its resources became linked to, and drained by, an external economy. Indian society and environment imploded under this colossal impact.

Mexico — and other agrarian transformations in Latin America. In most countries, national constitutions incorporated the demands of the poorest, and access to land was recovered by indigenous and campesino communities. To a large degree, the traditional knowledge of these communities was again applied. Ultimately, however, the lack of consistency in agrarian policy, the lack of real participation by rural people, and changes in the international order after the Second World War have resulted in the subservience of rural policies to industrialization.

Accordingly, colonial trade patterns — involving export of cheap raw materials and import of industrial products — have dominated the economies of most Southern nations since the Second World War. In addition and throughout this period, multilateral financial, technical, and aid agencies have promoted the replacement of local production practices in the South with technologies that are often environmentally damaging.

Recent decades have seen a further shift of resource control from local communities to centralized, commercial institutions. Community management and discipline in the use of natural resources declined further. Government loans and support have promoted further changes in rural production toward satisfying urban demands. As the monoculture of the Green Revolution began to take over, the genetic diversity on farms declined rapidly. Forests were sacrificed to meet urban and industrial needs. Unplanned and indiscriminate industrialization resulted in the proliferation of slums, pollution, and health hazards. The highly capital- and resource-intensive urbanization systems of the industrial powers, transplanted into impoverished economies, produced further disparities and inequalities. The gulf between the "haves" and "have-nots" widened and, as the "haves" captured increasing quantities of natural resources, environmental destruction wreaked further havoc on the "have-nots." Thus, a dual society has flourished in almost all countries of the South, with the gap between rich and poor growing simultaneously with environmental destruction and the erosion of community rights over the resource base.

In response to the social injustice associated with environmental destruction, protests began to emerge in the Third World during the 1970s and 1980s. These protests — for example, the Chipko Movement (the famous hug-the-tree movement) in the Garhwal Himalaya of India and the Set Setal urban youth movement in Senegal — signal the beginning of a rise in consciousness in the South.

Differing Perspectives on Key Issues

To date, the South has had little influence in defining the key issues in the global environmental debate. As a result, issues of world poverty and inequity have become isolated from, and over-shadowed by, global environmental concerns. Thus, although the environmental crisis has begun to force some changes in produc-tion and consumption, the bearing of these changes on critical socioeconomic and political conditions has been largely inciden-tal and, at times, negative (see Box 3).

A new context is needed for the global environment/develop-ment debate. It must define basic concepts, such as sustainability and the "global" environment, and basic issues, such as burden sharing and population. These questions are explored here. The framework used to develop the research agenda (presented in Part III) takes the alternative perspectives presented here as a point of departure.

Approaching Sustainability: Choosing Priorities

To date, Northern concerns have directed the global environmen-tal debate. These concerns reflect a definition of sustainability in which the physical environment is the primary focus and long-term intergenerational issues are key. Thus, primary moral obliga-tions have to do with maintaining the options and interests of future generations. A critical message from virtually all quarters of the South is that social concerns, economic issues, and intra-generational equity — the very obvious "here and now" dispari-ties in wealth and opportunities — are the keys to resolving the

Box 3

Costs of Dealing with the Costs of Pollution: An Example of Socioeconomic Fallout from Environmental Action

As one example of the often subtle socioeconomic implications of adaptations made to accommodate environmental concerns, to the extent that price adjustments to reflect environmental costs are being made by the North, the unintended effect is to contribute even further to North–South disparities. Because their economic base lies mainly in industrial production, environmental costs of production in many Northern countries are primarily associated with pollution. These costs are being steadily integrated into the price of goods as a result of public policies to control pollution; the costs being determined by the price of the control technologies.

Integrating the costs of land and resource degradation, the forms of degradation more commonly associated with the primary production economy of the South, is a much more complex matter. Firstly, the costs of rectifying these problems are more difficult to determine. Secondly, the prices of many Southern commodities are largely determined by monopolistic, transnational corporations. Thus, the Southern producers are "price-takers" and have to date been unable to collaborate in rationalizing supplies. Many Southern commodities also face stiff competition from substitutes.

The North is increasingly building into the price of its products — including the products it sells to the South — the expenditures it makes to control environmental degradation associated with pollution. However, there is nothing being built into the price of commodities shipped by the South to the North that reflects the associated costs of environmental degradation. Indeed, the terms of trade of several of these commodities have been consistently declining. The need to consider how the treatment of externalities can be equalized in internationally traded goods is but one small example of the kinds of factors that must be introduced to environmental decision-making.

environment/development crisis. Behind this message lies the notion of people-centred development. It is hardly surprising that the South is skeptical of the primacy given to issues such as atmospheric change within the "global" agenda. In the South, even the basic needs of a large proportion of the population are not being met, and economic and environmental priorities are largely ignored.

For example, the Global Environment Fund (GEF), sponsored by UNDP, the United Nations Environment Programme (UNEP), and the World Bank, finances projects that aim to prevent global warming, preserve biodiversity, reduce threats to the ozone layer, and control the pollution of international waters. These issues were selected by donor governments; they do not reflect the most pressing environmental problems of the Southern, recipient countries. Southern priority problems such as desertification and lack of clean drinking water could, for instance, have been included in the GEF. In comparison to funding for GEF projects, UNEP's anti-desertification fund has received almost no financial support, although it was set up in the late 1970s.

Moreover, given the Northern focus on the biophysical dimension of environmental change, analysis is done primarily within the natural sciences, and the topics that dominate the international agenda and dictate funding priorities are constrained by narrowly scientific perspectives. In comparison, key social dimensions of change are given relatively little attention.

Perhaps most disturbing is the sense that neither equity nor the environment itself are the concerns that underlie the recent Northern interest in "sustainable development." Rather, primary concerns continue to lie in sustaining Northern consumption levels and maintaining the conditions necessary for economic growth. Notwithstanding growing skepticism about the adequacy of the "techno-fix" approach, the associated position is that ecological problems can be technologically controlled in a market system, provided only that some adjustments are made to ensure that prices include environmental externalities. Even the depletion of natural resources is not viewed as a fundamental problem — it is assumed that new technologies will allow for continuous substitution. (Although there are fears that the growing Southern population and its increasing resource demands will mean less for the North and for future generations.)

In contrast, the environmental priorities of the South are underpinned by grim and undeniable human realities. In many countries of the South, environmental issues are issues of life and death. And, conversely, where poverty is widespread, lack of development may be a greater barrier to a reasonable quality of life than would the environmental impacts associated with current forms of development.

It is critical to any meaningful approach to "sustainable develop-ment" that environmental issues be integrated with issues of equity, social justice, human rights, and development. Fundamentally, the main cause of the environment/development crisis is unsustainable forms and levels of production and con-sumption in the North and their export to the South. It follows that, to resolve the crisis, more than technological approaches are required. Unsustainable output and expenditure levels in the North must be reduced, and socially and environmentally inappropriate development systems in the South must be reformed. A more equitable international order must therefore accompany the shift to more ecological and equitable national development. At the same time, constant attention must be given to the development implications of environmental decisions.

The Nature of "Global"

Selective and sectoral environmental issues now dominate the international environmental debate. It is clear that many players in this debate do not give "global" status to critical environmental problems that represent massive impediments to national and regional development and environmental quality in the South. These players, including many Northern governments, wish to separate out from the global agenda those environmental prob-lems that manifest themselves locally and regionally, thus limiting responsibility for these problems to the national level. As a result, the current international agenda sidesteps the systemic interna-tional causes of environmental degradation. There is an apparent desire, at least at the official level, to avoid any serious discussion of the restructuring of international economic relations. The ethic of caring and sharing is far from prominent in the arena of inter-national environmental debate.

Concretely, key Northern concerns focus primarily on long-term impacts involving selected, planetary-level, geophysical variables (ozone depletion, climate change). In the South, the most imme-diate and pressing environmental problems relate to the depletion and degradation of the biomass base, on which the majority of the population continues to be directly dependent. Indeed, as a large proportion of industrial output from the South is biomass based, economic activity in all sectors is threatened. An additional priority is the pollution, contamination, and resulting health impacts associated with inadequately controlled industrial development and misapplications of chemical technologies.

The land, resource, and health issues that preoccupy the South are as global in nature as those espoused by the North. The South's priorities must be reflected in the international agenda as global issues. The roots of many ecological problems, regardless of the scale at which they manifest themselves, can be traced not only to local and national factors but also to the global system within which nations operate. Thus, the definition of "global" in the context of environmental problems must include the following elements:

- Problems that are geographically widespread in effect;

- Problems whose causes may be local or national, but whose effects are transboundary;

- Problems that are local or national in scale, but recur within many regions; and

- Problems that reflect international economic and political dynamics (for instance, policies and practices of international agencies and transnational corporations).

Defining the Global Commons

The North tends to frame many of its environmental concerns within the context of the "global commons." Until recently, the concept of global commons has been primarily reserved for those regions or resources over which no individual or state ownership could be claimed: in particular, the atmosphere, the open oceans, Antarctica, and outer space. In the absence of such ownership, the overuse and abuse of the area or resource is deemed to be inevitable (see Box 4). Indeed, these global commons all currently suffer to varying degrees the negative effects of exploitation, pollution, and mismanagement by various nations, and all have been the subject of proposed treaties or international agreements for cooperative management. In some cases, treaties have been set forth to allocate ownership and distribution of resources.

Now, however, other environmental regions and features are being increasingly perceived as global resources, even though ownership, or at least potential control over ownership, is vested in particular nation states. Regions that are, in some quarters, being newly proclaimed as global commons include tropical rain

---

Box 4

The Commons: Collective Ownership or "No-Man's-Land"?

In Western tradition, "the commons" are areas or resources for which no formal and exclusive ownership exists. An alternative perspective, common to many indigenous societies worldwide, is to view the commons as subject to a form of collective ownership, in which members of the collective share both benefits and responsibilities. In other words, the commons are managed through equality in access and community discipline. The implications of this latter approach are very different from the "overuse and abuse" implications of the Western commons. Many forms of traditional collective land ownership — for example, the *bona* of Iran, the *zanjera* of the Philippines, the *acadia* of West Africa, and the common pastures of England — are managed and maintained to the good of the entire community and future generations. Social traditions, rather than legal arrangements, are usually key to communal maintenance of the quality and carrying capacity of the land. Given the prevailing balance of political and economic power, the danger is that the Western perception of common property will largely determine current debate on management of the global commons.

---

forests. Their status as a global resource is supported by claims to the effect that they are "the lungs of the world" and repositories of a significant proportion of the planet's biological richness.

Indeed, many of the planet's richest sources of biodiversity are found in some of the world's poorest nations. Given current rates of species extinction, there is increasing pressure from the North (most particularly, agribusiness and pharmaceutical interests) to have Third World genetic resources designated a universal heritage — a sort of nonterritorial global commons. Ironically, the loss of biodiversity in many of these areas has often come at the hands of technologies (such as the Green Revolution) and forms of exploitation promoted by the North, at the expense of indigenous practices that helped sustain genetic diversity.

We cannot deny the local and global importance of biodiversity. However, efforts to extend the concept of global commons to nationally based resources are a threat to Southern sovereignty over Southern resources and, consequently, to the rights of the Third World to benefit economically from endemic resources.

Given that Northern countries are unlikely to consider their natural resources in this light, the message from the North reads "What's mine is mine, and what's yours is ours."

Burden Sharing

Although the economic debt of the Third World has received abundant attention, the environmental debt of the North has been greatly underplayed. Conversely, the substantial contributions of many peoples of the Third World, and of the poor in general, in conserving their environment are seldom acknowledged in the international arena. For example, the work of north Indian and Nepalese farmers in terracing mountains to conserve soil is an enormous labour investment in environmental sustainability that has rarely been acknowledged.

The North bears primary responsibility for many of the problems currently on the agenda of the global environmental debate. It is the South, however, that is likely to experience greater hardships as a result of these problems (see Box 5). Moreover, just as poor countries have borne the brunt of the global economic crisis, the perception is that sacrifices believed to be necessary in the pursuit of sustainable development will also fall unfairly on the poor countries. There is a fear that development efforts will be made more costly by environmental measures imposed by international regulations. Indeed, current perceptions about the causes of, and solutions to, environmental degradation may, intentionally or not, foster international actions and decisions whose effect is to arrest development in the South. This would lead to a hardening of current global inequalities. As well, in addition to the fact that many resources taken from Third World countries are given little economic value, many natural resources (in particular, genetic resources) taken from the South are altered and sold back to Third World countries at high prices.

The issue of how the burden of adjustment will be distributed is critical to any meaningful global environmental negotiations. Elements of an approach to addressing this issue are proposed in Chapter 3. But, for now, it is important to recognize that international environmental conventions already adopted or currently being considered have significant economic and political implications for countries of the Third World. While the South would like to fully participate in global environmental

Box 5

Atmospheric Change:
Distribution of Responsibilities and Burdens

One global manifestation of the environmental crisis is the so-called greenhouse effect: alterations in the thermal balance through increasing concentrations of gases (such as carbon dioxide and methane) that trap radiation close to the earth's surface. This phenomenon is related primarily to the increased combustion of fossil fuels and biomass, and the massive loss of the earth's cover, which absorbs carbon dioxide, as well as some agricultural and animal breeding activities. It is conservatively estimated that by the middle of the next century the planet will experience increases of between 1.5 and 2.8 Celsius degrees, resulting in the highest temperatures in 120 000 years.

Through rising sea levels, global warming will result in the flooding of low-lying coastal areas. Thus, coastal populations will be affected. Changes in the monsoon winds are likely to bring floods in some cases and drought in others. In general, altered water cycles are likely to significantly affect agricultural patterns and potentials. Changes in sea currents are likely to result in damaging weather patterns such as cyclones.

All countries of the world do not contribute equally to the anthropogenic emission of greenhouse gases into the atmosphere; many countries of the industrialized North are among the largest contributors. The human repercussions associated with climate change will also vary considerably between different regions, but the distribution of these impacts bears no cause–effect relation to relative responsibility for global warming. Whereas the physical consequences of global warming — increase in sea level, droughts, cyclones, and changes in the hydrological cycles — will occur in countries of both the North and South, the capacity of First World nations to face these consequences is much greater. They are in a much better position to invest in the infrastructure (dikes, dams, wells, etc.), technological innovations, and technical capacity that will be required. Thus, the most vulnerable peoples are those in nations that have little economic and technical capacity for facing change.

Similar dynamics prevail in another environmental problem currently on the global agenda: the thinning of the ozone layer. This thinning is caused by the accumulation in the atmosphere of chlorofluorocarbons, chemical residuals from aerosols, refrigeration systems, and air conditioning. Penetrating through the depleted ozone layer, increased ultraviolet radiation stands to affect key primary producers, as well the health of more complex organisms, including humans. Again, the primary purveyors of the problem are the nations of the North, but the greatest burdens stand to be borne in the South.

management, a fair system of global environmental governance, built on the principle of equal human rights, is essential. We must be watchful for political biases in interpreting relative responsibility for environmental problems. Such interpretations are based on what is depicted as hard scientific fact; in fact, the data are often inadequate and open to various and frequently contradictory interpretations (see Box 6).

Perspectives on Population

Population is a major issue in the environment/development debate, with differing perspectives on its role in the current crisis. One mainstream view is that the large population of many Third World countries is a major (even the main) cause of poverty, resource depletion, and environmental degradation; population control is therefore seen as crucial to resolving the environment crisis. A key component in this argument is that in the sheer struggle to survive, large numbers of poor people destroy forests, harvest in excess of sustainable yield, cause soil erosion, and, in general, put tremendous stress on environmental carrying capacity.

Such a view is too simplistic. Relationships between humans and their environment are not fatalistic; they reflect cultural, economic, and technological factors that are potentially amenable to understanding and change. Notwithstanding the fact that the biophysical environment plays a role in determining the number of people that can be comfortably and sustainably supported in a given region, human relationships with the natural environment transcend passive dependence. Simplistic notions of carrying capacity therefore do not apply (see Box 7).

Indeed, in a modern, interdependent world, the population capacity of a given area can be greatly increased by importing a few critical items, such as plant nutrients. However, dependence on external input can also be excessive and inequitable. Many areas of the North, including densely populated Europe, are heavily supported by a wide range of imported goods. If a trend-through-time assessment was made of the amount of land in the Third World devoted to supplying resources to the North, it would undoubtedly show a dramatic increase over recent decades, despite decolonization. Many of these export-oriented uses of land in the Third World are highly ecologically destructive.

Box 6

The Data Game:
Who's Heating the World?

The same data and the same mathematical model can result in dramatically different conclusions, depending on the political assumptions that are introduced into the model. In one recent controversy, an environmental research organization's conclusions about national accountability for global warming were publicly challenged by another which, using the same emissions data, arrived at a very different set of conclusions.

The 1990-91 edition of *World Resources* (World Resources Institute (WRI), in collaboration with UNEP and UNDP; Oxford University Press, New York, 1991) concluded that "developing" countries as a group contribute to nearly half of the global warming problem: a remarkable claim given that it had been widely believed that global warming was largely the result of heavy fossil fuel use in industrialized countries.

The model used by the Washington-based WRI involved detailed calculations of national emissions of greenhouse gases (carbon dioxide, methane, and chlorofluorocarbons). These emissions were then used to calculate a single greenhouse index for each country, based on the differing climate-forcing ability of each gas. Total global greenhouse emissions, calculated by simple addition of each country's emissions, were found to be far greater than the quantity of gases that appear to be accumulating in the atmosphere every year. The difference between amounts released and amounts accumulating is accounted for by the existence of natural sinks for carbon dioxide and methane. WRI described the quantities of greenhouse gases accumulating in the world's atmosphere — that is, the emissions directly responsible for global warming — as net emissions. WRI assumed that each country was responsible for net emissions in proportion to its share of total global emissions. In other words, if a country was responsible for 10 percent of the total greenhouse gases emitted in the world in a particular year, it was also deemed responsible for 10 percent of the net emissions accumulating in the atmosphere in that year. Accordingly, WRI concluded that, in order of responsibility, the top five greenhouse polluters were the United States, the (former) Soviet Union, Brazil, the People's Republic of China, and India.

The Centre for Science and Environment (CSE), based in New Delhi, strongly disagreed with this set of conclusions, pointing out that WRI's model distributes the "absorption credits" of the earth's natural sinks in proportion to a country's emissions, in effect giving the biggest polluter the biggest share. CSE argued that the sinks are a global common heritage and their absorption benefits ought therefore to be equally distributed among all human beings. Using this logic, CSE assigned each nation a share of the sink equal to its proportion of the world's population. A nation's total emissions of greenhouse gases were then compared with its sink quota to determine its net contribution. Using WRI's data in its modified model (despite disagreement with some of the national data on deforestation rates and methane emissions), the CSE arrived at a dramatically different set of conclusions. India, China, and many other Third World countries no longer contributed to the carbon dioxide or methane accumulating in the earth's atmosphere.

The WRI–CSE debate brings the equity question into sharp focus in the context of global warming and underscores the fact that the interpretation of scientific data is often dependent on political assumptions and biases. The CSE report also points out the degree to which the South stands to be disadvantaged during global environmental negotiations because of its lack of policy analysts dealing with scientific data on global environmental change.

This points to another crucial issue in relation to population and environment: although absolute numbers in population clearly have a bearing on environmental conditions, more relevant factors are the volumes and patterns of consumption of different groups of people. Generally, Northern populations, with their much higher consumption levels, place a greater burden on the global environment than does the much larger population of the South.

Arguments that link environmental degradation to large numbers of poor people tend to overlook a common reality: it is frequently the alienation of land and resources, often to commercial interests, that is behind the degradation of the environment of local communities, and this is the process by which their members are rendered poor. They are the victims, not the culprits, of environmental degradation. For example, forest peoples seldom destroy their environment; more often, commercial logging or land clearing degrades forest resources and impoverishes those communities dependent on them. Similarly, traditional fishers whose resources are depleted by trawl fishing or pollution are rendered poorer by environmental degradation. In cases where the activities of poor people have strained the environment — for example, by opening up new areas of marginal agricultural potential — the cause is as much related to social problems as to population size.

Box 7

The Concept of Carrying Capacity

From a strictly technical perspective, the business of estimating the number of beings of any species that a given piece of land can support is usually extremely complicated and uncertain. The number of relevant ecological variables is enormous. More pointedly, in the absence of cultural considerations, any attempt to estimate the number of people that can be indefinitely supported in a given environment — the human carrying capacity of that environment — is an extremely abstract exercise and therefore of limited value. Carrying capacity is integrally related to the way in which land and resources are used. In other words, the number of people that can sustainably exist within a given environment greatly depends on the manner in which they interact with that environment. The different strategies by which human beings interact with environment is at the core of "culture." Cultural diversity is also why it is so difficult to speak of a "general model" for sustainable development.

It has been repeatedly argued that in India, for example, the population size has outstripped the country's capacity to cope. These statements are not, however, based on any rigorous scientific assessment of the productive potential of the land. Indeed, the most rigorous study undertaken to date indicates that India, through better management of soils and water, more adaptive forms of land use, and increased levels of agricultural inputs, could in fact feed three to four times the population that it contained in the late 1970s. This is of course not an argument for such an increase, but rather an argument against mechanistic perspectives on population.

All this is not to deny that rapid population growth is often associated with poverty and environmental stress. A rapid rate of growth strains the tasks of providing basic human needs. It also increases the difficulties of social, economic, and environmental management, and increases the challenge of providing environmentally sustainable employment. In addition, escalating urbanization results in new types and intensities of environmental stress as well as increasingly unmanageable social and economic chaos. Combined with inappropriate economic distribution policies, the low priority given to rural development worsens the situation by limiting options of the poor in relation to family size and by encouraging environmentally unsound migration. "Environmental refugees" are moving from areas that have been devastated by physical disaster (artificial or natural) or where access to economic resources has been severed or curtailed for other reasons. Migration from poorer to wealthier regions within and across countries is bound to increase if poverty persists, resulting in increased social tension.

The relationship between population growth and the environment must also be considered within a wider social context. While a large family can increase economic strain on the poor, poor families often prefer more children for economic security. Thus, reducing poverty would tend to reduce family size; efforts to control population without tackling poverty are unlikely to succeed.

In setting population policy, the unethical practices employed in some past and current "population-control" programs must be rejected (including forced or induced sterilization; the promotion of unsafe contraceptives, some already withdrawn in the countries of origin; and the use of birth control as a "conditionality" for receiving subsidies or loans). Instead, policies must address basic social problems and maximize democratic choices for families. Priority should be given to measures that reduce poverty and inequality and increase economic security — conditions that make it possible for poor families to limit family size. This should be accompanied by comprehensive education in family planning and by making safe family-planning methods widely and cheaply available. Improving women's literacy, education, and economic opportunities, as well as reducing household burdens, should also be a crucial component of population policy, improving incentives and options for family planning.

Placing the population factor in the right context is a complex matter that must account for characteristics of the biophysical environment, patterns of resource use and consumption, sociocultural conditions, and the socioeconomic roots of poverty. Accepting these complexities, priority should be given to widening the possibilities and choices for people, especially the poor, to plan their family size. But, however valid a priority family planning may be, it should neither be seen as a substitute for, nor should it deflect from, the changes in lifestyle — in particular, the reduction of wasteful consumption — that are necessary in the North and among Southern elites.

The birth rate is now slowing worldwide and population size in the South will eventually stabilize. Given current demographic realities, however, this will not happen in the short term. Reduced population growth will not substantially affect the reality of massive increases in the human population until well into the 21st century. Thus, efforts to address global change in the coming decades cannot hinge on population control. The major thrust must be to modify global patterns of production, distribution, and consumption.

CHAPTER 2
Causes of the Global Environment/Development Crisis

Together, actions at the local and national levels often have regional and global environmental impact. Conversely, economic, technological, and political forces originating at global or regional levels have significant and sometimes overwhelming effects on actions at community and national levels. Thus, in seeking to understand the causes of global environmental change, it is essential to examine national-level policies and actions, the international dynamics that influence these actions, and international activities directly.

Development dynamics within Northern countries have such a powerful effect on the world — particularly Third World countries — that what are ostensibly national-level decisions and actions in the North are actually international causes of environmental change. Key among these factors are overdevelopment in the North and the assimilation of Southern economies into a North-dominated global economy.

At the national level within the South, sociopolitical systems and development planning approaches — as well as dependence on the world market system — influence the nature and magnitude of environmental change. More specifically, types of productive processes, technologies applied, and patterns of economic distribution are key. As at the international level, the development model within many countries of the South is characterized by production and consumption patterns shaped by gross inequalities in wealth and income.

International Factors

Overdevelopment and Maldevelopment in the North

The industrial revolution saw the advent of powerful technologies that could effect rapid and radical change in the physical and socioeconomic environments. The technological capacity to massively transform nature was accompanied by an equally powerful socioeconomic force: private enterprise. This expanded the reach and impact of the industrialization process. The market system is characterized by competition between private firms; those that do not perform well — do not make sufficient profit — do not last. This fate is avoided by minimizing costs, by expanding market share, or by concentrating control over means of production. There is a built-in propulsion for companies to expand their size and markets and, in a chain reaction, the resulting market structure compels producers to find ways to further stimulate demand for their products. The emergence of transnational corporations (TNCs), a "logical" outcome of these market forces, jeopardizes national control over expansionist behaviour. Extraterritorial instruments to control TNCs are weak and almost nonexistent.

The economic system is therefore geared toward stimulating ever-increasing demand for nonessential goods and services. Thus, "overdevelopment" in the North is associated with a high-consumption lifestyle. The attraction of many modern consumer products is their immediate convenience; however, this convenience is often associated with hidden environmental costs. Firms also appeal to the rich and middle class to buy "fashionable" and "status-symbol" products. Built-in physical obsolescence and fashion sensibilities — key features of a "throw-away" product culture — are conscious tools to effect increased turnover. The result is superfluous and wasteful consumption. Moreover, although offering some advantages, credit systems (such as the credit card and instalment payment) have also enabled consumers to purchase products at levels that are well beyond their household means.

Beyond direct market forces, government policies and programs are also often geared to overproduction. The agricultural sector, for example, exemplifies Northern overdevelopment and its environmental perils; but, in this case, overproduction is mainly due to subsidies and protectionism. The resulting enormous stockpiles of some agricultural products have to be periodically destroyed. Northern agriculture is also ecologically destructive and energy inefficient.

The propulsion toward environmentally destructive economic growth is not limited to capitalism. Even in the formerly centrally planned economies of Eastern Europe and the Soviet Union, where the profit motive among competing firms was weaker, there was an impetus for unsustainable economic growth. The emphasis on a strong economy and defence industry perhaps initially reflected a perceived need for security against the powerful capitalist countries. It was also believed that the proliferation of goods made possible through modern technology (that is, by advancing the "forces of production") would contribute to attaining the socialist goal. Moreover, the consumer culture of capitalism, with its attractive range of well-packaged and well-promoted products, was transmitted through the media to the communist bloc, stimulating the appetites of consumers. The highly centralized economic management in communist countries, characterized by a lack of control and democratic participation by people in managing their resources, has had a degrading effect on natural resources and the environment. As well, there has been inadequate development of environmental regulations and technologies. Thus, the former Soviet Republics and Eastern European countries are also ill-prepared for the management of environmental problems.

Both market-oriented and centrally planned economies worldwide have used a large part of their national incomes and intellectual resources for armaments and defence. Because of the secrecy involved, it has been difficult to fully assess the negative impacts and opportunity costs of this use of finances and resources. In a situation where no costs have been spared to produce an ever-increasing arsenal of sophisticated weapons of human and ecological destruction, humanity has had to shoulder the burden of the arms race.

In socioeconomic terms, "overdevelopment" in the North is accompanied by, and indeed dependent on, "underdevelopment" elsewhere. While large parts of humanity (mostly in the South but also a growing minority in the North) cannot satisfy their basic and human needs, the major share of outputs and incomes is appropriated by a relatively small proportion of the population (mostly in the North, but also in the South); and the situation appears to be worsening. The economic activities and consumption patterns of Northern countries have had a far greater impact on the environment and global development dynamics than the relative size of their populations would suggest. Production processes in the North have depleted resources globally and have released most of the pollutants and toxic wastes that have contributed to contaminating the global commons. Thus, primary responsibility for global environmental change rests with the national economic, social, and technological systems of Northern countries.

The Assimilation of Southern Economies

Colonialism brought massive changes to Third World economies. The subsequent intensification of these changes through the spread of a world market economy controlled by the North is at the core of the international causes of environmental change. Economic propulsion led the West to colonize Third World territories to expand both the available storehouse of raw materials and the market for manufactured goods, technologies, and industries. Where direct force was previously applied, Third World countries are now advised, "encouraged," and economically coerced to continue exporting huge quantities of raw materials for meagre returns.

Thus, in the postcolonial period, as Northern TNCs have expanded to the far corners of the globe, the colonial pattern of world production and trade has become further entrenched. This process of "development" has also been greatly fostered by private commercial banks that provide loans to governments or the private sector; by multilateral agencies (such as the Food and Agriculture Organization of the United Nations (FAO), UNDP, and the World Bank) and bilateral aid programs that provide technical advice and aid and promote certain kinds of technologies; and by research institutes or foundations that provide technical and financial support.

The continued, postcolonial dependence of the South on the North has been a major factor in environmentally damaging policies and actions at the national level, especially in countries that have achieved independence relatively recently. World prices for most commodities are so low that export earnings are insufficient to cover import payments, resulting in balance-of-payment difficulties. In the past two decades, this crisis worsened as huge external loans were contracted for projects that were not viable. In many countries, the combination of low export prices and non-performing projects led to a crisis in debt servicing. Structural adjustment programs that accompany debt-rescheduling schemes have forced many Third World countries to further expand the volume of their commodity exports to service their foreign loans. In fact, the volume of raw materials exported from South to North has increased tremendously. This massive hemorrhage of resources from the South has had many environmental repercussions, among which are the destruction of forests for wood; the clearing of land for agriculture, ranching, or mining; the inundation of land for dams; and the depletion of nonrenewable resources, particularly metals and minerals.

At the same time, the export of investments and technologies from North to South has also greatly expanded. Some of the products, technologies, and industries that the Third World has imported from the North have been damaging to the natural environment and to human health. Many of the imported products are inappropriate and harmful. For example, baby food substitutes promoted by milk companies replace natural breast-feeding, which is nutritionally superior. Increased use of pesticides, some banned in the country of origin, has resulted in tens of thousands of deaths in the Third World. (Indeed, although the Third World accounts for only a small proportion of the total amount of pesticides used globally, a large majority of pesticide-related poisoning and deaths occur in the Third World.) Harmful chemicals used or generated during industrial production, or incorporated into consumer products, result in health problems such as cancers, blood disorders, and birth defects.

Growing public resistance in the North to domestic pollution appears to be contributing to increased corporate relocation of environmentally harmful industries to the South, to escape tight safety and environmental regulations. The Bhopal gas tragedy, where 3 000 lives were lost and 200 000 people were disabled, is a glaring example of the substandard safety practices of many multinationals in the Third World. Moreover, in addition to providing a market for hazardous products banned in the North, the South serves as a dumping ground for hazardous wastes. (Conversely, in the increasingly integrated global economy, pressures to conform to increasingly stringent and expensive environmental standards set in the North will grow, especially for products destined for international trade.)

Despite virtually universal awareness in the international community of the environment/development crisis, and the consequent need to regulate the market and corporations, substantial pressure is being created and actions taken — under the banner of "free trade" — to liberalize the market and reduce legitimate forms of public control over corporations (see Box 8). Free trade is not necessarily fair; when a strong party insists that a weaker party accept without conditions a free flow of goods and services, and relinquish control over investment, the weak party is likely to grow even weaker and the majority of benefits will accrue to the strong. Indeed, under such conditions, local enterprises in many Third World countries will falter, and the extent of foreign control and ownership of Third World economies will significantly increase. This would reverse the achievements of many Third World countries that have, through postcolonial policies and regulations, reduced foreign control of their economy by building domestically owned components. The use of trade sanctions to enforce the assumed resource prerogatives of foreigners is a form of attempted recolonization that would further frustrate South–North relations.

In terms of the role of aid agencies after the Second World War, many (if not most) of the programs they have financed or promoted have had adverse ecological effects. It is only in recent years, with growing public awareness, that consideration has been given to the environmental impacts associated with the policies, programs, and projects of the World Bank, the regional development banks, FAO, the General Agreement on Tariffs and Trade (GATT), and the bilateral aid agencies of Northern governments (such as the Canadian International Development Agency and the Japan International Cooperation Agency). The role played by research foundations in promoting ecologically harmful projects or programs has still not been adequately studied, but there are an increasing number of reports on the relationship between research funding, research institutes, and the promotion of specific technologies or technological packages, such as the Green Revolution. Moreover, many environmentally damaging technologies developed in the North and transmitted to the South have replaced indigenous systems that were more ecologically sound.

Many of these problems reflect in part massive imbalances in the generation and flow of information. Decisions are normally the culmination of a process involving three related components: information collection, analysis, and decision-making. Currently, there is a "pull" of information from the South by the North and a "push" of analysis and decision-making from the North to the

Box 8

The Uruguay Round:
Free Markets, Development, and the Environment

The Uruguay Round of GATT threatens erosion of the "development principle" currently acknowledged in GATT rules, which gives some degree of special and preferential treatment to Third World countries to facilitate their development. As one dimension, many Northern governments are now arguing that Third World countries should no longer be allowed to impose import restrictions on the grounds of balance-of-payment difficulties or to restrict food exports during periods of food shortages.

In the substantial negotiation areas, while the North is showing little interest in reaching agreement on issues of great concern to the South (such as the issue of access of Southern products to Northern markets), it is focusing on eliminating existing restrictions or obligations imposed by Third World governments on foreign companies. In the area of trade-related investment measures (TRIMS), the North is proposing that current national conditions on entry of foreign companies be abolished (such as limits to equity ownership, requirements for use of local materials, and requirements for level of exports); the Third World should be required to accept the presence of all applying foreign companies. A country failing to follow the TRIMS agreement could be subject to cross-sectoral retaliation.

The North is also seeking to bring the service sector within the scope of GATT or GATT-style regulations. Again, it is proposed that all GATT members be required to allow foreign service enterprises (in sectors such as banking, insurance, finance, professional services, media, and culture) to establish nationally, and that these enterprises be accorded "national treatment" (be treated no differently than local companies). As with TRIMS, retaliation for failure to comply could be cross-sectoral — in this case, directed not only against the contending country's service enterprises but also against its export products. In the case of both TRIMS and the service sector, the power of cross-sectoral retaliation would ensure compliance.

That the true motivation behind the "free trade" initiatives is self-interest rather than a consistent ideological position is demonstrated in another controversial area of the Uruguay Round. With respect to trade-related intellectual property rights (TRIPS), the North is propposing that Third World countries adopt strict patent and related laws that would in effect protect Northern companies and individuals (99 percent of existing patents in the world are Northern owned) and

> grant monopoly rights over technologies to the TNCs. This protection-
> ism would stunt technological development in the South.
>
> If adopted, the services and TRIMs proposals of the North would spell
> a regression back to direct economic colonization. Thirld World gov-
> ernments would have little or no power to restrict the behaviour of, or
> impose obligations on, TNCs.

South. The pull and push in the opposite directions is very weak.
Thus, the South relies on the North for analysis of issues relevant
to both North and South, and research that does take place in the
South is often driven by foreign funding and, hence, foreign
agendas. Now, even Southern research of very high quality has
no audience in the North; the often extensive knowledge of local
people has even less of a profile. As well, flows of information
and analysis within the South are weak. Southern leverage in
influencing analysis and decision-making also requires greater
South–South exchange.

Of course, these dynamics partly relate to inadequate indigenous
research capacity within the South, a problem that is further
explored in the next section. The issues of research capacity and
information flow, and their relationships to decision-making, are
also raised in Chapter 3 and Chapter 5.

National Causes in the South

Development Planning Approaches

Having been drawn into the world market as providers of raw
materials, the economic policies of most Third World countries
following independence have continued to emphasize cheaply
priced commodity exports. The environment remains outside
major policy arenas, including economic and fiscal policy, and the
government and elites, having largely adopted the same economic growth paradigm as the North, have shunned longer term
efforts at conservation and wise resource allocation. Thus, as
national economies interlock more intensely with the world market, the pace of resource depletion and environmental degradation increases.

Further justification for an essentially "hands-off" approach is
derived from the fact that the star of national planning, which
rode high through the 1960s and 1970s, has now fallen. The

impetus for planning arose largely from the perceived myopic nature of the market and its failure to deal with externalities and indivisibilities. However, the failure of national planning on a number of economic issues has pushed the pendulum back toward a reliance on the market system. The emphasis is now back on "getting prices right," with a surprisingly large number of writers proposing that a greater reliance on market forces is the way to deal with environmental problems.

Indeed, at a time when many Third World nations are increasingly subject to international economic pressures, the "rolling back" of the state and the weakening of central government authority has decreased regulatory capacity in relation to environment and resources. The state often lacks the capacity to adequately formulate and enforce appropriate policies, laws, and standards. As a result, companies can respond to market signals in complete oblivion of the externalities or diseconomies of their activities, and without the fear of state penalties. Referring back to the international causes, the weakening of state authority is aggravated by a process of regionalization, particularly shown by the intensified development of trading blocs. Given the power of the major trading blocs now taking shape, it is increasingly difficult for nation states to avoid becoming part of such blocs; and the prevailing trend is toward North–South rather than South–South alliances (it is estimated that the European, North American, and Far East blocs control over 65 percent of world trade).

Where resource policies and environmental controls do exist, they seldom address the social dimensions of resource use. Indeed, the main flaw in many Third World resource policies has been the simple failure to focus on human as well as environmental impacts. This is further evidence that current development planning approaches in many Third World countries favour mechanistic rather than humanistic approaches.

Social and Political Systems

The political and socioeconomic structures of many Third World countries — reflected in a concentration of land ownership and highly unequal access to natural resources, capital, credit, and industrial and financial assets — perpetuate environmental destruction and developmental stagnation. The political elite is often closely connected to the business elite. Corruption and patronage often lead to the approval or continuation of ill-advised, environmentally destructive, and socially damaging projects and activities. In many countries, companies bribe politicians or bureaucrats to buy or approve their products or projects or to grant them forest and mining concessions, for example, and to ignore the associated potential hazards. The formation of coalitions that might be capable of challenging these abuses — for example, trade unions and environmental organizations — is often blocked by perceived conflicts in goals.

These tendencies are magnified in some countries by a lack of true participatory democracy, often reflected in hampered freedom of the press. In turn, a generally lower level of environmental awareness, knowledge, and commitment of Third World policymakers reflects lower levels of public pressure. Where conditions of democratic openness exist, scientists, environmentalists, and the media have often promoted environmental issues to such a degree that governments must pay attention.

The allocation of land and resources is a political issue, but the political dimensions are often couched in either economic or philanthropic terms. For example, to bolster arguments for privatization of land and resources, communal ownership may be cited as an incentive to overuse and abuse the environment (see Box 4). A more profound analysis suggests that many traditional forms of land use are environmentally sound (see Box 2 and Box 9), but the communal decision-making structures that ensure balanced and respectful use of communal lands are weakened by the centralization of power. Mechanisms are usually lacking to effectively involve the public when making decisions about resource use.

This points to perhaps the most critical dimension of the politics of sustainability: sustainable development is the result of a political order in which society is capable of learning from and responding to mistakes in the use of natural resources. Experience suggests that both the potential and the incentive for learning are greatest when those making resource-management decisions are the ones directly experiencing the results of those decisions. Thus, within a framework condemning harm to the environment of other communities, empowering local people to control and manage their resources is generally the best guarantee of sustainable environmental management.

Box 9

Traditional, Sustainable Resource Use: Some Examples from the South

The demographic pattern and mode of production of the indigenous people of Amazonia allows a given area to be used over a long period of time. The population is dispersed in settlements along the rivers. Around the communal houses (called *malocas*) in these settlements, the resident extended family plants food crops in a pattern of established rotation. After several years, the *maloca* is moved some miles down river, and a new cycle is begun. This movement of *malocas* along the river results, in the long run, in a rotation of all the houses that are a part of the community — sometimes 20 or 30. The model is perfectly adapted to the poor soil conditions and fragile forests of the area.

In contrast, Amazonia is currently settled by concentrating the population in fixed areas. The consequences of this strategy are the overuse of surrounding areas to the point of exhaustion and the creation of dependent enclaves whose resource demands stretch far beyond the environs of the town and are destructive of traditional land use patterns of local indigenous populations.

As another example, hidden in the Sierra Nevada de Santa Marta is the remains of a civilization that lived there successfully and sustainably more than a thousand years ago. The Sierra Nevada is a coastal mountain range. From the base at sea level to the snow peaks, it has one of the longest vertical climbs in the world, and all microclimates of the neotropics are represented. The Indian population of the Sierra was concentrated in urban-style settlements whose economies were highly interconnected. This successful civilization, characterized by high population density and low environmental impact, was based on highly efficient and sustainable use of the region's productive capacity, the development of a technological complex highly adapted to the specific conditions of the particular environment, and a coherent and well-integrated social system.

Specifically, the settlement pattern involved many dispersed urban settlements of various sizes, distributed over the different altitudinal floors of the Sierra. Agricultural crops and cultivation practices were matched to the specific ecological characteristics and productive capacity of each level, and the people living on the coast fished and gathered salt. The settlements were interconnected by roads paved with stones; a system of exchange of goods among the different settlements enabled each community to obtain the specialized products from the various altitudes. Under these conditions, the carrying capacity of the region

> was high, permitting a relatively large population (up to 100 000 people) to maintain a high living standard in relative environmental harmony.
>
> In contrast, the Sierra is currently populated by immigrants whose imported systems of production are poorly adapted to the local environment. The environmental impacts of existing land use have resulted in extensive degradation of productive capacity and an associated impoverishment of the population, which now stands at about 20 000. Given low levels of social and economic integration, family units survive independently by extracting as much as possible from their immediate surroundings. The random occupational pattern is relatively insensible to the different microclimatic and other ecological features of the various altitudes. Soils are used without considering specific productive capabilities. Land is intensively exploited around the essentially self-sufficient settlement units to the point where erosion problems, soil exhaustion, and water shortages become critical. Emigration to other areas of the same region follows, and the pattern is repeated.

One of the most crucial but least recognized dimensions of the current environment/development crisis is the loss of community-level control over environment and resources. When communities are deprived of control over, and even access to, the resources on which they depend — as when land and resources are appropriated and transferred to commercial interests — the environmental and human repercussions can be devastating.

For example, in the forest communities of Asia, cultural dependencies on the forest are integral and complex. The diversity and wealth reflected in the knowledge of indigenous communities regarding natural resources is expressed in traditional technologies. The knowledge was generated by trial and error in interacting with nature over many centuries and was accumulated and transmitted from generation to generation. It is based mainly on diversified and sustainable use of natural resources. Shifting cultivation was environmentally sustainable over many generations. Thus, the environment has shaped the people; their economy, their way of life — in short, their culture — reflect, above all, human adaptation to the natural environment.

But outside logging interests, empowered by national governments to log the forests on which these communities depend, have no understanding of, or sympathy toward, the traditional shifting cultivation concepts. As a result, they disrupt the traditional patterns of cultivation. The destruction of the forest means the destruction of not only the people's economy but also the very essence of their culture. In the long term, this means a sacrifice of economic productivity, because people are generally unwilling or even unable to adapt once their culture has been destroyed.

As another example, the inequitable distribution of land in Brazil has led thousands of poor farmers to obtain farmland by clearing parts of the Amazonian forest by burning. If these farmers had access to already cleared lands, they would not have to burn existing forests. The negative impacts associated with these processes of alienation are often accelerated by the loss of traditional knowledge and technologies. Indeed, with the adoption of Northern development paradigms and technologies in the South, traditional capabilities are being lost at an alarming rate.

Finally, Southern countries, like those of the North, have been drawn into wasteful and irrational expenditures on arms and defence. In the East-West confrontation, some of the poorest countries were pushed into bankruptcy by war. Somalia, for example, ranks fourth lowest in the world in terms of per-capita income. In the early 1970s, however, 23.3 percent of central government expenditure was on defence. In 1989, 14 percent of Zaire's central government expenditure was on defence, equivalent to its combined expenditure on education, health, housing, amenities, social security, and welfare. Zaire's economy is in shambles, despite its considerable natural wealth. Most of the expenditures in arms are in foreign exchange. The combined foreign debt of Third World countries now exceeds 1.3 trillion United States dollars. The World Bank estimates that, in some countries, as much as one-third of the debt can be ascribed to the arms trade. Given their built-in obsolescence, money spent on arms has been largely wasted.

Patterns of Consumption and Distribution

The high levels of direct dependence on primary production in many regions of the Third World are no guarantee that the basic needs of people in these regions will be satisfied. Very unequal income distribution within most Third World countries ensures that a major share of the goods and services produced or imported for local use are luxuries for the rich and middle class.

Because of their lack of buying power, the real human needs of the poor are not translated into the production of basic goods and services.

The luxury products and services toward which production is distorted are patterned after those of the North. As in the North, the consumption patterns of the Third World economic elite are highly wasteful. As many of the goods and services have high import content, their consumption is not only resource- and energy-intensive (thus depleting resources) but also contributes to the outflow of foreign exchange and balance of payment problems. To raise the foreign exchange for these imports, the export of raw materials and natural resources is intensified, compounding such development and environment problems as massive debt and resource depletion.

In most countries of the Third World, industrial development and economic growth in general continue to be associated with greatly increased energy consumption. At a broad level, the legitimacy of increased access in the South to various forms of energy is clear, but the need for intelligent energy policies and programs is also clear (see Box 10). Major environmental effects are also associated with the increasing use of motor vehicles. Environmental quality and quality of life are both adversely affected by the increased use of energy and other resources and by the construction of transportation infrastructure.

Some Problems Related to Production

In global terms, the 1980s were characterized not only by a slowdown in economic growth but also by the declining prominence of primary products in the world economy and a decrease in the relative economic importance of industrialization in the countries of the North. In the majority of Third World countries, however, primary production remains the central economic sector and industrialization maintains its ascendancy. These two main sectors of production in many Third World economies — primary production and manufacturing — are highly resource intensive. This is a major source of environmental stress, especially in light of the inadequate checks and balances by the state, as previously discussed, and the prevalence of environmentally inappropriate technologies and production systems. These production systems usually coexist with the remnants of indigenous production

Box 10

Energy Consumption

Increasing energy consumption in the Third World is not so much a reflection of population growth as of development processes, including increased levels of activity and technological change in industry, agriculture, urbanization, and transportation. Increased access to modern (including alternative) forms of energy is a legitimate development requirement, especially in providing basic services. Indeed, environmental problems associated with the current reliance of many Third World people on biomass for energy (for example, deforestation for fuelwood) could be ameliorated through increased access to other sources of energy. However, not all activities contributing to increased energy consumption are desirable; indeed, strategies to rationalize energy use should address the relevance of the uses to which energy is put.

Taking the inevitability and legitimacy of increasing energy consumption in the South as a point of departure, Southern governments, industry, and the general population have nonetheless inadequately addressed the necessity of energy conservation, energy efficiency, and the development of alternative (particularly renewable) energy sources. A basic constraint is that transcendental breakthroughs in efficiency have not been achieved; many energy-saving technologies that exist in the North are not accessible in the South for financial or other reasons. Adopting technologies to improve energy efficiency is an important component of technological modernization, greater self-sufficiency, and enhanced international competitiveness in the South. However, the appropriateness of some technologies in Southern contexts must be critically considered. For example, repair of a highly efficient pump may require technical expertise not available in rural areas. A week of downtime during planting season, while the pump is being serviced at a distant urban centre, could be disastrous for the farmer.

With respect to fossil fuel consumption in particular, the greater availability of petroleum has to some extent softened the will to develop alternative sources. In the longer term, however, nations of the South will find that they have invested precious income in fossil fuel technologies that may well become obsolete, or at least prohibitively expensive, within the next generation. In sum, there is immediate need for both a rationalization of energy use in the North and a concerted research focus on more sustainable energy options in the Third World.

systems, which may or may not be significant, depending on the region or country.

In criticizing land and resource degradation in the South, Northern assumptions of moral superiority are clearly not justifiable, given the extent to which natural conditions and resources have already been destroyed and degraded in the North. Nonetheless, the serious environmental deterioration that is being caused by resource exploitation in the South must be recognized and addressed by the peoples of the South.

Primary production

In recent years, a declining proportion of the world's economy, as measured in monetary terms, has depended directly on primary resources. However, a high proportion of the economically active population in the Third World continues to depend on primary activities, and, at a subsistence level, there is extensive direct reliance on primary production. The exploitation of land, forests, and water resources, among other primary natural resources, constitutes the basis of survival of 60 percent of the population of the Third World. As the population continues to grow, the demand for food and other basic necessities will increase, and there will thus be greater pressure on natural resources. High exports of primary products and the associated disruption of production systems oriented to satisfying local needs are also major sources of pressure.

The distribution of primary production activities in the natural landscape does not always correspond to ecological realities. For example, the lack of adequate policies and technologies for the integral and multiple use of forest ecosystems has lead to their massive transformation for agricultural and livestock production. When ecosystems are transformed in ways that are grossly negligent of natural characteristics, the results in the medium and long term are, to say the least, counter-productive: severe soil and water degradation and, at the extreme, a general collapse of life-support capability.

An illustration is the loss of forest ecosystems through deforestation, which, in turn, causes soil erosion, loss of soil fertility, sedimentation of waterways, changes in or even depletion of hydrological cycles, and extinction of animal and vegetable species — in short, massive destruction of ecosystems and their genetic resources. In many cases, logging also causes irreversible damage to the economies and cultures of tribal peoples.

It is estimated that 2 million square kilometres of Latin America has been deforested in the last 30 years. Of Latin America's total annual clearcut of 50 thousand square kilometres (close to 80 percent of which is in the tropics), only 4.1 thousand square kilometres (8 percent) are regenerated in either a natural or induced manner, and the biological diversity of this regenerated fraction is lower than that of the original forest. More than 60 percent of the clearing carried out between 1971 and 1986 in Latin America was due to the expansion of the cattle frontier. Within Central America and the Caribbean, the deforestation of El Salvador and Haiti is dramatic. Haiti in 1923 had 60 percent of its surface occupied by forests; by 1974, this had been reduced to 7 percent. Fully 30 percent of Haiti's territory is currently unproductive.

In Southeast Asia, commercial logging is the main cause of deforestation. The wood from these forests accounts for most of the world's trade in tropical timber, much of which is exported to Northern countries, especially Japan. At current rates, most of the region's primary rain forest will be logged or degraded within 20 years.

Another main cause of soil degradation during the last four decades has been the expansion of the agricultural frontier beyond areas that have reasonable agricultural potential. Within areas of good agricultural potential, soil erosion has also rendered useless vast areas of production. In addition, intense agricultural technologies, which depend on high levels of agrochemicals, energy, and capital, have resulted in soil contamination, salinization, and water pollution. Latin America's 2 million square kilometres of eroded land corresponds to 10 percent of the region's surface area (equivalent to the area of Mexico). About 80 percent of Mexico's territory suffers from some type of erosion, and 30 percent of the area is considered to be subject to severe erosion. In the Third World, between 6 and 7 million hectares of cultivatable land becomes unproductive every year, a massive obstacle to development.

Manufacturing

Contrary to trends in the North, industrialization continues to increase in most regions of the Third World. While the 1980s saw small increases in the ratio of industrial to total gross national product (GNP) in many Third World regions, the ratio of industrialization for many Northern countries declined. For example, according to the World Bank, the ratio for the Organisation for Economic Cooperation and Development (OECD) declined from 36 to 31 percent between 1980 and 1988.

As more of the income base of the countries of the South shifts to manufacturing, the pressure on natural resources is maintained and environmental degradation persists or is aggravated. Indeed, the shifts in both type and quantity of goods produced often depend on more intensive exploitation of primary resources. Thus, increased industrialization in the South has come with all the attendant environmental repercussions: resource depletion; consumption of energy; generation of pollution and wastes and consequent contamination of water, soils, and air; occupational hazards; health threats to local residents; etc. Because of the sociopolitical dynamics previously discussed, standards of safety and pollution control are often far below what would be required in the North.

Several factors compound the problem. Primarily, the general scarcity of capital means that retrofits or process changes in existing plants (which are often old, poorly equipped, and heavily polluting) are not priorities. This is particularly true in cases where large investments would be required for what are seen as economically nonproductive ends, an obvious example being the cleanup of toxic sites. Also, in many cases, the technologies must be imported, requiring scarce or unavailable foreign exchange. It is often difficult for the South to obtain international assistance to address environmental problems related to older industrial plants; in many cases, these are no longer priority environmental issues within the North (already having been addressed by upgrades or retrofits, for example). International attention, guided as it is by Northern concerns, is focused on more recent problems. Finally, the need for foreign investment may make it difficult to insist on the best available technologies for new plants.

Scientific and Technological Dependence and the Homogenization of Production Systems

In the modern urban/industrial sector, the availability in the South of the scientific and technical capability needed to minimize human impacts on the environment is generally highly inadequate. Moreover, existing traditional knowledge on the wise management of the often rich natural resource base is not adequately recognized and is often being displaced. Third World countries today face problems of environmental degradation at a time when the global technological order is rapidly changing. Given limited scientific and technical capacities, nations are forced to choose whether they should address their grassroots realities or pursue the Northern development ideal. An entire range of new technologies is continuously evolving — the most critical of which include microelectronics, biotechnologies, and communication systems — and are affecting almost all aspects of development. The Third World is even lacking the capability to assess, or to control decisions on, whether and how to adopt and adapt to these emerging technologies.

The direction of most technological change is now toward greater capital and technical intensity and lower labour intensity. Therefore, with the goal of technological modernization, it is proving particularly difficult to reconcile the objectives of eradicating poverty and generating employment. There is an absence of appropriate policies to guide technology choices toward environmentally sound and socially just uses of natural resources. Consequently, Third World countries are often propelled into new technological territory more quickly than their domestic policy frameworks, management systems, and scientific capacities can effectively manage.

As a result, governments and other agencies in many nations of the South promote the adoption of inappropriate technologies, often supported by Northern aid programs. Indeed, the ways in which natural resources are appropriated increasingly exhibit a set of common traits regardless of location. Specific technological packages, developed for a particular set of conditions, are transferred to other regions with little adaptation to cultural, socioeconomic, or environmental differences. Based on the apparent success of these technologies and the technical feasibility of their application, support is given to developing means for their duplication (institutions for delivery, mechanisms for financing).

As evidence of a surprising degree of resilience and flexibility, many resource-management traditions have been maintained in some form, expressing themselves particularly during periods of crisis. Nonetheless, the loss of traditional knowledge of the many indigenous and campesino communities — an archive of empirical knowledge generated over centuries of experience and oriented toward sustainable production — is accelerating. The homogenization of styles of development, forms of production, and related technologies has resulted in both deterioration in natural environments and loss of cultural diversity. In the industrial sector, the same process has taken place: displacing small-scale indigenous production systems and establishing energy-intensive, large-scale industrial plants, with hazardous or polluting effects. The replacement of local technologies has resulted in both direct environmental damage and greater Third World dependency on foreign input.

For example, the technological package of the Green Revolution was hailed at one time as a "miracle" and was introduced into all regions of the Third World without regard for their basic characteristics. Since that time, it has usurped traditional technologies, displaced genetic variety, promoted excessive use of chemicals, depleted soil nutrients, caused problems with water supply and irrigation, induced pest immunity, and generally provoked ecological and cultural degradation. There is now a movement to return to more ecological forms of agriculture. Another example in the realm of primary production is the displacement of traditional fishers and their methods by modern trawlers and equipment. This has commonly resulted in the depletion of fishing grounds and the loss of livelihoods and sources of nutrition to fishers and their communities. In some Third World countries, trawl technologies had been introduced by Northern aid programs.

Conversely, a major barrier to more sustainable forms of development can be a lack of introduction and commercialization of appropriate technologies. For example, integrated pest management can help reduce pesticide use in agriculture; however, it also requires good scientific understanding of local ecological, crop, and pest specificities.

As another dimension of scientific dependence, environmental research by natural scientists of the North often cannot be verified by Third World researchers. It must be accepted on faith. In most Third World countries, there are no systematic mechanisms to monitor, document, or disseminate information about environmental change. Awareness has increased, but little is done. This is one factor in the problem of inequitable participation in decision-making on the global environment, and may be particularly critical in relation to the management and use of the global commons. In Latin America, for example, technological and scientific weakness has led to a dependency for basic knowledge about the resources and potentials of the semi-open seas, including reproductive cycles of commercial marine species. The tendency to globalize management of the "commons" will further strengthen the dominance of the North, given its superiority in terms of inventories and basic knowledge of resources.

Scientific data is often "exported" from the South for analysis and use in the North. In some cases — Costa Rica and some countries of Africa, for example — research by nonnationals is virtually unregulated, and much of the research undertaken by Northerners involves no sharing of skills or results with local researchers. Indeed, some natural areas in the South have virtually become Northern research laboratories. In contrast, resources are extremely limited for Southerners to study environmental conditions and sociopolitical trends in the North, even though these conditions and trends may have significant implications for Third World development and environmental management.

Similar concerns are relevant to the trading of debt loads for territorial or environmental patrimony. In some cases, these "swaps" are made without evaluating the long-term implications or, indeed, even a clear understanding of the perspectives of the particular program. Also, there are no adequate mechanisms to control the ransacking of indigenous species or to ensure that knowledge generated by research is shared with the people of the region. Thus, unexpected and often unproductive changes have resulted from some recent efforts to protect biodiversity.

CHAPTER 3

Responding to Global Environmental Change within a Fair and Sustainable Order

International Implications, Obligations, and Opportunities

The environment/development crisis has reached disastrous proportions for the planet as a whole and for peoples worldwide. As the 20th century draws to a close, our challenge is to determine how we are going to manage this extremely divided and increasingly overexploited world in the interest of all. The gravity of such problems as resource depletion, pollution and contamination, toxins and environmental health, and climate change require urgent solutions, many of which lie beyond the national level. International cooperation in several major fields is essential to resolve the environmental crisis peacefully and for the long term.

The environmental crisis is a profound opportunity to restore and strengthen international cooperation within a global agenda. It is an opportunity to focus the minds and wills of political and economic leaders, as well as people and their organizations, on broad and mutually beneficial strategies and mechanisms to ensure humanity's survival. The voices of ordinary citizens around the world — victims of environmental degradation and development gone wrong, and witnesses to the possible death throes of nature and humanity — must carry through forcefully to the decision-makers. We must insist on an end to the madness of unsustainable and unequal growth and on a beginning to cooperation in a spirit of genuine internationalism.

The physical changes required for sustainability — drastic reductions in the depletion and degradation of resources, and in the pollution, contamination, and toxicity that result from modern systems of production — cannot be accomplished solely by technological means. To properly resolve the ecological crisis, it will be necessary to change the high consumption characteristics that are now built into the socioeconomic system. In turn, this will require drastic changes in economic development models (including modes of production and technological systems), in

57

values and lifestyles, and in economic and political relationships. The ecologically damaging technologies and production processes that characterize modern systems must be changed, and traditional sustainable methods that are still intact or recoverable must be reassessed, defended, and promoted. A new process of economic structural adjustment is also essential: one dictated not by financial discipline oriented to debt payment, but by global and national ecological imperatives. The key question is how the burden of this new structural adjustment will be distributed, among nations and within nations.

Indeed, without equity considerations, proposals to address environmental destruction may translate into stagnation at current levels and styles of development in the Third World, with the North maintaining its already high living standards. This amounts to legitimizing a new form of domination over the Third World. Instead of structural reforms in the North, new mechanisms would be devised to compromise the Third World's sovereignty over its natural resources, as occurs when biological resources from the South are patented and sold back to the South at a hefty profit. Pressures on the South to limit its population growth would also intensify, to prevent an increased population from consuming Southern resources that the North requires to sustain its overconsumption. In fact, in a world of scarcer resources, Northern interests concerned primarily with maintaining the flow of materials and resources to sustain current production systems and lifestyles may use direct force to control or have access to these resources.

An important opportunity for reviving international cooperation on a comprehensive scale is the United Nations Conference on Environment and Development (UNCED), where over 100 heads of state or government will gather in Rio de Janeiro in June 1992. In the preparatory meetings for UNCED, major issues revolved around the control, distribution, and use of the world's increasingly scarce natural resources; the degree of culpability of different countries with respect to such global environmental problems as climate change; the related onus of responsibility for resolving such problems; and the options and capabilities for their resolution.

In June 1991 in Beijing, 41 Third World countries participated in the Ministerial Conference on Environment and Development.

The declaration of this Conference stressed that inequities in current international economic relations undermine the ability of countries of the South to effectively participate in global environmental efforts. This declaration constitutes a clear statement of the views of Southern governments on the principles on which the UNCED negotiations should be based. Economic and environmental issues must be linked within "a new and equitable international economic order" and the countries of the North must take the lead in eliminating environmental damage and assist Southern countries in overcoming their problems. Several mechanisms to meet these responsibilities were proposed. In addition, the statement reaffirmed the Third World's sovereign rights over their natural resources. Under such conditions, the South could agree to national adjustments favourable to the global ecology, such as a halt to destroying tropical forests, the conservation of biodiversity, and minimizing the use or production of harmful substances. Currently, however, the chances for such a bargain do not appear bright. It is more likely that governments will continue to argue for years to come, while the environment continues to be degraded and destroyed. The problems of humanity may be too complex and deeply entrenched for the Earth to be saved.

Elements of a Fair and Sustainable Order

This section summarizes the specific elements that must form the basis of negotiation for a sustainable future. The discussion primarily addresses the roles of international and national governmental bodies and major institutions; however, peoples' movements, NGOs, concerned scientists, and other environmentally conscious individuals have a major role to play. After all, these are the groups and individuals that first alerted governments to the worldwide ecological crisis.

Poverty, Affluence, and Needs

The phenomenon of poverty is linked to inequalities at both international and national levels, and is the direct result of a wide range of factors. Although poverty cannot be defined in strictly economic terms, from an environmental perspective, the material dimensions are key. Absolute poverty — the inability to obtain, on a day-to-day basis, adequate food, shelter, and clothing — is the living condition of 1.2 of the 2.7 billion people living in the tropical and subtropical regions of the globe. About 20 percent of the world's population is malnourished to the point of serious risk to growth and health. Each year, many millions die of starvation or hunger-related disease.

The key to addressing the complex set of circumstances that induce poverty at both international and national levels is to reduce the scale of inequality by

- Redistributing resources and incomes;
- Shifting the type of goods demanded and produced from relative luxuries to basic goods and services; and
- A corresponding shift in investment.

Place poverty at the top of the international environment/development agenda

To address poverty, the international economic order must be reformed. The alleviation and ultimate elimination of poverty must be at the top of any genuine agenda on development and environment. Indeed, a sustainable global order presupposes that the main axis of international policy formulation will be the development of the majority of humanity. The elimination of poverty must be seen as a means of enhancing productivity, not as aid or charity. In addition, a comprehensive strategy is required to substantially reduce outputs and consumption in the North, while ensuring a fair and equitable distribution of the burdens resulting from such a fundamental reorientation.

Address poverty and affluence in the North

As an internal condition, poverty must also be given priority at the national level. Northern governments should counter the disturbing trend to increasing poverty in their own countries by strengthening national social security systems. To reduce income disparities both internationally and nationally, Northern governments should drastically reduce corporate subsidies and increase taxes on luxury consumer items and on the incomes of the upper and middle classes. Investments in luxury products should be discouraged through planning and fiscal measures. The resources thus freed up could be used to address poverty in both South and North.

Restructure national policies and programs in the South

In the South, while alternative models of development are undoubtedly essential, a productive increment is also essential. Current stocks of capital and flows of goods and services are not sufficient to meet the legitimate needs and aspirations of peoples in the Third World. In addition, Southern governments must reorient their development strategies toward the eradication of poverty, the fulfilment of basic and human needs, and technological orientation to environmentally sound production systems. The eradication of poverty and the fulfilment of basic needs necessitate social policies for the redistribution of land, or at least access of the poor to land, and an emphasis on people-oriented policies focusing on health, nutrition, housing, education, and transport.

Southern governments must increase their understanding of, and attention to, the links between technologies, scale of economic activities, and poverty. The destruction of the technological and social bases of community economies, often related to the introduction of inappropriate technologies and scales of production, must be stopped. National development plans should ensure that development projects do not have net social costs. On the contrary, development has to be reoriented to protect and enhance the rights of small communities to their land and to basic facilities.

In most cases, where the issue of poverty has been accorded importance in a national agenda, the resultant plans and policies have not adequately reflected environmental linkages. The primary investment focus should be on regions and sectors where the links to environmental degradation are most severe. In fact, rural poverty is often most intense in environmentally degraded areas, such as rural areas with high rates of deforestation and degradation of agricultural lands. In this situation, the aim should be to generate sustained livelihoods by supporting ecologically sound systems of production. In this way, environment and development needs can be served simultaneously (see Box 11).

Support community-level initiatives

At the community level, efforts must be made to apply national policies in ways that benefit the poor. Pivotal to this is devolving control over resources back to where it originally resided: from international systems to the nation state, and from the state to

Box 11

A Program for Global Antipoverty and Ecological Regeneration

Many of the world's poor live in ecologically degraded regions; and, in these regions, the threat of impoverishment is generally greatest during periods of environmental crisis, such as drought. Helping hard-hit communities through employment opportunities in restoring and enhancing their surrounding environment and resource base provides both immediate economic security and the potential for an ecologically secure future. (It should be realized, however, that in some poor regions there is literally no labour surplus. In cases where poverty does not necessarily reflect a lack of employment, the creation of alternative employment opportunities should not draw people away from essential work.)

The Centre for Science and Environment, in New Delhi, proposes that such a program be used to back up an internationally guaranteed Right to Survival. The immediate aim of the program would be to put a floor to poverty, ensuring, at a minimum, a basic wage that provides people with sufficient purchasing power for survival. More progressively, however, if jobs in ecological regeneration were guaranteed to people in regions where environmental degradation or crisis was seriously threatening potential livelihood, these people would be able to stay to build their ecological capital, rather than joining the swelling ranks of environmental refugees. A key focus would be on improving local agroecosystems to create the potential for sustainable livelihoods. One of the additional benefits of such a program would be to relieve pressure on remaining wildlands and areas of high genetic diversity.

local communities. The socioeconomic legitimacy of the "people's economy" — small firms, small farms, etc., mainly family owned and operated — must be recognized as equal to, if not greater than, that of private-sector corporations or large state-run enterprises. Support for this economy does not require major subsidies and does not impose environmental strains or national financial burdens. It does require practical recognition by governments of its legitimate right to exist and thrive, recognition in the form of protected access to land, availability of small lines of credit without collateral requirements, accessibility of operating permits or licences for small producers and merchants, and possibly some marketing assistance. The right of the "people's economy" to exist and expand must be a central tenet of sustainable development. In sum, the operating principle should be better community access to resources to enable sustainable livelihoods based on local resources and appropriate technologies, and oriented to fulfilling basic and human needs.

Economic Order and Development Patterns

Given the critical influence of the global economic order on environment and development worldwide, even the most intense and well-oriented economic reforms at the national level cannot achieve what is necessary without accompanying reforms at the international level. This is not to deny the need for, and indeed centrality of, internal changes in Third World countries. But such changes will not be sufficient. Primarily, the current economic order blocks the path to development in the Third World. Thus, the following proposals are oriented to strengthening the position of Southern countries within the world economic system. The new regime must allow autonomous development in the South within this system.

Improve the terms of trade for the South

For good environmental and economic management in the South, unfair economic trade terms must be rectified. Primarily, current commercial conditions, which concentrate goods, services, and investments primarily in the nations of the North and marginalize the countries of the South, must be modified. There must also be North–South cooperation to reverse the massive and untenable flow of resources from South to North. Ecologically unsound trade must be discouraged, while preventing the use of environmental issues as trade weapons. In addition, the preferential treatment of Third World countries in trade arrangements should be continued, especially in the GATT, where some Northern countries seek erosion of this principle (see Box 8). "Free trade" must be tempered and balanced by the South's legitimate needs to control national development policy and build indigenous capacity.

Reduced prices for primary products have been particularly devastating for some Third World countries, both economically and environmentally. In Latin America, for example, reduced prices have led to the spread of export-oriented agriculture and expansion of the farming frontier and mining areas. Among other things, fair prices for primary products are essential — prices that reflect environmental and regenerative costs and the costs of complying with international conditions. In other words, prices of raw materials from the South must be significantly raised to reflect their real and ecological costs. This will not be possible without appropriate international public policies jointly developed by the producing nations of the South and the consuming nations of the North.

Specifically, one important step would be support from Northern countries for producer–consumer commodity pacts that would fix reasonably high prices for commodities and establish supply plans. Programs of the United Nations Conference on Trade and Development, including the integrated program for commodities, should also be reviewed and strengthened in light of the environment/development crisis of the 1990s. Northern governments must also phase out trade protectionist policies that block or limit the South's access to Northern markets, particularly in relation to basic industries — such as textiles, clothing, and processed raw materials — that are on the rise in the South.

Expansion of trade, investment, and technology transfer between the countries of the South is also essential for more balanced trade relationships. This initiative must come from the South, but should be facilitated, rather than hindered, by the North.

Deal with Third World debt and structural adjustment

The current structural adjustment policies and programs of the World Bank and the International Monetary Fund (IMF) impose additional burdens on the Third World poor. The transfer of resources to other countries during the 1980s, in large measure to service foreign debt, has been the central impediment to improving economic conditions in many Third World countries, particularly in Africa and Latin America. Without a favourable, or at least balanced, flow of resources, regional development will not be possible, as the poor countries require an accumulated increase in production to cover even elementary needs.

The structural adjustment programs imposed on indebted countries should be significantly revised. In lieu of current approaches, mechanisms should be established that relieve debt burdens and thus release financial resources that Southern countries require to deal with their development and environment problems. At the same time, the countries of the South must pursue alternative development strategies that fulfil people's needs without leading the national economy into new external indebtedness.

Regulate transnational corporations

A comprehensive framework should be established to regulate the conduct and effects of TNCs, which are globally the most powerful forces impinging on environment and development. In particular, more effective regulation of TNCs is required in the areas of investment, finance, trade, health, environment, wages, and technology.

Ensure equitable distribution of costs and benefits

The responsibilities, risks, costs, and benefits of environmental protection must be equitably allocated through global negotiations, and considerable attention should be devoted to approaches to, and components of, this "global bargaining" process. This process will inevitably be complex and difficult. The stakes are high, the issues are very politically charged, and the approach taken to the required interregional and intertemporal comparisons depends on the interests at stake and the values applied. These comparisons are also potentially subject to religious, racial, and other prejudices. Nonetheless, there must be a means of weighting relative responsibilities and an associated distribution of costs borne and benefits earned by different individuals, social groups, or countries. Incentives and disincentives must account for the differential impacts of countries on the global environment. The resources of the world are finite, and the rich should not persist in taking a disproportionately large share. Ultimately, the countries of the North — with high levels of responsibility for causing global environmental change, greater financial resources to devote to solutions, and control over basic levers of power (aid, trade, and debt) — must address the issue of sustainability from the foundation of equity and must bear the greater burden for a broad transition to more ecological forms of production.

Taking energy use as an example, the countries of the North, with their much higher total and per-capita fossil fuel consumption, and associated higher emissions of greenhouse gases, must

- Ensure more rational use of energy in the North;
- Work with the South to create an international framework that allows all people equitable access to the atmosphere;
- Provide technological and financial assistance to nations of the South to enable them to achieve maximum efficiency of energy use;
- Assist vulnerable Third World countries in coping with the impacts of climate change; and
- Provide technological and management support for sustainable, integrated use of forest ecosystems and eliminate international economic pressures that encourage short-sighted exploitation of tropical forests.

The Political Order

Knowledge about, let alone participation in, the global environmental debate is limited to a small proportion of humanity, counted largely among the well fed and well housed. Most of the world's peoples are, at best, spectators to this debate. Greater popular awareness of environmental issues and greater participation in their resolution are essential. Indeed, the global environmental debate must be democratically anchored in the national and local politics of every nation. The need for environmental management should not be posed as a trade-off against democratic rights. Credible institutions committed to equitable solutions are also essential at the international level.

Democratize resource management and environmental action

At the national level, democratic systems of government and true participatory democracy are crucial for protecting the environment and promoting sustainable resource use. Policy changes should support the decentralization of planning. Also key are freedom of the press and freedom from monopolistic ownership and control of resources and production. Where political will and leadership on environment issues do not exist, it is necessary to question how to generate them.

What form should a national government take to ensure that it responds to people's genuine interests and aspirations? Dictatorships are not the best way to manage natural resources and ensure that long-term concerns are well accounted for; neither are multiparty parliamentary systems, by themselves, adequate. Even within political democracies, the impact of existing environmental and natural resource policies and laws on people's participation in management must be examined. Vital questions about the types of village and urban institutions required also need to be addressed.

Systems of participatory democracy must be clarified. In particular, the kinds of laws, institutions, and processes required to increase people's control and management of their natural resource base must be determined. There must be opportunities for local peoples to exercise their traditional knowledge in managing their own environments. Where they exist, respect must be accorded to common property resources such as grasslands, forests, and aquatic systems, especially those of importance to the poor. People dependent on natural resources (in particular, women, indigenous peoples, nomads, and fishers) should not be marginalized or impoverished for the sake of "development." Women in particular must be empowered with equal opportunities for education and equal partnership in development. At a more prosaic level, equality must be nurtured through the sharing of daily tasks.

Information on global change should be reaching both policy-makers and citizens. The technocratic perception of environmental issues is a key factor in removing them from domestic political discussion. Environmental concerns should not be the reserve of the technocrat. As a related point, while the role of the state in setting policy and managing major programs is key, the role of NGOs, social movements, and local communities is also important. NGOs must have better access to information to support advocacy work, and national and regional NGOs need information about activities and impacts at the local level. Coalitions of people that reach beyond political, religious, and racial boundaries are needed, as global environmental threats obey none of these boundaries. A particularly important gap lies in the formation of Southern NGO coalitions.

Recognize the sovereignty of Third World countries

The bedrock of a sustainable future is the freedom for communities and nations — within a universally accepted framework that prescribes penalties for harming another community or nation — to control the use and management of their natural resources and thereby determine their own form of economic and social development. Each society can then experiment and learn from its own mistakes. Sustainable development cannot be imposed by an external agent.

Sovereignty is especially critical in relation to natural resources and economic policy. This relates in part to the right to determine the terms under which TNCs can invest in a country (a right being challenged in the current Uruguay Round of GATT negotiations).

Create fair, credible, and democratic international institutions

To support international and equitable sharing of responsibilities for global environmental change, institutional development is essential. International concern for environmental change is producing a normative order that orients investments, commercial movements, and technological relations. This order and the resulting regulations will not necessarily be sensitive to the needs and demands of Third World nations. Indeed, experiences of the Third World with international organizations have led to a belief that the rich countries are unwilling to foster institutions that are responsive to the particular needs of the South. This points to the need for a critical examination of the degree to which the existing world regulatory order, including existing international environmental structures, ensures equitable treatment of all states and respect for their sovereignty.

With respect to international economic institutions, the Bretton Woods institutions (the World Bank and the IMF) and other major international economic actors (including TNCs, the international banks, and GATT) are Northern controlled. These organizations promote policies without addressing their implications for the exploitation of natural resources or for environmental conditions in general. They have thus been largely responsible for promoting the transfer of environmentally unsustainable and socially unacceptable economic models and technological systems from North to South.

The operations of these institutions must be changed so that they promote just and ecologically sustainable policies. As well, the principle of democratizing world economic institutions must be implemented through a program of action that gives the South equitable decision-making power and that is oriented to reducing the concentration of control over investment, production, and trade. Moreover, these institutions, with decision-making powers that affect the lives of so many people, must be made more democratically accountable. Decision-making processes should be transparent and accessible to local communities, as well as to Southern governments. In particular, those who stand to be affected must have the opportunity to participate in program design, impact monitoring, etc.

Institutionalized mechanisms are required for measuring "environmental debt" and reflecting it in a comprehensive system of international accounts. This, in turn, depends on defining an acceptable set of indicators of environmental change.

Finally, the links between environment and peace are strong. The role of international institutions in preventing war is key, as peace is essential to develop the regional cooperation that is required to build sustainability.

Knowledge Systems and Technology

All nations must participate in debates on the global environment as well-informed sovereign states. A two-way flow of information between South and North is crucial. Also, participation in global environmental debates requires greater research capacity within the nations of the South. It is critical that the Third World have access to the knowledge, skills, and technologies that will be vital in the coming decades. Currently, participation is militated against by a low level of research on environmental issues, as well as by repressive political environments.

Improve information flow and the balance of influence

If the countries of the South are to participate as autonomous nation states in the global discourse on the environment, they will have to form their opinions based on firm scientific understanding of the relationships between their national interests and global environmental needs. Research by indigenous scientists is key. In addition, Southern research must have greater penetration and influence in the North.

At local, national, and regional levels, environment and population need to be linked through the concept of carrying capacity. Data bases for analyzing trends in resource quality, quantity, availability, and carrying capacity are needed. The kinds of inter-disciplinary research that are required can only take place with increasing levels of cooperation between sectors and disciplines. Fundamentally, the social research required to understand the human implications of physical environmental change is weak, in both North and South. It is critical that long-term research efforts be linked to short-term needs and goals. The emphasis must be on clear priorities that make sense at the local level and over the short term.

Reorient resource management

Alternative development models require a strategy of natural resource management that minimizes burdens on basic resources — soil, water, forests — and minimizes the exploitation of scarce or sensitive resources. Some elements of such a strategy have already been suggested; in sum, it should

- Combine traditional knowledge and modern technology to improve productive systems and employ regional diversity;

- Integrate productive activities with ecosystem management to ensure the preservation of natural systems and processes; and

- Modify international policies of financing, pricing, markets, etc., to support the viability of production alternatives, and to allow producers to control and manage the productive process.

Perhaps more fundamentally, there must be a reduction in the extraction and production of many primary commodities.

Given the limits to renewability and the vulnerability inherent in overspecialization, achieving the required increments in produc-tion cannot be based on greater extraction of a few resources. The productive potential lies in diversifying the resource base. The potential for diversification in the Third World is in part sup-ported by the fact that many countries of the South continue to harbour very high levels of biological diversity. For example, original vegetation covers 42 percent of the surface area of Latin America, despite extensive degradation. The rich knowledge of different campesino and indigenous communities parallels the natural wealth and is expressed through traditional technologies that have evolved over many generations. These communities rely on a diversified use of natural resources and operate in harmony with the ecosystem, assuring sustainability. Research and management efforts by local resource users must be supported.

A broadened understanding of global responsibility for certain resources is also essential. For example, tropical rain forests, although concentrated in a few countries, benefit all humanity through atmospheric regulation and biodiversity. Therefore, if a country in which natural forests are currently logged for export decides to impose environmentally motivated restrictions on logging, compensation for financial losses that may be incurred should be a global responsibility. Similarly, it is the responsibility of "global consumers" to pay the full ecological and social costs of consumption in a world market where mineral and biomass products are available from distant lands, but are often produced and transported at high ecological and social cost.

Diversify technologies

Drastic changes are required in technologies and production processes. Traditional forms of resource use and traditional technologies were generally energy efficient and ecologically prudent, although their production levels and economic returns were often low. Modern production systems and technologies generally produce larger volumes of goods over time, but rely upon high levels of energy and other resource inputs. The result is a lack of ecological sustainability. The need today is to integrate the ecological wisdom of traditional practices and technologies with the production potentials made possible through modern science and technology, so that increased productivity can be obtained in an ecologically benign manner. Technologies to assist in determining ecosystem potentials and to manage land information are also essential. Investment flows must therefore not only promote growth but also attract technologies.

With respect to industrial technologies, in addition to reducing material and energy intensiveness, strict limits must be placed on the use of toxic substances and hazardous technologies. Policies should be implemented to promote clean fuels, and subsidies for fuels that emit greenhouse gases should be removed. Codes of conduct for the transfer of technology are also needed.

Promote adaptive capabilities

The development of human resources should ensure adaptability in the face of the globalization of knowledge and attitudes. Also, a balance must be struck between globalizing forces and the maintenance of local integrity. By necessity, then, development approaches must be anchored in history and philosophy to ensure that the analysis and ultimate prescriptions are holistic and moral. Environmentalists and social scientists must work to provide relevant and balanced information, to undertake education and advocacy, and to assist people in developing new resources, technologies, and strategies.

Processes of Cultural Change

Efforts to ameliorate global environmental change should strengthen the capacity of peoples to sustainably use their natural resources according to their needs, skills, and aspirations, within the context of an environmentally conscious lifestyle. Values, attitudes, motivations, and capabilities are key, but are perhaps the most complex and difficult aspects of the global environment/ development crisis. A systematic analysis of perceived needs and desires is necessary, as is an understanding of the ways people balance short-term and long-term goals.

Support cultural diversity

The rich variety of relationships that people have had with their natural surroundings are reflected in the diversity of cultures worldwide and in the wide range of religions, philosophies, ethics, values, and lifestyles that characterize these cultures. In general, communities directly dependent on the biophysical environment develop a strong respect for, and a sense of "rootedness" in, the natural world. Unfortunately, the integrity and influence of the associated social norms and values are deteriorating in the face of the dominant, consumption-driven, "throw-away" culture.

Global homogenization of culture and values must be counteracted by recognizing and supporting cultural diversity. Cultural diversity, like biological diversity, must be seen as a resource whose loss diminishes development potential. It may then be possible to foster an enriched appreciation of less material-intensive sources of human satisfaction and fulfilment. Whereas human demands on physical resources must be contained, personal fulfilment through nonconsumptive activities should be freely pursued. Also, in these times of rapid change and enormous pressures, a sense of cultural pride can act to protect ecologically adaptive traditional knowledge and skills.

Promote respect for nature

Individual, institutional, and societal appreciation of, and respect for, nature are essential foundations for a truly sustainable future. The values of many traditional cultures in relation to the natural environment are an important source of wisdom. A better understanding of the conditions that foster a sense of connection with nature is essential, so that these conditions can be promoted at the household level, in the school system, in the business community, and in the various other sectors and institutions responsible for shaping our values and our future. New parameters for development are needed that value the environment. Economic growth, as measured by GNP, per-capita income, etc., is completely inadequate in terms of expressing both environmental and equity concerns.

Promote gender equity

Environmental degradation leads to an excessive work burden on women, who play culturally determined roles of fuel, fodder, and water carriers in almost all Third Word societies. To ensure that women have powers commensurate with their responsibilities, as well as opportunities to expand their spheres of activity, gender equity is a value that must be widely adopted. Equity as measured by equal access to the control and use of resources does not come naturally; it must be part of a deliberate strategy. Increased participation of women in the economy and increased female literacy could be key to generating a demand for family planning, leading to the possibility of stabilized population growth. Experience in Sri Lanka and the Indian state of Kerala has shown that female literacy is strongly linked to the processes of demographic transition. Thus, the population issue should be perceived, most of all, as an issue of women's rights and women's development.

PART II

Research on the Social Dimensions of Environment/Development Issues

CHAPTER 4
Roles, Problems, and Potentials

Clearly, researchers on social issues have a key contribution to make toward understanding the processes of planetary environmental change. In spite of this, the focus of development on rapid economic growth has neglected broad-based social research; research that is essential for sound planning. In a world dominated by commercialism, management, and administration, researchers on social issues have had little or no political or decision-making influence. The emphasis on the biophysical dimensions of change also reveals a bias toward technocratic management based on supposedly "hard" facts, facts acquired within a natural science framework. Environmentalists themselves have primarily focused on scientific data to build their arguments, reinforcing this bias in the popular mind. By both design and default, therefore, researchers on social issues in both the South and the North have been assigned a marginal role in defining and addressing global environment/development issues.

At the same time, social scientists have neglected or been inadequately informed about issues central to the global environmental debate. In fact, they frequently address issues that have important environmental implications, but are often not adequately aware of these implications. The environment has been seen primarily as the province of the physical and biological sciences; the social sciences have neglected to take adequate account of the interaction of environmental problems with socioeconomic structures.

There is increasing recognition that the roots of — and solutions to — environmental problems lie in social and economic institutions at local, national, and international levels. A solid understanding of social conditions and processes is key to successful development. Indeed, experience clearly indicates that many development initiatives fail not because they are scientifically or technically flawed, but because they do not account for the social, political, economic, and cultural systems within which they were meant to operate.

Thus, integrating environmental concerns with development planning, and the very concept of sustainable development, brings into focus critical social and economic issues. To acknowledge the essential role of social science research in development planning is to accept that noneconomic factors are as important as economic goals. Social science research gives development a human face.

Roles of Social Research in the Environment/Development Context

The primary purpose of research on social issues is to understand human relations; it should clearly not be limited to an "academic" exercise. Analysis directed to problem solving, including the formation of social policy, is also legitimate and pertinent social research. However, conceptual and methodological development would be impeded if research focus was dictated solely by social problems and priorities. Moreover, given the pressing nature of environment/development problems, attention must be focused on bringing together basic and applied research related to environmental issues. Social research should also focus on means of enhancing cooperation between sectors and regions to develop shared understanding andgoals. Interdisciplinary sharing of information is one essential component.

The appropriate implementation of research is to be encouraged; but, this is not explicitly or necessarily the role of the researcher. Other actors must be involved in carrying the research through to practical application. Social work or activism that does not involve study, analysis, and the development and sharing of knowledge is not social research. Researchers may become involved in practical applications of the research, however, and this can enrich the research process.

Social science research related to environment/development issues can be conducted in both academic and nonacademic settings, and directly within the community, as action research. Indeed, social science research on these issues is not, and should not be, restricted to social scientists. Researchers from a range of backgrounds and disciplines should heed social issues.

Basic Understanding and Knowledge

The most conspicuous role of social research in relation to the environment/development crisis is to investigate the nature of relationships between social conditions, values and attitudes (motivations), human activities (primarily economic and technological), and environmental quality. These investigations may contribute to developing the methods of research and analysis required to predict, prevent, or control environmental and developmental degradation.

Predictive Analysis

Social science also has a predictive or projective function. Such a role requires the formation of research frameworks and studies to project future trends. It may, for example, involve monitoring trends in socioeconomic behaviour and analyzing the environmental implications of these trends (for example, implications for resource use and probable consequences of predicted changes in resource use). Social research may also define probable responses in relation to particular sets of decisions and choices, and thereby help to clarify desirable options.

Policy and Institutional Analysis

Social research can broaden the policy and planning process in relation to environment/development issues to include considerations beyond those of an economic and technical nature. It can also address key social policy issues. For example, how should the burden of adjustments required for sustainable development be distributed between countries, between social classes within countries, and between current and future generations? Institutional analysis can contribute toward improving existing national and regional institutions. It can identify the need for new institutions and develop strategies for regional cooperation and regional environmental management.

Education

Social research should help to heighten the understanding of the philosophical and practical implications of environmental issues among all sectors. It is particularly important for local people to understand the environmental and related socioeconomic implications of both locally generated and externally imposed change. For example, developing comprehensive and accessible frameworks to analyze environmental change would allow nontechnical people to absorb and use the information. Also, social research should raise the awareness of decision-makers to the needs of local people, particularly those people who are highly dependent on their environment.

Advocacy and Empowerment

Social research should not only contribute to people's under-standing but also enable their involvement and empowerment. It should help to stimulate the acceptance of responsibility by indi-vidual citizens, communities, and governments, as well as educa-tional, religious, and financial institutions. Marginalized people in particular need tools to defend themselves against abuse and absolute poverty. Social research can help people to articulate their interests and needs before regional development plans and projects are implemented. Research should also promote respect for the spiritual beliefs and values of other cultures. Ultimately, the value of social research may go beyond describing existing beliefs, values, and attitudes, and actually stimulate their positive evolution.

As implied earlier, there is also a place for social research in proactively identifying alternatives for the survival and develop-ment of communities. An example would be alternative decision-making processes and structures that would enable local people to have more control over their natural resources, and to exercise that control democratically and in the interests of environmental sustainability.

Key Limitations and Problems

Although the wide-ranging environmental effects of human activi-ties are now of acute concern, the social sciences — notwith-standing increasing sensitivity — do not reflect this concern in their scope of study. Many challenging conceptual and method-ological questions have been raised in relation to the role of the social sciences in the environment/development arena. The expertise and insight of social researchers worldwide could do much to answering these questions.

Inherent Complexity of Environment/Development Issues

The relationships between people and their environment are inherently complex and many modern causes and effects are new to humanity. Human–environment interactions are multidimen-sional, often characterized by relationships that are reciprocal and random. Given the changing velocities of these processes, as well as the changes in the type and intensity of their outcomes, an appreciation of historical relationships is essential.

Inadequacy of Existing Frameworks

At one extreme, it has been suggested that changes within social science paradigms — perhaps even fundamental paradigm shifts — are needed to make the social sciences relevant to environment/development problems. At the other extreme, the lack of knowledge about the social dimensions of environmental issues is seen to reflect the simple lack of attention that has been devoted to these issues. There is no consensus on the question of paradigms. However, the need for a new framework to address emerging interdisciplinary challenges has been frequently articulated, and some elements of this framework have been proposed. Unfortunately, there has yet to be a clear focus to galvanize the research community.

The lack of a specific conceptual framework for addressing environmental issues has forced researchers to depend on existing disciplinary approaches, although these do not correctly fit the complex, interwoven realities of human–environment relationships (see Box 12). In many cases, environmental issues are addressed by simply adding "one more variable" to an already existing analysis. The lack of a clear framework may also partly account for a certain "faddishness" in environment/development research. The focus shifts from impact assessment, to women in development, to resource-based analyses, with little real integration or coherence.

Lack of Interdisciplinarity

Perhaps the key limiting factor in most current research on ecological problems is the artificial and misleading isolation of the social and natural sciences, and a lack of tradition of interdisciplinary work by social scientists.

One sector that exemplifies the need for an interdisciplinary approach is agriculture. A critical set of policy issues relates to trade-offs between short-term and long-term productivity. Fundamentally, new criteria for efficiency are required. Complex questions arise regarding trade-offs in the use of hybrid seeds and pesticides and the roles of traditional and modern agricultural practices. Such issues cannot be left entirely to biophysical

---

Box 12

Examples of Disciplinary Limitations

Although it is difficult to establish whether a particular discipline's limitations are inherent to its theoretical structure or reflect the focus of its practitioners, it is clear that the dominant approaches in most disciplines have failed to adequately address the majorenvironment/development issues. Within the economics profession, for example, there is a preoccupation with variables (such as growth of national product) whose measurement excludes such key development/environment variables as the "hidden" contribution of women to the economy, the "downstream" environmental costs of economic activities, and the cultural homogenization often associated with economic development. In more recent years, the prevailing political orientation in the countries of the North — reflected in part in the rise of neoliberalism and a focus on static allocative efficiency and short-term stabilization measures — has tended toward unbridled faith in the market. This faith is maintained largely by underestimating the "externalities" of activities of producers and consumers, by ignoring the long-term implications of current economic activities, and by removing equity issues from the economic development agenda.

The sociology of development, another important intellectual discipline, tempers the growth centredness of economics by contemplating issues of equity, basic needs satisfaction, and social relations. Practitioners within this discipline are concerned primarily with issues such as ownership of productive assets, distribution of incomes, and factors affecting productivity. It is recognized that the unequal distribution of assets, incomes, and power are structural forces that result in inequitable, unbalanced development, regardless of the rate of economic growth. Nonetheless, as with economics, there is a prevailing belief in the desirability of economic growth and a disregard for the problems inherent in attempting to sustain this growth. A related dominant assumption is that technological modernization is desirable and positive. There is inadequate questioning of the ecological, social, and developmental consequences of interactions between humanity, nature, and technology.

---

scientists; they have major implications for economic policy, social policy, and development planning as a whole. Similar issues and policy dilemmas arise in all sectors, including industry, transportation, energy, housing, and health.

Despite the urgency, few researchers on social issues are attempting to come to terms with what "sustainability" means in the context of their work. Few are equipped with an operative knowledge of the different facets of the environmental crisis. At the same time, physical science analysis has not been adequately extended to include social causes, effects, and possible solutions to environmental problems. In sum, whereas the instruments of social science analysis are critical, the knowledge and tools of both the physical and social sciences must be combined to understand and resolve the environmental crisis.

Efforts are being made toward interdisciplinarity. For example, there is an increasing number of interdisciplinary programs in universities, as well as joint working groups and panels in a range of institutional settings. The increased sensitivity of development sponsors — largely because of pressures arising from project-specific impacts — is also stimulating an environmental focus in social research. Moreover, social research in the South has addressed issues associated with environmental resources and natural disasters. Nonetheless, the overall situation of disciplinary isolation has not greatly changed. Environment/development problems are too rarely analyzed within an integrated framework.

The results of unidisciplinary research can be disturbing. For example, many economists involved in environmental research take a quantitative and neoclassical approach; an approach that is promoted by many influential research sponsors. The resulting "solutions" tend to be antihumanist, their main thrust being increased privatization. The ongoing dominance of economic analysis in development decision-making is producing very real and disturbing effects. People traditionally reliant on their local environment are being disenfranchised in the name of environmental protection.

Decline of Equity Considerations

The preceding example reflects the dangers of addressing complex environmental problems without dealing with concerns of equity. In the 1960s and 1970s, most development research demonstrated at least some sensitivity to issues of equity. Equity must be reintroduced and reinforced as a central consideration in any research related to environment/development issues.

Inappropriate Units of Analysis

Social analysis is sometimes performed in relation to administrative regions and economic categories. Seldom, however, does it focus on particular ecological regions or natural resource boundaries. Despite some global commonalities in the appearance of environmental problems, the implications for each region are unique. This uniqueness is a function of distinct natural, cultural, and social conditions, which, together, determine the form in which people relate to and use their environment. In other words, regional conditions dictate the regional relevance of particular environmental concerns; they should thus be reflected in the design and focus of research activities. The global concerns associated with climate change, for example, are relevant worldwide. However, their relative priority in a given region would depend on the vulnerability of that region to climate change, the existence and perceived severity of other environmental threats, and the degree to which that region contributes to climate change. Thus, to understand the human dimensions of global environmental change, the causes and effects of global change must be examined from the regional perspective, regions being defined on the basis of environmental and developmental coherence.

CHAPTER 5
Challenges and Emerging Trends in the South

Challenges for Southern Researchers

One of the major barriers to social research on environmental issues in the South is that social scientists traditionally confine themselves to socioeconomic issues, detached from their biophysical framework. In a broader sense, there is a lack of interdisciplinary tradition. These are generic problems. There are several problems more specific to Southern research and analysis on environment/development issues, including data deficiencies, Northern domination, and institutional barriers. For the South to develop a distinctive and functional understanding of major environmental issues, both the generic and specific constraints on the role of the social sciences must be addressed.

Data Deficiencies

Researchers in all regions of the South face serious data problems. Compared with their Northern colleagues, Third World social researchers are at a great disadvantage: they lack the basic data necessary to analyze the social significance of environmental phenomena. Low research budgets have limited the acquisition and analysis of data and, to date, research capacity continues to fall far short of research needs. Resources for conducting primary research in particular are extremely limited. Moreover, much of the data that do exist are unreliable or outdated, and statistics are seldom in an appropriate form. These problems are compounded by the fact that considerable work on environmental issues is produced as consultancy reports. Such reports are usually not accessible to the research community — the underlying data is considered the sole property of the consulting firm or reports are classified confidential when considered controversial or embarrassing to the authorities. In some regions, the proportion of environment/development research that is caught in this "grey" literature is truly intolerable; in many cases, it denies people access to information that is fundamental to their livelihoods and futures.

Dominance of Northern Perspectives and Approaches

Southern social research on environment/development issues is, like many other areas of research, dominated by Northern perspectives. Many factors have promoted this domination, including

- Conceptual vacuums (lack of alternative ideas and perspectives) in the South, partly a reflection of the newness of many of the issues;

- Influences in the training and background of national professionals that foster uncritical adherence to Northern ideologies and methodologies; and

- The prevalence of Northern financial support and research facilities, through which selected hypotheses, approaches, and often conclusions are promoted.

Primary indicators of domination include an unquestioning acceptance of imported ideas, approaches, and interpretations, and their propagation through work carried out in the local or national context, irrespective of their true applicability. Based on these indicators, there is no doubt that the "dominant view" of global environmental issues is accepted to a certain extent by many Southern professionals. Both academic and state-supported projects have borrowed ideas and approaches from the North, and the associated views and interpretations often strongly influence conclusions and recommendations. However, Northern domination is far from absolute. As work progresses and higher levels of understanding are achieved, national professionals are able to develop their own perspectives on social problems, including global environmental issues.

To propose relevant and culturally respectful solutions, social research on environment/development issues must truly reflect local and regional culture and history. Traditional assumptions and approaches must, therefore, be challenged. However, a critical perspective on "Western" ideas needs to be articulated with caution. It has become a fad among many Southern scholars to label everything as "Western" and then decry it. This can lead to the curbing of what could be very useful research. Critics must rise beyond the level of repudiation and assist in developing an independent, alternate set of perspectives. Also, certain concepts and tools, although developed in the North, remain universal and should be used without fear of domination. The challenge to Southern social scientists is to use these concepts and tools, adapted as necessary, to develop their own agenda and solve their own problems. Anti-Westernists should also beware of uncritical and unquestioned romanticism for the past. Several environmentally friendly technologies of the past — for example, manual grinding of grain — were also "women-unfriendly," placing excessive demands on women's labour.

Financial Dependence and the Research Agenda

Southern researchers rely heavily on Northern money. This makes it difficult for them to direct their efforts according to nationally or regionally relevant priorities. Thus, key areas of importance for the South are inadequately studied. For example, there is little to no Southern research on key Northern institutions and activities that influence environment and development globally and in the South, including the green movements in the North, which have potentially tremendous implications for Northern politics and, thus, South–North relations. The research agenda must be redirected toward greater self-generated understanding of both dynamics within the South and impacts of the North upon the South.

Large development institutions that commission or finance environmental research rely, in most cases, on their own experts. This is partly because of a real or imagined lack of local expertise and partly because consultancy firms in donor countries have often cornered the market on such work. Thus, when local specialists are involved, they often serve as subcontractors to donor-country consultancy firms. The division of labour in these contracts generally confines local research to gathering clearly specified data. Analysis is then done by the foreign consulting agency. Given economic conditions and poor salaries in many Third World countries, such subcontracts are sufficiently lucrative that they attract some of the best scholars.

Such contracts seldom lead to the production of academically respectable output by local researchers. The documents produced are rarely subject to peer review. Indeed, they are rarely even available to local researchers — they are often only circulated internally, considered for official use only, or even classified as confidential.

Lack of Influence of Southern Research

The challenges raised by the dominance of the North are related not only to the "decolonization" of Southern approaches to research and the establishment of research priorities, but also to the establishment and amplification of the influence of Southern research on policy formulation, globally, regionally, and nationally. Policies and programs of the major international and bilateral financing and aid organizations continue to be heavily if not exclusively guided by Northern research, regardless of the credible and often innovative research from the South.

In fact, although the extreme underrepresentation of Southern-generated analysis reflects the biases of Northern institutions, it also reflects the reality that Northern researchers continue to produce a much larger body of literature on the South than do Southern researchers! This is not to deny the existence of high-quality and important research from the South; rather, it emphasizes the need for more support for research by Southerners.

The Actors

Roles and Problems of Universities

In much of the South, environmental research, like most other areas of research, takes place primarily in universities. However, the relatively rigid boundaries of traditional disciplines have made it difficult for universities to embrace what is essentially an inter-disciplinary subject. Thus, there are few universities where environmental issues — physical or social — have been integrated into existing programs and courses. Even though there are now special curricula and research programs in many universities to address biophysical environment issues, the social aspects of environmental problems have been largely neglected. Even where social issues are being integrated, the analytic approach generally remains weak. Where discrete interdisciplinary teaching and research programs on the environment have been established, their novelty and rarity tend to place great demands on the host institutions.

Beyond problems specific to introducing environmental studies in existing institutions is the crisis faced by these institutions as a whole. Grave economic conditions, compounded in many cases by austerity measures applied through structural adjustment programs, are undermining the financial base of postsecondary institutions. Research programs — never a priority even in the best of times — are often most deeply affected. Universities are invariably overcrowded, and staff are demoralized by poor pay, inadequate equipment, and excessive workload. In many cases, laboratories and libraries have virtually collapsed. Environmental programs, therefore, become dependent on consultancy research commissioned by international funding agencies or NGOs — research that is often project specific, such as environmental and social impact assessment. The opportunity to undertake independent research oriented toward comprehensive and long-term analysis is uncommon.

Roles and Problems of NGOs

Increasingly, relevant environment/development research is taking place outside universities, particularly in NGOs. This is partly because of the inadequate response and research capacity of the universities and partly because nonacademic institutions and popular movements have a different set of perceptions and needs in relation to environment/development issues. In some regions, the NGO community has played a key role in initiating research on the environment and in shaping its major thrust; however, patterns and results differ from region to region. In some cases, NGOs with holistic approaches undertake sophisticated, credible research, whose relevance is often enhanced by integrating practical community experience. Indeed, the trend toward integrating environment/development analysis has been greatly stimulated by NGOs and social movements.

In other cases, however, there are notable shortcomings in NGO research. In many regions of the South, NGOs, like universities, depend on consultancy research and research sponsored by Northern-based NGOs. This reflects the fact that consulting is the only relatively steady and secure source of research funding. Whereas some research sponsors are sensitive to locally defined research needs or will allow the recipient organization a significant degree of autonomy in allocating funds, donor-driven research more commonly reflects the perspectives and needs of the donor organization. On the positive side, however, NGOs have wrested some environmental issues from domination by consultants and have promoted greater media attention and public debate on the environment.

Given their typically "activist" positions, NGOs tend to work with local activists, although they are not necessarily the best local researchers. Also, many NGOs tend to adopt what are — intentionally or not — rather anti-intellectual positions. In many cases, the approach involves uncritical use of participatory research and rapid evaluation methods. Some of this sort of research is informative; however, it is seldom a basis for understanding the long-term needs and problems of an environmentally sustainable development process. These research efforts are far from exhaustive and need to be complemented by fundamental research.

NGOs in Southeast Asia and the Pacific

There are many NGOs and study centres in Southeast Asia and the Pacific that specialize in environmental issues. Also, NGOs working in related areas — for example, community development, basic needs satisfaction, health, and consumer issues — often undertake research into community-level environment/ development problems that affect their main area of concern. The research undertaken by fledgling NGOs may be rudimentary and highly community specific; but, as experience and information build, so does the breadth, sophistication, and general applicability of the NGO research. The research generated or supported by NGOs, often based on action-research methods, is generally richly empirical and very grounded. Therefore, it is of great practical relevance.

There is a growing trend for NGOs in Southeast Asia and the Pacific to build their own research capacity, and an increasing number of professionally trained researchers and former university academics are joining NGOs as full-time research staff. Alternatively, academic researchers may work through NGOs. But, unless the research is commissioned or somehow controlled by the NGO, the experience may be frustrating and of limited advantage to the organization. Thus, where outside academic expertise is to be used, a combination of "in-house" research capability and directed input from university academics is most acceptable from the NGO perspective. Some NGOs in Southeast Asia have also helped to establish policy research institutes, which are free to undertake independent analyses.

NGOs in Africa

In Africa, local people are beginning to take over the development and environment research institutes and NGOs originally established by expatriates or outside agencies. However, there is little funding available for indigenously defined research priorities. With economic conditions and structural adjustment, government funding for research has all but dried up, leaving almost exclusive reliance on external funding. Foreign national and international environmental organizations have begun capturing research funds that were once the province of the universities. Funding from bilateral and multilateral agencies is also being diverted to Northern NGOs. Research efforts are therefore biased toward the particular and often narrow interests of foreign NGOs — for example, wildlife conservation — at the expense of compelling endemic needs, such as social research on the degradation of natural resources.

The research undertaken by NGOs in Africa is often rudimentary, project or community specific, and oriented toward short-term, quick-fix solutions. Given the urgency of the famine problem in Africa, for example, NGOs of non-African origin have focused on immediate, short-term, action-oriented "fixes." Although some of this research has grown in breadth, sophistication, and general applicability, in many cases its value and applicability remain limited. Indeed, some of this work can hardly be deemed research at all; it is more like filling in checklists. Moreover, because the intellectual demands of this type of work are quite low and the rewards are rather lucrative, many researchers are casually including environment in their list of specializations.

NGOs in Latin America and the Caribbean

In some countries of Latin America and Caribbean, risks of a degeneration in basic research capabilities and a distortion of research priorities arise from opportunistic responses to research funding. In this region, the amount of money available for environmental research has generally been increasing. Much of the money comes from research foundations and, in many cases, nationals have considerable authority in determining how the research money will be used.

A key issue, however, is who is capturing the funding. In most parts of Latin America and the Caribbean, research capability lies primarily with the universities. However, partly because of the red tape involved in funding public university research, foundations are increasingly channeling research money to NGOs and, in some cases, directly to communities. This may explain the recent proliferation of NGOs, some of which are one- or two-person operations that do not have a clear constituency. Some NGOs in the region have contributed significantly to the understanding of environmental issues; but not all have the capacity for disciplined, credible research. Thus, an entrepreneurial as opposed to scientific approach to research may prove detrimental to developing a comprehensive, integrated understanding. As elsewhere, consultancy firms are capturing substantial funding for impact assessment, which is now law in some countries. This again is pulling some of the best researchers away from the universities and generating an information base that is inaccessible to the research community and the public.

Government Research Institutions

Governments are also important direct researchers. In many countries, the state directly runs research stations, research centres, or policy-oriented think tanks. Such centres or institutions generally have some measure of freedom from typical public-service constraints, but are usually faced with three problems:

- A mandate that is limited to addressing those issues that the government deems relevant;

- Limitations on research freedom, even within identified areas, through restrictions on the kinds of themes that can be explored or through control over distribution of research output; and

- Financial constraints that often reflect a more generalized cutting back of the state.

Despite these constraints, government research institutions remain potentially useful sources of knowledge. A key challenge is to make the work of these institutions less bureaucratic, more transparent, and more accessible.

Foreign Research Institutions

Foreign research institutions play a critical role in many Third World countries. Some actually maintain research teams in the South. These researchers often do excellent work by international standards; but their "enclave" character tends to undercut the relevance of their work to local communities. In most cases, the research is addressed to issues identified by their home institutions, and the approaches used are not always appropriate to local situations. Furthermore, these institutions tend to integrate outward and have little local intellectual anchoring. Any interaction they do have with local intellectual communities is often sporadic and paternalistic.

For example, collaboration between the institute's researchers and their local counterparts is often marred by a division of labour in which the foreign researchers carry out the conceptual work and analysis and the local researchers are confined to gathering data. Such a division of labour does not contribute to creating local capacity to identify research areas, develop research methods, and analyze empirical results. In the worst cases, such research draws on local intellectual resources — human and bibliographical — without proper acknowledgment and with no obligation to communicate research results to the local community.

Role of Local People

Historically, local people have had limited access to information that would help them to perceive the significance of their actions in the global context or the implications of global dynamics on their own lives. Local people living at the subsistence level do, however, experience environmental change in a direct way and are usually aware of the causes. Although such knowledge may not derive from conventional scientific processes, it can contribute greatly to an understanding of environment/development dynamics.

In the past, local people have seldom had the confidence or influence to bring their experience and knowledge into "external" spheres of decision-making. Recently, however, local people in some regions have become increasingly active and empowered. This reflects the growth of communication networks and, in some cases, is the result of environmental disasters. Examples include the emergence of women's groups in the Pacific islands to protest nuclear testing and the solidarity of indigenous forest dwellers against logging in Southeast Asia. Also, some very grassroots associations are forming to address basic situations and issues; in some cases, oral communication networks are quite effective at gathering and disbursing information. (The problem for more formal research organizations is how to tap into these networks.) Thus, traditional interests and knowledge are beginning to penetrate the research and decision-making establishments.

Themes and Trends in Research

Common Themes

Despite a widely diverse set of concerns and institutional orientations, there are certain broad themes that research in the South tends to emphasize. These can be contrasted with the dominant Northern perspectives.

In much Southern environmental research, nature–society interactions are key, in particular, the implications of environmental change for society. Even though Southern environmental research tends to address both intragenerational and intergenerational dimensions, "here and now" issues are central. Thus, predictions and recommendations focus on the short or medium term. Analytic approaches are relatively simple and are oriented to addressing change processes within current problem-solving modes. This increases the ease and potential of associating causes of, consequences of, and responses to change. In contrast stands the Northern tendency to focus increasingly on intergenerational issues, on long time horizons, and on impacts involving selected geophysical variables affecting the fundamental equilibrium of planetary systems.

Generally, Southern research also tends to focus on geographically discrete environmental changes; Northern research is dominated by more systemic changes. In other words, Southern research tends to focus on localized types of activity, where cause and effect are geographically close. Thus, an activity and its associated impacts do not cause change elsewhere. When widely replicated, however, such activities may, together, be enough to affect the global situation. In contrast, systemic environmental change is essentially independent of the locale of its cause. Impacts resulting from an activity in a particular place may, independent of local effects, trigger system-wide adjustments. Global warming, largely caused by carbon dioxide emissions into the atmosphere, is an example of systemic change.

Research Topics

Taking Southern social research as a whole, some trends are apparent. Analytic and methodological social science skills are increasingly being applied to the problems of environment and development and to the management of human and environmental resources. The trend has been stimulated and primarily led by NGOs, social movements, and the researchers associated with them. This reflects increased contact among social action groups working on environmental issues through the growing number of information and activity networks.

Insights gained from this sharing of experiences and research have highlighted the degree to which international factors are at the root of many national and local environmental problems. Equity, environment issues, and the links between poverty and the environment are therefore emerging as subjects of increasing research and intense debate in the South. NGO researchers in particular are focusing more and more on these factors, and the findings are being used in discussions with representatives of international agencies, such as the World Bank, about the impacts of their policies and projects.

Another issue that is attracting considerable research interest in many Third World countries is the relationship between structural adjustment, debt, and the environment. This relationship takes two forms. One is the effect of strategies based on increased exploitation and export of raw materials implicit in adjustment strategies. The other is the problem of "environmental conditionalities" that are either being counseled or actually imposed. Research in Latin America has paid particular attention to these issues, and some research in Africa is also beginning to look at them. Related to this is the whole issue of "debt for nature" swaps. Problems of managing internationally shared natural regions (that is, the global commons and regions that straddle more than one national jurisdiction), such as the Amazon, Antarctica, and the Pacific Ocean, are also attracting special attention among researchers in Latin America. In addition, Latin American researchers have paid particular attention to problems of genetic manipulation and the erosion of biodiversity.

For more than two decades, drought and desertification have been viewed as the major environmental challenge in much of Africa. Thus, it is not surprising that these problems have received more attention than any other aspects of environmental change. In this respect, many authors have sought to uncover the factors responsible and have advanced various hypotheses about the causes. The conjectures arising from such studies, however, are rarely substantiated with conclusive data. Also, in this large body of literature, direct and systematic treatment of the relationship between the changing patterns of natural resource use and global environmental change are rare.

Concerns related to soil erosion have also been prominent, perhaps most particularly the crucial role of land degradation in the agrarian crisis. On the technical side, range science is largely concerned with interventions to improve the land for cultivation (for example, rotational system, legume seeding, intercropping, riding and heaping, and ploughing and planting densities). Studies in agronomy and farming systems reflect a new sensitivity to the ecological values of traditional farming practices. It is now realized that most of these practices are environmentally sustainable and thus have enabled local peoples to cope, if not thrive, in their environment for centuries. In Latin America, questions of erosion have been conceived on the basis of large geographical areas such as the Andes, where erosion is a major concern.

The flood of recent discoveries of surreptitious toxic waste dumping in some countries of Africa and Latin America has generated heated — but rather unsystematic and uncoordinated — debate, mainly carried out in the mass media. These discoveries reveal the vulnerability to abuse of many Third World countries and highlight the lack of scientific and technological capacity for monitoring, detecting, and providing adequate information on most aspects of global environmental change.

Other issues that have been featured in the literature of the South relate to urban, industrial, and human settlement problems (for example, urban decay, housing problems, industrial pollution, and population growth). The link between urban environmental problems and unprecedented rates of urban growth has stimulated research on the "push" factors of rural environmental degradation and the "pull" factors of urban life.

PART III

The Social Research Agenda and the Institutional Requirements

CHAPTER 6
Values, Principles, and Approaches

In developing the proposed research agenda — that is, in select-
ing and explaining key research themes and topics — we, the
Commission, were guided by the values, principles, and
approaches outlined in this Chapter. We believe that they should
also guide all research efforts on environment/development
issues.

Values and Principles

Attention to Equity and Poverty Issues

A review of environment research from the South reveals a recur-
ring concern with matters of equity. This likely reflects the immediacy and saliency of intragenerational distribution issues and
poverty in the South. As one of the highest priorities of development is to improve quality of life, the emphasis on equity must be
maintained and reinforced in both identifying research requirements and in undertaking research. This point bears greater
emphasis in light of the ascendancy and prevalence of
approaches that either seek to expunge equity issues from policy
analysis or, at best, relegate them to secondary, if not formal and
token, considerations.

Attention to Democracy and Human Rights

An emphasis on the purely physical symptoms of environmental
problems tends to encourage a technocratic view of both the
problems and the solutions. However, to the extent that environmental processes affect and are affected by human actions, they
are linked to politics and, therefore, to issues of values, power,
and governance. Thus, in determining the focus of research and
conducting the research itself, particular attention must granted to
issues of basic human rights, as well as the decision-making
methods and the distribution of power in society as these affect
environmental processes or responses to these processes.

Related to this is the question of national sovereignty and the
rights of nations as enshrined in various international charters.
The global nature of many problems will likely require that global
monitoring and regulatory agencies be established. This will

almost invariably entail a "surrender" of some aspects of national sovereignty. Respect for both human rights and the rights of nations to sovereignty means that accession by nations and their citizenry to international agreements on environmental monitoring must be voluntary and democratic. Research on the environment will have to be sensitive to these rights.

Gender Sensitivity

Our point of departure — the human dimension of global environmental change — calls for an agenda and a research approach that is gender sensitive. Even though studies on "women and environment" have sensitized the research community to the differential impact of environmental processes on women, they have been carried out in a "ghetto" of their own and are often merely perfunctorily appended to principal analyses. In addition, such studies have tended to be confined to areas that, through gender bias, have been designated as female economic activities — namely, those related to subsistence and family. As a result, gender considerations are usually not adequately represented, if at all, in such areas as economic policy and environmental management. Researchers, when elaborating proposed research themes, must consciously and meaningfully consider the gender dimensions of the topic at hand.

Approaches

Interdisciplinarity and Process Orientation

Environment/development issues are, by definition, complex. As well, the entire mosaic of interactions between human societies and their environments can vary over different historical periods. These realities make it essential to articulate and explore development/environment issues within an interactive, interdisciplinary, spatial, and temporal framework.

In applying this analytic approach to human–nature interactions, the human environment can be perceived in two broad categories: the natural environment and the socioeconomic system. The two continually interact through numerous feedback loops. The socioeconomic system itself is a mosaic of the technological, cultural, economic, political, legal, and administrative subsystems of a human community inhabiting a specific natural environment.

These subsystems are intimately interconnected and determine the pattern of a human community's interaction with its surrounding environment. A human community may overexploit its natural environment, causing it to deteriorate. But, as the two are joined through a feedback loop, the deterioration of the natural ecosystem will ultimately damage the socioeconomic system.

The human–nature interactions of a particular community are further affected by interactions with external human communities. Through economic exchange and the transfer of knowledge or technology, cultures living in different natural environments within the same nation will interact. Cultures from different nations may interact either indirectly through economic exchange, the transfer of knowledge or technology, and the spread of foreign lifestyles, or directly through political domination (as in the days of colonialism) or economic domination (as a result, for example, of heavy indebtedness and externally imposed conditions).

What does this mean for research? Environmental processes are both physical and social, and occur over time in a multifaceted and complex manner. As such, they can only be fully grasped if the strengths of various disciplines are applied — not in fragmented and compartmentalized ways but as part of an integrated approach. To capture both the global and historical nature of environmental change, such an approach must be temporally and spatially comparative. In other words, it must be sensitive to the differential impact of environmental processes on different physical and social spaces, and it must seek to understand their dynamic evolution over time.

This is not to deny the special competence of each discipline. Nor is it to deny the fact that certain themes are more amenable to research in one discipline than in another. Rather, it is to insist that disciplinary competence can only be brought to full potential within a consciously interdisciplinary framework. The dialectical and synergetic interplay of different disciplines will not only promote an holistic perception of the environment but will also enrich individual disciplines. In developing the research agenda, our commitment to an interdisciplinary approach is clear. Not only is it reflected in the way that the specific research topics are articulated, but also in the organization of these topics within integrative issue areas or themes.

Focus on Regional and Local Perspectives

By its very existence and composition, the Commission highlights the importance of exploring the causes and effects of global environmental change from regional perspectives. In developing the research agenda, we have attempted to allow for the flexibility necessary to address the tremendous variations between regions — variations in terms of biophysical conditions, levels of material development, sociopolitical systems, cultures, human interactions with the physical environment, the environmental impacts of different lifestyles, and the ways that environmental problems manifest themselves. Research that captures regional and local perspectives and experiences with respect to environmental issues is essential. This will not only help to correct the currently skewed perception of global environmental problems (favouring Northern concepts and concerns), but will also capture the full complexity and variety of the impacts of global environmental changes and ensure a sensitivity to local conditions and needs.

Attention to Global and Transboundary Dimensions

We have explored, in some detail, the international causes of key environment/development problems. Attention must also be given to the ways in which environmental problems manifest themselves both internationally and globally. Environmental impacts on the global commons are one category. The more general case involves any of a wide variety of environmental problems with transboundary dimensions.

Global commons, defined by lack of national ownership, include Antarctica, outer space, the deep oceans, and the atmosphere. Threats to the commons may originate primarily in particular regions, but impacts may be felt globally, and the severity of effects on humans does not correspond to culpability.

For example, although some regions of the world bear a much greater responsibility for the climate changes now occurring (being the major consumers of fossil fuels and the major beneficiaries of deforestation), the environmental repercussions will be experienced worldwide. However, the nature and severity of human experience of the environmental repercussions will vary greatly (see Box 5). Ironically, it is the least culpable countries that often will be most affected by environmental impacts and the resulting societal impacts and human devastation. This is primarily because of their lack of capital to invest in infrastructure and technologies to cope with environmental and societal change.

There is also a wide range of transboundary environmental problems, including transboundary (but not global) air pollution (acid rain, for example), transboundary trade in toxic products and waste, transboundary impacts on water quality and quantity, and international tourism.

CHAPTER 7
The Research Agenda

Research Themes

The research agenda is structured around three sets of physical environment issues, and five social issue areas. A "cause and effect" analysis of the three physical issues can be pursued by analyzing the social dimensions within the five social issue areas. We believe that these eight issues provide a reasonably straight-forward, comprehensive, and interactive set of themes, covering the key dimensions of the environment/development crisis.

Physical Environment Issues

Resource depletion and degradation

Resource depletion and degradation are associated, either directly or indirectly, with primary resource exploitation or with activities and infrastructure — such as those connected with urbanization, transportation, and international tourism — that extend over land and water, and thereby affect or encompass associated resources. Impacts include losing productive lands or habitats through competitive uses, erosion, loss of fertility, etc.; decreasing stocks of nonrenewable resources; declining populations and yields of species; and losing biodiversity through species extinction or reduction in intraspecies diversity. These human-induced losses translate into a reduced potential for development, particularly sustainable development.

Resource problems may be depicted in sectoral terms.

- **Land and soils:** Land scarcity reflects the intensity of competing uses and, in particular, the pressures of urbanization and cash cropping. In many regions, food crop production and traditional uses of the forest and other natural systems are under severe and mounting pressure. Loss of fertility and erosion of soils are coincident problems.

- **Water:** Increasing water consumption in a wide variety of sectors — especially urban, agricultural, and industrial — is severely depleting surface and groundwater resources in many regions. Indeed, water supply is increasingly becoming a major source of conflict, perhaps most strikingly, in the Middle East (although in some regions, water scarcity is as much a reflection of pollution and salinization as of overconsumption). Watershed disturbances from forestry, agricultural, urban, and other uses are variously resulting in problems of siltation, increased runoff and flooding, and reduced water catchment. In coastal areas, the destruction and deterioration of buffers between land and water (reflecting the assumption that such areas lack economic value) is resulting in erosion and declining water quality.

- **Biodiversity:** Plant and animal populations are being depleted and destroyed through direct exploitation and habitat destruction resulting from activities in other sectors (in particular, the exploitation of forests). Erosion of intraspecies genetic diversity is also provoked by trends toward using a very limited number of varieties in agriculture.

- **Forests:** Commercial activity is a primary cause of the depletion and damage of forests. There are also associated impacts on soil, water, biological richness (number of species and species populations), climate, as well as forest dwellers and other communities.

- **Aquatic habitats and fisheries:** Mangroves, wetlands, coral reefs, and other highly productive and sensitive aquatic environments are being directly destroyed through land reclamation and urban industrial development. Indirect damage results from a variety of pressures causing coastal erosion. The loss of productive potential in these systems is reflected in declining fish stocks. Direct depletion of fish stocks is primarily related to commercial overfishing and the use of inappropriate technologies, like trawlers.

- **Energy resources:** Rates of energy production and consumption are rapidly depleting petroleum and other fossil fuels. Hydroelectric production degrades aquatic systems and often affects the availability and productivity of land.

- **Other nonrenewable resources:** Mining activities are depleting many minerals, including base and precious metals, as well as qualitatively and quantitatively ravaging lands and habitats.

Pollution, contamination, and toxicity

Problems of pollution, contamination, and toxicity derive from different aspects or stages of the same activities responsible for resource depletion and degradation. Key sources of impact are extractive and industrial activities, energy production and consumption, urbanization, agriculture, and transportation. With over 100 000 chemical substances in commercial use worldwide, pollution and chemical hazards are omnipresent. Toxic chemicals (including wastes) are associated with industrial production and industrial (pharmaceutical, agricultural, textile, etc.), commercial, and consumer use.

Impacts include the degradation of water (including surface water, groundwater, and oceans), air and atmosphere, and land and soil resources, as well as radiation and noise pollution. These impacts disrupt ecosystem functions, reduce ecosystem productivity and fertility, threaten human health (including increased morbidity, mortality, and developmental handicaps), and provoke atmospheric change (including ozone depletion and global warming).

Occupational, public, and consumer health threats arise from the production and sale of unsafe products and the generation and inadequate disposal of toxic wastes. Such problems are particularly virulent in the Third World. The threat of contaminating the resource base (water, soil, etc.) is also greater in jurisdictions where regulatory capability is relatively low. Less dramatic but more insidious than acute toxicity is chronic, generalized ecotoxicity — where the life-support systems of living organisms become toxic not as a result of a specific chemical but because of the complex interactions of many chemicals within the environment. New and emerging technologies, including biotechnologies, pose new, less understood types of hazards.

Natural disasters

The natural disasters of extreme climatic events — hurricanes, tornadoes, tropical storms, floods, droughts — and tectonic movements — earthquakes, tidal waves — have the potential to take a massive toll in both human and environmental terms. Many regions of the South are already prone to a variety of natural disasters, including hurricanes, storms, drought, and flooding. The human costs of such events in the Third World are frequently devastating. While conventionally defined as "natural," the frequency and severity of at least some of these phenomena appear to be increasing as a result of human activity. In particular, global warming appears to be associated with greater frequency and severity of climate-related disasters.

Social issue areas

The five social issue areas correspond to the elements of a fair and sustainable order articulated in Chapter 3. Thus, they forge a link between the research agenda and our analysis of the necessary orientation of the global development/environment debate. Following each issue area are the key dimensions for research.

- **Poverty, affluence, and needs:** Inequality; poverty; affluence and overdevelopment; basic needs issues; population and resource use.

- **Economic order and development patterns:** International economic realm; national development models and styles; market mechanisms and the environment; economic–ecological valuation and development theory.

- **Political order:** International political order; role of the state; democratization, participation, and accountability; gender; legal and regulatory systems; conflict over natural resources.

- **Knowledge systems and technology:** Traditional knowledge and technological systems; modern science and technological systems; appropriate technologies.

- **Processes of cultural change:** Cultural diversity; homogenization of cultures; values and ethical systems; education and media.

The Interactive Research Framework

The framework of the research agenda is presented in Figure 1. The key physical problems that must be understood are placed in the central box; the five social issue areas are positioned around this core to highlight the cause and effect dynamics between the two.

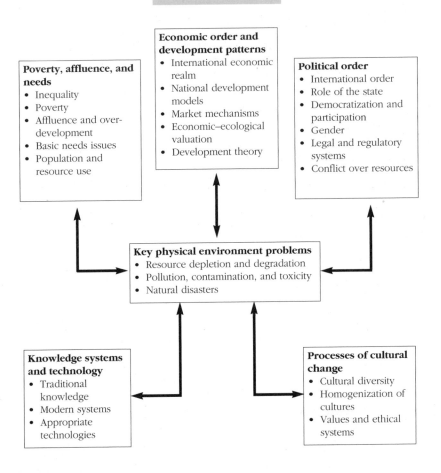

Figure 1. Framework for the research agenda.

Our approach has two related implications for social research. First, researchers on social issues are encouraged to take key environmental problems as a point of departure and to contribute to holistic analyses of their social causes and effects. Second, social researchers are encouraged to deepen or widen the areas of their research in the five social issue areas (poverty, politics, economics, technology, and culture) by being sensitive to environmental issues. In other words, the research agenda is framed in a manner that encourages research into the social dimensions of environmental issues as well as the environmental dimensions of social issues.

CHAPTER 8
Research Topics and Research Support

The list of research topics presented in this Chapter is far from exhaustive, and the thematic organization is not definitive. A range of alternative themes can be envisaged; but overlaps in the research topics would be virtually unavoidable and, indeed, overlaps between research themes and research topics reflect the inherent relatedness of the issues. Most research topics can be pursued at various geopolitical levels (local, national, regional, and global).

Theme: Poverty, Affluence, and Needs

Topic: Inequality
Relationships between socioeconomic inequities and environmental problems

- Relationships between socioeconomic inequalities (in wealth, asset ownership, access to land and income, education, etc.); overconsumption on the one hand and poverty or basic needs problems on the other; and environmental problems.

- Structures of social inequality that contribute to poverty and to the poor's inability to have harmonious relations with the environment: a key example is landlessness and lack of land security, which, in some countries, puts pressure on the poor to destroy forests.

- Ways in which environmental problems exacerbate social inequalities (in income, health, opportunities, access to resources, etc.) and differences in the ways various socioeconomic groups experience or are affected by environmental degradation; factors influencing these differences.

Topic: Poverty
Relationships between poverty and environmental conditions

- Environmental problems that create or exacerbate poverty and mechanisms by which this occurs.

- Implications of poverty for modes and levels of resource exploitation.

- Ways in which rural poverty affects efforts to protect natural areas and efforts related to environmental protection and conservation in general.

- Implications of poverty and joblessness in terms of ability to adapt to environmental change.

- The economic, social, and cultural rights of the poor, and violation of these rights in the process of "development"; the phenomenon of environment migrants and refugees, forced evictions, etc.

- Impacts of development projects and associated environmental problems on communities: sources of livelihood, access to land, level of self-sufficiency, etc. Specifically, for each sector and for each resource, what communities stand to be affected by environmental problems and how (in terms of socioeconomic status, health, quality of life, etc.). For example, in relation to forestry, what are the impacts of deforestation on indigenous peoples and on farm communities (related to soil erosion, water pollution, etc.)? In agriculture, which farmers are most affected by problems relating to pesticides, pest control, water contamination, etc.? In fisheries, which groups are facing the most serious threats related to reduced catch, damaged nets, etc.? In industry, who are the workers most affected by occupational hazards, and which residents face the threats of emissions, effluents, or wastes from local factories?

- Potential economic benefits of policies, programs, and projects versus socioenvironmental costs, including implications in terms of social equity (who benefits and who suffers?).

- Approaches to ending the cycle of poverty and environmental degradation (for example, enhancing rural employment opportunities and income diversity).

Topic: Affluence and Overdevelopment
Environmental and resource implications of overdevelopment

- Manifestations and explanatory mechanisms of overdevelopment and unsustainable lifestyles, including links to income inequality and to the systemic need to generate growth and effective demand.

- Environmental effects of overdevelopment and maldevelopment, including their role in global ecological stress.
- How to deal with unsustainable consumption and how to share the adjustment burden.

Topic: Basic Needs

Relationships between satisfying basic needs and environmental conditions

- Effects of pollution, resource degradation, and resource scarcity on basic needs (food, water, housing, health, and safety), especially of the poor; what are the environmental health problems (including home safety and product safety) and who is experiencing them?
- The urban social and environmental crisis: causes, manifestations, and solutions.
- Alternatives for squatters and urbanites unable to meet basic needs.
- The social and environmental costs of transportation, especially the costs of private motor vehicles, and alternatives for private and public transportation; implications for transport policy.
- Ways in which environmental problems are exacerbated through inadequate social planning and social services, including the following: environmental impacts of the lack of social infrastructure and social services for the poor (for example, lack of sewage treatment or proper waste disposal, leading to water pollution); the lack of resources and planning in social sectors such as housing, urban layout, transport, health, and garbage; and inadequate governmental and employer attention (resources, regulation, enforcement) to occupational safety and environmental controls.
- Appropriate methods for providing social services to fulfil basic and human needs (for example, food, nutrition, water, sanitation, health, housing, and transport).
- Entitlement to food, shelter, health, and education as basic human rights; implications for development and environment policy.

Topic: Population and Resource Use

Relationships between population characteristics, types and levels of resource use, and environmental conditions

- Links between environmental stress and population size on the one hand, and, on the other, between environmental stress and the consumption levels and styles of resource use of various income and occupational groups.

- The complex interlinkages between population, family size, poverty, inequities, gender relations, and environmental problems: which way does causation run, etc.?

- Relationships of local inhabitants to the local environment and resource base in rural, semi-urban, and urban areas.

- The carrying capacity concept in relation to population, environment, and development.

- Characteristics and requirements of a biomass-based subsistence economy; economic impacts on this subsistence economy resulting from environmental degradation and environmental transformation caused by the penetration of the "formal" economy; relationships between subsistence livelihoods (fishing, gathering, food cropping, etc.) and environmental quality; the marginalization and impoverishment of groups dependent on natural resources as a result of ongoing economic and social development.

- Social implications of population policy options, such as top-down "population control"; democratic family planning in conjunction with overcoming poverty and increasing educational and economic status of women, etc.; elements of an appropriate population policy.

- Population, health, and women's rights, including the impact of reproductive technologies on women's health and the safety of various contraceptive methods.

- The implications of AIDS (acquired immune deficiency syndrome) on health, demographic, and social policies in the South.

- Implications, in different socioeconomic structural contexts (for example, land-distribution patterns), of demographic growth on resource use and the provision of social facilities and employment opportunities.

- Environmental impacts of demographic mobility and vice versa.

- Alternatives to rural–urban migration (for example, by improving living conditions and opportunities in rural areas).

- Requirements for, and social costs of, relocating coastal human settlements (especially slum areas).

- Regional and global implications of increasing demands for, and use of, energy.

Theme: Economic Order and Development Patterns

Topic: International Economic Realm

Relationships between international economic factors and environment/development pressures and problems

- Identification and analysis of international factors causing national environmental problems: international trade and investment, including patterns and divisions of world production and trade, terms of trade and prices for Third World commodities, rules governing world trade in the GATT, and bilateral trade relations; actions and powers of TNCs; indebtedness; structural adjustment; and transfer of development models.

- Environment/development issues related to the new international economic order; impact of economic globalization on the environment.

- Impacts of globalization, economic liberalization, external indebtedness, structural adjustment programs, and declining terms of trade on patterns of resource use, related environmental pressures, and capacity for environmental protection.

- Environmental implications of the overall flow of financial resources from South to North and North to South, including implications for capacity for environmental protection.

- Environmental impacts of the World Bank, multilateral aid programs, commercial banks, and international agencies such as FAO, GATT, and UNDP.

- The role of TNCs in environmental degradation: practices regarding use of toxic substances, sale of unsafe products, disposal of waste, promotion of unsustainable lifestyles, exploitation of and damage to natural resources, etc.

- Environmental implications of international tourism.

- Third World efforts for fairer North–South economic relations and lessons from experience to date.

- Implications of, and options to satisfy, the emerging need for global environmental agreements to address the impacts of international economic relations.

- Forms of, and approaches to, reforming international public institutions (for example, GATT, IMF, multilateral banks, and UN agencies) in relation to the needs of the environment and development.

- Appropriate policy packages and instruments to deal with Third World resource and environmental problems that result from indebtedness, structural adjustment, declining terms of trade, etc.

- Mechanisms to ensure that Northern nations share environmental costs associated with trade and export policies.

- Approaches to environmental regulation of the practices of major private economic enterprises (forms of regulation, mechanisms of enforcement, etc.).

- Impact of environmental conditions on economic and environmental management in Southern countries.

Topic: National Development Models and Styles

Relationships between national approaches to economic development and environmental quality

- Economic development approaches and general characteristics of the economic practices of the countries of the North, in terms of their implications for global and regional resource use and environments.

- Reasons for, and environment/development implications of, Southern adoption of dominant Northern development models.

- Structural similarities in the ways in which the impacts of global change manifest themselves regionally.

- Environment/development implications of explicit and implicit principles and priorities in development planning and economic policies that stress short-term economic growth and commercial interests; pressures on decision-makers to focus primarily or exclusively on economic potential.

- Relationships between distribution of income, ownership, and control of economic assets; patterns of production and consumption; and environmental impacts.

- Environment/development issues related to specific economic sectors, including transportation, agriculture, forestry, fisheries, mining, industry, tourism, urbanization, and construction.

- Current relations between human labour, natural resources, and technology, and their implications for sustainable development strategies, including adequate levels of employment in sustainable livelihoods.

- Development implications of economic expansion based on resource depletion; short-, medium-, and long-term effects of resource depletion on employment, revenue, exports, balance of payments, etc., and impact of resource scarcities on cost and availability of production inputs and capital goods; implications of economic dislocations caused by resource scarcities for national policies relating to foreign trade.

- Specific economic effects of environmental problems, including ecological degradation caused by development projects; economic costs of disruptions or dislocations of local communities as a result of pollution, industrial siting, tourism, adverse effects of new technologies, etc.; economic effects of increasing pollution and toxic waste (rising costs for treatment or safe disposal, effects of ailments on labour productivity, etc.).

- Economic losses and impacts on agricultural productivity and potential as a result of losses in biodiversity, soil nutrients, indigenous knowledge, etc.

- Requirements for transition to sustainability in the North, including alterations to unsustainable patterns of production and consumption, and their implications for the South.

- Strategies for incorporating sustainability into economic growth programs with special relevance to developing countries: that is, presenting the economic content of an alternative development strategy.

- Impetus and mechanisms for developing and adopting development strategies based on local values and technologies; economic and social policies to support and promote sustainable modes of production based on the recognition of diversity and the goal of integrated resource use.

- Resource potentials, state capacity, and social, technological, and financial conditions required to support endogenous development; the viability of such a development path in the current world order.

- Economic (including employment) impact of microexperiments in environmental regeneration and management; translating the lessons into alternative national policies.

- Approaches and mechanisms to incorporate environmental considerations in sectoral policies; appropriate forms and combinations of regulatory and economic instruments for increasing industrial, social, and individual environmental responsibility.

- Mechanisms for national appropriation of technological development as an instrument of development.

Topic: Market Mechanisms and the Environment

Environment/development implications of the "free" market

- Contradictions between sustainable development and neoliberal strategies, including self-regulating market, domination of the price system, and downplaying of state action.

- The role and impacts on environmental conditions in Third World countries of the international market, competition among firms, and monopolistic or oligopolistic structures.

Topic: Development Theory and Economic–Ecological Valuation

Environment/development implications of development paradigms and ways of assigning value to environment and resources

- Analysis of paradigms of development, including the concept of development as economic growth; changes in rationality implicit in new models of development.

- Explicit and implicit assignment of economic value of natural resources; impacts of undervaluation of ecological resources.

- Revisions of interpretive approaches to development, especially traditional paradigms with respect to demography, poverty, the market, and the state.

- New paradigms of development that incorporate environment, needs fulfilment, and equity at local, national, and international levels.

- Integration of social science frameworks in quality of life concepts and models.

- Means of incorporating environmental considerations in quality of life indicators; tools for integrating environmental considerations into economic cost–benefit analysis of development projects and the measurement of national economic growth and development.

- Means of more accurate costing of the values of a clean environment, and the need for cost–benefit analysis that accounts adequately for ecological functions; appropriate Third World methodologies for valuation of environment and resources.

Theme: Political Order

Topic: International Political Order

Environment/development dimensions of international relationships

- Environmental problems with international transboundary dimensions (for example, atmospheric pollution, nuclear power and weapons, transboundary resources, transboundary movement of waste, international tourism, voluntary and involuntary migration, biotechnology, and loss of genetic diversity).

- Environmental problems requiring North–South and general international agreements (for example, sharing of responsibilities and burdens to resolve environmental problems, questions of national sovereignty in relation to natural resources, enforcement of international policies, reform of international institutions, regulation of TNCs, and intellectual and technological property rights).

- Reassessment of North–South relations in general, particularly in political and economic areas, as a basis for developing international-level agreements on resolving environment problems; existence and implications of lack of influence of the South in global fora and negotiations in various areas including politics and economics; related barriers to the promotion by the South of its interests in relation to equity and globally fair environmental protection.

- Impacts on civil society and implications for sustainable development of neoliberal models, democratic transitions, new social agents, neocorporatism, etc.

- Issues related to the global commons that reflect the interdependence or asymmetry of international relations; legal aspects of defining and managing the global commons.

- Political aspects of biodiversity and biotechnology; mechanisms to prove and to ensure recognition of Third World contributions to global knowledge, as leverage for greater equity in the distribution of benefits; demonstrations of interdependencies to foster global solidarity; mechanisms for negotiating in situ conservation and national control of biodiversity.

- The nature and influence of both "green" political parties and nonpolitical environmental movements in the North and the political implications of their growth for the South.

- The character of environmental coalitions among the countries of the South and the implications of their growth for countries of the North and South and for international relations.

- Political and environment/development implications of reduced powers of governments of the South as a result of the dictates of international agencies, TNCs, etc.; the related general propagation of an open-market system.

- The political and legal implications of the global environmental conventions being proposed and the use of aid, trade, and debt as political levers for changing environmental behaviour in countries of the South.

- Implications of international treatment of the principle of national sovereignty in relation to natural resources and to ecological problems, including those with transboundary effects.

- Enforcement of environmental policies in the international arena (who has the right and, in reality, who has the power?); roles of the UN Security Council, the General Assembly, the major powers, etc.

- International conditions conducive to the transition to environmentally sound development in the Third World.

- Basic principles on which to base agreements on responsibilities, burden sharing, financing, etc., related to sustainable development.

- Negotiating mechanisms for formulating international environment/development agreements, particularly between countries of the North and South; international mechanisms for settling environmental disputes.

- Design and implications of legal, financial, and other programs of internationally shared environmental action, including institutional arrangements related to coordinating planning and implementing programs for environmental protection and economic reform, and strategies for managing the global commons to control emerging problems such as global warming.

Topic: Role of the State

State policies and actions affecting or affected by environment/ development issues

- State policies contributing to environmental problems.

- Political implications of unsound development models and related environmental problems, including redefined notions of sovereignty.

- Existence and adequacy of legislation and enforcement regarding environmental protection and the rights of people to secure livelihood, food, health, shelter, etc.

- Relationships of the state, TNCs, and national corporations with respect to the depletion and degradation of natural resources; exploitation of natural resources at the expense of the territory and rights of local communities.

- Systems of corruption, monopoly, and misuse of power, and improper linkages between political and business interests; implications for the legislation, regulation, and management of natural resources, and for environmental protection.

- Social and political conditions necessary to fully integrate social issues, environmental issues, and ecological options, at all levels of government decision-making, in planning and implementing sustainable development.

- Mechanisms for national control of technology as a tool of development and for the use of environmentally sound technologies.

Topic: Democratization, Participation, and Accountability

Environment/development implications of varying levels and styles of democracy

- Environment/development implications of varying degrees of political freedom and varying degrees of political space for social movements, local communities, and NGOs to contribute toward ecologically sustainable solutions.

- Implications of the nonrecognition of people's rights (rights to livelihood, food, health and safety, clean environment), including the marginalization and impoverishment of groups dependent on natural resources as a result of ongoing economic and social "development" processes; implications of suppression of, or lack of mechanisms for, the influence and participation of local communities, women, NGOs, and other public interests in decision-making related to development policies, programs, and project implementation.

- Political responses to resource scarcities and environmental degradation; tendencies toward centralization of power, and implications for individual and collective rights; risks of intensification (by the state or other vested interests) of repressive measures as problems increase.

- Impacts of NGOs on environmental issues, including acquisition of financial resources and execution of actions.

- Increasing influence of environmental public interest groups as a result of the growing intensity and explicitness of environmental problems; related opportunities for social, environment, and consumer groups to play a more effective role in advocating environmentally sound development policies.

- Environmental implications of state reform, democratic transitions, social participation, and the revaluing of traditional cultures.

- Criteria for sociopolitical systems that create positive conditions for environmentally sound development, that are equitable, and that satisfy basic needs.

- Public participation in planning, implementation, and control of development: strategies, models, and mechanisms for cooperation and equitable, participatory decision-making to ensure local community participation in environmental management.

- Mechanisms for, and implications of, returning or preserving local control of local resources as an option for protecting the environment with social equity; nature of laws and institutions needed to increase people's control and management of their immediate natural resource base.

- Characteristics of successful community initiatives to resolve environmental problems.

Topic: Gender

Role of women and implications of the repression of women in relation to environment and development

- Women's perceptions of, and dependencies on, the environment; women's roles in environmental change; women's roles in resource and environmental management.

- Time-use studies of women's work in relation to natural resources and the environment.

- Gender perspectives on current development processes and associated natural resource exploitation processes.

- Impacts of development processes and associated environmental stress on women's health, economic position, and status; impacts of development processes and resource and environmental degradation on women's roles in food production.

- Nature of institutions needed to empower women in environmental management and mechanisms to develop more gender-balanced decision-making in environment/development policies.

- Ways of improving women's rights and freedom in terms of decisions regarding reproduction.

Topic: Legal and Regulatory Systems

Relationships between regulatory regimes and environmental protection

- Manifestations and implications of state and institutional weakening and the related loss of regulatory capacity and control, in relation to environment, natural resources, and territory.

- Causes and consequences of inadequate state legislation and policies for environmental protection; environmental impacts of inadequate legislation, ineffective enforcement, and corruption.

- Characteristics of national environmental protection agencies in the South; implications of the absence or inadequacy of environment units within key government agencies, such as economic development or planning agencies.

- Existence and adequacy of public interest laws to help victims of environmentally damaging policies and activities; implications of the absence or inadequacy of such laws.

- Development of international laws and legal mechanisms to deal with liability of transnational and international agencies in relation to environmental abuse associated with their policies and practices.

- Managing common property resources; improving management through an understanding of successful approaches in traditional societies and in present-day projects and micro-experiments.

- Traditional laws and norms that protect the environment; challenges and implications of implementing traditional laws for environmental protection.

- Conflicts and complementarities in reconciling traditional and modern environmental laws.

Topic: Conflict Over Natural Resources

Implications of growing resource constraints for local, national, regional, and international violence

- Probabilities of, and regional geopolitical implications of, new or more intense conflicts over resources as environment and resources are degraded and depleted; implications of the intensified use of nonrenewable resources (especially energy).

- Degree to which conflict over resources is an underlying cause for political problems such as ethnic conflicts, nationalist drives, secession movements, and tensions that threaten national unity; possible loci of future conflicts (for example, between and among social classes and groups, local communities, consumers, corporations, the state, foreign governments, and international institutions).

- Implications of the tendency of dominant development models to erode the power of local communities over natural resources and to transfer this power to the state, often acting on behalf of, or together with, commercial interests (forest dwellers losing their land to timber companies; rural villagers relocating to make way for dams).

- Effectiveness of environmental and social impact assessment in relation to the interests of local communities.

- Probable shape of future political institutions and arrangements in response to accelerated resource depletion and other environment problems; implications of increasing chaos and potential "ungovernability."

- Impacts on environment and development of armed conflict, related not only to direct environmental destruction but also to destabilization and social destructuring.

Theme: Knowledge Systems and Technology

Topic: Traditional Knowledge and Technological Systems

Environment/development contributions of traditional knowledge and implications of the erosion of this knowledge base

- Adaptations of communities to their environment; traditional resource management practices; roles of people in local resource management; roles of informal leaders in enhancing local awareness and participation.
- Existing and potential contributions of traditional knowledge to modern economic growth.
- Influence of modernization and technological development on traditional, sustainable patterns of resource use and environmental relationships; natural and social impacts of introducing uniform, unsustainable technological models.
- Means for determining and valuing investments made by the poor in ecological sustainability.
- Development of suitable systems, both global and national, for compensating those who hold valuable traditional knowledge about the characteristics and sustainable uses of their environment and resources.
- Approaches to rescuing and revaluing traditional knowledge about natural resources and their management.

Topic: Modern Science and Technological Systems

Environment/development perils and potentials of modern science and technology

- Technological factors that contribute to environment/ development problems: modern technology as the physical instrument facilitating rapid and powerful depletion of resources, greater pollution emissions, increasing concentrations of toxic wastes, displacement of labour, concentration of power (through corporate and bureaucratic control of powerful technology), etc.

- Environmental problems impacting on technology, including resource depletion and degradation resulting in the reduced utility or life span of technologies.

- Processes and impacts of technology transfer; technology as an instrument of economic interests of TNCs or local big corporations, introduced through investments, loans, aid, or trade; promotion of inappropriate technologies within the North and from North to South.

- Displacement and replacement of environmentally sound local technologies by modern technologies and development projects; sectoral implications (for example, in agriculture, fisheries, industry, transport, health and nutrition, and housing); social and ecological implications (for example, loss of biodiversity, erosion of genetic resources, and increased dependence on imported inputs).

- Impacts of biotechnology on various areas of production; ability of countries to control and generate biotechnologies.

- Relocation of hazardous industries and wastes to the South and the export of banned and hazardous products to the South; regulatory policies of Northern governments that permit or promote such relocations and exports.

- Health hazards and potential hazards associated with nuclear technology, biotechnologies, toxic substances, products, and wastes.

- General social impacts associated with particular types of modern "development" projects (for example, nuclear energy, natural gas, hydroelectric development, and dam construction); postproject studies to address social, cultural, psychological, and economic impacts, and to integrate findings with physical impact assessments and research.

- Possibilities for technological change that respects unique cultural and ecological conditions.

- Mechanisms for increased efficiency in energy use.

Topic: Appropriate Technologies

Development of knowledge and technologies to support sustainable development

- Identification of current environmentally unsound practices in various sectors; requirements for a transition to more environmentally sound practices.

- Assessment of sustainable resource potentials in countries and regions; development and implications of technologies based on the sustainable use of these resources.

- At the national level, means of defining and promoting environmentally appropriate and sound technologies in various sectors, including agriculture, fisheries, forests, water management, energy, and industries; instruments (institutional, financial, informational, etc.) to encourage development of environmental (including restorative) technologies.

- Needs assessment, development, and application of technologies to rehabilitate damaged ecosystems (forests, soil, marine systems, rivers, etc.).

- Technologies for absorbing a growing labour force.

- Role of social and environmental impact assessment in development decision-making; development of such impact assessment and its integration into planning and decision-making.

Theme: Processes of Cultural Change

Topic: Cultural Diversity

Environment/development value of cultural diversity and implications of its loss

- Impacts of development processes on local cultures, ways of life, consumption patterns, recreation activities, etc.; relationships between environmental problems and disruption of local cultures; socioeconomic and cultural transformations resulting from environmental changes at local and regional levels; human adaptations to environmental degradation.

- Disruption and erosion of cultural diversity as a consequence of migration, development processes, and other social changes.

- Environmental implications of the deterioration of cultural wealth; implications of sociocultural change, including social disintegration and marginalization induced by "development," in terms of exacerbating social conditions (such as poverty) that negatively affect the environment.

- Relationships between biological diversity and cultural diversity.

- Cultural perceptions of the environment and resources, including roles and functions; cultural perspectives on the effectiveness of actions to achieve sustainable development.

- Critical assessment of traditional cultures in relation to sustainable resource management.

Topic: Homogenization of Cultures

Mechanisms and environment/development implications of increasing homogeneity in values and aspirations

- Influence of modernization and technological development on culture.

- Changing consumption patterns in the North and the South and their impact on the environment; mechanisms by which consumer patterns are spread, and relationships to communications, cultural paradigms, and technological styles.

- Mechanisms and processes by which traditional cultures survive, resist, and adapt in the face of homogenizing influences.

Topic: Values and Ethical Systems

Relationships between values and behaviours affecting the environment

- Paradigms of human and social development, in particular, the implied environmental viewpoint of aspirations to "modernity"; attitudes, values, and behaviour in relation to the environment.

- Environmental aspects (positive and negative) of religion, ethics, and values; roles of religious institutions and moral teachings in promoting environmental awareness.

- Factors influencing population and consumption levels, including ethical aspects.

- Environmental perceptions of dominant social groups, including industrialists and business people.

- Relationships between environmental changes and changes in human attitudes, formal values, and social structures.

- Changes in norms required for sustainable development; motivations and social springboards for changes in attitude and behaviour.

Topic: Education and Media

Transmission of environmental values, attitudes, and lifestyle or consumer orientations

- Values, attitudes, and perspectives that promote unsustainable economies and lifestyles.

- The role of international media (including print, film, television, popular culture, consumerist culture, and advertising and marketing techniques) in promoting inappropriate lifestyles; impacts on cultural diversity.

- Promotion of existing modes of thinking regarding nature and development through dominant educational and disciplinary paradigms; perpetration of these influences through the educational system, universities, research foundations, etc.

- Implications of approaches to the development of human resources in the Third World, including the influences of education abroad and of international support of research institutions and NGOs.

- Mechanisms for improving awareness and capacity in the media, educational institutions, etc., to promote more environmentally sound values, attitudes, perspectives, and knowledge.

Institutional Development and Research Support

The pace of social, economic, and environmental change compels a more thoughtful and systematized approach to research on development/environment issues, both globally and in the South.

Moreover, the growing value of knowledge worldwide is undeniable — a trend that is likely to become increasingly pronounced. Knowledge will come to play a role similar to that played by capital today. The advantage will lie with those countries capable of acquiring and applying knowledge on critical development/environment issues.

Institutional development and restructuring are therefore of tremendous importance. Knowledge must be obtained and diffused, and mechanisms must be established to apply this knowledge to resolving environment/development problems and to cultivating a sustainable future. The social dimensions of environment/development issues demand particular attention. Social research on these issues must be stimulated, and its relevance enhanced.

Climate and Conditions Needed for Environment/Development Research

International and national support for developing and operating Southern research institutions is highly inadequate, especially for institutions dealing with environment/development research. Significant funds for science, research, and education on environment/development issues should be allocated to universities. Support to independent research institutions is also needed; this could be initiated through seed funds for institution building and support toward eventual self-sufficiency.

To support Southern research institutes, money should be reallocated from currently wasteful expenditures (such as arms or the superfluous consumer products of the North). Without denying the need for a greater international sensitivity to Southern research priorities, there is little moral grounds to blame the North for promoting inappropriate research in the South when governments and organizations in the South are not supporting their own research institutions and when research and education are considered to be issues of secondary importance.

Other constraints that must be addressed include institutional barriers in accessing accurate information; political interference in research focus, research results, and information flow; and inadequate linkages with extension programs. Above all, guaranteed academic freedom and open access to information are essential

— including access for local people and the general public. Multilateral institutions and private-sector corporations must make their information base more accessible. Tools of mass communication must be employed. Broad coalitions to develop and maintain information networks can also provide invaluable information to nonexperts, enabling local people to act as agents rather than objects of change. Such networks also stimulate public support for the free exchange of knowledge and information.

Greater support is also required for the distribution of Southern publications in the North, as is Northern responsiveness to Southern prescriptions for program development relevant to the South. Southern scientists, experts, and institutions should be partners in Northern programs delivered to the South. North–South exchanges are critical because of the global nature of many environmental problems.

In general, major changes must occur in communications between the citizens of the South and between citizens of North and South. Communication between academics, politicians, scientists, and business people must improve. The transnational exchange of ideas, culture, and knowledge are truly the "commodities" that must be opened up to free trade, rather than the materials, energy, pollution, labour, and capital that are now being moved globally.

Principles and Goals to Guide Institutional Development and Actions

Encourage the research community to adopt ecological sustainability as a development objective

The objective of ecological sustainability must be added to the other development objectives acknowledged within the social sciences (namely, basic needs satisfaction, economic growth, a fair distribution of assets and income, and healthy social relations). Researchers must therefore be supported in efforts to come to terms with what "sustainability" means in the context of their work and to incorporate relevant approaches within their research. Social researchers must equip themselves with a knowledge of the different facets of the ecological crisis.

Ensure local anchoring of research and the development of local research capacity

To successfully pursue the research agenda we have proposed, research institutions must have strong local anchoring. Sporadic, short-term visits by experts do not build a firm foundation for understanding local socioeconomic, cultural, and biophysical conditions. In particular, the practice of flying in experts from the North not only downplays local research capacity but also produces disjointed and incomplete knowledge of cumulative processes. The distinctive nature of environmental problems can only be captured by the permanent presence of committed observers. Here, local researchers have a vital role and a comparative advantage. Emphasis on local capacity is justified not only on scientific grounds but also because of the importance of strengthening the participation of local communities. The identification, highlighting, and systematic strengthening of local and regional research capacity is key.

Support the development of indigenous science and technology

Importing technology and expertise from the North fosters finan‚ cial, social, and scientific dependency. At the same time, inappropriate methods and materials find their way into the Third World. The countries of the South must develop their own science, a science built on the basis of their own needs, both cultural and environmental.

Encourage South–South exchange

A South–South exchange of information and knowledge is essential for improved research capacity in the South. It is also critical because many regions in the South share not only similar development problems but also similar ecosystems and natural resources. Governments and institutions from the South should support South–South training of scientists and South–South exchanges of experience. Partnership programs and interregional research networks among southern institutions for research into common problems must also be financed and promoted.

Support interdisciplinary approaches

Environmental research should be supported by organizing inter-disciplinary academic units. These groups would integrate, in an holistic manner, the capacity in the South for solving environmental problems. Educational training should include lectures, seminars, and courses designed to foster interest in, and an understanding of, environmental problems among social scientists.

Environmental research and study centres must include social science practitioners from a wide range of disciplines, including economics, law, sociology, and anthropology. Support for the participation of women and indigenous cultures must also be part of the costing of environment/development research.

Encourage interinstitutional, interregional, and intersectoral cooperation and consultation

Mechanisms are needed for national and regional consultations among social researchers and practitioners working in various settings, such as universities, other research institutes, governments, and NGOs. Working cooperatively to collect and manage information on socioenvironmental problems, social researchers and practitioners can play a key role in planning and decision-making. But, to do this, they require access to relevant and accurate information.

Create linkages between research and application

It is also important to ensure the dissemination, practical testing, and application of research results. Policies should be developed through an interactive process of scientific analysis, program development, and field results. This requires a high level of cooperation between research institutes, researchers working in other settings, and those involved in delivering development and social programs.

Promote public participation and exchange

We are often told that we live in a global world. However, we seem to be learning less and less about the lives of people in other countries and in other regions of the same country. This cultural isolation can be and has been used to manipulate workers and consumers. Institutions must therefore devise creative ways of passing their research results onto a broader public, perhaps through creative uses of popular media and methods. Of utmost importance are the linkages between Southern and Northern workers, farmers, and artists of all kinds for mutual education and communication. Through such linkages, and not through proclamations and declarations from "above," people will recognize their common concerns and interests in relation to development and the environment.

Bibliography

AAS (African Academy of Sciences). 1989. Environmental crisis in Africa: scientific response. Proceedings of the International Conference on Drought, Desertification, and Food Deficit in Africa, 3–6 June 1986. Academy Science Publishers, Nairobi, Kenya. 130 pp.

Abalu, G.O. 1976. A note on crop mixtures under indigenous conditions of Northern Nigeria. Journal of Development Studies, 12(3), 212–220.

Adedeji, A., Shaw, T.M., ed. 1985. Economic crisis in Africa: African perspectives on development problems and potentials. Lynne Rienner Publishers, Boulder, CO, USA. 290 pp.

Agarwal, A., Narain, S. 1991. Global warming in an unequal world: a case of environmental colonialism. Centre for Science and the Environment, New Delhi, India.

Agarwall, B. 1986. Firewood supply in the Third World. Institute of Economic Growth, New Delhi, India. Studies in Economic Development and Planning No. 40. 209 pp.

Ahmed, I. 1988. The bio-revolution in agriculture: key to poverty alleviation in the Third World? International Labour Review, 127(1), 53–72.

Akpata, T., Okali, D.U.U. 1990. Nigerian wetlands. Man and the Biosphere National Committee, Lagos, Nigeria. 198 pp.

Ayanda, J.O. 1988. Incorporating environmental impact assessment in the Nigerian planning process: need and procedure. Third World Planning Review, 10(1), 51–64.

Balasubramaniam, A. 1984. Ecodevelopment: towards a philosophy of environmental education. Regional Institute of Higher Education and Development, Singapore. 82 pp.

Benneh, G. 1974. The ecology of peasant farming systems in Ghana. Environment in Africa, 1(1), 35–49.

Boege, E. 1988. Los Mazatecos ante la nación. Contradicciones de la identidad étnica en el México actual. Ed. Siglo XXI Editores, Mexico City, Mexico. 307 pp.

Castanon-Morales, J.L. 1982. Problemas de alimentación y nutrición en el Tercer Mundo. Problemas del Desarrollo, 12(47/48), 9–24.

Castro, M.E.B. de, Menezes, J.E., Siqueira, C.B., Lira, C.L. 1983. Trópico semi árido: resumos informativos. Vol. 4. Centro de Pesquisa Agropecuaria do Trópico Semi Arido, Brasilia, Brazil. 328 pp.

Cheru F. 1989. The silent revolution in Africa. Debt, development, and democracy. Zed Books Ltd, London, UK. 189 pp.

Chia, L.S., ed. 1987. Environmental management in Southeast Asia: directions and current status. Faculty of Science, National University of Singapore, Singapore. 211 pp.

Chiriboga, M., Piccinno, R. 1981. La producción campesina cacaotera: problemas y perspectivas. Centro de Arte y Acción Popular, Quito, Ecuador. 117 pp.

CIMMYT (International Centre for Maize and Wheat Improvement). 1987. The future development of maize and wheat in the Third World. CIMMYT, Mexico City, Mexico.

Co, J., Tan, M., ed. 1987. Restoring health care to the hands of the people. Proceedings of a series of symposia on Health Policy Development sponsored by Bukluran para sa Kalusugan ng Sambayanan (Task Force People's Health), March–May 1986. Health Action Information Network, Quezon City, Philippines.

Constantino, R. 1985. Synthetic culture and development. Foundation for Nationalist Studies, Quezon City, Philippines.

Constantino, R., Constantino, L.R. 1988. Distorted priorities: the politics of food. Foundation for Nationalist Studies, Quezon City, Philippines.

Consumers' Association of Penang. 1976. Pollution: Kuala Juru's battle for survival. Consumers' Association of Penang, Penang, Malaysia.

—— 1978. Padi pollution in Kuala Kedah. Consumers' Association of Penang, Penang, Malaysia.

—— 1980. The Malaysian fisheries — a diminishing resource. Proceedings of a seminar organized by the Consumers' Association of Penang, 16 July 1977. Consumers' Association of Penang, Penang, Malaysia.

—— 1982. Development and the environmental crisis. Proceedings of the symposium on the Malaysian Environment in Crisis organized by the Consumers' Association of Penang, the School of Biological Sciences, Universiti Sains Malaysia, and Sahabat Alam Malaysia, 16–20 September 1978. Consumers' Association of Penang, Penang, Malaysia.

—— 1985. Pesticide problems: legislation and consumer action in the Third World — the Malaysia experience. Consumers' Association of Penang, Penang, Malaysia.

—— 1990. Rural Malaysia: poverty, basic needs problems, and policy proposals. Consumers' Association of Penang, Penang, Malaysia.

Cruz, C.A., Segura-delos Angeles, M. 1984. Policy issues on commercial forest management. Philippine Institute for Development Studies, Manila, Philippines.

Cruz-Majluf, G. 1982. Tecnología y desarrollo en el Tercer Mundo. Problemas del Desarrollo, 12(47/48), 223–234.

CSE (Centre for Science and the Environment). 1991. The CSE statement on global environmental democracy. CSE, New Delhi, India.

Danusaputro, St. Munadjat. 1981. Asian–African identity in world affairs — its impact and prospects for the future, with special reference to international and environmental law. Binacipta, Bandung, Indonesia. 240 pp.

Dei, G.J.S. 1988. Coping with the effects of the 1982–83 drought in Ghana: the view from the village. African Development, 13(1), 107–122.

De La Torre, E. 1986. Touching ground, taking root: theological and political reflections on the Philippine struggle. Catholic Institute for International Relations, London, UK.

Dourojeanni, M.J. 1982. Recursos naturales y desarrollo en América Latina y el Caribe. Universidad de Lima, Lima, Peru. 436 pp.

Downing, T.E., Kangethe, W.G., Kamau, C.M., ed. 1989. Coping with drought in Kenya: national and local strategies. Lynne Rienner Publishers, Boulder, CO, USA. 411 pp.

Echeverria-Zuno, A. 1984. Problema alimentario y cuestion rural. Ed. Nueva Imagen, Mexico City, Mexico. 323 pp.

ECLAC (Economic Commission for Latin America and the Caribbean). 1989. Desarrollo sostenible en Colombia: sus tendencias y limites. Estrategia, Economica y Financiera No. 129, 21–28.

—— 1990. Magnitude of the poverty in Latin America in the Eighties. ECLAC, Santiago, Chile.

—— 1990. Preliminary balance of the economy of Latin America and the Caribbean. ECLAC, Santiago, Chile.

—— 1991. El desarrollo sustentable. Transformación productiva, equidad y medio ambiente. ECLAC, Santiago, Chile. 146 pp.

—— 1991. Inventarios y cuentas del patrimonio natural en América Latina y el Caribe. ECLAC, Santiago, Chile. 335 pp.

Emil Salim. 1986. Pembangunan Berwawasan Lingkungan. Lembaga Pusat Penelitian Pertanian, Bogor, Indonesia.

Environmental Liaison Centre. 1986. Sustainable development: report of the proceedings of the Global Meeting on Environment and Development for Nongovernmental Organisations, 4–8 February 1985, Nairobi, Kenya. Environmental Liaison Centre International, Nairobi, Kenya. 109 pp.

Ezaza, W.P., Othman, H. 1989. Political instability and ecological stress in Eastern Africa. *In* Hjort af Ornas, A., Salih, M.A.M., ed., Ecology and politics, environmental stress and security in Africa. Scandinavian Institute of African Studies, Uppsala, Sweden. pp. 131–144.

Faniran, A., Areola, O. 1976. The concept of resources and resource utilization among local communities in Western State of Nigeria. African Environment, 2(3), 39–51.

Farmers Assistance Board. 1982. Profits from poison: a look into the socio-economics and politics of pesticides. Farmers Assistance Board, Quezon City, Philippines. 115 pp.

Feder, E. 1982. Algunas observaciones sobre el empleo. Problemas del Desarrollo, 12(47/48), 197–205.

—— 1983. La crisis presiona para enfatizar cultivos exportables. Problemas del Desarrollo, 13(50), 9–16.

Feder, E., Torres, G.C., Salazar, J.A.C. 1985. Ensayos sobre cuestiones agrarias. Terra Nova, Mexico City, Mexico. 169 pp.

Fernandes, W., Kulkarni, S., Joshi, G., Shiva, V., Sharatchandra, H.C., Bandyopadhyay, J., Kannan, K.P., Baxi, U., Gadgil, M., Prabhu, P. 1983. Towards a new forest policy. People's rights and environmental needs. Indian Social Institute, New Delhi, India. 155 pp.

Gonzalez, C.L. 1983. La cara externa de la política anti-crisis, el problema alimentario y el salario real. Instituto de Investigaciones Económicas y Políticas, Universidade Guayaquil, Guayaquil, Ecuador. 27 pp.

Greslov, F., Zutier, P. de, ed. 1989. Recursos naturales y desarrollo. Debates y experiencias sobre ecología, sociedad y naturaleza en las Montanas Andinas. Ed. Horizonte, Lima, Peru. 280 pp.

Gutman, P. 1989. El medio ambiente en los grandes proyectos. Revista Interamericana de Planificación, 22(85).

Herrera, F. 1985. Despertar de un continente: América Latina 1960–1985. Asociación Latinoamericana de Institutiones Financieras de Desarrollo, Lima, Peru. 611 pp.

Higgins, G.M. 1982. Potential population supporting capacities of lands in the developing world. Food and Agriculture Organization of the United Nations, Rome, Italy.

Hjort af Ornas, A., Salih, M.A.M., ed. 1989. Ecology and politics, environmental stress and security in Africa. Scandinavian Institute of African Studies, Uppsala, Sweden. 255 pp.

Hong, E., ed. 1983. Malaysian women: problems and issues. Consumers' Association of Penang, Penang, Malaysia.

—— 1985. See the Third World while it lasts: the social and environmental impact of tourism with special reference to Malaysia. Consumers' Association of Penang, Penang, Malaysia.

—— 1987. Natives of Sarawak: survival in Borneo's vanishing forest. Institut Masyarakat, Penang, Malaysia.

Ibe, A.C., Quelennec, R.E. 1989. Methodology for assessment and control of coastal erosion in West and Central Africa. United Nations Environment Programme, Nairobi, Kenya. Regional Seas Reports and Studies No. 107.

Ikporukpo, C.O. 1985. Petroleum exploitation and socio-economic environment in Nigeria. International Journal of Environmental Studies, 21, 193–203.

INDERENA (Instituto de Desarrollo de los Recursos Naturales Renovables). 1990. Policy of the National Government in defense of the rights of indigenous peoples and the ecological conservation of the Amazon basin. INDERENA, Bogota, Colombia. 240 pp.

Institut Masyarakat. 1982. Appropriate technology, culture and lifestyle in development. Institut Masyarakat, Penang, Malaysia.

Institut Masyarakat and Consumers' Association of Penang. 1980. Kuala Juru: a people's cooperative. Institut Masyarakat, Penang, Malaysia.

ISAS (Institute of Southeast Asian Studies). 1991. The environment and economic development in Southeast Asia. Proceedings of a workshop, 27–28 September 1990, Singapore. ISAS, Singapore.

Janvry, A. de. 1986. Perche i governi fanno quello che fanno? Il caso delle politiche dei prezzi degli alimenti. QA Questione Agraria, 24, 25–58.

Juma, C. 1989. Biological diversity and innovation: conserving and utilizing genetic resources in Kenya. African Centre For Technology Studies, Nairobi, Kenya. 139 pp.

Khan, M.H. 1986. Landlessness and rural poverty in underdeveloped countries. Pakistan Development Review, 25(3), 371–402.

Khor Kok Peng, M. 1989. Housing for the people: why Malaysia has so far failed to meet housing needs of the poor. Consumers' Association of Penang, Penang, Malaysia.

——— 1991. Penang Hill: the need to save our natural heritage. Friends of Penang Hill, Penang, Malaysia.

——— 1992. The future of North–South relations: conflict or cooperation. Third World Network, Penang, Malaysia.

Kio, P.R.O. 1976. What future for natural regeneration of tropical high forest: an appraisal with examples from Nigeria and Uganda. Commonwealth Forest Review, 55(4), 309–318.

Kiriro, A., Juma, C., ed. 1989. Gaining ground: institutional innovations in land use management in Kenya. African Centre For Technology Studies, Nairobi, Kenya. 191 pp.

Kleiner, A. 1984. Manifiesto de las organizaciones por la defensa de la ecología en Argentina. Libreros y Editores del Poligono SRL, Buenos Aires, Argentina. 81 pp.

Kumar, S.K., Hotchkiss, D. 1988. Consequences of deforestation for women's time allocation: agricultural production in hill areas of Nepal. International Food Policy Research Institute, Washington, DC, USA. IFPRI Research Report No. 69. 72 pp.

Lago, P.F. 1975. Ecologia e poluição: o homem e o ambienta Catarinense. Editora Resenha Universitária, São Paulo, Brazil. 214 pp.

Lajo-Lazo, M. 1983. Efectos de la agroindustria transnacional en el desarrollo agrícola y alimentario. Problemas del Desarrollo, 13(50), 117–150.

Leff, E. 1986. Ecología y capital. Hacia una perspectiva ambiental de desarrollo. Universidad Nacional Autónoma de México, Mexico City, Mexico. 147 pp.

——— ed. 1986. Los problemas del conocimiento y las perspectiva ambiental del desarrollo. Ed. Siglo Veintiuno, Mexico City, Mexico. 476 pp.

——— compiler. 1990. Medio ambiente y desarrollo. Ed. Porrua, Mexico City, Mexico.

Lim, J.Y. 1987. The Malay House: rediscovering Malaysia's indigenous shelter system. Institut Masyarakat, Penang, Malaysia.

Maihold, G., Urquidi, V.L., compilers. 1990. Diálogo con nuestro futuro comun. Perspectivas Latinoamericanas del informe Brundtland. Ed. Nueva Sociedad, Caracas, Venezuela. 179 pp.

Maliyamkono, T.L., Bagachwa, M.S.D. 1990. The second economy in Tanzania. Heinemann Educational Books (East Africa) Ltd, Nairobi, Kenya. 197 pp.

Manrique, N. 1988. A donde va la promoción campesina? Debate Agrario No. 4, 53–73.

Mascarenhas, A. 1989. Environmental stress and political security in Southern Africa. *In* Hjort af Ornas, A., Salih, M.A.M., ed., Ecology and politics, environmental stress and security in Africa. Scandinavian Institute of African Studies, Uppsala, Sweden. pp. 233–255.

Mascarenhas, A., Ngana, J., Yoshida. 1985. Opportunities for irrigation development in Tanzania. Institute of Developing Economies, Tokyo, Japan. JRP Series No. 52. 114 pp.

Mascarenhas, O. 1989. Population and development in Tanzania: a review of information sources. Dar es Salaam University Press, Dar es Salaam, Tanzania. 214 pp.

Mascarenhas, O., Mbilinyi, M. 1981. Women in Tanzania: an analytical bibliography. Scandinavian Institute of African Studies, Uppsala, Sweden. 256 pp.

Menendez, I., ed. 1982. Economía y desarrollo rural en América Latina. Ed. Nueva Imagen, Mexico City, Mexico. 207 pp.

Menendez, I., Gomez Oliver, L., Olmo, F. del. 1985. Clases sociales y desarrollo rural. Ed. Nueva Imagen, Mexico City, Mexico. 288 pp.

Mercer-Quarshie, H. 1976. Yields of local sorghum (*Sorghum vulgare*) cultivars and their mixtures in Northern Ghana. Tropical Agriculture, 56(2), 125–133.

Modina, R.B. 1987. IRRI rice: the miracle that never was. ACES Foundation Inc., Quezon City, Philippines.

Mohamed Idris, S.M. 1990. For a sane, green future. Consumers' Association of Penang, Penang, Malaysia.

Moyo, S., ed. 1991. Zimbabwe's environmental dilemma: balancing resource inequalities. Zimbabwe Environmental Research Organization, Harare, Zimbabwe. 165 pp.

Muni, S.D. 1991. After the Cold War: a Third World perspective. Ecodecision, September 1991, 36–38.

Myers, N. 1990. The Gaia atlas of future worlds. Anchor Books/Doubleday, New York, NY, USA.

NEST (Nigerian Environmental Study/Action Team). 1989. The Nigerian environment: nongovernmental action. NEST, Ibadan, Nigeria.

—— 1991. Nigeria's threatened environment: a national profile. NEST, Ibadan, Nigeria. 290 pp.

—— 1991. Towards sustainable development in Nigeria's dry belt. NEST, Ibadan, Nigeria.

Odhiambo, T.R. 1989. Statement of the problem. *In* Environmental crisis in Africa: scientific response. Proceedings of the International Conference on Drought, Desertification, and Food Deficit in Africa, 3–6 June 1986. Academy Science Publishers, Nairobi, Kenya. pp. 16–29

Odingo, R.S. 1990. State-of-the-art review of social science research on Eastern Africa. *In* Drought in Africa. Proceedings of a workshop held in Timbuktu, Mali, 24-28 November 1986. International Development Research Centre, Ottawa, Ont., Canada. IDRC-MR277e,f, 115–157.

Ofreneo, R.E. 1980. Capitalism in Philippine agriculture. Foundation for Nationalist Studies, Quezon City, Philippines.

Okali, D.U.U. 1980. Nigerian rainforest ecosystem. Technology Man and Biosphere National Committee, Ibadan, Nigeria.

Okigbo, B.N. 1989. Development of sustainable agricultural production systems in Africa: roles of international agricultural research centres and national agricultural research systems. International Institute of Tropical Agriculture, Ibadan, Nigeria. Distinguished African Scientist Lecture Series. 65 pp.

Pombo, V.S. 1983. La crisis alimentaria en la periferia: un enfoque alternativo. Problemas del Desarrollo, 13(51/52), 195–246.

Prah, K.K. 1989. Land degradation and class struggle in rural Lesotho. *In* Hjort af Ornas, A., Salih, M.A.M., ed., Ecology and politics, environmental stress and security in Africa. Scandinavian Institute of African Studies, Uppsala, Sweden. pp. 117–129.

Rahnema, M. 1991. Global poverty: a pauperizing myth. Interculture, 24(2).

Recio, P.M., ed. 1986. Caring enough to cure. Council for Primary Health Care, Manila, Philippines.

Romero-Rodriguez, J.J. 1982. Agricultura y nuevo orden económico internacional. Revista de Fomento Social, 36, 51–61.

Sachs, I. 1982. Ecodesarrollo: desarrollo sin destrucción México. Programa sobre Desarrollo y Medio Ambiente, El Colegio de Mexico, Mexico City, Mexico. 210 pp.

Sada, P.O., Odmderho, F.O. 1988. Environmental management in Nigerian development. Evans Brothers, Ibadan, Nigeria.

Sahabat Alam Malaysia. 1984. Environmental crisis in Asia–Pacific. Declaration and resolutions of the SAM (Sahabat Alam Malaysia) seminar on Problems of Development: Environment and the Natural Resources Crisis in Asia–Pacific. Sahabat Alam Malaysia, Penang, Malaysia.

—— 1984. Environment, development, and natural resource crisis in Asia and the Pacific. Sahabat Alam Malaysia, Penang, Malaysia.

—— 1984. Papan radioactive waste dump controversy. Sahabat Alam Malaysia, Penang, Malaysia.

—— 1984. Pesticide dilemma in the Third World: a case study of Malaysia. Sahabat Alam Malaysia, Penang, Malaysia.

—— 1985. The crisis deepens: a review of resource and environmental management in Malaysia 1975–1985. Sahabat Alam Malaysia, Penang, Malaysia.

—— 1986. Hazardous industries and workers' health. Proceedings of a seminar organized by Sahabat Alam Malaysia, 8–9 December 1984. Sahabat Alam Malaysia, Penang, Malaysia.

—— 1987. Forest resources crisis in the Third World. Proceedings of a Conference held 6–8 September 1986. Sahabat Alam Malaysia, Penang, Malaysia.

—— 1988. Global development and environment crisis: has humankind a future? Proceedings of the conference on Global Development and Environmental Crisis. Sahabat Alam Malaysia, Penang, Malaysia. 802 pp.

—— 1990. Solving Sarawak's forest and native problem. Sahabat Alam Malaysia, Penang, Malaysia.

Salau, A.T. 1990. Integrated water management: the Nigerian experience. *In* Mitchell, B., ed., Integrated water management: international experiences and perspectives. Belhaven Press, London, UK. pp. 188–202.

Salih, M.A.M. 1989. Political coercion and the limits of state intervention: Sudan. *In* Hjort af Ornas, A., Salih, M.A.M., ed., Ecology and politics, environmental stress and security in Africa. Scandinavian Institute of African Studies, Uppsala, Sweden. pp. 101–116.

Sanitsuda Ekachai. 1990. Behind the smile: voices of Thailand. Thai Development Support Committee, Bangkok, Thailand.

Sen, A. 1987. Africa and India: what do we have to learn from each other? World Institute for Development Economic Research, United Nations University, Helsinki, Finland. WIDER Working Papers, WP19. 50 pp.

Sen-Sarma, P.K. 1987. Forest, environment, and development. Ashish Publishing House, New Delhi, India. Environment Management in India, 1, 181–191.

Siam Society. 1989. Culture and environment in Thailand: a symposium of the Siam Society. Siam Society, Bangkok, Thailand. 558 pp.

Silitshena, R.M.K. 1990. Social science research on drought in Botswana, Lesotho, and Swaziland: a state-of-the-art review. *In* Drought in Africa. Proceedings of a workshop held in Timbuktu, Mali, 24–28 November 1986. International Development Research Centre, Ottawa, Ont., Canada. IDRC-MR277e,f, 97–114.

SKEPHI (Indonesian Network on Tropical Forest Conservation). 1990. Kedung Ombo: between development myth and marginal reality. SKEPHI, Jakarta, Indonesia.

—— 1990. Selling our common heritage: commercialisation of Indonesian forest. SKEPHI, Jakarta, Indonesia.

Soemarwoto, O. 1981. Environmental education and research in Indonesia universities. Regional Institute of Higher Education and Development, Singapore. RIHED Occasional Paper No. 4, 61–62.

Soto-Holguin, A. 1988. La ciudad pérdida de los Tayrona — historia de su hallazgo y descubriento. Ed. Gente Nueva, Bogota, Colombia.

Sricastava, V.K. 1990. In search of harmony between life and environment. Journal of Human Ecology, 1(3), 291–300.

Sunkel, O. 1981. La dimensión ambiental en los estilos de desarrollo en América Latina. Economic Commission for Latin America and the Caribbean, Santiago, Chile. 136 pp.

Tan, M. 1988. Dying for drugs: pill power and politics in the Philippines. Health Action Information Network, Quezon City, Philippines.

Third World Network. 1988. Toxic terror: dumping of hazardous wastes in the Third World. Third World Network, Penang, Malaysia.

Toledo, A., coordinator. 1982. Petroleo y ecodesarrollo en el sureste de México. Centro de Ecodesarrollo México, Mexico City, Mexico. 263 pp.

Toledo, V.M., Carabias, J., Mapes, C., Toledo, C. 1985. Ecología y autosuficientoa alimentaria. Hacia una opinión basada en la diversidad biológica, ecológica y cultural de México. Ed. Siglo XXI, Mexico City, Mexico. 118 pp.

Toledo, V.M., Carabias, J., Toledo, C., Gonzalez-Pacheco, Y.C. 1989. La producción rural en México: alternativas ecológicas. Fundación Universo Veintiuno, Mexico City, Mexico. 402 pp.

Tudela, F., coordinator. 1989. La modernización forzada del Trópico. El caso de tabasco. Proyecto integrado del Glofo. El Colegio de México, Mexico City, Mexico. 475 pp.

UNDP (United Nations Development Programme). 1990. Development without poverty. UNDP, Quito, Ecuador.

Unesco (United Nations Educational, Scientific and Cultural Organisation). 1976. Report of a symposium on ecological effects of human activities on tropical and subtropical forest ecosystems, University of Papua New Guinea, 28 April–1 May 1975. Unesco, Paris, France. Australian Unesco Committee for Man and the Biosphere Programme, Publication No. 3. 214 pp.

UNFPA (United Nations Fund for Population Activities). 1990. Estado de la población mundial. UNFPA, New York, NY, USA.

UNICEF (United Nations Children's Fund). 1989. World state of infancy. UNICEF, Madrid, Spain.

Vandana, S. 1987. Forestry crisis and forestry myths: a critical review of tropical forests: a call for action. World Rainforest Movement, Penang, Malaysia.

—— 1991. The violence of the Green Revolution: Third World agriculture, ecology, and politics. Third World Network, Penang, Malaysia.

—— 1991. Biodiversity: social and ecological perspectives. World Rainforest Movement, Penang, Malaysia.

Vergara, N.T. 1985. Expanding populations and shrinking resources: the economic setting and development potential for social forestry. *In* Rao, Y.R., Vergara, N.T., Lovelace, G.W., ed., Community forestry: socio-economic aspects. FAO Regional Office for Asia and the Pacific, Bangkok, Thailand. pp. 3–17.

World Bank. 1990. World Development Report, 1990. World Bank, Washington, DC, USA.

—— 1991. World Development Report, 1991. World Bank, Washington, DC, USA.

World Rainforest Movement. 1990. The battle for Sarawak's forests. World Rainforest Movement, Penang, Malaysia.

—— 1990. Rainforest destruction: causes, effects, and false solutions. World Rainforest Movement, Penang, Malaysia.

WRI (World Resources Institute). 1991. World Resources 1990–1991. A Report by the World Resources Institute, in collaboration with the United Nations Environment Programme and the United Nations Development Programme. Oxford University Press, New York, NY, USA.

Members of the Commission

Anil Agarwal

Since 1980, Dr Anil Agarwal has been the Director of the Centre for Science and Environment in New Delhi, India. From 1977 to 1980, he worked with the International Institute for Environment and Development in London and, from 1984 to 1986, he was the chairperson of Environmental Liaison Centre International in Nairobi, Kenya. Recognized worldwide as an authority on environment/development issues, Dr Agarwal has received several national and international awards, including the Padma Shri from the Government of India, the Global 500 Award from the United Nations Environment Programme, the A.H. Boerma Award from the Food and Agriculture Organization of the United Nations, and the Vikram Sarabhai Memorial Award from the Indian Council of Social Science Research. Dr Agarwal has written, coauthored, and edited numerous books on environment- and technology-related issues.

Julia Carabias

Born in Mexico, Julia Carabias is currently with the Ecology Laboratory, Faculty of Sciences, Universidad Nacional Autónoma de México (UNAM). She holds membership in, and is affiliatied with, the Botanical Society of Mexico, the National System of Research (Mexico), Consejo Universitario UNAM, the Consejo Consultivo Programa Nacional de Solidaridad, and the Comité Editorial Routa Agrociencias. Ms Carabias is also the Program Coordinator for the Programa de Aprovechamiento Integral de Recursos Naturales, UNAM, and has authored, coauthored, and edited several articles and books on issues of the environment and natural resource management in Mexico and Central America.

Martin Khor Kok Peng

Martin Khor Kok Peng is currently the Director of the Consumer's Association of Penang, Third World Network, Penang, Malaysia. He received his training in economics and social sciences from

Cambridge University and the Universiti Sains Malaysia and has worked on behalf of the United Nations University as Project Coordinator in Malaysia. Mr Khor Kok Peng is Editor of *Third World Economics* and Managing Editor of *Third World Resurgence*, both publications of the Third World Network, and has authored many books and articles on the Malaysian economy and the state of North–South relations.

Thandika Makandawire

Thandika Makandawire is currently the Executive Director of CODESRIA, the Council for the Development of Economic and Social Research in Africa, in Dakar, Senegal. Dr Makandawire has served on the Selection Committee of the Rockefeller Foundation Fellowship Programme, on the Joint Committee for Africa of the Social Science Research Council, and on the Executive Committee of the International Social Science Council. From 1982 to 1984, working with the Government of Zimbabwe and various international donors, he was instrumental in establishing the Zimbabwe Institute for Development Studies. One of the leading social scientists in West Africa, Dr Makandawire has authored, coauthored, and edited many books and articles on the economics, politics, and other social aspects of development in Africa.

Adolfo Mascarenhas

Born in Tanzania, Professor Adolpho Mascarenhas is a leading social scientist from the Tanzania Authority on African Drought Issues and currently the Director of the Graduate Studies Program at the University of Dar-es-Salaam in Tanzania. He received his doctorate from the University of California at Los Angeles in 1970, served as the Director of the Brailup University of Dar-es-Salaam, and was an advisor to Unicef and WHO in 1977 and 1978. Prof. Mascarenhas has published extensively on the issues of African regional planing, environment/development, agricultural production, and health.

Alvaro Soto

A Colombian anthropologist, Dr Alvaro Soto is currently President of the International Center for the Environment in the Tropics (INCENT-NEOTROPICO), heads the Secretariat for the Latin American Environmental Network, and is an Associate Member of the Institute for Research on Environment and Economy of the University of Ottawa in Ottawa, Canada. He has served as Senior Fellow at the International Federation of Institutes for Advanced Studies, as Director of the Department of Anthropology at the University of Los Andes in Bogotá, Colombia, as the Director of the National Parks System of Colombia, and as the Director General of the Colombian National Institute of Anthropology. Dr Soto has published various articles and books on environmental issues and the indigenous peoples of South America.

Erna Witoelar

Erna Witoelar is currently a Member of the Board of the Indonesian Consumers Organization in Jakarta, Director and Chief Editor of its monthly consumer's magazine, *Warta Konsumen*, and President of the International Organization of Consumers Unions. She founded the Indonesian Environmental Forum (WALMI), a network of environmental NGOs, and has served as its Chairman and as a Member of its Board. In addition to holding several positions with various international organizations, Mrs Witoelar was member of the Advisory Committee on Industry and Sustainable Development for the Bruntland Commission and a Member of the Board for Environmental Liaison Centre International in Nairobi, Kenya.

The International Development Research Centre is a public corporation created by the Parliament of Canada in 1970 to support technical and policy research designed to adapt science and technology to the needs of developing countries. The Centre's five program sectors are Natural Resources, Social Sciences, Health Sciences, Information Sciences and Systems, and Corporate Affairs and Initiatives. The Centre's funds are provided by the Parliament of Canada; IDRC's policies, however, are set by an international Board of Governors. The Centre's headquarters are in Ottawa, Canada. Regional offices are located in Africa, Asia, Latin America, and the Middle East.

Head Office
IDRC, PO Box 8500, Ottawa, Ontario, Canada K1G 3H9

Regional Office for Southeast and East Asia
IDRC, Tanglin PO Box 101, Singapore 9124, Republic of Singapore

Regional Office for South Asia
IDRC, 11 Jor Bagh, New Delhi 110003, India

Regional Office for Eastern and Southern Africa
IDRC, PO Box 62084, Nairobi, Kenya

Regional Office for the Middle East and North Africa
IDRC, PO Box 14 Orman, Giza, Cairo, Egypt

Regional Office for West and Central Africa
IDRC, BP 11007, CD Annexe, Dakar, Senegal

Regional Office for Latin America and the Carribean
IDRC, Casilla de Correos 6379, Montevideo, Uruguay

Please direct requests for information about IDRC and its activities to the IDRC office in your region.

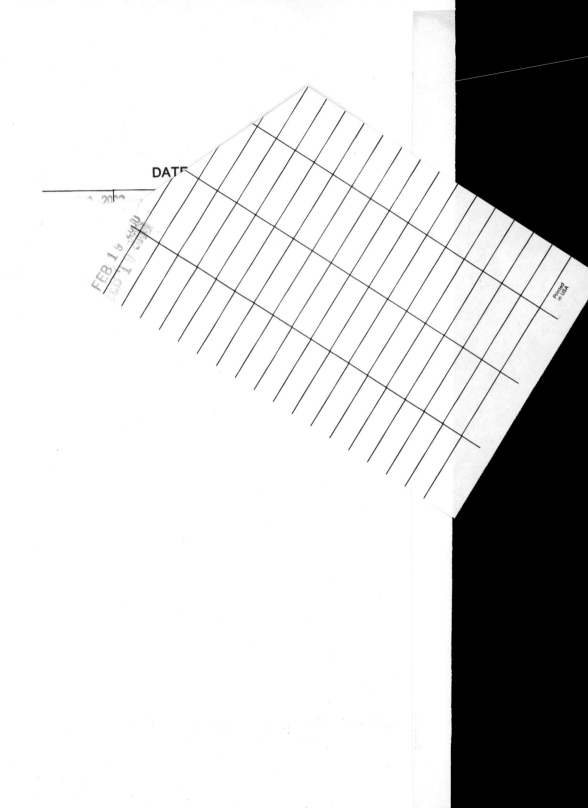

DATE

FEB 1 9 4410

"*GOSSIP*"

"*GOSSIP*"

A Spoken History of Women in the North

edited by Mary Crnkovich

Canadian Arctic Resources Committee
111 Sparks Street, 4th Floor
Ottawa, Ontario
K1P 5B5

Canadian Cataloguing in Publication Data

Main entry under title:
Gossip: a spoken history of women in the North

ISBN 0-919996-44-2

    1. Women—Canada, Northern. 2. Women—Canada,
Northern—History. I. Crnkovich, Mary
II. Canadian Arctic Resources Committee.

HQ1453.G68 1989   305.4'09719   C89-090456-1

CARC 1990 Publishing Program

Publications Manager: Alan Saunders

Production Manager: Anne Kneif

Cover: *Conversation*, sculpture by Mary Takkiruq, Gjoa Haven, N.W.T.

Cover design: Anne Kneif

Printed and bound in Canada by M.O.M. Printing, Ottawa

To Ana and Annie

Contents

ACKNOWLEDGEMENTS

On behalf of the Canadian Arctic Resources Committee and myself, I would like to extend my appreciation and sincere thanks to all of the women who took the time to learn about this project and to participate.

I also express my appreciation to the Government of the Northwest Territories Women's Secretariat; Women's Program of the Department of the Secretary of State of Canada; and specifically Kate Irving, Nancy Greenwood, Jackie Claxton, and Judy Wright who made their institutional resources available to us and provided both their time and commitment to the project throughout its duration. I would especially like to thank Janet Billson for her persistent encouragement and support. I would also like to acknowledge the foresight of John Merritt in proposing the idea of the "Women in the North" project and "letting us run with it".

This project would not have been possible without the talents, energy, and sense of humour of Ann Ray, Assistant Editor and Anne Kneif, Production Manager. I would also like to thank the rest of the CARC staff who helped make *Gossip* a reality. The tedious and unrelenting task of transcribing the tapes was done by Jan Wetter, Kyria Mancini, Colleen Hennessy, Janet Ma, and Toby Schnider, to whom I owe a great deal. To Angela Bernal and Louise Holt, I thank you.

I am indebted to Sharon Cohen, Linda Archibald, Leslie Macintosh, Sheila McIntyre, and Bev Baines for their vision and inspiration. Not last nor least, I would like to thank my partner Duncan Noble (and his incredible Mac) for always being there!

INTRODUCTION

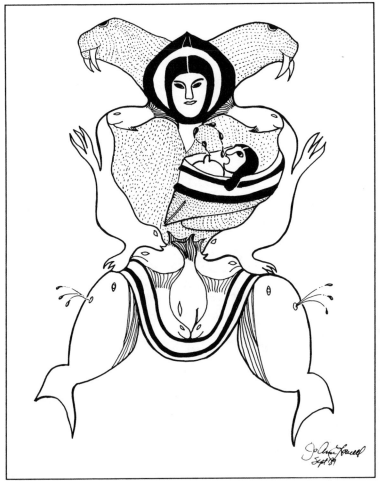

In Our Spare Time...

As the co-ordinator and editor of the "Women in the North" project, I have had the privilege of following its development from beginning to end. My involvement in a project of this type and magnitude has been a rewarding experience. As such, I thought it would be appropriate in this introduction to reflect on its history.

The project, like its creators, underwent many changes since its beginning in 1987. *"GOSSIP": A Spoken History of Women in the North*, is a culmination of these changes and was only made possible through the efforts of many women. It commemorates the women of the North, their strengths and their contributions to their communities and families. It is a sample, an introduction, an exploration. It has uncovered a diversity of life-styles, viewpoints, and experiences among the women who have participated.

The changes experienced by women in the North are vast. The impact of these changes has been empowering for some and devastating for others. There are some who have used this time of change as an opportunity to get involved in formal politics and to ensure they have a role in shaping the future of the North. There are others who have felt powerless and have attempted to cope with the impact of change on their families and communities in isolation of everyone around them. While for some women the change is too slow, for others it is too fast and has passed them by.

There are many valuable insights contained within these pages. There are portraits of the lives of northern women and there are origins of new theories about women and their roles in society. Diversity among women is reflected in their terminology. There is no underlying consensus or common denominator of meaning for such concepts as "equality" or "feminism". In fact, some women rejected the use of these terms because they were not a part of their lives while others felt comfortable with them and continued to explore them. The articles demonstrate how women, and especially native women, have been written out of the history of the North. These women have written "all the things [they] should have been able to read" (Alice Walker, 1978).

This book is a "first" for many reasons. It is the first time such a collaborative research project has been undertaken, where a number of women from distinctly different cultures have written about the lives they share north of 60°. This project sensitizes us to our differences as women and the importance of learning more about each other. It is a touchstone for further feminist research. *GOSSIP* symbolizes and celebrates the significance of and value in women recording their own ideas in their own words. Often these experiences and viewpoints have been re-created through the interpretations of male historians and anthropologists. Within feminist writing experiential writing is recognized and valued as a significant contribution. However, more recently, the preponderance of feminist works about the experiences of white women of Euro-Canadian descent has been recognized and is beginning to be balanced with the words of women from different cultures.

The insights and analyses offered in *GOSSIP* are northern-based and women-centred. It is not a scholarly piece, but, like scholarship, has its place. Women are seldom afforded the opportunity to tell their story in their way. *GOSSIP* gives them this chance.

GOSSIP marks the first time women in the North and South have worked together to bring a project to fruition. The forum was made available to ensure northern women expressed "themselves" on issues in their lives. However, like other works which have been written on the North and its people, it is not fully representative. *GOSSIP* does not express the viewpoints of all women in the North nor does it exhaustively canvass all of the issues. To that extent, it is unfinished.

Origins and Methodology

The origins of this book are southern-based. It began as one part of a multi-year study on economic and social issues in the North which the Canadian Arctic Resources Committee (CARC) was undertaking. It was an attempt to ensure that the particular issues and aspects of the many general issues confronting women would be recognized in the larger study. The funding was obtained through the Women's Program of the Department of the Secretary of State of Canada.

The project was originally designed to include women throughout northern Canada; however, this first step proved to be anything but easy. Due to the geographical vastness of the country and diversity in cultures, it was decided to redefine the "North". The geographical scope was narrowed and, for the most part, our focal point became the Northwest Territories.

The Northwest Territories amounts to one-third of Canada's land mass with a population of 52,240. Within this vast territory, there are four major cultural groups—the Dene, Métis, Inuit, and Euro-Canadian. Within each of these groups, there are many smaller groups each with their own dialect and customs.

The objectives of the project were two-fold: to provide an opportunity for women to gather, express, and reflect on their views and experiences as women living in the North; and to raise awareness among southern Canadians about northern women, their perspectives, and their contributions.

As co-ordinator, I drafted project outlines and summaries for others in the North to review. My focus of interest was the relationship between ethnicity and feminism.

Within this framework, one possibility which northern women could explore was whether native women thought of themselves or were thought of in a "proprietary" way, as "things" possessed by men; and whether they shared the feelings of objectification experienced by white women in a southern Euro-Canadian culture. Certainly, based on historical records and anthropological accounts, this presented a possibility when past practices such as the exchanging of wives, polygamy, tattooing of women, and female infanticide were taken into account.

There was also the possibility of going beyond the "identified" contributing factors of violence against women such as alcohol, and focusing on possible cultural factors. After reading or hearing Inuit tales* such as *Sedna*, *The Faithless Wife*, and *Ululigarqnaaq*, in which women can be viewed as the "victims" of violence, the similarity to the Euro-Canadian fairy tales strengthened this idea. It was not difficult to wonder whether alcohol only exacerbated an already serious problem of violence against women which existed well before the white man came.

These ideas and queries have never directly been addressed or even explored; perhaps the time has not come, perhaps it never will, perhaps they have no place in the North. The assumptions and questions presented were culturally biased. The type of critical analysis and re-examination I had hoped to encourage northern women to engage in appeared to be even more assaultive and insensitive because they were so disconnected to the social reality of these women.

To ensure my own perspectives did not overshadow the design and outcome, I contacted and met with several women in the Northwest Territories. These women inevitably provided insights and perspectives which reflected a variety of opinions on numerous topics which they themselves considered to be "the issues" in the North.

It was suggested that rather than initially categorize possible subject areas for submission such as women and the law, women and politics, women and health, or women and work, we should instead listen to what the women wanted to say. It was felt that the project would be more manageable if it focused on the issues commonly identified by women; if we moved beyond this and sought out people to write about specific topics we would lose sight of our objectives.

The first crucial step of the project was to get word of its existence to the women of the North. Their involvement was essential if the project was to be a success. Since travel was financially impossible, the only other options available to do this were radio, television, or mail. Television and radio stations were contacted and the northern newspapers all ran articles describing what was wanted. Interested northerners were encouraged to call CARC collect.

---

* Gedalof, Robin (ed.). *Paper Stays Put: A Collection of Inuit Writing*, (Edmonton: Hurtig Publishers).

The first response came from a northern woman shortly after the first radio news story was broadcast. Unfortunately, the excitement of receiving a response so early in the life of the project was short-lived. The caller explained that she had a great recipe she would like to share in the book. As we talked a bit more she explained that she had created her own business from this recipe. Adhering to the objectives of the project and my own commitment to print what women in the North had to say, I told her to send it along. I did explain the objectives behind the project and tried to convey enthusiasm in her interest to participate. None the less, it was hard not to think about receiving a recipe as the first response.

For a period of time after this first call there were no other responses. Becoming more desperate, I decided personally to contact as many women as I could by way of letter. The Women's Secretariat of the Government of the Northwest Territories agreed to include the CARC letter with their newsletter. It was mailed out across the territories and the rest of Canada. The letter explained the project objectives and emphasized that this was a northern women's project which depended on northern women getting involved. To provide a better under-standing of what the project was about, several suggested topics were presented as guidelines. Attached to the letter was a postage-paid response card.

The "suggested" topics may have prevented women from developing their own topics or choosing to express themselves through a format other than writing; however, in an attempt to circumvent this problem, return phone-calls were made promptly to those women who mailed back a response card. They were told that this was a project which would be directed by those who participated. They were encouraged to express themselves about anything they chose and in a style and format with which they were most comfortable.

Those unable or unwilling to write in English were encouraged to produce a tape which we would transcribe and translate if required. Although translations were done with great care and sensitivity, the inherent problem of failing to express the true experiences or feelings of the orator in translation does exist.

The responses eventually arrived. Women had taken the time to identify many issues they faced in the North and expressed their interest to talk or write about them.

In the earlier stages of the project, it was difficult to overcome the barriers which kept our project from reaching many native women in the communities. This failure was primarily attributable to communication barriers. In order to have a full representation, many oral interviews or informal gatherings to simply talk with these women were required. The high costs of translation and transcription limited the number of interviews relied on.

Participants and Contributors

Of the many women who responded about half submitted articles. One woman ran as a candidate in the federal election for the western Arctic and won. Another woman decided she would write her own book. One contributor withdrew when her child was born, but eventually did find time to submit an article.

One woman suggested she would be prepared to write how practices like customary adoption were being practised in her "mixed" marriage. She later explained that she feared ramifications from government bureaucrats if she wrote about the customary adoption of their child. She was not prepared to risk losing her child.

One contributor "delivered" her contribution almost a year past the deadline. She is a midwife and wrote in her rare spare moments. Her article was written throughout a two-year period, in many different places, awaiting the births of many babies. In the end, when she came to my home to review some changes on the final draft, we were interrupted by her pager to which she immediately responded. I only heard one side of the conversation:

"Well those sound like contractions..."

"Do you think you are having the baby?"

"Well, maybe I should do a check..."

"Mary..."

Then I was asked if it would be all right if my midwife friend could do the check at my home as it was the most convenient place for both of them. Shortly thereafter, the awaiting mother arrived at my door. When the check had been completed, it turned out the time wasn't quite right and off went my midwife friend and this pregnant woman.

Then there was the phone call back in the winter of 1988, collect, at 1:00 a.m., from "Susan in Yellowknife". By this stage into the project I was accepting all collect calls at all hours anticipating it was another woman willing to participate in the project. This caller was living in a small cabin outside the Yellowknife area—she only came to town to get supplies. On this recent visit she came across a news item about the project in the local paper. She wanted to write her story about being a fisher and trapper and her experiences with the other trappers and fishers who were mostly men. She explained that she lived happily with her dogs in the bush without electricity, indoor plumbing, or other modern amenities. I gave her the information she wanted and encouraged her to write and to call again, collect. I am still waiting to hear back from her.

There were women from the South who had received the letter through the Women's Secretariat and responded with their ideas. The southern contributors are women who either originally were residents of the North and have relocated to the South or who have worked extensively in the North and are now attempting to publish their work.

"GOSSIP": A Spoken History of Women in the North

The submissions which arrived, for the most part, surprised me. At first I could not reconcile my vision of northern women with what I was receiving in the mail and hearing on the phone. The spectrum of viewpoints was unpredictable. I had stated repeatedly, and truly believed, that the views of women had to be expressed in the manner they themselves chose. In achieving this objective, I had to refrain from my desire to rewrite, substantively edit, or overlook certain submissions.

Reading and rereading the articles, and writing and talking with the authors, proved to be an experience which was often painful and enriching at the same time. I learned to become tolerant of the women's views which were often opposite to my own. I learned to stop labelling or categorizing submissions. I learned respect for others, and by the end of this project I became vigilant about my conviction of keeping the submissions as true to their original form as possible.

Critics of some manuscripts questioned the lack of professionalism or "polish". Others were concerned about the length or repetition of some pieces. These criticisms at first seemed valid; however, the criticism such articles incited reminded me not only of the value and importance feminist scholarship has attributed to work of this nature but also how vulnerable such work has become even among feminists. There is a need to continually ensure that women's experiences are the source of feminist theory. To that end, this means women of different colour, culture, race, and class must have the opportunity to express themselves and not be held to standards which neither reflect their ideological, cultural, educational, or economic experiences nor render them invisible. To disconnect ourselves in this way further removes women's writing from our own reality and perpetuates the oppression which does exist for all women.

GOSSIP is a written translation of women's talk about new social, political, cultural, economic, and environmental crises which have had an impact on their lives.

The word "gossip" has generally been used to discredit women's comments, but feminist literature has explored and developed alternative interpretations. The intent is to make the reader more aware of how a term like "gossip", when used pejoratively to describe communication between women, has tended to isolate them from one another by trivializing their everyday experiences. It is in this way that their accounts and perspectives have been neglected or marginalized in written records.

The bias in favour of "written records" in the history of the North has not only isolated women, but has also ignored and devalued the oral tradition of native people in northern Canada.

GOSSIP does not aim to separate women from their cultural communities nor does it only represent a Euro-Canadian feminist perspective on women in the North. Rather, it focuses on the varied perspectives among women coping with and initiating change.

The submissions included in *GOSSIP* are only a beginning. It is the anticipation of all those who have participated in this project that many more projects of this kind will follow. It is our hope that more opportunities will be available to women from the North and South to work together to ensure the voices of all women will be heard and their stories shared. Accordingly, future endeavours of this kind should be funded to ensure original works in native languages and native-language translations of English-language originals are made available. The need for contact in a more substantial form other than mail or telephone, necessitates any future projects be northern based.

There is significant power in words, especially those woven together to form "history". It is our intention that the words of the women which make up *GOSSIP* will promote a greater awareness of the North and its people and contribute to an historical record that is as yet incomplete.

Mary Crnkovich

Chapter I

CHANGING ROLE OF WOMEN AND THEIR FAMILIES

Summer Camp Scene by Kiakshuk

A Good Life

Annie Okalik
Based on an Interview by Angela Bernal
Translated by Sadie Hill

To begin with, I would like to say that I am grateful for having been asked to talk about what Inuit life was like back then and how it is today. It would be better for me to voice my thoughts so that someone else may be reminded of what the traditional Inuit way of life was like and how it differs now, especially for those of us who have gone through a transition of life-styles.

My way of living is very different now than the way it used to be. And though we are provided with some comforts from modern culture, it isn't the same kind of comfort and peace that we had. While we still lived our traditional life I bore some children, and after we moved to the settlement of Pangnirtung, I bore more. My two sets of children were raised in completely different ways. My eldest ones lived like I did; my younger children were born having to enter school. So my younger children are inclined more to modern living and my older ones to the traditional Inuit way of life.

In those days, there was no other place but our homes and parents. We honoured our parents then, and no one else. If we were told to do something, we did not refuse or talk back, nor were we to be lazy. And often, because there was more than one set of grandparents, they'd be treated and respected the same way by the grandchildren and they, in turn, took care of us. I have benefitted greatly from my grandparents' advice, and I still remember the stories my grandmother used to tell me. My grandmother was really in charge of the children then, compared with today. She would tell me stories about her life when she was growing up and she'd tell me that our life now is so easy because there are no shamans to govern the lives of Inuit. But, looking back, it really wasn't any easier, though our lives were made easier then by heeding the traditional laws.

When we, as young girls, grew old enough to start learning our future roles in life we'd be taught different things. We'd be so filled with pride if we managed to accomplish a certain task and move on to another lesson. The elders would teach us based on our abilities. We were taught such things as tanning sealskins and caribou skins, cutting patterns for clothing and sewing, chewing skins to soften them, and making *kamiks* [boots]. And all those lessons proved to be useful in our lives.

Our life seems to have been completely turned over. An example of how life has changed for Inuit is that most of the young men do not know anything about hunting. Because I was the eldest child in our family, I would accompany my father during his hunting trips. We'd hunt by dog-team during the winter and on foot in the summertime; we'd also trap for fox. My father was a very quiet man; he never scolded me during my childhood. In fact, we became the best of friends. What helped was the fact that I knew my limits and respected the rules. We would share all the tasks at hand. I remember I would get so sleepy after everything we needed was inside our little igloo and our *qulliq* [oil lamp stove] was turned on. He would say his prayers both at bedtime and morning. I have benefitted by the way my father lived his life.

Both of my grandmothers, too, would always say their prayers. They have helped me in many ways. I have always wanted to lead my life with the same kind of wisdom. They would always put the Lord first to begin their day, to protect and lead them. I also remember when a number of people moved from Broughton Island to the small village of Pangnirtung. My father and some other men would conduct church services every Sunday morning and evening. The way things are now is proof that our life has degenerated, simply because we have forgotten to put God first in our lives.

On the subject of childrearing, I know it has changed in many ways too. Children now are permitted to go over their parents' heads; I feel that the old way of childrearing is a lot better. Children would accompany their parents to church services and would never start misbehaving; in those days, baby-sitters were not so readily available. Today, children are walking and running around during worship, and the mothers do not even take steps to correct them; it is no wonder the children now are like that. As mothers we have the responsibility of correcting our children starting at an early age. I do not want to be misunderstood on this subject. I just want it known that children have to be steered in the right direction before they're set in their ways. I am not saying that all of our traditional ways of life are better, but there is a very big difference when compared with today's way of life. I strongly believe that it is time for us to try and better our way of life.

Compared with our life now, we did not use drugs or alcohol, and I have seen how much these things have wrecked the lives of Inuit, especially the young people. I remember that when the supply ship came during the summer months, two of the Inuit employees of the Hudson's Bay Company store would consume alcohol, but they were moderate in their intake. Today, along with new things being introduced to the North, it seems that people will drink much too much, with no limits at all.

I am not trying to say that all of the old ways of life were better, but in regard to alcohol intake now, it does seem that life was a lot better than it is today. I want also to point out that excessive drinking did not happen right away. It seems that the introduction of television to the North was one of the influences in the degradation of the Inuit way of life. The things shown on television such as drunken people, murders, and robberies, have opened more doors to a poorer-quality way of life for the Inuit. I have also become aware that this is the same in all Inuit communities across the North. What I would like the most is to have no alcoholic beverages advertised on television, because these advertisements just encourage people to consume alcohol. Inuit should not be using alcohol at all; it isn't a part of our traditional way of life, and it has played a major part in lives lost in Inuit communities, especially among young people.

On the subject of marriage, single women were not to become pregnant without a husband. And even though I gave birth to my eldest child while married, the child wasn't my husband's. In those days our husbands were chosen for us. When a man chose who he wanted for his wife, the girl's parents would be approached, and, if they approved, the marriage would be arranged. Girls then had to marry men who weren't even their boyfriends; their feelings weren't taken into consideration at all. The marriage was based on how good the man would be for the girl, and sometimes her parents would not approve of the marriage. In short, a girl in those days got married to the man her parents wanted for her. It did not matter to them whether the girl was repulsed by her parents' choice or not; they just did not have a choice in the matter. It was maddening, especially on first meeting. To begin with, you did not want that certain man, so you'd just sit there with not a thing to say. Later on, though, after some time had passed, the man and the woman grew to love each other and become partners in each of their roles in life. Today, they get married to people they want, so I don't understand why so many couples are getting separated or divorced, especially when they already have children. I truly disapprove of that; I feel it is wrong.

I strongly believe that children are emotionally hurt by their parents' divorce. It is obvious that children suffer a great deal; their whole appearance changes as though they'd lost a lot of blood. It has a lot to do with missing their parents being together and having a good home. They act as though they'd lost a loved one through death. And now we, the elders of a couple who divorce, just sit back and let it happen when we should be doing something to correct that. What is wrong with the elders now is the fact that we just watch our children divorce and marry someone else. Though our traditional way of life was better in a lot of ways we are now too greatly influenced by the *qallunaaq* [non-Inuit] culture.

Since time began, all married couples have had disagreements. But the way it was then, we did not even think of divorce on grounds of disagreements. We would iron things out because there always is a way to work problems out; forgive each other and forget. That is what I want our young people to become aware of. Today, when married couples have the slightest little problem in their marriage, they get a divorce, or they will take another man's wife or another woman's husband. Another reason why so many couples get divorced is that they start feeling that they no longer love their spouse; even ministers are like that now.

Another big cause of divorce today is when either spouse has committed adultery; they refuse to reconcile. Adultery has been committed since time began, and hard times and problems for married couples occur, so they have to work at keeping their families together through thick and thin. I myself know what it's like to hear that your own husband has cheated on you with another woman. When I again heard of what he'd done I was so filled with anger toward the woman I started planning on what I would do to her. And while sitting there planning, I remembered what the Bible said concerning those who hurt us deliberately and those who are sinners. And when I thought of that, peace and quietness within myself seemed possible, and I got the comfort I needed to overcome that anger.

I have also noticed that reading the Holy Bible is not done any more, whereas when I was young I would read my Bible every night at bedtime to find out what life was like in the Old Testament times, from the time God created the world. Reading the Bible has been beneficial to my own life. The prophecies written in the Bible talk of what is to come, that the world will come to an end, that there will be nothing left. It makes me wonder if what Jesus said was to come—whether His second coming is not where we are standing now. For example, men and women having multiple affairs as though they were animals. But, we, unlike animals, have souls. We are not supposed to live like that. In the book of Isaiah it is written to heed what will come to pass in the future so that we can be prepared.

I have also gone along on caribou hunting trips to the big lake near Nattilik during the summer. And while we were there on the barren-land, away from the sea, we found old clam shells. Those were the evidence of the Great Flood. Today it seems that we have come to that same place before the Great Flood; I truly believe that we have to start preparing for that day.

On the subject of adoption, it has been done all through history. Childless couples would adopt a baby and raise it on broth when milk was unavailable. Today, childless couples are not the only ones who adopt—it has steadily been on the increase. Another thing is that the government handles adoption now. Most times the child's grandparents are not even consulted on the subject; the government just goes ahead and sends the child to another community. Sometimes the grandparents aren't even notified, when they could give advice about what may be better. We, the grandparents, if we tried hard enough to have a voice on these matters, could give a knowledgeable input. We're just not taking initiatives to make a stand. Some of our old culture is still a lot better than the way of life today, and we, the elders, have the wisdom and the knowledge.

Midwifery was another thing that we took care of ourselves, without a thought to using hospitals to give birth. This was because we had the knowledge to assist women in labour. Pregnant women were advised to try to stay active as long as they weren't ill, to continue with tasks as long as they were not too heavy to handle, and not to stay in bed too long after waking up. This advice, I know, was told to pregnant women in all northern regions, because it was passed by word of mouth and by songs. We were told not to stay in bed too long after waking so the embryo could grow at a normal rate, and to move around so the fetus would not make an imprint in the pelvic area. This would make labour and giving birth easier and shorter. In Pangnirtung, we did not think to go to the nursing station when we were about to give birth.

After my first child was born I became a godparent to a male child, and since then, I am a godparent to several boys and girls. My godchildren and I exchange gifts and celebrate on each other's birthday and during Christmas. In those days, the person who was the first to handle and tend to the newborn became a godparent. We used to enjoy assisting a woman in labour even if it was in a small tent or shelter during the springtime.

I also remember the time when I was still a young girl and someone came to our camp with word that they had been sent to fetch the woman in labour, that the nurses wanted to tend to her at the hospital. She was the first woman to give birth in a hospital, and from then on women started going to hospitals instead of being assisted by midwives. I, too, gave birth to my younger children at the hospital, but had my older ones assisted by midwives. I did not like giving birth at the hospital. I found that you are made to wait too long. Today, women who give birth have no idea what it was to have their babies with Inuit midwives. I do not approve of the way women are treated now. Although there really weren't that many deaths due to childbirth, now it seems that women are treated like they're made out of glass. And though we're just Inuit, we would assist in childbirth quite well without losing that many lives, and when it went well, we'd be so happy. We didn't mind in the slightest if it was in the middle of the night when we were fetched to assist the woman in labour. There would also be times when the woman giving birth would lose a lot of blood; some women would even faint because of loss of blood. I myself lost too much blood more than once while giving birth. And because all births differ from each other, we did not even worry about death. Another thing I want to point out is that women in labour used to be tended to every step of the way. Now it isn't like that any more. I know this because I, too, have given birth both at the hospital and with midwives.

From the time I was a small child, RCMP have always been in the town of Pangnirtung. I remember when those who'd broken the law would be sent to Pangnirtung from all over the North to do time. For instance, a man who had killed his in-law was in Pangnirtung with his wife and children for about five years. There was also a man from Arctic Bay who'd killed his wife. He was there with his new wife for quite a long time. Another was from Baker Lake. He was also sent with his wife and their grandchild. It turned out that he had sexually molested his grandchild who was under his care. They were to spend quite a number of years in Pangnirtung, and they later spent time at different communities as well.

Recently the Inuk employee of the RCMP informed everyone that the RCMP sergeant was expected to come to Pangnirtung and wanted to hold a meeting with the elders on how they felt about the RCMP up North. And though we did not go over the people who manage things in our community, I voiced what I had witnessed regarding the conduct of the RCMP. I pointed out the wrong things they've done, like sending people to our community without actually putting them in jail. I also pointed out that though they didn't have too great a control over matters then, they now control way too much. Another thing that I have to say about the RCMP is that they would hire Inuit men whose wives couldn't bear children so that they could take advantage of them.

What I also brought up was the fact that young people who haven't committed major crimes are being brought to court, even the very young ones who aren't even grown up yet. When it comes to young people, we, the elders, are quite capable of dealing with their wrongdoings in our traditional way. I really disagree with the fact that our young people who've committed minor crimes are readily given to the police. I get so angry in my mind in defence of our young people being brought to the police and brought before the court, when, if we tried hard enough, we could handle it ourselves.

Again, what I want to establish is that in our traditional way of life, we used to deal with discipline and punishment. Before the meeting with the sergeant, we had also met with a judge who had been in agreement with what we had to say on the subject of our young people being taken to court. He assured us then that he only sits at the bench when someone has been accused and brought before him. So if we could just agree on this subject and make a stand together, I'm sure we can do something about it because it seems like they get encouraged instead to commit more crimes later on, instead of turning their lives around for the better. These are the things I have seen happen.

What has also been discussed numerous times is the reason for our young people committing crimes—that they just do not have much else to do for entertainment. Compared with life back then, there are plenty of things to occupy the young people. Though we didn't have much entertainment back then, there were chores and tasks to be done, but today there are numerous kinds of entertainment brought up North from the South, and if we could get our young people to take advantage of them I strongly feel it would help. There are also plenty of jobs that our young people are capable of doing if they would only take that extra bit of time to learn the trades instead of wasting their time wandering around doing nothing. In those days we were taught things we needed to know for our future livelihood. We were taught all the necessary things that we'd be using for the rest of our lives, like making clothing and other things. And because there are so many things to do now, it just isn't right to say something like, "But there isn't anything to do!"

I am also amazed that the young women can hold down good jobs now and learn different trades. I am very much in favour of our young people completing their education. The need to qualify in southern technology is always growing and will become useful to know for future job opportunities. Inuit have a chance at job competitions in the future only if our young people continue and complete their education. There are numerous people who have started school and not completed it. And because they have not completed their education they cannot qualify for job opportunities that come up. There are so many things now that our young people could learn and master, whereas we were not taught any other than the necessities for survival and livelihood. Compared with the old days, the cost of living has steadily grown. This means we all have to depend quite a lot on our income.

Though I should be talking about what I am grateful for, I have said nothing but what I am in opposition to. There are many things that we should be grateful for that modern life has brought us, even though it didn't seem to matter too much at the time whether times were hard or not because it was our way of life; things like *kamiks* had to be tended to every day—drying, softening, and mending them. Today, mothers do not need to worry about those things quite as often. Another thing that women had to do was make sure that there was enough oil for our *qulliq* which was the only source of heat for warmth and to cook food with. Water and ice had to be fetched during the winter. All those things that we had to do then have been replaced by other conveniences available today. I don't even think that I could make a pair of waterproof *kamiks* from sealskins any more.

In early spring we'd start mending and preparing our summer tents, and, at the same time, we'd have to clean and dry the sealskins while the sun was out. In the fall we would gather firewood, sometimes even after the snow had come, which would be placed in the lining of the tent to winterize it. Now it seems that we all tire too easily, probably because we don't have to work quite as hard as in those days. Our elders would advise us and control our lives then. It isn't like that any more.

I would also like to add what my grandmother used to say to me in one of her stories about her own mother. She said the year her mother got married she, for the first time, could not accompany her family to Nattilik on their hunting trip for the summer. Just before they left, her mother sat alone outside, singing one of her songs. The words were: "In the future, white people will be coming to Inuit land." My great-grandmother was probably a shaman and had predicted the future. Today there are quite a number of *qallunaaq* living in the North. And as it turned out, my great-grandmother and the rest who'd gone hunting never came back and nobody has ever found out how they all died. Their belongings were the only things found.

Also, the late Anglican minister used to say that he thought the day would come when houses would reach the river and be across it as well. What he said then has also come true, for now the houses in Pangnirtung indeed have reached the river. The other person who told me that the Inuit will one day live in houses was a doctor. When he said that, I told him it was impossible because there was no way I could believe him. Now we do all live in houses like he said we would.

Editor's Note: Annie Okalik died in the summer of 1989, one year after this interview.

In Our Opinion

Alice Hill

The traditional role of native women has been to manage the home and the family. Has this role changed much over the last 60 years? To answer this question, we must look at two age groups—our respected elders and the young native women. And we must look at two ways of life—living off the land and living in modern urban communities.

Modern technology, in the form of computers, television, radio, telephone, and household appliances has changed native women just as it has other ethnic groups in Canada. Traditional women still live off the land and survive year-round in our harsh northern environment. We have young mothers at home taking care of their babies, and we also have native women out working in all walks of life. Many women have adapted to an urban life-style, and are attending high school, university, or government training programs. We have women chiefs, businesswomen, and women highly skilled in the arts and crafts industry. Yes, native women have come a long way in 60 years.

The traditional relationship between men and women was one in which men generally provided for the family while women were responsible for family upbringing. Women may have walked several paces behind men, but this was not to signify superior status; it was to ensure the safety of the women and children.

Sixty years ago, a native woman would travel with her family by dog-team from bush camp to other communities. Two or three days from Fort Franklin to Rae Lakes and Lac la Martre was common. The Dene would meet on the trail and stop to smoke tobacco, and to exchange news about families and events of importance to them. Women talked of midwifery—who had had a baby and where.

But the nomadic life is gone. Our people are colonized in communities so that they can be managed according to European standards of education and health. It did not matter to Europeans that we had our own medicine and our own ways of

11

curing the mind and healing our wounds. Our culture and traditions were ignored. It didn't matter to Europeans that families were separated during the school term from September to June, the best season for trapping. We adapted to their demands in a society based on the fur trade, and we helped them explore our land. In fact, native women played a vital part in negotiations between native bands, traders, and explorers during the 1700s.

Because we are Dene children, we have all been exposed to the nomadic life of our parents. We were taught well, taught to work hard and be responsible. In the bush, a native woman was kept busy all the time. She cooked meat from the hunt, dried meat and fish, repaired fishing nets and snowshoes, tanned hides, and sewed clothing. She was responsible for teaching her daughters about menstruation, birth, and breastfeeding. She was responsible for setting up the tent—laying spruce boughs for the floor, erecting the wood stove, cutting wood, and stringing lines.

Winter or summer, the camp was a healthy environment. Caribou, moose, fish, and small game provided a nutritious supply of food, and most ailments, whether minor wounds and cuts or major fractures, were treated on the spot.

Today in the Northwest Territories, there are five central hospitals and 19 nursing stations; however, five communities have no medical health care facilities at all. Pregnant women are often forced to leave their families and travel to the nearest hospital where they are subjected to discrimination and the cultural shock of urbanized living. The Dene woman handles the situation by being strong within herself, by hiding her anxiety about her children and family.

Some native women who cannot read or write do not understand medical terminology or hospital paperwork, and they are unaware of their right to a second opinion. They trust the doctor's analysis and treatment, and they view such individuals as important figures. Nurses assume an even more important role, as they not only fill in for the doctor when the latter is absent, but actually live in the communities and witness the family violence resulting from alcohol and solvent abuse. They see child abuse and neglect, and a lack of family planning. They see sick children and elders with chronic illnesses caused, in many cases, by excessive smoking.

The attitude of native women to tobacco has changed considerably in recent years. Although aboriginal people introduced smoking to Europeans and have traditionally used tobacco in pipe ceremonies and other rituals, there appears to be a greater awareness of the associated health risks. The Government of the Northwest Territories Department of Health has attempted to inform the Dene about smoking problems, but it has not always been successful. Television and radio advertising in the Dene languages could help improve the situation.

Alcohol abuse is a persistent problem in the Northwest Territories, but, again, women's roles and attitudes have changed considerably. Although restrictions have been imposed in many communities, bootleggers and home-brew continue to feed the demand. The native woman is just as susceptible to drink as her husband or friends; in some cases they become alcoholics and must face the negative consequences—fights and arguments, yelling, accusations, and jealousy. Children often become caught in such situations. They are understandably frightened, and sometimes run away from home.

We wonder why the government consistently subsidizes liquor instead of food. Do they make that much revenue that they can't introduce a more responsible policy? Will the public not allow it? In any case, they are not helping the situation.

Alcoholism is a disease which destroys the mind and makes the body sick. Those who choose to quit must have strength and willpower. They should have access to counselling if a treatment centre is near and the support of other people, especially the family. Drinking to extreme is no longer acceptable; native leaders are speaking out and are attempting to serve as positive role models. We must continue to have programs such as Northern Addictions, and we must initiate programs in communities. Alcoholics Anonymous must expand to more communities, and toll-free telephone lines should be made available.

The combination of alcohol and violence has changed the role of the native woman. She must play the role of listener and take in abused women and children. They may be relatives, they may be friends, but the pattern is almost always the same: they return to their home and drink to forget. The problem is no different from that in any other slum area.

What does the native woman hear? She hears of mental depression from the lack of a steady income, from institutionalization, from inadequate parenting skills. Being unable to comprehend the white business world and the pace of technological change can be devastating. Although there are many places to turn for help, there is also fear of reprisal from within the community, and of bureaucratic processes and procedures. Paperwork and red tape are perceived as obstacles. But thousands of victims have received help through various organizations, so we must work with them and with local political representatives to seek legislative change.

Our people are poor in material wealth, but rich in spirit. They smile easily, they share things, and they are kind. They love their children and their elders and are respectful to those who are friendly in return. But the poverty they suffer is real. I have seen some women with hardly anything in their food carts and wondered about their diet. Educating northerners about nutrition is an important objective of the home management program sponsored by the Native Women's Association of the N.W.T. The program explains the benefits of country foods and the need for a balanced diet providing the necessary vitamins, proteins, and carbohydrates.

It is important to stress that cross-cultural orientation must work both ways. Professional heath care workers must try to understand Dene culture and communicate with the individual.

The role of native women has also changed with regard to housing. Where once we lived in tents and cabins, we now live in houses, despite the fact that many are overcrowded. Sanitation has improved with waste disposal and running water, but a large number of homes still have honey buckets and depend on water delivered by truck. But does this necessarily mean that native women are adopting more sanitary practices? This, of course, is a matter of individual choice, but there should also be more public education. Television and radio ads would help get the message across, and nursing stations should be stocked with translated videos for the communities.

Another change involves the native woman's role as a parent. At one time, families gathered in clans and took care of one another. However, with the introduction of European systems of education, children were forced to leave home to attend school; the native woman cried for her children, and the children did the same. Although schools have now been established in many more communities, the family is still separated during the winter months when the men leave to hunt and trap. The native woman stays behind so that her children can attend school, and she must assume responsibility for the upkeep of the family within the community. During these times, welfare is often the only option, unless the woman's husband has had a successful hunt and the freezer is stocked with meat and fish. In some cases, the native woman earns some cash through the sale of arts and crafts. In other cases, she relies on relatives to share food and lend a helping hand.

What about community problems in general—alcoholism, solvent abuse, violence, civil disobedience, sexual abuse, illiteracy? These are tough questions. Such problems have a psychological effect on the individual, who often finds them difficult to comprehend, let alone deal with. The Roman Catholic Church teaches a social order to which the Dene adhere, but the church cannot solve everything. For example, the sexual abuse of children is a problem that requires special care and understanding. The child's self-esteem and self-image are low, and there is the sense of physical violation. The child may no longer trust adults and may be afraid to speak up. Our objective is to find a committed support group where children can go for help in the communities.

The traditional role of native women as care-givers to our elders has changed with the establishment of retirement homes and hospitals. The chronically ill, those confined to hospital, are often cut off from the community and forgotten. Are they receiving traditional native foods? We have to get involved in hospital boards so that the necessary changes can be made.

Many patients have to travel great distances to receive medical treatment. Do these patients have access to translators and assistance when they are away from their homes? Are they treated with courtesy and respect? We need more liaison workers in all the communities, and we need translators in the health care field. The Native Women's Association has lobbied government to hire more translators and to train more native people in health care professions.

Health care in the Northwest Territories has come a long way in recent years with the advent of micro-surgery, new laser equipment, and other methods, but funds for research must continue to be available.

Native women work and contribute to the tax system just like everyone else. We have our opinions, too. I feel that the earth we live on is like a spaceship travelling in space. We must take care of the environment, the land, and the water, thereby taking care of our health. Let's work together to keep it clean from pollution and contamination for the future of our children and ourselves.

Editor's Note: This article has been adapted from an address to the Cross Cultural Health Conference, Whitehorse, Yukon, 3–5 May 1987.

"Boy, Have Things Changed"

Maata Pudlat
Based on an interview by Angela Bernal

I was born in a camp with my twin brother. At that time we were still pretty much Inuit and we had no southern things to get mixed up with. We were living in huts, we travelled by dog-team, and slept overnight in igloos when we had to. I lived with all my brothers and sisters. We used to have very large families, even though we were struggling. Maybe because the more we struggled, we got closer. We seemed not to have everything, but had most things that we needed. I don't think we depend on each other any more, so that's why we're not that close. We're close, but we're not as close as we were before—even our children. They have most things that they need, whereas before, in my childhood, we always needed something because we didn't have very much. We would share. We would find love and comfort by helping others. What we had was for others to share. We didn't have very much but I think we were happier. Due to a lack of food, due to a lack of nice things, we would appreciate things more from inside rather than just outside; just from your visual eye. But I remember liking most things—oh, I used to like little things so much. If I saw that little glass over there a long time ago, 20 years ago, boy, that would turn me on! I would appreciate things more. We never considered ourselves poor. We were very rich in the heart because we had love and closeness.

But now, I see that jar with so many beautiful things inside...so what? It's just a jar with so many colourful beads. I see it everyday, it really doesn't touch me any more. In the olden days, boy, things were just so beautiful. Look at today, we have TV, we have everything, lots of things. When I try to sleep sometimes at night, I think to myself, "How did I pull through all of this?" So many changes in such a short time! Nobody else in the world has seen so many changes in such a short time like Inuit.

I went to school. I had to go to school because I was ordered. We were still in the camp when the government came to our parents, and they told us, "Your children have to go to school." My parents had no choice. And if we didn't go to school, we wouldn't receive family allowance, Baby Bonus; that's what our parents were told. They had no choice. That's what really gathered the North—the education, the school, the government. Our parents had no powers. In the old days, white man was somebody *big* with a lot of power. We had things to give, but never received. You know what I mean. [Laughter] Always giving and never receiving anything from them—that's what made them so powerful, I guess. When I think things like that—so many changes—I realize my children haven't had a glimpse of what I saw in my life, because everything just changed so fast. Sometimes I wonder, "How did I cope with it?"

Here I am working, being a mother, but I am a mother in a very different way than my mother was. When I was a child, not too long ago, just over 20 years ago, I was a child in a real Inuit way, a very Inuit way, the old traditional way. I was clothed in skins when I was a baby. We had no materials or fabrics. So, in a very short time my kids had no way of seeing what I went through.

I was born in a camp not very far from here 33 years ago, with all my relatives and one leader. All the camps used to have one leader. That used to be just great. We would respect our leader in our camp. There were so many camps scattered all around; there wasn't a settlement.

My sister had to leave us. She's older than me. When the government officials came to our camp, they approached my dad and said my sister had to go, she was at that age; she was the first child ever to be away from the family. Boy, that was something! We used to cry. My dad would worry, my brothers would worry, we couldn't sleep. We kept thinking, "Oh, she must be crying", because we had never been apart. Most fathers, most parents, couldn't face the fact that their little loved ones were away, somewhere, in somebody else's house. Even today, we have never really learned to be apart from our families. Maybe that's why there are no well-educated men and women. To be well-educated, like most well-educated professionals, you have to be away for so much time. Even today we don't like that. We don't even like to be away from our settlement too long. That's maybe one of the reasons that kids don't always graduate from school. It's very, very hard for most Inuit to be apart.

I was about eight years old when I went to school. I went to school till I was 16. Finally my dad moved, like most parents who couldn't be away from their loved ones, from their children. They had no choice but to move. I guess that was the government's idea in the first place, to get the parents to where the children all go to school. I don't know what they had in mind. So most families started coming to the settlements in the 1960s. That wasn't very long ago when you come to think of it, eh? Cape Dorset. That's where the missionaries, Hudson's Bay, and government were. Then families started moving in. They had no choice, because it was so hard for so many families to be apart from their children who were attending school here.

When we moved here, we were put in a very small house. They weren't even matchboxes. We had no toilets, no kitchen, no rooms, just one little square room. That was just good enough for somebody's bedroom. There were so many of us then. Inuit had very big families in those times, because there was no birth control or anything. So, when we got into the settlement, we sort of got confused. Our dogs were shot (our dog-team was our only transportation) because the RCMP didn't like the fact that they were loose. We never used to tie down the dog-team dogs. You tie them down and they'll lose their muscles. So we tried that in the settlement, and the RCMP didn't like it because many families lived in this town at that time. The RCMP went around and shot all our dogs. Boy, we cried. When you lose your dog, it's like losing one of your family. Dogs don't just mean dogs to us. They're your supporters, they're the ones who let you live. So, they were like gold to us—how a white man thinks of gold. Boy, we were crying. Even adults cried from losing their precious leader dogs. And more things came, and booze started coming in and most tried it. Because we're very sharing, when someone— even a white man—offers something, in our tradition, it is very impolite to refuse what they're giving. It's very unkind, it hurts the one who's offering. We're so used to sharing and doing things together. I think that's what happened with booze and drugs. We've got more common sense now; and it's not all going to be traditional ways, but I guess that's how it started. Booze was coming in and everybody sort of got excited and tried it.

But we were all confused, even our parents. What were we going to do? There weren't any jobs or well-built houses except for government employees. They had wonderful houses with bathrooms, bedrooms, kitchens, running water, lights! I remember, the first time I saw those light switches, I didn't know what it was, so I clicked it up, and a light went on. Boy, that scared me! And as children, we were always so scared of white people, like the RCMP. We would hide when they came into our camps. But now, I can walk all over them. [Laughter] That wasn't very long ago either. I was *so* scared of white people. Maybe because my parents were the same. Not really scared, but just didn't want them around, I guess. But they invited themselves in. [Laughter]

I'm not being prejudiced or anything against the whites. I am just telling the facts. Like I said, we have learned a great deal in no time at all, and we have coped without having extreme reactions.

When we were given rules and regulations, they came mainly from the South where they didn't know *anything* about us. Like the government from Ottawa, the federal government, they were all southern people. Those politicians who had never seen us were making all the regulations for us. And that didn't fit at all. All the things that were the law—they made laws that were useless to us. It wasn't how we deal with people. It wasn't too long ago either that we started speaking up for our rights and said what we wanted to see in our communities. That was about ten or 15 years ago, when we started getting power over what we want to see or do. So that's far better than it used to be, too.

I try and live a balanced life, but I'm caught in between! I know how to be Inuk, but not fully Inuk like my parents were. I'll never be that, I know. And I know the whites' way of life, but that will never make me a white, so I am in between. I am living both ways. I try to go out on the land as much as possible with my children. We live down there and that's when we feel free, that's when I feel so close to my ancestors. Down there, where there's no government—out on the land where my ancestors were. That's when I have good feelings, "Boy, this is me, I'm an Inuk!" Or else, I wouldn't be enjoying this like my ancestors did, and that hurts me. Sometimes it hurts me so hard, just in there. I don't know the feeling. We go with our kids all the time. We travel long distances, sometimes to Lake Harbour by canoe. The kids enjoy that and most of my age group are caught in between. They know how to be a bit of white, a bit of Inuk, but they're living both sides.

It would have been far better when white people came up North, a long time ago, if they had listened to us in the first place—learned from us, did things the way we did, and then listened to us and just accepted our culture. If they had learned from us, worked with us, instead of walking all over us, I think everything would have worked out better today. I think we would have more traditional ways today. But that wasn't to be, so we have to make the best of things. That's why we try to work hard, make the best of things. Everything's *so* expensive, and there's not very much money, and there's not very much employment. They let us learn, they let us get educated, but they have no jobs to offer us in our towns. So what's the use of education? I am a kindergarten teacher, but a lot of times I think most Inuit people never really want to get away from home. But they get us educated, they let us go to school, but there's no jobs offered. All the good jobs are down South. What jobs you see here today are all taken, and there's not very many.

If you were brought up with love and understanding and courage, no matter how hard it is you'll strive and try to go on. You're not just going to give up if you were brought up in a family where nobody just gives in. There are strong and weak families everywhere in the world, but here in the North you have to be very strong.

We were never given the right direction, the right co-ordination. We were never taught what to do if you're caught in between, but we have managed to cope with it. I think we're just trying our best. But what is our best if we don't really do something about it? We have to act together in most communities. But maybe when we get our Nunavut. The reason we are really fighting for our Nunavut is because I think it's about time. We're getting tired of people running our lives from down there. It's time to yell out and shout, "We've had it!" It's been too long. We've been letting things run ignorantly, when *we* know what all the problems are.

Between Two Cultures

Suzanne Manomie

Marriage

I have been living on Baffin Island now for 18 years, 17 of them married to a first-class Inuit carver. I can still remember some of my earliest impressions. When we were first married in 1971, I used to think we had marital difficulties because we were Inuit and *kadloona* [non-Inuit]. Then I realized our misunderstandings arose partly because we were a man and a woman, but eventually I knew it was mostly, as in every relationship, because we were two individual human beings. We had to learn about each other's background and culture. We had to learn to compromise and get used to one another. Most often we had to learn to forgive one another.

There was one basic tenet that we, with our individual backgrounds, agreed upon for different reasons. My husband had been taught since birth that thoughts and wishes should come first. The man was definitely supposed to be the leader of the family. I agreed that the man was meant to be the head of the house because that is how God planned it when He created Adam and Eve. Both men and women have an invaluable role to play. In the Inuit past, women sewed the clothes, tended the lamp, and looked after the children. The men had the strength, endurance, courage, and patience to bring home the food. Survival would not have been possible without both.

In today's world, where women often have to work outside the home, men can't suddenly forget thousands of years of conditioning. It would be good, of course, if they could also bring courtesy, kindness, and consideration to the relationship. They often do. A leader has responsibilities as well as privileges.

Over the years God taught me that life would be much more pleasant and our home would be a place of harmony and love if I tried to follow His plan for the family. God's rules do not presuppose that your husband will be perfect. None of

21

us even come close. But, if women wear "the unfading beauty of a gentle and quiet spirit", God will honour their obedience. I have experienced this often in our marriage. I was given the strength and love to see us through difficult times because I was able to do things God's way. I often failed, but thankfully, 17 years later, we are still together and peace and understanding are present.

Customary Adoption

During the 17 years of marriage, we have adopted six children by customary adoption. Sometimes the system works well and other times it doesn't. I have come to feel very strongly about the whole subject.

I think that when the system is functioning as it was originally intended, it is superior to the white man's way. The children don't grow up with the trauma of finding their roots; they know from the very beginning. Usually the adoption is kept within the extended family. The child can feel very positive about how much he or she was wanted. We are good friends with the natural mothers of our children and they often visit.

Unfortunately, the system does allow for some of the evils of the white man's world. There are some people who drink and take drugs excessively or who gamble incessantly. These activities lead to the neglect and abuse of children. Sometimes teenage mothers feel forced by their culture to give their baby to a father, father-in-law, or older brother from whom they have experienced sexual and other physical abuse. How terrible it must be for those mothers! I feel that the fine, caring elders that live in every community should form screening committees for prospective adopters. Something must be done to stop the placing of these precious little ones in homes where the whole community knows they will be neglected and abused.

There is another objectionable practice within the system which has been around since the beginning. Sometimes when people adopt girls, they treat them like slaves from the time they are old enough to be of any help. Surely something can be done to stop this barbaric custom. Our children, whether natural or adopted, are not our possessions. They are a gift from God, loaned to us for a while to love and care for, and to teach the right way.

In our own personal experience many of the things I've already mentioned have occurred. There are four and a half years separating our first two daughters. During the intervening time we were promised babies to adopt several times, only to be cruelly disappointed at the last minute. We would go to a great deal of trouble and expense to prepare for their coming and then the mother would change her mind after the baby was born. Often this was not their personal choice.

Once a big brother insisted on having the child if it was a boy. Unfortunately, this particular person had a lengthy history of drunkenness, crime, and violence. Yet the young mother didn't feel she had a choice. It must have broken her heart to send her little son into the home of this violent man.

On another occasion, a teenager promised us her baby before it was born. As she went into labour, her boyfriend's father, an old man who was a patient in the hospital, sent his daughter to say, "If it's a boy, I want it!" It was a boy.

We are grateful to God for the six wonderful children He has allowed us to have. It has been a learning and growing experience for us all. With His help I hope that our children can help to promote love and understanding between Inuit and *kadloona*, simply by existing.

Women Loving Women—Northern Style

Helen Fallding

I have lived in the Yukon on and off for the last ten years. Over the course of that time, I have been asexual and confused, part of a heterosexual couple, a closeted lesbian, a half-closeted lesbian, and now a gay activist. I imagine that most Yukoners believe there aren't any gay people here. Many lesbians lived here for years before they found another member of "the family". But I am beginning to believe that there are many of us—that our lack of community is not really related to our numbers.

It's not easy to get northern lesbians to tell their stories. Confidentiality is a touchy issue in small communities where any detail about your life immediately identifies you to the whole town. Because of this and because I only had a few weeks to pull together this submission, I chose to use fiction to communicate something about our lives. These portraits are caricatures and aren't intended to do justice to the reality of anyone's life or thoughts.

In these stories are embedded some of the reasons why we don't find each other and why, in some cases, we run from each other. For many northern lesbians, invisibility is what makes living here possible at all. But a few of us feel strangled by it. I wanted to see our existence acknowledged in this anthology of northern women's voices.

Conversations That Might Have Been

I own and run a corner store. Sue and I started it up from scratch 20 years ago. We drove up here in a van to spend the summer fishing and we've never left. We're not exactly rich, but the business is pretty solid. I even give courses now at the college, for women who want to start up a business! Sue's not fond of the technical end of things, the bookkeeping and so on, but she manages the customer service

25

aspects. She's the sociable one in the family. Without her around to drag me out to parties, I probably wouldn't know anyone in this town. The store is my life really. Nothing is going to get in the way of that.

There are one or two couples that we see on the weekends. Women who've been here for almost as long as us. When we were young and crazy, we used to go to a lot of parties, but you get tired of the soap operas and jealousies that go along with that. Anyway, I don't have a lot to say to these city girls that come and go these days.

Our customers don't know we're a couple. It's none of their business really. I don't think anyone questions it one way or the other.

* * *

I was born in this same town. We lived in the bush mostly, but gramma had a house in town. My mom came into town to have her babies. I was here to help with a new baby once and the priest came round. He took me off to mission school. I cried for months. Billie was my best friend, because she could speak my language and wasn't afraid of nobody. When we quit school, she got a job in construction. I moved to Edmonton for a while. I slept with a guy once and that was enough, thank you. I came back and found Billie and we've been together since. Except that one winter when my family took me out to the bush with them, 'cause they figured Billie was a bad influence. I got sick of them and just walked out all by myself in the middle of January. They don't bug us now.

All those people we went to school with have a million kids and they look right through us, just like white people look through Indians. I met these two white girls once who were like man and wife. They were pretty friendly, but Billie didn't like me to talk to them. She says one of them had the hots for me.

* * *

Look, I need to let you know right away that there's no way you're using my name. And I want to look over what you write before it gets published. I am not in the sort of position where I can afford to be known as a lesbian. I co-ordinate a program for children. I make good money and I do a lot of important work in this community. My reputation needs to be spotless. I've chosen to be celibate. No relationship lasts forever, and I can't afford gossiping ex-lovers.

I agreed to talk with you because I feel it's important for liberal people to know that they can make life safer for gay people in the North. When you hear speculations about who in town might be gay, let your friends or co-workers know that those discussions are inappropriate and even dangerous. And don't ask us invasive questions about our lives—most of us are very private people. If you know a young person who is coming out, advise them to leave the territory. I worry about the *naiveté* of these newcomers from the city. This is not Vancouver. It's not even

Saskatoon, for God's sake. I wish someone would warn these women that if they're not extremely careful, they are certainly risking their careers and they may be risking their lives.

* * *

I once heard someone from the Women's Centre say that she couldn't find any gays in the territory. I thought that was hilarious. That lady's been going to too many meetings and not enough ball games! I can't say I've ever lacked women's company, and I think the secret is that I play a lot of sports. Sometimes it seems like half the players are gay. Of course, you have to be careful because even straight girls look that way up here. Nine out of ten gay girls won't admit they are if you ask them straight out, but it doesn't take a genius to notice how many of them live together. And those that live alone are not averse to a little warmth on a cold night, whatever the hell they call themselves in the morning. I think this place is Canada's best-kept secret. A woman can get a good job, buy a piece of land, play competitive sports, and meet women. The straights don't hassle you about being queer, because it never crosses their minds that someone is up here, except when they started talking about putting us in the Human Rights Code. I know the government meant well, but I think it's one of the stupidest things they could have done. It just stirred everything up. The creeps and religious weirdos came out of the woodwork and some of us went through a lot of shit. No one in their right mind would take a complaint to the commission anyway—unless they were the martyr type.

I must admit that I don't know a lot of gay guys. I guess they're not into coming North to build cabins and shoot moose. They'd probably be more worried about being beat up too. Some of the bars are pretty rough, but we women know how to take care of ourselves.

I don't know whether I can live here long term. But then again, I'm pretty sure I can't live in the city at all. What a trade-off: clean air, an affordable home, and meaningful work combined with total isolation as a lesbian; or pollution, poverty, and a supportive community. Living in a mid-sized city might be the worst of both worlds.

I often tell my city friends that this place is like 1950 revisited. Lesbians alone tormenting themselves with guilt and believing they're the only ones, or else being invited to secret parties where they vow never to breathe each other's name in public. Needless to say, I don't get invited. I insist on living as if this was 1989. Once, after a night of dancing in a local bar with my lover, I was approached on the street by a woman I didn't know. She hissed at me that we were putting everyone else in danger by flaunting ourselves. So much for my idea of starting a support group!

When I first got here, my heterosexual acquaintances drove me nuts by avoiding the "L" word and never referring to my relationship. But they've come a long way. They're my main suppport now, but there are things they'll never understand. I'd like to send a message to every "out", politically active lesbian in Canada: "Get the hell up here before I go crazy!"

* * *

I've finally decided to leave this place and move South. After all these years, I realize this place is not a home. It's hard not to be bitter about it. Lee and I built this home with our own hands. Then she up and died before we really had time to enjoy it together. People expect me to stay on as if nothing much had happened. But I'm lonely. No one understands what we meant to each other, because we were trying to protect Lee's career. It's too late to tell them now. Lee taught at the local primary school. A whole generation of kids in this town learned how to read with her. Everybody loved her. At her funeral, they talked about what a private person she was, but so ready to listen to other people's secret sorrows. They talked about how she had never married or had children, but had spent her love on the kids of the community instead. They talked about how she was survived by her beloved brother and sister, nieces and nephews. They didn't know what to say about me, so they said nothing at all.

I swear my life is not going to end like that. I'm going to move to the city and become an eccentric old lady. I'm going to speak the truth every day of the rest of my life. But I can't do it here. Lee's ghost is here, whispering in my ear, "Its important not to upset people, it's enough that we know that we loved each other."

* * *

Why not come out to the trapline with me this winter? I could use another pair of hands. Frank hasn't been out since the first year we got married. He isn't really the type. Anyway, it don't hurt to have a bit of time to yourself. Thank God we never had kids. I'd probably have had to give up the line. Indian ladies seem to pull it off—husband, kids, a trapline, keep the freezer full of moose, the whole bit. But us white chicks don't seem to have it in us. I used to have a trapping partner—you remember Mary? We had a big fight around the time I got married and she took off for Vancouver. I don't really want to get into it right now. Anyway, it's been a long time, and a woman gets lonely. I've been watching you. You seem lonely too sometimes. So why don't you come out to the line with me this winter?

The Feminist Conservative

Anne Crawford

Before I came North as a young lawyer eight years ago, I lived and grew up in an Anglo-Canadian city in southern Canada. In the context of both that culture and my profession, I am a feminist, and reasonably vocal in identifying and addressing the inequalities I see. In the context of northern life, however, that activism has been left by the wayside, and you are now reading the words of one who might best be described as a feminist conservative.

The transition happened almost without my noticing; and when I have attempted to explain the change, I am often at a loss for words. How has it evolved that I now sit and watch things that I might earlier have decried as sexist, or put time and energy into activities and groups that promote a reasonably traditional view of women's role in this world?

In part, this is because, in the North I know, there is not one world; there are, in fact, two. There is a native world and a non-native world, and the two only touch in special places with special people—when the wind blows in large, blue gusts from China.

I don't wish to suggest that there is no contact or communication between people of different cultures. There is usually daily contact and communication, to a varying degree, depending on how and where one chooses to live. While northerners have been able to communicate and live together in ways that are a credit to most, there are still distinct worlds among us.

In the non-native world, of government and courts and career, I suspect you would still see me in the context of the feminist who moved North. It is when I moved into the world of community life, that largely native world, that my caution and conservatism emerge.

From early experience one learns that there is a problem of even identifying "sexism" in the northern context. What at first encounter may appear to be a sexist act or idea likely has a very different origin.

Consider the problem of identity. One of the things that feminists have fought against is the idea that women could, or should, be defined in terms of their relationships to men. The concept that an individual should stand on her own and have independent worth is fairly basic.

Recently, my younger sister, who lives in the same community as I do, was introduced in the following fashion:

> "This is Linda. She is the younger sister of Anne. Anne is married to Neil who is a lawyer at *Maliiganik Tukisiiniakvik*. Anne is a lawyer too."

Indeed, I often hear myself introduced in Inuktitut in a very similar manner:

> "This is Anne. She is the lawyer who is married to Neil. Neil is the lawyer at *Maliiganik Tukisiiniakvik*."

Now, one could easily see in such an introduction exactly the sort of definition by male relationships that rightfully raises feminist ire. However, on closer examination, both of these introductions make sense. The introduction places the individual in the context of her family, which is the essential definition in a northern community. This definition by family is the way of life for men and for women. An assertion that anyone would want to "stand on her own and have independent worth" is, to a certain degree, a rejection of family and of community.

Also, with a recognition of the mobility of non-natives in the North, the introduction carries the family tie until it comes to rest at a place that has some northern stability. Lawyers and sisters and husbands can come and go; but *Maliiganik Tukisiiniakvik*, the locally controlled Legal Aid Society, already provides a reference to the familiar. With that tie, the new person can be placed in the proper community perspective.

There are still further complications in identifying sexism in its northern setting. For me, much of the difficulty stems from the sexism built into my own culture and upbringing.

I cannot deny all connections with those southerners who, in bringing tuberculosis and hospitals and airplanes to the North, also managed to transport Anglo-Canadian forms of sexism. Much of what we might now oppose as sexist was introduced by our own forbears, so we look a bit foolish in admonishing others in the North for practising now what we have followed in the past. I recall, for instance, a friend's description of her amazement at the compulsive behaviour demonstrated by southern teachers at the federal day-school in her northern community. These people insisted that boys line up and enter the school through one door and girls through another. Boys hung their coats on one side; girls on the opposite. All day long these divisions continued.

The same divisions occurred at my school in the South, but I don't remember ever questioning them. To an eight-year-old Inuk, who had been used to playing as an equal with boys and girls of her own age, the system was bizarre—and it was quite beyond her understanding what relationship hanging one's coat had to one's gender.

Coming from a world of English where non-sexist language is a recent and often controversial issue, one is impressed by the gender-neutral structure of Inuktitut. Personal names carry no gender; one Nowdlaq or Eelia or Akeshoo may be a man or woman.

There is no distinction between "he" and "she" in the language. In their Inuktitut translations, even constructs like boyfriend, younger sister, or older brother need not be gender-specific. English has a fair distance to go to meet the structural equalities of this language.

Although I hear discussions and complaints among young Inuit women that their husbands are not helping as they should, I see a fairer distribution of labour in some Inuit homes than in many non-native homes I visit. I recently visited the home of an elderly Inuit couple where the husband was doing the laundry while the wife entertained. In that household, without running water, doing laundry was a substantial chore, yet there seemed no indication that the situation was anything other than routine.

Another incident which stands out in my memory is that of the oldest woman in my community strongly supporting the admission of women as Anglican priests. All people were equal in God's eyes, asserted the woman, and the church was in no position to determine those who received the call to ministry on a basis as irrelevant as gender.

In recalling these examples, I begin to wonder if I actually have anything to offer on the subject of equality—or whether I should spend more time as a student of my neighbours.

This brings me to my third reason for caution. I believe that change, or "progress" as it is styled in the South, is not necessarily a "good thing". For change to be a positive feature, it requires that people accept and control that social evolution for themselves. Imposed change is destructive, even if it is, by some esoteric and objective standard, "good".

When I find myself disagreeing with the "way things are" in the North, I remember that respect for others means patience in accepting others' choices even when I might make different ones. And that patience is tried and especially needed when I fail to understand or to agree with those choices.

This is not to suggest one is duty-bound to hide one's own views from others for fear of creating some destructive influence: quite the opposite. The feminist case is more effectively presented by deeds than words; that is, by example than by expostulation. I believe that empowering women and communities to make choices for themselves creates the potential for positive change. And that process of empowering, whether by example or by providing information, is a more productive use of energy than deliberately setting out to provoke changes of one's own choosing.

This is particularly true of outsiders. Just as there are distinctive native and non-native worlds in the North, with only modest overlaps, there are similar divisions in the world of women. Despite many parallel features, the worlds of native and non-native women are generally lived apart.

Take the example of sewing. Sewing outdoor clothing is important for Inuit women. Besides being a traditional skill which women enjoy, the winter clothing available in stores is expensive and often ill-suited to the North. Families on the land rely on the clothing women produce. Every *amautiq* [hooded parka] must be produced in someone's home, and pride requires that children and husbands, and especially babies, are well dressed.

This is not necessarily true for non-native women. As I sat in my front yard with sailcloth needles and waxed threads around me, mending the seat cover on the skidoo, I was approached by a swarm of curious native children. "Where did you learn to sew?" inquired the children. "*Qallunaaq* [white] women don't sew."

The children have reason for their broad assumption. Non-native women rarely sew, and for the most part don't go out on the land. Store-bought clothing is usually adequate and more appropriate for their needs. When they need northern clothing or an *amautiq*, they generally arrange to buy these from Inuit women in the community. One might argue that the difference is only of incidental interest. Indeed, most women, native or non-native, wouldn't spend too much time pondering such trivialities. Occasionally though, these trivialities bring the ways that women socialize, communicate, and make plans for their communities into clearer focus.

A typical meeting of the Apex Anglican Women (a largely Inuit organization whose meetings I occasionally attend) would be held at the *qammaq*—an insulated, round-roofed building on the beach. It was built by women, with seating platforms for coats, supplies, and babies. Some women would arrive earlier in the afternoon to start the fires and light the oil lamps.

The meeting would begin with some singing and prayers, followed by talk about community events and people. There is usually some country food served— raw frozen caribou or char, dried fish, fermented seal or walrus, frozen eggs, dried ribs, or bone marrow—whatever was available from people's homes.

Throughout the evening, women help themselves from a kettle of tea on the stove; children wander in to talk to their mothers, play or sleep, and arrive and depart, as the meeting progresses; and there are stories, jokes, and gossip in Inuktitut. When there are people in need we are asked to help out or contribute goods, and the necessary community work is organized. Everyone sews during the meeting.

A typical meeting of the Baffin Women's Association (a largely non-native organization whose meetings I occasionally attend) would include about the same number of women. Meetings are held at the library or another public building, and members arrange for care for their children so that they can spend some independent time with other women. Participants arrive reasonably promptly and tend not to leave until the end. We usually sit on chairs. At coffee break, there are sweets or cookies which one of the organizers has picked up before the meeting, and good fresh coffee.

We often have a speaker and there are lively discussions in English on issues we see as affecting women in our community and on how best these issues can be addressed. We plan to effect change, and organize to do so. No one sews during the meeting.

While these instances are true to life, they have clearly been chosen for the purpose of contrast. Sometimes the distinctions may not be as vivid, yet the attitudinal differences of native and non-native women invade every other corner of life, affecting our goals and priorities as fundamentally as they affect how we choose to hold meetings.

The small differences, like sewing, multiply into bigger differences, like the meetings. The final result is the unavoidable acknowledgement that I cannot, in conscience, engage in individual action or confrontation which affects lives I am not fully a part of, and which alters them in ways I inevitably will not fully understand.

Finally, I must be a cautious feminist because of the nature of the northern community. The size of the communities in the South permit, and in some cases even require, confrontation and radicalism that would almost invariably be destructive in a northern context. Similarities exist, of course, but the differences between the two regions are as significant as the consequence of leaning overboard on an ocean liner and leaning overboard in a canoe. Those who choose to lean out of ocean liners take risk upon themselves; those who do likewise in canoes are almost certain to affect the course of the vessel, and impose risk on the other passengers.

To carry the analogy one step further, imagine the canoe in waters already choppy with winds of change. The sound choice would be to direct the available energy to keeping the boat stable and upright, and not to exercise one's personal choice as to the final destination. One might wish to convince the crew that a particular direction was advisable but it would be a foolish expense of energy to paddle in a direction which the rest of the crew rejected.

Having already identified the preceding paragraphs as my final argument it is only fair to confess that what follows contains more emotion than logic. The emotional element is basic: I like many things just the way they are.

I like it that women are the ones who clean the church in my community. We get a chance to talk and work together, to go over the past week's events, and to spend next week's bingo winnings, all the while polishing the brass candlesticks and collection plates.

I like that time on a holiday afternoon, or after dinner, when women congregate around a pot of tea to talk. Children rattle in and out of the room, and men amuse themselves elsewhere. "Married women's talk", I call it—thoroughly and unabashedly domestic—of men and children and personal lives; talk of families, in a way which reflects their strengths and the responsibilities of women in a native community.

I like the time when several families are travelling together on the land. The men are off hunting, the women rummaging through *qamutiiks* [sleds] and grub boxes, unpacking and organizing for tea, with one eye on the smaller kids who struggle to climb as high and slide as far as their older brothers and sisters.

This may be "women's work", but it is work which is done in community with other women, in the context of families and of common purpose. I don't long to drive a skidoo or go hunting with men. Sometimes I do that and it's fun, but it is different from the steady, quiet pleasure of women working with women.

It is these positive memories, added to the caution that experience has recommended, which have caused me to re-evaluate how I live in the North as a feminist. This tempering of opinion was neither immediate, nor is it complete, for there are still times when I enjoy giving a fast and pointed reply to an offensive act or comment. Life would be dull if we were all conservative feminists all of the time.

Although I once feared that I had sold out on activism altogether, those fears now appear unfounded. Knowledge and understanding have compelled me to an activism with steady, small footsteps, rather than the tilting run which was once the pace I chose. And at the new pace I am steadier on my feet, with more time to choose a path, while I enjoy the land I am travelling.

Women of the Kitaq

Women's Kitaq Group Hut, Pangnirtung
Based on an Interview by Angela Bernal

The reason they have this *qammaq* [hut] is that they want to show the younger generation how they used to live and to see the actual *qammaq*. This is what they used to live like a long time ago.

At that time they used to have sealskin, not canvas. The inside used to be like this. And they used to have twigs for insulation. They used only *qulliqs* [oil lamp stove] then; they didn't have stoves. It was one lamp, run on seal oil or whale oil. They used it for cooking and melting water.

We were born outside Pangnirtung when there were no *qallunaaq* [non-Inuit]. We learnt by watching our mothers when we were very young. They always knew how to make things.

The young people here, they don't participate very much. But during the winter, in adult education, they learn how to make traditional clothing. They're going to try and start activities here in the *qammaq* for the younger people if they get funding from the territorial Department of Economic Development. They're trying to get funds. Women come every Thursday, anybody who wants to come and sew. And they come here on Saturdays. Sometimes they come and sometimes they just want to buy something, some clothing from people. The women try to welcome as many young people as want to come.

The younger relatives of women who come here are not able to come very often. For example, I don't like to come here. I have kids. You work all day, and there is no time. I want to stay home.

I get my mom to make my things. That's the bad part, I guess. She just provides us with what we need. I like traditional clothes because they are cheaper and warmer.

The name for this ladies' group is Kitaq Group. *Kitaq* is the thread used for sewing the skins. They used to wear sealskin outside and they used special thread for sewing the skins. It was called *kitaq*.

At the outpost camps the men catch the seals. The women dry them and clean the skins. They dry the meat. Sometimes they go fishing with the men. In winter-time around here, only the ladies go fishing by themselves, in school time. But they haven't seen women going on a boat by themselves and hunting by themselves. Not by boat, only by skidoo. I fish. I don't use the net. I don't know how. The ladies can go fishing. We've done that a lot of times. Without the men. Men and women both cut up the seal. It depends on who's around. It depends on the weather, too. You can have it finished by the next day if it's good weather. If it's not, it takes longer.

Guided by Our Bellies

Lynn Brooks

A t this time of year, if you look outside, the Northern Lights are quite exquisite. They are beyond description—blue, green, and yellow, flashing and dancing across the sky. It's quite chilly outside and my flowers are starting to freeze.

I'm thinking about the North—the smell, the feel, and the look. It cleanses your senses to the point of explosion and the feelings rise inside. You become quite emotional about this land, this piece of Canada that you discovered at some point in your life and have come to call home.

I came to the North in 1969. I had a small child, and was pregnant with another. I was literally running away from a violent marriage...[but] I really had no sense of what I was running to. Coming to Yellowknife in those days was like coming to a small boomtown, I suppose—25 men to every woman—a kind of place that you had read about in books.

I didn't feel like a pioneer, although certainly the women who had come in the 1930s and 1940s must have. Some of them who I know well are still around.

Barbara Bromley springs to mind. She came here when she was very young, stayed, and raised a family. She is a woman who has influenced the development of Yellowknife—if not the North. Her work for the senior citizens and the Aven Senior Centre in Yellowknife, which has become home to many senior citizens who cannot go home or live with a family, is a good example.

I think of Helen Parker, wife of the former Commissioner of the Northwest Territories. She came as a nurse, and probably had absolutely no idea of the kind of impact that she would have in the development of the YWCA, the Heritage Society, or in the preservation of historical buildings in the North. Those are a few of the accomplishments that are attributed to her.

The more I think of Yellowknife and the North, the more I think of women. I know that's an odd thing to say, because it seems such a harsh and forbidding environment at times, particularly out on the land in winter. Certainly you cannot survive even a few miles outside the settlements if you don't have your wits about you. So, it makes for a hard life in many ways.

But I have to relate to my own development because I know how I felt about things when I came. I really had no concept of myself. I wanted to survive; and I saw when I came to the North many other women coming for the same reasons, usually with a child or two. They were coming here and looking for a place to be themselves, to raise their children, to be secure, to earn a living.

I worked at the Bank of Commerce, and I know, as a group of young women working for the bank or government, we did not have much sense of female identity. We certainly had no sense of feminism. Although we were greatly pursued by many men because of their large number, many of us did not feel adequate or desirable or good enough, particularly because we had children or bad marriages in our backgrounds. It seemed that women in Yellowknife were, if they were not native, white women with "shady backgrounds". That's one way of putting it, I suppose.

When I think back on it, I realize how completely innocent most of us were: how little we knew then what the North was, how little we knew about what it took to be a native woman in the North, and how little we knew about what it took to be a woman on our own. We almost lived as our bellies guided us from day to day to survive in the best way we could: working, raising our children, and talking to each other about childrearing and the financial problems which were continually present.

None of us ever had enough money. We were all out of groceries long before pay-day and scraping odds and ends together to throw together a stew or a hash to feed everyone. We were always worrying about actually having enough money to pay the baby-sitter, if not constantly worrying about having a baby-sitter. At that time the idea of quality care for our children was something that was a dream. I don't think that many of us had any idea that we or our children had a right to it. I think that many of us thought of ourselves as "lesser than". We were certainly prime candidates for feminism.

There were no two ways about it, we needed it. We were living with no connection to the women who lived in other settlements in the North, and with really no concept of what their lives were like. We didn't have the opportunity to try and relate to native women, even those who were living in the valley or the delta. It was really a very divided community in that way. I'm not saying people didn't coexist or that people didn't get along. I'm saying they simply had very little to do with each other. I think that this changed very slowly. It was a maturing, a general maturing of northern women, as they began to find each other. I'm not quite sure how that happened, but I do believe that the feminist movement, without question, had something to do with it. I believe that women in the larger communities in the North as well as women in the small communities, began to believe that things needed to change. I think they began to recognize the consequences of their lack of power to run their own and their children's lives. I think that women in the smaller communities discovered this differently and at a different rate because the impact of feminism in the North hit women differently.

For some reason, during the 1970s an awakening began. We saw the development of the Native Women's Association; we saw native women coming together, talking together, working together, developing some of their skills which they had always used to support their families—sewing, making crafts, and that sort of thing. When these women came together through the Native Women's Association, they talked about issues. When they went back to their communities, they talked about issues in their communities. With the development of the Government of the Northwest Territories Women's Secretariat in the late 1970s and early 1980s, again you had women who were board members and native women from across the North who came together and talked about issues like spousal assault, child care, sexual abuse, and the complete lack of economic opportunities for women in smaller communities. The lack of educational opportunities and the lack of control that women had over their lives became very evident to women throughout the North.

Women are the holders of the culture, women are the talkers, women are the craft-makers, women are the story-tellers, women are the healers. Perhaps it's not good to generalize about these things, but I'm talking about what usually happens. There are some extremely powerful women, some incredible women in the smaller communities, who have worked so hard to put together women's support groups and be a resource in their community.

Some of these strong women that I can think of are women like Mary Teya from Fort McPherson, who has been a rock in that community. She has been a resource for women who are being battered and for children who are being abused: a mini family-counselling service on two legs. She is a powerhouse of kindness, consideration, and outreach in her community. Bertha Allen is another women who has been a political giant among the women in the North. She has been president of both the Native Women's Association and the Status of Women. She has remained active in politics at both the municipal and federal levels. Despite all of this, she has continued to work tirelessly for the rights and advancement of women. She has done this within her own, totally traditional marriage: her husband goes out and gets his whale. They live a life that is enriched by the traditional values of their culture. And yet, she is a champion of women's education, advancement, and business.

Other women come to my mind. Eliza Lawrence, who is one of many children who grew up south of the lake, and is very traditional. She once told me that when she was young, her dream was to grow up and marry a good hunter and live happily ever after. As a member of the legislative assembly who spoke out for a transition house for battered women to be placed in Yellowknife, you could see that she has come far beyond her dream of marrying a good hunter. She has come far beyond that.

Edna Elias has been involved in every level of politics in Coppermine. She has also held the position of president of the Status of Women. She is a woman who has great organizational skills. She has been recognized as a champion of women's rights and her concern surrounding sexual abuse has been admirable and high-profile. Accordingly, this has made an impact on the way sexual assault has been thought of in the North.

We are often told by people in the justice system that the abuse of women is traditional in native cultures. The women that I have had the privilege to know around this great land will tell you that this is absolutely not true. They do not feel that abuse is part of their tradition, or that subjugation is traditional or defines culture. Who defines culture? Is culture defined by one-half of the population?

I could talk about many individual women and they could pass before me in a great parade as I try to talk about feminism in the North. Mary Brown, who is a native woman married to an oil executive in Norman Wells, worked tirelessly, to the point where she made herself ill, over women's issues such as child care, employment, wife assault, and sexual abuse. She was trying to be a total resource for her community.

You can say these issues are not women's issues, they are people issues—and I suppose they are. But, because they affect me in such a devastating way, they become our issues and women take ownership of them. That is how I see feminism in the North. Women have worked to develop ways of dealing with these issues, caring for and supporting each other, reaching out to each other, and ultimately, reaching out to their husbands, fathers, sons, and brothers to bring them into the circle of what the family ought to be, could be, or perhaps, used to be.

You talk a lot about alcohol in the North and how it affects our lives, how it impacts on women and children, and how it has destroyed the culture. When I think about the native women that I know and the suffering alcohol has brought into their lives, I think about women like Muriel Betsina, Bertha Blondin, and Florence Barnaby. I could go on and on naming names and names. These faces come up before me and I know their strength; I know their solidness and cores of iron. I know how they take care of their families and try to impart the true, wonderful things about their culture. They try to keep alive qualities of love, caring, sharing, and the good traditional ways. They could teach you about the land, about the animals, about the things that are available on the land, and how to cook, clean, and use them. They could teach you to exist on the land without all the trappings of white society. For example, Muriel Betsina has taught my own daughter how to make mukluks and mitts, to bead and embroider, and much more. She has taught her about being a woman.

I can only talk about what I have learned from women in North. When people say to me there is no feminist movement in the North, and that the feminist movement could not possibly survive in the North, I say to them, "The North is one big beautiful kaleidoscope of women—working, being, surviving, caring, loving—and trying to dig down deeper into themselves and pull out the solutions to some of the truly terrible problems of northern society."

I do not wish to exclude men from this process, and don't wish to say that they do not contribute. I do not wish to say that they do not champion the cause of human dignity, because many of them do. Many have supported me and many other women in achieving our goals. But I have to think of the younger women of the North also.

For instance, Kathy Turner, whose young husband is going to school, has been raising her little son with great fear of making a mistake and is very unsure of herself. None the less, she is involved in actively promoting quality child care in hopes that it will become a household word in the western Arctic. She has spoken to groups and addressed politicians, as the western Arctic representative of the Canadian Day Care Advocacy Centre. Her personal development in such a short time against such odds is just incredible to me. I can remember when we all had our children with us, because there was no one else to care for them, while we put together proposals and worked out strategies to develop methods of getting in touch and networking with other women in smaller communities.

I feel that being a woman in the North is a privilege because of the women I have met. I believe that feminism is everything that is right, good, and beautiful. It is everything that you can preserve which is the best in us: caring and sharing, keeping values, women and children with self-esteem and feeling good about themselves, and the beauty of culture being passed on from one generation to the next. This is the epitome of feminism, as far as I'm concerned. My whole self-image, and the self-image that I have tried to pass on to my daughter, has come from the deep and beautiful feminism of the North.

New Choices for a New Era

Janet Mancini Billson

Introduction: From Tradition To Modernity [1]

" I was born in a little camp about 60 miles from here, at Shark Fiord. My whole family goes there every year, not to sleep over or anything, just to get it back in mind, in memories." This poignant statement reflects the sense of loss many Inuit women feel when they speak of the traditional life out on the land prior to being moved into "settlements" by the Canadian government after World War II. Not that it was an easy life—in many ways it was very hard—but many of the contemporary problems caused or exacerbated by alcohol abuse and unemployment were manageable or non-existent when virtually everyone lived in small camps of a few families each. It is as though the Inuit have crossed 5000 years of history in a generation. As one teacher in Cape Dorset says, "Nobody else in the world has seen so many changes in such a short time as the Inuit have."

Now, many Inuit families still try to spend time out on the land, hunting and fishing, clam digging, or berry picking, as the seasons dictate. This is out of necessity, for few families can afford to feed themselves solely through wage employment and buying from the northern stores. It is also for pleasure, for regaining a diminishing sense of family unity, harmony between Inuk and nature, and a time when male and female roles were more clearly delineated and parents had more control over their children. Many women, especially those over 30, refer to going out on the land as the happiest time for them. For example, when one woman was asked about the happiest days of her life, her eyes filled with tears: "When we go camping...I will never forget the good times we had then."

The following memories and reflections of Inuit women and men take us back to that time and bring us forward to an examination of contemporary problems in Inuit communities. They highlight the complexities of women's choices as they move from a traditional life-style into the dawn of the 21st century. The reflections are derived from interviews conducted during the summer of 1988 with 50 women and eight men, all ranging in age from 13 to 98, in the eastern and central arctic regions. [2]

The Traditional Ways

Life in Camp: "It's only a story now..."
"It was maybe harder than these days. There were no skidoos. They used dog-teams. That must be hard," reminisces Mary, 45, who grew up in a camp and still likes to go out on the land on weekends. Leah, who is 72, remembers: "People used to walk a lot; they used to do everything, even sew. They used to make *kamiks* [boots] and *amautiks* [hooded parkas]. Back then, some things were fun, but some things weren't. We used to make a lot of things, mostly everything. When the sealskin boots wore out, we repaired them. We didn't have other people around. It was mostly our own people."

Mainah, 46, recalls her childhood in the camp: "I remember my mother. When I was little, she would always look after sealskins, like scraping off the blubber, drying them, stretching them, and making them into things like *kamiks*. In the summertime, when the skins were dry enough, my mother would gather all the skins and sew them together to make a tent. And in the winter-time, when the men were catching caribou, she would dry them, make clothing out of them—a parka, and something that looked like pants—using the caribou-leg skin for the pants, and some sealskin for pants also. She would also make mitts out of sealskin."

Qatsoo, 98, remembers the cycle of life very clearly: "In early autumn the women would start getting ready for the winter. We would start making tents and sealskin clothes for the men first, and their *kamiks*. Men's clothes would always be made first, before the ladies' and the children's. When it was winter-time and there was ice, we would start preparing the caribou skin for the men's clothes, because we were so used to it, we would do it every year—making the clothes for different seasons. We used the *tessikoon* [made from metal and wood] to make it easier to sew on the hides.

When the winter came around, the men would go hunting by foot on the flow edges. Once it was all ice they would go by dog-team. When the spring came around, in March or April, they would go somewhere on the ice where they could have an igloo, and they would go hunting for baby seals. After they were at their igloos, they would go back to Kekerton and live in their permanent houses, *qammaqs*. Once we had the baby sealskins, we would start making them into clothes for the summer. We mainly went hunting for seal pups because we needed the skin and the meat is good, too. At that time anybody who went hunting didn't eat all day, but they would bring a ringed-seal skin that you can blow up to use for water. We scraped the fur off the skin, and when we sewed it we would always

44

keep it wet so it would be easier to sew, and the thread we would use would be braided before we started sewing it. Every time the thing would get old it would always tinkle!

"In the springtime, men would make some *qamutiiks* [sleds] that would just fit the boat so they could go hunting down by the flow edge. Every male would go except for the elders and the children. At that time they never used to have a campstove, but they would have a fire to make some tea. Every Saturday, the whalers would give out biscuits to the women only, and they would give tobacco to the men. Saturday is called *csivataavik* in Inuktitut, which means 'the day we get the biscuits'. When the men were out hunting at the flow edge, then we women would go out hunting by dog-sled, and we would catch some seals, too. But the women didn't go very far. We would just go out and hunt and then we would go back.

"After the men were at the flow edge trying to catch some whales, they would go back to Kekerton and stay for a few days and would try to get ready to go hunting again for walrus. When we got some walrus, we would take the blubber to a big pot, and after walrus hunting, we would say 'that's the end of the hunting for the year.' When we were getting ready to start the *qulliq*, we would start hammering at the fat so it wasn't just one big blubber. By then we had enough food for the whole year. We would stay at the camp and take our time cleaning our stuff, and maybe get ready to go caribou hunting again. But we wouldn't use the big boats that we used for whale hunting; we would go by different boats and bring along a kayak. As you can see we did a lot of hard work at that time."

To the staples of seal, caribou, fish, beluga, and berries, the Inuit added the bannock and tea that they adopted from the Scottish and American whalers who penetrated arctic waters during the 19th century. Pauloosie, 40, explained: "When we ran out of tea, there's some leaves on the land that we could make tea out of. Life would be hard, but at the same time it was always fun. Some didn't even know what to do, but still they had a good time...[life consisted of] mainly hunting, surviving; the men hunted for food and my mom looked after us, made the clothing, made suppers to eat, looked after the house. I was happy. I remember bad times and good times. There was the food shortage that I remember—hunger. It was in early spring, when there's a lot of snow and nobody can go hunting. The whole camp. It was bad. You get up, and have nothing to eat. I remember my father went to hunt and just drank water. He was gone all day and never got anything. That's why we were hungry—completely out of blubber: no light, no heat, but nobody died then. We started using our own wood [used to support the house] for heat. A lot of times we tried to eat something that was not real food. Maybe old skin for making boots. If you got a little fire you heated it, to make it softer to eat. It was very difficult. But it wasn't that bad. We didn't have to kill the dogs for food. This is sad, but it's only a story now. And there was a lot of happiness also. Especially in the summertime, when there was good hunting, and we went up to the summer camp to hunt for caribou. Being childhood, it was always fun. I think our traditional hunting, as long as we keep our language, our tradition, will be alive."

Geela, 39, remembers living in *qammaqs* and going out every year to a different camp to have a summer break from the main camp: "There were about 12 families in our camp. I remember when we were starving almost, when whales would come into our main camp and everybody would go wild. My mom said those things [sniffing, drug use] were never done out there, out in the camps. But they were doing it, I've heard. Not a lot out there, maybe a few times. I was so surprised to hear it, because I was told it was never done! And drinking. There's an old man I go to see almost every day. He was living out on the land when he was a boy. He's seen people drunk way back then. They got the whisky from the traders and whalers."

Traditional Gender Roles: "Both men and women were leaders..."
According to some women, although males were accorded ultimate authority in many matters, in fact, leadership of the camps was shared between both members of a head couple. Qaida, 42, remembers: "My grandfather seemed to be the captain of the community. He and my grandmother used to be the highest in the camp. They would look after the whole community for health; I remember my grandmother would be the person to deliver the babies." Although women are not depicted as having perfectly equal status, their expertise in things female constituted the basis for a certain indisputable authority. Qaida continued: "Both men and women were the leaders, because men couldn't look after the women in those days, or still, now. My grandfather couldn't deliver the babies, or he couldn't sew for his family or help out other families who needed help. It was the woman who looked after the women's side. She would teach us how to sew; how to make things; how to cook; how to survive; and how to scrape the hides and dry them the proper way. All those sorts of things that men couldn't do. They could, but in those days they didn't!"

Anna, a 45-year-old administrator, remembers: "The women used to stay in the camp and look after everything while the men were hunting. They were the planners. They looked after the future for their children and their grandchildren. The men, all they did was bring the food, most of the time." Decisions by either male or female were made with a respect for their partner's skills and needs. Because of the harsh arctic climate and terrain, the woman's skills at seamstressing were critical for survival, as was her ability to store and prepare food. Thus, the traditional gender roles were relatively balanced.

Yet, just as the man was still the boss for the whole camp, so within each couple, if there was a decision to be made, the male often took precedence. Would they sit down and discuss it? "It wasn't like that then. The wife would have to agree." The male's authority was paramount out on the land, as it is even to this day, according to Anna. "He's the boss, and his wife will say, 'yes sir', because on the land, he knows what he's doing, and his wife is his servant."

Arranged Marriages: "I grew to love him..."

One choice that contemporary Inuit women can make for themselves is that of a marriage partner. This was not so until relatively recently. The tradition of arranged marriages functioned to ensure that all adults found partners during the childbearing years—an important concern for small populations in a treacherous climate. Arranged marriages also ensured that bloodlines were protected against intermarriage and that camps were linked with each other. According to some older women, they also served as a buffer against prostitution, promiscuity, or early pregnancy without the stability of a relationship. Now, elders fear that some young girls in the larger settlements may get swept up into prostitution; they lack control and discipline; and their marriages are more likely to end in divorce. Maata, a widow in her 60s, complains: "The girls get more babies without being married. I didn't really like marrying my husband, but then later I did...I grew to love him. Most of my age group are married like that, by the parents. Now, most of the younger ones are ending up with divorce, like my daughter. She has three kids. She got married like that on her own without us arranging it. I don't like it. The other two girls were arranged by us. When we were living in Bonaccord I never knew about divorce, but now they are getting divorces."

Lucy, 39, had an arranged marriage. "When a man wanted someone for a wife, he would go get her from another settlement, or from the same town. The parents would just give her to the man, for a marriage. They married, but not from their same settlement. We used to gather in Pangnirtung, a lot of people from different settlements; that's when I met my husband-to-be. Parents had to say yes, if they wanted him for a son-in-law. Women didn't know their husbands when they became husband and wife. That's the part where women seemed smaller than men. The parents would say 'yes' and that's it; even if they didn't want him, they went through with it."

Traditionally, the arrangement of a marriage marked the passage from childhood into adulthood. As soon as the male was married, or living with a woman, he entered adulthood. As Maata adds: "Now you've got your own way, and now you can handle it. Raise your family. Now you are independent. No more dependence on your family. The man was expected to provide for his pregnant woman; but now, very often, if a woman gets pregnant, she will stay with her parents and be dependent on them. Before, when they started living together, they had to move from the house. Or, if they lived within it, the man would provide everything, seal for clothing, things like that. That was the man's responsibility." For the female, both the onset of menses and the arranged relationship with a man marked her transition into adulthood.

At 86, Kudloo looks back at her marriage: "My mother arranged my marriage; we were never married by a minister, though. I used to go hunting and fishing with my husband. I liked it. But I don't like all this divorce now. I believe in God, in that book—the Bible—that they shouldn't be separated. It's both the man's fault and the woman's fault. When they get angry at each other, they get divorced or separated."

Traditionally, the men of the camp were instrumental in arranging marriages, as Meeka, a seamstress in her early 50s, relates: "At that time I had a boyfriend, and my grandfather on my mother's side, he arranged it just because my grandfather was related to that guy and he wanted him to be with me, so it was all arranged. I didn't really want to, but I had no choice. At that time, men used to arrange the marriage, and usually the mothers would write each other and say my son wants to be with your daughter, and if the son wants to be with her daughter, then the son would go to the camp and be with her."

Some were married by Anglican ministers, travelling into the missions for their wedding. Others said, "one man, one woman" to each other to seal their commitment. "They would talk and make promises to each other. Even though they would go through bad times, they knew they would always be together. They would go through the good and the bad."

For many elders, marriage followed a period of living together and the birth of the first child. Leah, 78, recalls that she started living with a man when they moved up to another camp. They lived there for four years and in the fifth year she gave birth to their first child: "We were formally married by a reverend when we had two kids and there was one on the way, but I never knew it! We were married by this reverend who permanently moved here." Rosie, 82, remembers: "We got married long after we had three children. We got married here in the settlement when we moved here. We had nine more children, but they all died. Two right after each other, a few months apart. Some died in the ocean. They all died. I only have three left."

Leah believes that arranged marriages were a "bad" custom: "I remember one time we were at the church on Blacklead Island; there was a reverend there who was baptizing the man who was to become my husband. That was before we even met. I was the only one there. That night when I was home in bed, with everything on, clothes and blankets and everything, I heard the door open and close. So I was there hiding in the blankets. I used to have beautiful long hair. There stood a man with long hair, moustache, bearded. I was really scared! He was there to go to bed with me, but I was wearing my clothes and I put on my new parka which had beads on it, and at the back there were some pennies that made noises like bells. When I sat down they made *so* many noises, but my mother never woke up or never said anything, which made me hate my mother for ignoring it. So he joined me in my bed. I just lay there because I didn't know what to do. I was scared, because I was always told that I wasn't supposed to hang around boys. When we were in bed I tried not to touch the guy, but I think that I touched him when we fell asleep. It was really creepy. I thought he was creepy." Leah and her man started living together after that night, but he stayed with her because: "My mother thought that I had to learn some more. He stayed with me until I was old enough, then we moved to my husband's camp and we stayed there. We stayed with my mother-in-law until I knew how to sew a tent and get ready for the things that my husband needed." She was 16 years old; a year later her first baby was born. After they became a couple, Leah was saddened by the fact that whenever she went out visiting, her husband would go after her because he thought she would be with someone else. "He was really jealous."

The Move to the Settlements: "I don't make *kamiks* any more..."

Many emphasize that the Inuit way of life was different in the camps. Both men and women had fewer choices; survival was the common goal around which life turned, day after day, winter after winter. Hard work extended to the children as well. "There was no easy going," Joanasie, 42, reflects. "The only problem in the old days, when they have a lot of food, they have a lot of good times, and they start to go after another man's wife or another woman's husband. That's the only time they created problems. When they are hard working or there are hard times and they try to fight starvation, that sort of thing, they never have that kind of fooling around. They have to stick together in order to survive. In those days they did not have much opportunity. When they came into the settlements in the 1960s, they started to come together with a lot of people. In the old days, the camp might be 40 or 50 or less. They never got beyond 50 people. So when they come together it suddenly becomes 200 or 1000 people. The culture and the way of living started to change then."

Adjusting to a new rhythm of life was difficult for many elders. When Qatsoo came to the settlement, her work was harder: "I missed the land. I wanted to climb that mountain behind the hamlet—I never did. It's too far. The mountains are too far. When the men were out hunting and they were to be back any day, we would start boiling some seal meat with the *qulliq*. I love eating boiled seal meat. Because there weren't any camp stoves at that time; men would not eat all day while they were out hunting, that's why the women would get the meat ready. When we started living in Pangnirtung, that's when we started seeing camp stoves. We used to go out with the dog-teams, but now I don't do anything much."

And, with a decline in hunting and the availability of sealskins, many women stopped making the traditional clothing that had been such a central part of their life on the land. As Mary points out: "I don't make *kamiks* any more. I used to watch my grandmother and her sister. By watching them, I used to learn."

Generally, life out on the land was "good" and families seemed happier. Most of the women concur that they were not aware of family violence, or if it existed, it was considered despicable and was extremely rare. Was spousal assault as much a part of life in the camps as it now appears to be in the settlements? Qatsoo recalls: "I remember one case in my camp of a lady being hit, but I haven't seen or heard of another case besides that couple. It's much worse now. There are members of the mental health committee who say that there are traditional ways of correcting the problems...something to do with going to the parents or the elders. They would talk the problem over and then I guess it was corrected. I guess maybe people back then had more respect for the elders. Back then they didn't have alcohol, they didn't have drugs, they didn't have planes where the man could just take off. Mom used to tell me that I just had to hang in there, that my problems with my husband would eventually be solved. But she didn't know what I was going through. My ex used to see his friends and wouldn't come back for days or nights. Didn't bother to call me or anything. They couldn't do that back then because they didn't have all these other influences. It was a lot easier to correct the problem than it is today."

Contemporary Life: The Dilemmas of Choice

Remaining Single: "Just stay together..."

Far from the traditional pattern of virtually universal marriage among the Inuit, remaining single or living in common law are becoming the norm. Although contemporary Inuit women now can choose their own mate, decide whether to marry, and decide whether to divorce, the freedom to make choices is not without cost. For younger women, raised in settlements and with greater educational and economic opportunities, divorce is still relatively infrequent because many have chosen not to marry in the first place. This is a complex decision, stemming in part from the fear of having to announce a divorce to a small community, and in part from the threats of alcohol abuse, spousal assault, and infidelity that might place a woman in jeopardy, trapping her in a marriage she no longer desires.

The response to a question as to why one social services worker *did* get married reflects the pervasiveness of changing attitudes toward marriage. Jukeepa, 47, explains: "That was the time when the mother and father told the people to get married. I got married when marriage was still going on. There's hardly any marriage going on these days. Once a year or once every two years." Expenses are not high and are not perceived by the women as an important reason for not getting married formally. Weddings are usually performed by a minister and are open to the community: "You get married at church so anybody goes there, and then after the wedding, they usually have people over to the parish hall to have tea and baked stuff. Anybody goes there, too, so it's not like you have invited guests. It's not like you have down South."

A 30-year-old artist echoes the trend toward remaining single: "I'm not married. I guess I don't believe in marriage. No, I do, but it just never comes by. I've been with him for 11 years. No marriage yet, although we have talked about it." Beyond inertia is the possibility that economic instability discourages many couples from marrying. When we asked what is the biggest problem facing women, about half of the women interviewed mentioned economic problems (low income, lack of education, poor-paying jobs). The other half were split between domestic violence and lack of communication or discipline between parents and children. When asked directly whether economic instability might be a factor in declining marriage rates, there was some agreement. In many Inuit communities there is little work; what exists is often seasonal or low-paying. The traditional role for the Inuk male was to provide for his family, to be a good hunter and a good fisherman, and to protect his family, take care of them and feed them. But if jobs are scarce, and you are a 23-year-old male who gets a woman pregnant, your choices may be limited. "Some people just live together and help each other support their children, because they love each other and they love their children. But it's hard sometimes. They start to get problems...and split up for awhile." Others, like 48-year-old single parent Anna, neither married nor lived with the man with whom she had her first and only child at 16. She raised her by herself, without much help from family. "It wasn't too hard."

A church person feels that many avoid a trip to the altar because they fear marriage "might break up the relationship. They think, after you get married, and you need a divorce, it's a really hard thing to do and you're going to feel guilty about it. They may want to have the perfect relationship before they get married. That's another problem, because a marriage is never going to become perfect. It's a never-ending job. Two different people living together and working together and sharing together; it's never finished."

Many women speak vaguely of the decision not to marry. For example, two women in their 30s, who work full time and are regular church-goers, describe their situations. The first says: "We thought about it and we're still thinking about it. Seems like we're waiting for the right time to get married, but we've been living together more than ten years. When we finally have a quiet time in the evening, we try to talk about it. But it seems hard to discuss it when the kids are around. It doesn't make any difference; it just changes your last name, that's it. But in the religion days it was better to be married under God." Her friend agrees: "My boyfriend wanted to get married when we had our first child, but I don't know what happened. We agreed and we never got married!" After five years of living together, they are now considered to be married under common law, which takes some of the pressure off the decision to marry in the church. "Or, if you're a working couple, you have a thing that you fill out. If something happened to you, who would be the one to get it? You usually put your common law partner's name—just like a husband and wife thing. We're protected, in a way. We could get each other's pension."

For Sheila, 22, living with her boyfriend in their own house feels comfortable: "I've never really thought of marriage." She isn't sure she would like marriage, although her boyfriend has mentioned it. "We never really talk about it." After two years living together, she continues to use her own last name; her first child also has her last name, but the second has his father's last name.

A not uncommon situation, however, is for the man to walk out at some point. For example, Eena, 22, is unemployed and on welfare; she lives with her parents. She has two young babies, a year apart, each with a different father. Marriage was out of the picture: "They didn't want to have any kids. They didn't want to have anything to do with us. Both fathers." She is angry that neither man wanted to take any responsibility for their children or for her well-being. She did not plan her life to turn out this way: "Not the first one because we were planning to get married, and he left us. The other guy I met in another hamlet. I didn't find out that I was pregnant till I was back here and he already found a girlfriend and they got married." Her parents have been very supportive, adopting one son and allowing Eena and the other son to live with them. Her current boyfriend "doesn't mind" that she already has two children. If they marry, she would take only the youngest son with her. Right now she is not too worried, since they have only been going together a few months and "we haven't really talked about" marriage. Perhaps, "someday".

Sheila believes that even without a formal marriage, "You can have the social workers help you get child support from the father. Or, if you want to go through court, you can find legal aid and you can just call them up—there's one here in town." Many women feel that a formal marriage would not have protected them anyway; alimony and child support are mythical benefits in the case of under-employed or unemployed men. Instead, the extended family provides the cushion, as a 32-year-old health care worker explains: "A lot of us, if we run into that situation, have a lot of support from our families, our brothers or sisters or parents."

Younger women (under 30 or 35) feel they have a say in marriage choices now. "If we don't want to marry, we can say no; I know I would say no, and I would go my way." The message is clear: if a woman does not lose her protective rights by avoiding formal marriage, she has less incentive to take the vows. If the relationship fails, she does not have to face the humility of divorce.

The Stigma of Staying Single: "A subtle class distinction..."
According to an adult education specialist, even among those who are upwardly mobile and achievement-oriented there is still the dream of marriage and the status it might accord a young woman. "When I asked the young women in my class to write in confidence about their deepest hearts' desires, there were some girls who were 'living together' with men, and one of them felt that she wanted to get married. There is a subtle class distinction, even in spite of everybody saying that it's all right and we can just live together. People who are married seem to be a different class than people who just live together. A lot of young people who used to just live together are getting married now."

Some older women think that the younger generation, "doesn't really try as hard in a relationship as the older ones who have been married a long time." An 86-year-old great-grandmother disapproves of the resistance to marriage and the higher incidence of divorce than in her days: "Up here, a lot of the younger kids say, 'Well, my boyfriend lives with me sometimes, and then I kick him out and then he comes back after a week or so, and we have an argument and he leaves again. It's just up and down all the time.' Most of them, I think they get along pretty good."

Jukeepa, who met her husband at a community dance and has been married 27 years, has a little more sympathy for the women who are a generation behind her. She was 20 years old when they had their first child and 22 on their wedding day. Although she has not experienced these problems in her own marriage, she thinks fear of assault and alcohol abuse might be one reason the younger women hesitate to marry.

Contemporary Adoption: "I don't feel like I lost her..."

Another factor in the decision not to marry is that pregnancy does not necessarily lead to a wedding; customary adoption of children offers another way to ensure that children will be cared for properly.

The traditional custom of adopting children in and out of Inuit families persists into the late 20th century, and without the expense, psychological trauma, or isolation of children from their natural parents that is common in other contemporary cultures. Adoption is handled privately between families and friends; registration of the transaction with social services is, in most cases, informational rather than a matter of government intervention. The process of adoption is viewed as natural, as logical, and as an efficient means of ensuring that families who want children can find them and that mothers who are not in a position to give a child a good future can be comforted by knowing he or she has found a welcoming home. The custom may stem in part from the stark reality that haunted women living out on the land: children might be conceived and born in the absence of birth control virtually every year—but a woman could carry only one child in the hood of her *amautik* at a time. New little ones had to be raised by other women, or they risked freezing to death or starvation.

Eena, whose family of seven brothers and sisters includes one adopted in one adopted out, says: "I guess when one family wanted a baby another family just agreed to give the baby away. Or if the mother didn't want the baby, whoever wants the baby adopts the baby."

However, as with arranged marriages of an era ago, women were not always given the right to make their own choices. In many ways, men orchestrated the family structure. If a man wanted to adopt a child out to someone he knew wanted a baby, he could make that decision unilaterally. "Back some years they would do that. The lady didn't have any right to say no or yes. Even if the wife says no, if the husband says yes, that's it," Kudloo recalls.

For example, friends of Eena's parents wanted to adopt; when her mother was pregnant with her fourth child, they asked her if she would be willing to adopt the newborn out to them. When her mother refused, they asked her father, who agreed. "So Mom never really agreed with the adoption, but my father did, so that's why she was adopted out." That was 30 years ago, when the families still lived out on the land. Two children had already died, so that left her mother with only one child at home.

Adoption is also used to keep extended families together, and to balance the sex ratio within each family unit. Sophie, in her early 30s, has eight children: two adopted out, five at home, and one more she adopted in last year. She has been married since she was 18 years old. The oldest child is a girl and the second one is a boy; the third-born, a girl, was adopted out at her husband's request. After three more boys were born, the last male was adopted out, at her request: "The one I adopted in is from my sister. I didn't want anybody to adopt her from outside the family. The first one I adopted out was my husband's idea. And the second was mine. It was a boy and I had too many boys." Adopting her two children out made Sophie "feel awful", but she accepted her husband's decision because, "he's my husband and he's the boss." However, other women feel that now the wife/mother has more say in whether or not a child should be adopted in or out: "I think, myself, if I didn't want to adopt a child out I wouldn't. But I don't know how I would feel later on. Maybe I would agree later on, but not right now. I don't want to adopt out."

Sophie comes from a typical family, though: six males, six females, and one male adopted out to a family short on males. Julie, 35, a health care worker, has four children at home, and one adopted out: "I have two boys and two girls with me, and my common-law husband. My first baby, born when I was 18, was premature and adopted out." Adoption can also be used in the case of failed birth control. One woman in her 30s, who has a stable marriage and who works part-time as a clerk for the Government of the Northwest Territories in her hamlet, has "three children with me and one adopted—actually four." In her case, her first two children were born before her marriage; it was the second child who was adopted out: "I didn't want to get pregnant. I was taking birth control pills and somehow I got pregnant, and I didn't want to keep it." She adopted the baby out to her sister. When the sister died, her husband kept the child, who was then four.

Teachers confirm that girls in high school are more likely to have and adopt out their babies than to turn to abortion: "There were a couple of girls who had had babies and they gave them up for adoption. One of them, who was only 16, said, 'I don't want to become a bum like my sister.' Her sister's boyfriend was tyrannizing her, and she had no way of getting out of that situation. So she gave her daughter up for adoption to her parents, and she came back to school and is trying to get ahead."

It is not unusual for the girl's own parents to adopt her infant. Peepeelee, 17, stated, "If a girl my age got pregnant, and she didn't want to keep it, usually her mother would take it." Middle-aged parents, then, often have infants and toddlers, having adopted the babies of their teenage daughter(s); and many adopt when they are getting older, in order to ensure a helping hand during their senior years. This pattern underscores the desirability and utility of children. A seamstress in her 40s has two natural sons, the first one born in a settlement when she was 23. In addition, she has "lots" of adopted children, again balanced by sex: two boys, two girls. The younger ones still live at home, insurance against old age. Similarly, Daisy, 64, was 17 when she married, but 16 when her first child was born, fathered by a different man. She kept the baby, and her husband adopted him. In turn, Daisy adopted a baby, her youngest son, who is now 18: "I really like him. He can help. He does what I ask him to do." Annie, 19, has four brothers: "Originally five, but one is adopted by our uncle on my father's side. And I have four sisters." The children range in age from nine to 32 years old. The mother is 48, which means that she might have been denied the adoption had physiology alone dictated the acquisition of children.

Perhaps the most fascinating aspect of Inuit customary adoption is the fact that many children continue to have routine contact with their natural parents. This is in striking contrast to the shroud of secrecy that usually surrounds adoption in the South. Some report not only contact, but close relationships. Almost always they at least know who their parents are. In small settlements or out on the land, that information would be especially hard to keep secret. Although there may be cases in which Inuit children are not informed of the identities of their natural parents, or there are hard feelings about being adopted out, they are the exception rather than the rule.

In one case, two sets of twins were born to a couple within a year of each other—the second set, girls, were adopted out to the mother's sisters. Now adults, the twins agree that they never felt rejected by their mother. Says Helena: "I quite understand why it was. My mother told me what it was all about when I got older; maybe in my 20s we talked about it. But I knew about it before then, because when I was 11, I had TB, and on my way to the hospital down South, my real parents were living in Iqaluit, so I landed there and had to stay over night. That's when I met my real parents. They lived in a camp when I was born, and moved to Iqaluit later." Their relationship is friendly and they visit each other regularly: "I'm very close to them." Helena has adopted one of her own children out: "My daughter stayed with me last night. We see her a lot, so I don't really feel like I lost her. I'm not as close to her as my daughter at home. Maybe when she gets older. But I don't care whether I see her or not."

It is difficult to discern whether or not adoptive children from outside the family have the same status as adoptive grandchildren or a couple's own natural children. Occasionally, a child would be introduced to interviewers as, "That's the fifth child, but she's adopted."

The Guilt and Fear of Divorce: "God will condemn you..."
Another factor in declining marriage rates is the fear of divorce, which for many Inuit women is fraught with an overlay of sin and guilt, the legacy of 19th century missionary zeal. According to an Inuk minister, communication was difficult and the Anglican position against divorce was overdrawn in order to impress upon Inuit couples the sanctity of marriage and the importance of commitment. In retrospect, the minister guesses that, "The impression was, you shall not divorce your wife—if you do it, you break God's law." The missionary put it that way for protection of marriage, but it urges people the other way around. There's no love in it. There is a condemnation in the promises they make. "If you break this, God will condemn you—they are afraid of that."

As one woman said: "I'm not criticizing our religion at all. I'm an Anglican and Mom and Dad are both Anglicans and they are very active in the church. There was a point where the older people didn't agree with any separation or divorce because of the rule. Mom had that on me for so many years, and I felt so guilty. Back then, but not today."

The Stigma of Divorce: "It must be your fault..."

In addition, Inuit women suffer, as do all western women, from the social stigma associated with divorce, not to mention the usual legal and economic difficulties. Consequently, the incidence of divorce is low among Inuit women in the communities we visited. For older women, whose marriages frequently were arranged and for whom divorce was not a socially or religiously acceptable alternative, divorce is almost non-existent: "We were taught not to get a divorce when we get married. It's against the law, or Inuit belief." People perceive the woman as: "the one who is supposed to keep everything together. It must be your fault that you're getting a divorce." Are parents then more likely to be critical of a woman who chooses divorce? An elder, Kudloo, says: "Whenever I hear about somebody who just separated or divorced I always feel unhappy. I also love them, but I would not show it because they're from the same community, but it's like they're strangers. It's hard to let your love show to them if you don't even talk to them."

Lena, 36, is separated and says it is her parents who are most critical: "It's not my friends. My family, my mom especially, she doesn't believe in divorce or separation. Other people just talk. The woman is supposed to keep it all together. It's usually the woman who has to make up if there has been a fight. It's always the woman. I was talking to a girl yesterday. She was very badly abused, mentally and physically. The boyfriend's mother came to her and cried right in front of her, 'Don't leave him, go back to him. I'll pay your airfare to go to be near him.' He's in jail right now. They don't have any idea what the woman goes through, especially mentally. They don't see what's there. They can see the bruises if she was beaten, but they don't see what's inside." This comment underscores a common understanding: the woman who is physically abused may be in no worse shape than the woman who is mentally abused. A man can destroy her self-esteem without raising his hand.

Traditional Mechanisms: "It's not working..."

If divorce is not the answer, some feel that returning to the traditional mechanisms of conflict resolution and problem-solving might be appropriate. One elder believes that: "It would help the couples now if the parents sat down with them and told them about the long life ahead of them, like they did traditionally. As long as they don't shout at each other, sitting down and talking about it is the best way. With my children, before they did anything bad I would tell them right and wrong. That's the only way it would work—tell them that they're not supposed to do any bad things."

But for Sara, 39, whose husband has been physically abusing her for years, the traditional mechanisms did not work in a contemporary setting. Rather than proceed with a divorce, Sara decided to tell family and friends that her husband was hitting her, utilizing the traditional method of turning to the extended family for help. But the hitting stopped only to be replaced by mounting verbal abuse. She cannot understand why her husband seems so unable to communicate positively, especially when he claims that he still loves her and wants their marriage to work. "To my understanding, from what I've been through and from the other girls, and the men I've talked with about spousal or family violence, it's the way they were brought up that's not working in today's pace."

Yet, Sara is a homemaker who is deeply involved in traditional life-styles—hunting, camping, and cooking. She respects the idea of the old mechanisms. Now she is reserving her right to take the parts of tradition that work for her: "As for me, I was brought up to accept anything, because love and sharing and forgiveness will cure it all. It will take time, but it will work. That's the kind of life I was brought up in. Now I'm ready to tell my parents, 'Look, what you taught me—it's not working. What I'm going through right now, what you taught me, I'll use it, but to a point where I don't have to take it any more.' I'll use their method, not because I was brought up that way, because it's how I understand things. Nobody does things because they were told to do it. They do it because that's how they know it." Her family cannot understand why she would not keep trying. "I just can't take it any more. I don't really know who I am. I have to say 'no more' for my own mental health."

Early or Single Motherhood: "I'm climbing up the ladder..."
Typically, the consequence of choosing to live separately is also to raise one's children alone. It is almost always the woman who takes custody and care of the children after divorce, separation, or desertion.

Many Inuit women have adapted to single parenting, often at an early age. Rebecca, now 30 and never married, had her first baby at 20. Lucie, 20, has two toddlers, the first one born when she was 16; her mother had her first child at age 17. Neither married. Their situations are not at all uncommon. Since leaving her husband in 1984, 33-year-old Rachel has raised her three children herself. The first was born when she was 16: "It's hard, I can tell you that, but rewarding as well. I'm finding, since I've been separated, I guess I didn't really know myself then, but I'm climbing up the ladder. It's a lot easier for me now with my children than I had at that time in a bad marriage."

Echoing the belief that it is better to stay single than to marry, Rhoda, 45, claims that raising her children after divorce is easier than it was during a tempestuous marriage: "I didn't want my children around when we were fighting; I didn't want my children to go through what we were going through. That was the reason we got a divorce."

Toward the Future

Overall, the relationships between women and men, parents and children, are positive and constructive considering the dramatic impact of rapid social change on Inuit life. Many younger women hold optimistic views of the future, as male and female roles are beginning to regain their balance. They characterize couples in the new generation (under 25) as "happy" and not as plagued by the assault that characterized the transitional generation (those who are now in their late 20s or 30s).

What do Inuit women want for their children? The possibility of delaying childbearing and marriage until a later age. One women expressed her views: "From my side, women have changed a lot. I know for me, for my kids' future, I don't want them to have to settle down at an early age like me." Education for their children also holds important keys for successfully rebalancing gender roles through improved economic opportunity for both men and women.

In the context of shifting gender roles and greater choices for women, some feel that through better communication couples can find ways to make meaningful commitments. For example, one minister is offering workshops and classes for couples who are contemplating marriage: "I usually do three weeks' counselling about marriage. It really helps them a lot. I usually show them a filmstrip about marriage, and talk about the common prayer book, step by step, explaining what we really mean when we say this, or that. I usually talk to them about my own marriage, and what I used to think when I was younger, what experiences I have with helping couples, how they can solve their problems. It really seems to help a lot."

Some who are active in the church believe that rewriting the services would help clarify the commitment in terms that Inuit men and women could relate to more easily. More fundamentally, many agree that a new emphasis on the traditional values of sharing would help couples redefine marriage. As one church activist in his 30s explains: "Inuit, even young people, should know to share. I learned from my parents to share everything. Our food is caught for the community. This is our custom. Today, my age, they should know to share. Today, if I'm not working and my wife is working, we could support each other. We shouldn't really be afraid of anything. This is our life; the sharing, no matter what. Sharing in the home and the family."

A return to these old values would help couples face economic hardship and uncertainty. Spousal assault committees and support groups, or changes in national RCMP policy, might also soften the conflictual male—female relationships that trouble many Inuit families. It is obvious that these troubles are shared by many families all over Canada. For the Inuit, it is also clear that they are not so much problems as symptoms of exceedingly rapid social change. [2]

Notes

1. Interviews were conducted by the author in Pangnirtung, and by Angela Bernal in Cape Dorset, Clyde River, Spence Bay, Broughton Island, Pangnirtung, and Iqaluit. Names are fictionalized in order to preserve the confidentiality of those who participated in the research project; their voices are intermingled to protect their identities further. All interviews followed a similar outline of questions and were open-ended. Appreciation is extended to Kyra Mancini for her painstaking transcription of over 50 taped interviews; to Sheila Qappik and Peona Shukulaq for their sensitivity in interpreting interviews with women in Pangnirtung; and to the following for their very generous support of this project: Canadian Embassy, Washington, D.C., for a faculty research grant, 1988; Rhode Island College for faculty research grants and a 1988 summer research stipend; the Pangnirtung Hamlet Council, Mayor Johnny Mike, and Secretary—Manager Alan Angmarlik for permission to conduct research in Pangnirtung and for logistical assistance; the Social Science Division, Government of the Northwest Territories, for facilitation of the licensing process; and David Sissmore, Principal, Arthur Turner Training School, Pangnirtung, for assistance with lodging. This article is dedicated to Qatsoo Eevik, a Pangnirtung elder.

2. For a discussion of the impact of rapid social change on Inuit and Dene communities, see the author's "Social Change, Social Problems and the Search for Identity: Canada's Northern Native Peoples in Transition," *American Review of Canadian Studies*, Fall 1988.

Changing Women in the North

Toni Graeme

The role of women in the North appears to be getting more difficult, more stressful, and more thankless. The economic necessity for women to work outside the home is greater, and yet there is still the responsibility of keeping the family together. As well, there are the ever-increasing social problems, like drug and alcohol abuse, assaults, depression, and suicide. Whether or not these problems afflict our families, their increase is bound to have a serious effect on us. I would like to shift the emphasis around and focus on the "changing woman in the North." This is where the optimism is. It is the change that we as women make in our own lives that will determine our role in the North—and anywhere else for that matter.

Women are taking more control over their own lives: when to marry, when to start a family, when and how to get an education. More women are setting career paths to suit their interests, even if they are ones that have traditionally been male-dominated.

The federal and territorial governments keep too few statistics on women in the North to be helpful to us in looking at women and their numbers in various areas. But because our communities are so small, and communication and net-working so good, we can see some progress being made.

Two years ago, only 8 per cent of the management positions in the Government of the Northwest Territories were held by women. Today, that number has risen to 10 per cent. Although a 2 per cent increase seems small, it is, none the less, an increase. Three out of four women who make up the increase are native northern women—this is progress.

Nationally, more women than men are successful in small business, and there are a surprising number of women active in business in the North, particularly in the western Arctic. In Yellowknife, it is estimated that almost one-third of the small businesses are owned by women. These businesses range from arts and graphics enterprises to clothing stores, restaurants, and travel agencies. There is still room for growth in small business in the tourism and service sector but women are becoming more aggressive in learning how to start and run a business, and in identifying sources of government and bank financing.

Wherever we live, the quality of the social fabric of our lives is incredibly important. With the territorial government having to respond to an ever-increasing rate of social problems, women are taking a lead role in identifying particular problems and initiating local solutions. They are bringing people together to analyse the situation, to locate resource people who can help, and to find funding to establish projects or services. A prime example of this type of initiative is Nutaraq's Place, the newly opened transition house in Iqaluit, a project undertaken by the Agvvik Society. It took almost three years of planning before its doors were opened to those in need but their persistence and commitment paid off and is typical of the women throughout the North who are successful at whatever they are determined to do.

In the 1984 federal election we saw a woman running in the eastern Arctic and two in the West. Greater numbers of women are taking leadership roles in native and other non-governmental organizations. Doing so means we are not only making a contribution to our community but are also learning how groups work, the impact they can have, and, in a small way, gaining organizational and corporate experience in goal-setting and budgeting.

Every day I hear of women establishing their own network which they hope will rival and replace the "old boys network". Like everything else on earth, we are evolving. As with every generation, the future of our daughters and granddaughters to be freer than ourselves and to pursue their goals, rests with us today.

I think we have many exciting challenges ahead of us in the next few years in the North, and I have every confidence that women in all communities will rise to the occasion.

Traditional Practice in a
Contemporary Family

Mary Ellen Thomas
Based on an Interview by Angela Bernal

The traditional Inuit culture is going and a new culture is being created in a new time and a new era. I think though, that the basic values will be the same. Here in Iqaluit we have an urban community. You can find people from many countries of the world...in 3000 people! That allows us to have our own family life the way we want it.

For a long time, it has been predominantly white men who have married Inuit women—there's a long history of that in the North, from the early traders back to the early pioneers. They needed the skills that the women had to help them adjust to the community, and for survival. That history is long. It's only recently that white women have married native men, and it's becoming more common. There are many families like ours.

My oldest child is adopted. She became part of our family in a strange kind of way. It's a long story. She is the natural child of my husband's sister. There is a traditional belief that if you have three children of the same sex; if you give the third child away, then you will get a child of the opposite sex. So, his sister had two girls. When this child was born, she was the third girl, so she was given up for adoption. Adoption is very much a part of this culture. About one in five children is adopted. People adopt for many reasons. For example, in my husband's family there are five or six natural children, followed by five adopted children. Children are thought to be part of your life. There's no starting or stopping of childrearing age. Children are totally part of your life from birth to death.

The one reason that she was adopted was because she was the third girl child. She was first given in adoption to her grandparents (my husband's parents). They live on the land in the traditional community. It's called Kuyate. It's two houses, about 60 to 70 miles from here. When the child was born they had to be notified to come and pick her up. The hospital would not keep the child, and the mother was afraid that if she took the child home she would be unable to give her away. So she called me from the hospital and said, "Would you please come and get this child and keep it until my parents come?" So I did, and I took her home from the hospital when she was two days old.

I gave her away when she was five days old, when my husband's parents were able to come. Shortly after they took the child, when she was three and a half months old, his mother became ill. So she came here to hospital and they discovered she had cancer. She was too ill to look after the baby so we kept her. When she was five and a half months old, the adopting mother died of cancer. It was then December and it was too cold to take a five-month-old baby on the land and try to travel home to their community, so they left the child here for the winter. The original understanding was that when the summer came they would take the child.

However, when the time came, they realized there was no woman at the camp who could look after the child. There was only a girl who was 11 years old, and she didn't have the skills or ability to look after a baby. So the father said to us, "Would you like to keep the baby?" We loved her very much by this time. We were attached to her and she was attached to us. We did not want to deny his rights, so we told him that we would let him think about it for awhile longer and see if he still wanted us to keep her. We thought perhaps when she was two, and was walking and able to get around, that he would take her back. So we waited until she was two, and asked him again if he wanted to take her or if he wanted us to keep her. He said to us that we could keep her. So, we have adopted her by custom, really by tradition—whoever's able in the family looks after the child. Now we are thinking about the possibility of legally adopting her. I don't know if we will do that or be able to do that.

Traditionally, if the adopting mother died as quickly, she would have gone back to the natural parents, but by this time the natural mother was pregnant again and she couldn't take care of two small babies. So the next person in the family who was able to care for her would have the responsibility for doing that. But, for example, [my adopted daughter] still calls my father-in-law her father; her brothers are still her brothers; and she calls my husband not dad, but brother. She calls me daughter-in-law. Those are the terms she is used to—calling them by the relation of the person that they're named after, not their birth relation.

She is also named after the mother who passed away. So the natural mother calls her (daughter) mother. Because my husband is named after the sister of the mother, they call each other older sister, younger sister. Naming is very important because it gives everyone a place in the community, no matter what their age is. A child can be a mother or a father. It gives a relationship to everyone that you have responsibilities to.

I guess that's one of the strangest things that I have had to adjust to. For example, when I first came here, I saw an older person come up to a child that was about three years old and shake his hand. And I said to myself, in white culture we would never do that. So I went to someone and asked, "Why did she do that?" It was because that child is named after her husband. So, here was a woman of 60, greeting a three-year old as if he were her husband, and talking to him as if he were her husband, because that is that child's responsibility. That part of the culture is hard to understand sometimes—the importance of naming. They have an identity very early.

It gives everyone a place in the community and it gives them numerous people to which they have responsibility. It's part of the culture that you aren't just there with your family, you're part of everybody, and you have multiple relationships to many different people. It allows you to be part of the community. It's one of the nicest things I think I've found. I had a close friend who I was always planning to travel with. We were going to go to England. We thought this would be a great idea, for two single people, at that time, to go to England. She died unexpectedly and there is a child who was given her name almost immediately after she passed away. I recognize that character in this child who is now nine years old. My plan to travel with my friend was left incomplete, but now the opportunity that one day I will go to England is there, and I can complete that action with this child. It's not left unresolved. The feelings and emotions you have are not just left when someone passes. You are able to complete them. It's important to me, and it's part of the culture.

I really have not come to understand things as much as I would want. The longer I am here the less I understand. It's a very complex culture. When you ask many native people why something is, they don't know either, they just know that it exists. It's very hard to find out things because people sometimes don't know.

My natural daughter was born in the hospital, with the traditional midwife. The doctor was there, but as an observer. He allowed the midwife to deliver her. I was following instructions from the midwife. Breathing is an expression of white culture. That's something they teach you in this white culture. Inuit don't teach you breathing, but they teach you things like how to position the baby so you're comfortable, how to hold your body, and how to relax. Those are the things that she talked to me about. I think that one of the most satisfying things is that our hospital allowed me to do what I wanted to do. I'm not sure if they would have interfered or not had there been major problems. The doctor did help at a point in the delivery; he did take over, but with the midwife's help. Both were there and both participated in the delivery. She was comfortable with me being in the bed, and she instructed me to lay back, not completely back—most people don't do that [the native way of kneeling] anymore.

My husband was nervous, and scared, I guess, of what delivery was all about. Traditionally, the man would go away when the labour drew near. That's what he did. He left and went to his brother-in-law's place. Then I had the baby and his brother-in-law called in by radio and let him know the child was born, and then he came back. It was a feeling of "I don't want to bother you," or "I don't want to make things worse for you," and so he left. He was very nervous about that part of it. I could talk to him as much as I wanted about it, about shared responsibilities, about the joy, but he was not happy with that. There are many Inuit men who do go with their wives to the hospital, but even for him to talk to someone who had done that, he was very nervous about it. He had to follow his own feelings, and I had to let him, as much as I wanted him to be there. I had to let him. I couldn't force him to do something he didn't want to do. So I had two people who were very comfortable with me—a traditional midwife and a real strong friend of the family, who is bilingual.

My natural daughter is named after my husband's sister, who died. My husband asked his father what she should be named, and he said since my mother and father had both passed away in January, that she should be named after my parents because of their recent deaths. Her father and I talked about it. To him, he had not really resolved the death of his sister, so it was important to him to name her Lulu. But she has lots of other names too, and she will get more names yet, till she develops, till she's about one year old. She's got eight or nine names already. When a child cries unreasonably people think that it's because there's someone who's not named yet, who has to be named. That's also part of this culture. It also doesn't matter if she has boys' or girls' names.

She has four or five boys' names already. It started with the name that she will resemble, or she may take on the characteristics of one of those persons. Whether they're male or female, it doesn't really matter because this culture has no word for a male or female identity to things. For example, in English there's always the pronouns *he* or *she*, but in this culture there's no concept of gender.

When my daughter was about a year old we were on the land at my father-in-law's house on the bay. Her older brother went and brought a small bird back to the house so she could kill it, so it would be her first animal that she killed. He was very proud, everyone was very proud that this small bird was her first kill. She was upset by the bird being in the house and about it being killed. The family didn't understand. They were very proud of something. She had gained some identity as a hunter, as a person who has taken the spirit of an animal. For example, there are many rituals when a boy kills his first seal, caribou, or whale. There are rituals and patterns in the way people behave. I didn't understand that. They couldn't understand why I was upset either.

I try not to stop my children from learning, experiencing, being a part of both cultures. I cannot make my child a white person. She is part of both. I want her to be part of both, so I have to do things that allow her to be part of both. That's the hard thing sometimes, when you let go and when you hang on.

My husband is a hunter, and people always ask me what he does, and when I tell them he hunts, they look at me. I see a question mark come into their eyes and they say, "So he is unemployed?" I'll say, "No, he's hunting." The concept is very hard for some people to understand. They assume that because he is a hunter, he is suddenly nothing. That is really hard to accept among people of my culture, to understand what it means to be a hunter. It is also becoming rarer—there are very few native men who have the ability and resources to hunt. So in our family, I am working to help him follow his career and I'm quite happy to do that. We have tried him working and being a part of my culture, because he has a good education, but he's unhappy when he's participating in the labour force. He's very unhappy. He tries hard, but when he's unhappy then I'm unhappy and our whole family is unhappy. I'm quite glad to work and allow him to do the hunting part of his life-style. And when I'm able during the summer months, I like to participate with him as well. We go out on the land for a month or two; we live on the land, and follow the traditional life-style. I'm hoping our children are learning their skills there as well.

There's always a lot of work to be done at camp. When we first got together I would say, "Are you embarrassed that I don't have the skills to be able to do those things?" or I would feel that he would somehow be ashamed that I wasn't able to do the things that he needed to have done. I wasn't able to sew the sealskins properly or take the right amount of fat off the skin for things, and I would feel that I was letting him down somehow. I've tried to learn many of the things, and I'm not very good at them, but he's a very good teacher. There are other women in the family who can do the things that I cannot do, and there are things that I can do that they can't do, like filling out government forms and contacting agencies.

I speak as much Inuktitut as I can. My husband speaks to the children. I am not fluent in the language and you can't translate it. There are just so many things in it that don't translate. The flow in our home is back and forth from one language to another. It's very comfortable.

I've always been lucky that I've been employed as an adult educator. The primary theme has always been teaching reading and writing in English, but that's not what I do. The advantage of my job is that I work with the local education council which is elected in the community to look after the learning needs of the adults. It has always given great ideas about the community's needs. You use that, along with your own experience about what you feel the community needs, and what the individuals themselves want, then you try to pool all of that into some kind of learning activity. Over the years adult educators have addressed many kinds of needs that women have had, such as nutrition or mental health. We ran a community newspaper at one point where we used it to address learning and talked about communication in our own community. We've talked about the needs of elders and tried to incorporate traditional skills into our projects. Over the years, I've had many, many kinds of experiences using what people feel they need in their own community. I think we've served our communities very well. I think that I've learned more than the people I've taught. I've learned all kinds of things about the communities, the culture, and the peoples' interests and experiences. I really appreciate that.

Chapter II

MIDWIFERY AND BIRTHING

Birth by Mayoreak Ashoona

The Family Centred Maternity Care Project

Lesley Paulette

Family Centred Maternity Care

The birth of a baby represents, as well, the birth of a family. The woman giving birth and the persons significant and close to her are forming a new relationship, with new responsibilities to each other, to the baby, and to society as a whole. Family centred reproductive care may be defined as care which recognizes the importance of these new relationships and responsibilities, and which has as its goal the best possible health outcome for all members of the family, both as individuals and as a group (McMaster University, n.d).

The philosophy and practice of family-oriented maternity care has been endorsed by numerous professional associations, both in Canada and the United States. This model recognizes that the family is at the centre of the childbearing and childrearing experience. It recognizes and responds to both the physical and the psychological needs of the birthing woman and her family members, and is respectful of the family's needs and rights before, during, and after childbirth. Family-centred maternity care offers choices to the family, strengthening family bonds by encouraging shared and informed participation in all aspects of the birth process, within the bounds of medical safety.

Project Background

In April 1987, the Native Women's Association of the N.W.T. undertook Phase 1 of the Family Centred Maternity Care Project. The project was undertaken because native women had been saying for some time that maternity care in the North today does not always take into consideration the full needs of the native woman and her family. One problem which had been identified repeatedly was the separation of the birthing woman from her family and her community at the time of her child's birth, when often she must travel to a hospital far from home.

The phrase "Family Centred Maternity Care" was chosen as the name for this project because it describes a contemporary concept that comes very close to our understanding of the traditional way that native society met the needs of birthing women and their families. The family-centred experience of childbirth and childrearing was very much a part of native culture.

The project was launched with a small grant from the Department of Secretary of State of Canada. Phase 1 was designed to provide the membership of the Native Women's Association with an overview of the issues of maternity care in the North today, so that the membership might make informed decisions about taking further action. Phase 1 was also seen as a first step in a continuing process of active involvement of native women in decision making about their own health and health care. The improved health and well-being of native women and their families is a goal which can be approached by promoting holistic health education, family-centred maternity care, natural childbirth practices, and quality midwifery. The project has developed a data base about women's and maternal/infant health in the Northwest Territories. As native women gather and analyse information about their own experiences, review literature, carry out interviews, and make community lists, they develop tools that can be used to bring about desired and appropriate changes. Some of our findings, and the recommendations based on them, are presented here.

Community Visits: The Age Factor

As it turned out, the older women were much more open to talking about their birthing experiences than were the younger women. The elders were eager to share traditional knowledge they thought may be of some benefit to the people in the future. Equally significant is the fact that, traditionally, the very personal and intimate experience of childbirth was shared, rather than private. It was natural for older women to tell their stories without embarrassment or hesitation. The simple passage of time may also have made it easier to talk about birth experiences when they can be placed in the perspective of a lifetime. For young women today, in the smaller communities, birth is no longer a shared experience. Women usually go into labour and give birth away from even the closest members of their own family, in a hospital far from home. Birth has become a very private experience, and, therefore, one not easily or openly talked about, even in intimate circles. As a result, the focus of the community visits shifted more toward documenting traditional birth experiences, and less emphasis was placed on trying to identify women's current concerns and needs at this time. However, discussions with women in the communities were very valuable in helping to clarify the direction which the project should take in the subsequent stages, and some of the methods which could be used to encourage the greater participation of all women, old and young alike.

The Traditional Experience

Prior to the arrival of doctors, nurses, nursing stations, and hospitals in the North, when aboriginal people lived in a traditional way, childbirth and child care were family-centred experiences. Young women were taught by their mothers about their menstrual cycles, and about the roles and responsibilities of women at the time of puberty. Mothers chaperoned their daughters carefully, and babies were rarely born to women who were not already partnered with a man who could provide for his family. Women married at a young age, often as a result of an arrangement made by their parents.

Following marriage, a young woman was also taught to recognize the early signs of pregnancy, such as the absence of menstrual periods. As soon as she discovered that she was pregnant, she was expected to tell her mother right away. In some regions, it was considered taboo to hide the fact of one's pregnancy, and was said to lead to a harder labour for the woman. As soon as her pregnancy was revealed, a young woman was counselled by her mother and other female elders about the right way to look after herself and her baby during pregnancy:

> They told us to walk a lot. That way the baby would always be moving and would be born healthy. And we were not allowed to eat a lot of bannock and greasy foods or sweet foods, because the baby would get big and fat. (Fort Rae elder)

By the time a young woman was ready to give birth to her first baby, she was usually already acquainted with childbirth firsthand. Young married women were encouraged to attend the births of others, so that they might learn by observation and explanation from older, experienced women:

> When a woman went into labour, all the women went over there and us young girls would have to accompany them. Our mothers and our grandmothers showed us how it's done and explained everything—the reasons why they're doing it that way. And, as soon as we knew that the baby was born, as soon as we heard it crying, they made us all kiss the baby. (Fort Franklin elder)

As the time for her baby's birth approached, the young mother prepared the things she would need. She gathered a good supply of moss for her baby and for herself. She sewed a moss bag and prepared a cord made from twisted fibres or sinew for tying off the baby's umbilical cord. She also made a pad of moss, sometimes covered with fabric, to position under herself at the time of the baby's birth. Finally, she would go out into the bush and cut a dry pole to have ready as a cross-bar on which she could lean for support during labour and delivery. In all her preparations, she might be assisted by her sisters or friends.

When the mother went into labour, the news spread quickly to others in the camp or the village, and soon she was surrounded and supported by other women. Her mother, grandmother, sisters, and friends might all be there, taking turns walking with her, rubbing her back, and supporting her during contractions. Almost always, her husband was there with her, unless he was out hunting or checking traps at the time and could not be contacted:

> My husband's relatives were always there to help me. But only when my husband lifted me up (during contractions), that's when my baby would be born! Of the ten children we had, he was there for nine of them. (Fort Franklin elder)

Particularly in the days when people lived in small family camps in the bush all year round, it was common for the father to take a very active role in the birth. And, sometimes, when birth took place on the trail, a woman's husband was her only midwife.

In most communities, there was at least one woman who was recognized as an experienced birth attendant or midwife. She might have acquired her skills as an apprentice, alongside her own mother or grandmother. Or she might have demonstrated a special interest in or aptitude for midwifery at a young age, and learned from experience as a result of attending, with enthusiasm, at as many births as she could.

A midwife would be called on by the family to come and help, especially if the labour seemed long or difficult. She offered her skill, her experience, and her reassuring presence. Sometimes she also brought with her herbal medicines that helped the labouring woman along.

Usually, labour and delivery were normal, and minor complications were handled as they arose by the midwife and the attending relatives. The mother was encouraged to be up and walking during labour. As labour became really active, and the time of birth approached, the mother assumed a squatting or kneeling position. The dry pole, lashed across two upright poles, or hung by two ropes from the ceiling like a swing, provided a cross-bar on which she could lean:

> Each time she would get a pain, they would help her up so she could lean on that stick. And they would support her back, pushing with their hands on the lower part of her back. And then when the pain was relieved, they would lower her down again. And that's how our babies were born—in those days you never saw a woman lying on her back to have her baby, never! (Fort Rae elder)

As the baby's head began to deliver, someone prepared to catch the baby from behind or in front. Rarely was it required to deliver the head, and tears to the mother were unheard of. The baby was given directly to the mother, while the placenta was delivered and the cord cut. Different people in different regions observed their own particular customs regarding the disposal of the afterbirth, but it was never disposed of casually. It might be wrapped in a bundle and placed in a tree, burned in the fire, or else preserved and dried to make a particularly potent medicine for treating sickness; the placenta was respected for its power and its special relationship to the child. Likewise, the stump of the umbilical cord, when it dried up and fell off, was kept or disposed of in a ritual manner. Even the amniotic fluid, when the bag of water broke, was regarded by some people as blessed water that was beneficial to anyone who touched it.

Following the birth of her child, the young mother, especially the first-time mother, was counselled in the art of motherhood and child care by her relatives and more experienced friends. Children were breast-fed, sometimes for as long as two or three years. This served as a natural form of family planning, often resulting in several years' spacing between children. Every woman had her own particular way of rearing and caring for her children, so the new mother would take from these offerings that which would be useful to her.

The elders interviewed recalled very few serious complications among the births in which they had participated. They pointed out that the traditional life-style was hard and strenuous, but that people were vigorous and healthy. Also, their diet was comprised chiefly of natural foods from the land. These factors, they maintain, contributed to the ease with which they gave birth, and to the general good health of mothers and their infants.

There were, however, occasions when serious complications arose, and birth attendants had to deal with them as best they could. Most of these problems occurred in the third stage of labour, that is, the delivery of the placenta. Several accounts were related of retained placentas that had to be removed, either manually or by cord traction. One elder recalled how she had stayed with a woman for two days and nights until she was able to remove the retained placenta and control the bleeding. She learned later that the same woman died after a subsequent birth as a result of a similar complication. In one story told by the women of Fort Rae, a woman suffered a prolapsed uterus a month or so after the birth of her child, and was nursed by the other women in camp who used hot compresses and massage until the condition corrected itself.

One woman in Fort Franklin recalled the breech birth of her daughter, following an unusually long and difficult labour. Another explained how she and a group of other birth attendants had worked successfully to do an external version, turning a baby from a transverse position to a vertex position so that it could be born:

By God, we sure did a lot of turning, each of us taking turns, until we got that baby turned around! And then everything was all right. (Fort Franklin elder)

In times of really serious birth complications, the aid of a medicine man was sometimes sought. Medicine and prayers, and the faith of all in attendance, were credited with saving the lives of more than one mother and child. There were cases, however, where it seemed that nothing could be done. Such was the story of the death of a baby, resulting from apparent shoulder dystocia. In such circumstances, the grief of the family was shared by the entire community.

Childbirth was indeed an experience that brought members of the family and the community together in a unique and very intimate way. The elders suggested that in the days when families gave birth together in this way, the bonds between family members were stronger than they are today. In particular, men seemed to have a different kind of appreciation for their wives, and a closer relationship to their children. The elders spoke fondly and with enthusiasm about their experiences, and explained that the act of helping another woman in childbirth was considered to be God's work, an honour and privilege to perform. Thus, the act of women caring for one another had a spiritual dimension as well as a purely practical dimension. It was with sadness and regret that the elders noted that, in today's scheme of things, there seems to be no room for native women to help each other in this way any more:

Delivering babies, you're doing the work of God, just like looking after the sick or the elderly. It helps you to stay good. But nowadays, they take young pregnant girls off to the hospital, just like the sick elders, and its seems they have no use for us any more. (Fort Franklin elder)

Transitions: The Changing Birth Experience
In the span of only two or three generations, the experience of childbirth for native women in the Northwest Territories has changed radically. Childbirth has been totally removed from the life of the smaller communities, and everywhere it has largely been removed from the sphere of the family. These changes can perhaps be best understood in the broader context of the overwhelming changes that have occurred in all areas of life for northern native people since the late 19th and early 20th centuries.

These great economic, social, and cultural changes have had serious consequences for the physical, mental, and emotional health of native people. In settlements characterized by poverty, poor nutrition, inadequate housing and infrastructure, and social and cultural upheaval, people have succumbed to infectious disease, accidental and violent death (often alcohol-related), and suicide rates much greater than the average Canadian population. Infant mortality rates, especially in the post-neonatal period, have been as high as three and four times the national average.

In the mid-1950s, the Canadian government responded to the grim health conditions in the North by developing an Indian and Northern Health Service within the Department of Health and Welfare. Aggressive measures to curb the alarming morbidity and mortality rates were taken in the form of public health programs, construction and staffing of nursing stations in the small communities, and extensive referral and evacuation of patients to secondary- and tertiary-level care centres in larger settlements and southern Canada. The percentage of births in the Northwest Territories occurring in a hospital or nursing station rose sharply, from 38.9 per cent in 1953 to 90.6 per cent in 1968 (Medical Service Branch, 1963; 1968).

During the 1960s and early 1970s, a period when infant mortality rates declined appreciably in the Northwest Territories (Brett et al., 1976), maternity care was provided primarily in the nursing stations. Many of the nurses were British, hired because of their advanced training in areas such as midwifery. While O'Neil (1985, 1986) has pointed out the problems that sometimes ensued when medical personnel from a totally different cultural background practised their brand of medicine in northern native communities (O'Neil, 1985;1986), the skill and experience of these nurse-midwives has been credited with the maintenance of "acceptable" perinatal and maternal mortality rates in a high-risk population under conditions of isolation (Baskett, 1978). The services in place at the time, of consultant physicians and the police, such as the routine evacuation of all primigravidae, all grand multiparae, and all other high-risk pregnancies, also functioned to increase the likelihood of optimal maternal and infant outcomes.

But since the mid-1970s, the policies in maternity care have changed, either due to difficulties in hiring foreign-trained nurse-midwives to work in remote northern communities, or to changing attitudes about acceptable risk levels in obstetric care. Current policy dictates that all expectant mothers in the western Northwest Territories are sent out from the smaller communities to give birth in a hospital, either in the larger centres of Inuvik, Yellowknife, or Hay River, or to Edmonton (Kaufert et al., 1987). A similar situation exists in the eastern Northwest Territories and northern Québec. Today, no births take place in nursing stations unless they are unexpected premature deliveries. In these cases, the deliveries are attended by nurses who have no particular training in midwifery. Similarly, routine pre-natal care is now the responsibility of these same nurses who have limited training and experience in maternal health.

Much has been written about the evolution of health services in the North by those with an interest in public health policy, but little has been documented from the point of view of those men and women who have been directly affected by those changes. Their perspective is included in the next section.

The Current Experience

One of the elders in Fort Franklin, whose childbearing years spanned the period of transition from home to hospital birth, commented on the differences she experienced:

I enjoyed it a lot more in the bush because of the fact that everyone was there to help out. Your mother guided you, preparing you for what's coming. Just the togetherness...everybody together, helping one another and guiding you. But being in the hospital, you're on your own until you're just about to have your baby. Only then do you see people helping you, just at that time.

...I'd always had my babies in the squatting position. But when I had my oldest son, they took me to Fort Simpson. I didn't like being on my back, I wanted to be in the squatting position, so I stayed in that position until just the last minute. Then they had to push me down on the bed to have my baby that way, even though I didn't want to have it that way.

The elders note that it has been years since they have seen or heard of a birth taking place in their community. The implications of this are numerous. First, most young women have never seen a baby being born before they have their own first child, and tend to be ill-prepared for the experience that awaits them. Second, when women are sent out to larger centres to deliver in a hospital, they usually travel out alone, leaving their husbands, children, if any, and other family members at home. The separation of the mother from her home and family, for a period of two weeks to a couple of months, contributes to many problems for everyone concerned. The loneliness and isolation of the mother, aggravated, in some instances, by the conditions and attitudes encountered in the boarding home in which she is billeted pending the birth of her child, constitute stress factors which jeopardize her total health in the final weeks of the pregnancy. When the child is born, the woman goes through the experience of childbirth without the support and reassuring presence of her family. Indeed, in the role of patient in a "total institution," the native woman experiences medicalized childbirth in a cultural context which may bear little or no relation to her own cultural identity or experience. The absence of the baby's father and siblings at the birth delays, and perhaps ultimately compromises, the process of family bonding. Meanwhile, in the absence of the mother, her husband and children manage as best they can at home. Fathers often experience trouble balancing their jobs and their responsibilities at home, while the cost of additional child care puts further stress on the family finances. Children may experience increased health problems in their mother's absence, as a result of emotional stress coupled with some measures of neglect, or, at the least, disruption in their usual routine (Kaufert, n.d.).

Finally, the removal of childbirth from the sphere of family and community has undoubtedly contributed to the breakdown in the traditional practices of sharing knowledge and support between the older and younger generations. Young women no longer confide in their elders as soon as they know they are pregnant. Sometimes this is because they are single, and they fear the elders will disapprove of a pregnancy out of wedlock. Further, the overwhelming emphasis placed on hospital deliveries and the medicalization of childbirth today has served to devalue the wisdom and authority of the elders. The health care system defines doctors and case-room nurses as the only legitimate birth attendants, and nursing station staff, together with the consulting physician, as the only legitimate dispensers of pre-natal care. The experience of childbirth in the hospital today is so different from the traditional experience of birth at home that elders are ill-equipped to prepare young women, as they have little idea themselves what goes on behind hospital doors (O'Neil et al, 1987).

What was once an experience that united different generations of native women in a cyclical ceremony of life-renewal, has now become one more stark example of the gulf across which the older and younger generations struggle to communicate today. Many young women are wholly ignorant of the traditional knowledge which their grandmothers have about female health and childbearing, and can hardly conceive of what it must have been like to give birth at home, in the squatting position, surrounded by half of their relatives and in-laws.

Similarly, the elders I spoke with found it disturbing to contemplate their granddaughters giving birth on their backs with their feet in stirrups, deprived of the support of their husbands and other family members. They fear that drugs have taken the place of personalized attention as a means for helping women cope with the intense sensations of labour. Two-thirds of Indian and Inuit women receive analgesia at least once during their labour and delivery (Spady, 1982). Further-more, the elders were puzzled and appalled by the number of new mothers who shuffle around and sit gingerly on rubber doughnuts while their stitches heal. The collective experience of the elders had caused them to take for granted an intact perineum in childbirth, and the very notion of deliberately cutting a woman's vagina (as in an episiotomy) was totally beyond them. Yet, native women routinely experience an episiotomy (Bouchard, 1987), and women who have an episiotomy experience more severe tears than women who are not cut (Spady, 1982; Bouchard, 1987).

The Perspective of Health Care Professionals

While young native women are no longer learning from their grandmothers how to care for themselves in pregnancy, how to prepare for childbirth, or how to care for the newborn, they are not getting information on these subjects from other sources either. Native women do not make very good use of the pre-natal care and pre-natal education that is available to them through nursing stations; this factor contributes to increased morbidity and mortality (Spady, 1982: Graham-Cumming, 1967). The perceptions of several health care professionals, shared in conversation with me, are that many native women, particularly in the smaller communities, lack basic knowledge about their bodies and their pregnancies. This perception was validated by the concerns of the elders who are worried that young women simply don't know how to look after themselves any more. Caught somewhere between the traditional experience of their grandmothers and the high-tech hum of the case-room, young native women appear to be somewhat alienated from their own bodies and their own health care. The cycle of fertility, childbearing, mothering, and ministering to other women, as it was re-enacted from one generation to the next, today seems fragmented and weakened.

Health care professionals complained that native women tend to be "non-compliant" about reporting to the nursing station early in the pregnancy, keeping regular pre-natal appointments, and showing up for pre-natal classes. While the reasons for this under-utilization of services need to be examined more closely, there are indications that differences in values, expectations, and cultural background may be deterring some women from making use of obstetrical services provided by non-native practitioners. The significance of this cross-cultural dynamic with respect to the relationship between indigenous women and government health workers providing maternity care has been reported elsewhere (Sargent, 1982). One problem commonly pointed out by medical personnel is the difficulty in pinpointing the expected date of delivery of women who have kept no track of their menstrual periods, have waited for several months before presenting themselves for their first pre-natal checkup, and have not been able to recall when they felt "quickening" (Round, 1987; Spady, 1982). The resulting uncertainty in dates has often caused women to be sent out to hospital weeks in advance of their delivery, further aggravating the hardships to the family described above. An extensive program of early ultrasonic screening of all pregnancies has been instituted in an effort to pinpoint due dates.

Another approach would be to encourage women to take more responsibility for keeping track of their periods and reporting early in pregnancy, thus facilitating the calculation of due dates (Round, 1987). A further dimension of this dilemma, however, is that women sometimes delay reporting their pregnancy in a deliberate effort to confuse their due date. They hope that they may be able to have their baby unexpectedly at the nursing station before the date on which they were scheduled to fly out to hospital, thus eliminating the problems associated with being away from home. While this tactic, which has been known to work on occasion, may raise many concerns with the medical authorities, it is clearly indicative of the intense dissatisfaction which some women feel about current maternity care in the Northwest Territories.

Recently, native women have expressed their discontent, particularly Inuit in the Keewatin region. They have called for a return to births in the communities, attended either by nurses or traditional native midwives. Some medical researchers and practitioners in the North have, in fact, concluded that midwives are the most appropriate providers of pre- and post-natal care, and should be the principal birth attendants at uncomplicated births (Bouchard, 1987; Gagnon, 1987). However, the general response from the medical community has been less than enthusiastic.

While those in positions of authority within the federal and territorial departments of health acknowledge the problems created for native women and their families under the existing system, they fear that a return to birthing in the communities would lead to a decline in the status of maternal and infant health. They point to the shortage of trained nurse-midwives currently available in Canada, and express grave concerns about the technical capability of indigenous midwives who have no modern medical training (Round, 1987). The question of midwifery, they point out, is further complicated by the current political and legal debate over the licensing and training of midwives in Canada (Round, 1987). Other concerns focus on the feasibility of providing medical back-up in the small communities and reliable evacuation measures in the event of an emergency. In the wake of a hard-fought battle to bring down maternal and infant mortality rates in the past 20 years, it is clear that the medical community favours a conservative definition of acceptable risk in obstetric care; it is reluctant to relinquish its position that hospitals are the only safe place for birth (O'Neil, 1987: Round, 1987).

Concerns Regarding General Health:
Toward a Holistic Approach

Much of the debate about maternity care and childbirth in the North has become polarized around the issues of midwifery and place of birth; concerns are also evident about the persistent "high-risk status" of the native population. Social and economic conditions in the communities are such that the woman's general health and life-style may not be contributing to a healthy pregnancy. Nutrition is widely recognized as one of the prime determinants of a healthy outcome in pregnancy. Yet, the substitution of store-bought foods for traditional diet, coupled with the high price of quality foods in the North, has seriously compromised the nutritional status of native women. Maternal smoking and alcohol abuse point to greater risks in pregnancy and birth (Spady, 1982; Bouchard, 1987), as do a high proportion of teenage and single mothers, as well as older women who have borne many children. The fact that native women do not make extensive use of pre-natal care or health education available to them is cause for further concern.

The introduction of skilled nurse-midwives and primary care facilities in the communities in the 1960s and early 1970s may have occasioned some real improvement in maternal and infant outcomes in the neo-natal period, but it is not immediately obvious that the recent shift to hospital births outside of the communities has brought further improvement. Caution must be exercised in interpreting small crude numbers projected into proportionate mortality rates, but there is evidence that infant health indicators in recent years are levelling off and even possibly showing a decline (Medical Services Branch, 1983; O'Neil, 1986). The post-neonatal period has always been, and continues to be, the most dangerous period for native infants (Basket, 1978; Medical Services Branch, 1962), due in large measure to the physical and social conditions that prevail in the communities. The illnesses which continue to plague native children—otitis media, gastro-enteritis, streptococcal infection, pneumonia, and influenza—have collectively been referred to by some as the "northern infant syndrome". It is obvious that these illnesses in the North, as in other native communities in Canada, are largely preventable through better living conditions (Bain, 1982).

All of these factors point to the need for a holistic approach to preventative health measures, and suggest that a narrow emphasis on providing increasingly sophisticated obstetrical care would be grossly misguided.

The economic, social, and cultural dysfunctions within communities must be addressed, not only at the local level but also within the broader context of regional and national political economies. Native people themselves must play a central role in both the process of community development and the review and reform of current health care delivery systems (Bain, 1982; O'Neil, 1986; Health and Welfare Canada, 1985).

Directions for the Future

Health conditions among native populations, and the manner in which health care services are currently delivered in the North, reflect the colonial legacy that has profoundly influenced northern society. Along some dimensions of morbidity and mortality, indicators in northern native population rival and, in some cases, surpass those of Third World countries (Young, 1983). The manner in which maternity care is provided in the North today is reminiscent of the expropriation of childbirth by the medical professions which occurred elsewhere in Canada in the first half of the 20th century (Canadian Broadcasting Corporation, 1985).

In the view of the author, the challenge is to find safe and appropriate ways of bringing childbirth, and the responsibility for maintaining maternal and infant health, back to the family and the community. This challenge must be taken up by people in the communities, the organizations that represent their concerns, and agencies responsible for providing health services. The concluding sections of this report set forth recommendations for further action which the Native Women's Association might appropriately take in an effort to meet this challenge.

Recommendations

1) Start in the communities to strengthen existing resources

I believe that the interaction between the younger and older generations, which I witnessed in the course of doing interviews with the elders, is the key to reintegrating elements of the childbearing cycle. A community-based research process is needed in order to foster an open dialogue on childbirth and childrearing. Women of all ages have a contribution to make.

The initial focus around which this community-based research process can develop is the recording and documenting of the traditional knowledge about female health, pregnancy, childbirth, and childrearing, of which the elders are the custodians. Young women in each of the regions served by the Native Women's Association can be trained in the methodology of documenting oral tradition, as well as in the fundamentals of maternal and infant health. These regional re-searchers/facilitators, necessarily fluent in their own language, will then be prepared to do field-work in their region, interviewing older women and men about the childbearing cycle. The data which they gather will be valuable in itself as a record of cultural knowledge, and as the basis on which culturally appropriate health promotion materials and curricula might be developed. (It is important that this work be done in each of the regions, as there may be great cultural variation from one region to another.)

The regional facilitator will play a vital role in encouraging younger women to express their own feelings and to articulate their current concerns and needs with regard to maternity care. The process will also serve to strengthen and enhance the human resources which exist within the community, and will start to reactivate the network of mutual self-help and self care that was, traditionally, the backbone of community health care in native societies. Finally, the process will provide a bridge across which different cultural perspectives and models of health knowledge and health care (the traditional and the modern scientific) can be drawn closer together.

It is proposed that monies be sought to fund this process over a period of two years. At the end of the first year, a workshop might be held, with representation from each of the regions, as well as delegates from other regions of the Northwest Territories. (The Inuit Women's Association has expressed interest in working with the Native Women's Association on this project.) The workshop would generate supplementary documentation (audio-visual) to support the field work done in each region throughout the first year. In the second year, discussion tools developed from the material generated in the first year will be used to facilitate discussions with younger women, which will lead to a statement of native women's needs, concerns, and priorities from a community perspective. This statement of needs and concerns will be useful in itself, and will also serve to sharpen the focus of further efforts to examine the current maternity-care policies and practices in the North.

2) Study the existing system closely
There is a need to take a close look at the existing manner in which maternity care is delivered in the Northwest Territories, to identify the strengths and weaknesses of the system, and to evaluate the outcomes that can be documented. We also need to study in greater depth such facets of maternal and infant health as current and proposed strategies for minimizing the risk status of maternal and infant populations. Part of this review will be accomplished through the community-based research process outlined above, as women express concerns arising from their own personal experience. Other aspects of this review, however, will require a complex analysis of various types of data, including the statistical data which, to date, has been problematic.

At present, the Native Women's Association has a standing invitation to work collaboratively with the Maternal, Perinatal, and Infant (MPI) Committee of the Northwest Territories, and other potentially interested groups yet to be identified, to carry out such a review. This collaborative approach has been proposed as an alternative to separate reviews. Furthermore, it is clear that review of the existing system is timely, in light of the imminent transfer of all health services to the territorial government, and that the MPI Committee will be going ahead with some sort of review, with or without the participation of other parties.

Past experience has taught native people to be alert to the dangers of being co-opted whenever "collaboration" or "consultation" with government has been proposed. The danger of being used merely to lend legitimacy to a process which, ultimately, remains in the control of the government gives native people reason to pause before leaping into collaborative relationships. The potential for co-optation may be no less present in this proposed collaborative venture than in any other. On the other hand, there are potential advantages to working in a co-operative relationship with government health agencies. These advantages exist to the extent that the concerns and questions raised by native women are addressed in a serious way by the (government's own) research process, rather than remaining marginal to it. Full participation by the Native Women's Association in all phases of the process, from the initial design to the analysis and interpretation of the findings, could be the strongest possible insurance that the system will actually make maternity care in the North more responsive to the needs of native women and their families.

In my opinion, it is worth further exploring the option of engaging in a co-operative research process with the MPI Committee of the Northwest Territories, and with other groups who have already demonstrated a concern in this area. These groups include the Inuit Women's Association, the Northwest Territories Registered Nurses Association, and the Keewatin Inuit Association in collaboration with the Department of Community and Preventative Medicine, University of Manitoba (Kaufert et al, 1987). It is essential, however, that the Native Women's Association define a mechanism whereby the association's involvement in the process will remain accountable to its membership. At the least, this would involve a member of the association's Board of Directors being designated a member of the collaborative team, in addition to the association's staff being committed to work on the study. Preferable, however, would be a project advisory group within the association, consisting of representation from the Board of Directors, at least one or two interested women from the communities, and consultative services of several professionals in the fields of health research and practice, not employed by either the federal or territorial governments. This advisory group would meet periodically to give direction to the association's research and planning efforts, both at the community level and at the level of collaborative involvement with government agencies and other groups. Staff hired to work on Phase 1 of the Family Centred Maternity Care Project would be responsible for following through on the directives given by the advisory group, and, in turn, would feed to the group current information and updates on the progress of the research activities.

3) Heed the lessons learned by others elsewhere

A further piece of the puzzle which is essential to consider is the experience of aboriginal peoples in other parts of the world who have sought to improve health conditions and delivery of their health care services. While the conditions in northern Canadian native communities are, in some respects, unique, many parallels can be drawn with the situations described elsewhere.

Last, but certainly not least, are the important developments occurring right now in other parts of Canada and the United States with regard to the recognition and licensing of midwives. Task forces in Québec, British Columbia, and Ontario have been studying very closely the multitude of medical, social, and legal aspects of the midwifery issue. The Ontario Task Force on Midwifery has recently released its report, including recommendations on the training, licensing, and practice protocols which might govern the practice of midwifery in Ontario. There seems little doubt that midwifery will eventually become sanctioned in Canada; the many questions which remain centre on "when, how, and under what conditions?"

Toward Proposals for Change

The recommendations set out above are not an attempt to put forth, at this time, specific proposals for change in policy or practice in the existing northern health care system. It is strongly felt that such proposals would be grossly premature. The issues are complex and the stakes high. Careful attention must be given, at this time, to a process of research and planning which will in time lead to concrete proposals. From the point of view of the Native Women's Association, it is vital that women in the communities participate in this process. If women are not involved at a grass roots level, then any changes to the system that the association might lobby for in Yellowknife will be just one more thing done to native women without their active participation.

Research and planning need not mean simply another voluminous study that just sits on the shelf and gathers dust. Approached in the right way, the research process can, itself, be a powerful tool that helps individuals, families, and communities recognize and draw on their own inner resources. It is apparent that some of the needed changes to the maternity-care system in the North will only come about in the wake of a painfully slow research and planning process and considerable political debate. But it is equally apparent that some of the most fundamental and far-reaching changes, which will ultimately affect the quality of maternal and infant health in the North, will come about as a direct result of the efforts of women and men, young and old, in the communities, to make whole again the circle of the family.

References

Advisory Council on the Status of Women. *Midwifery: A Discussion Paper.* Winnipeg, Man.: Advisory Council on the Status of Women, May 1987.

Bain, Harry. "Community Development: An Approach to Health Care for Indians." *Canadian Medical Association Journal*, 1 February 1982, pp. 223–224.

Baskett, T.F. "Obstetrical Care in the Central Canadian Arctic." *British Medical Journal*, 2 (1978): pp. 1001–1004.

_____. "A University Department's Involvement with Medical Care in the Canadian North." *Canadian Medical Association Journal*, 3 February 1978, pp. 298–300.

Bouchard, F. "Having a Baby in Northern Quebec: Lessons for the Future." In *Circumpolar Health 87*. Edited by H. Linderholm, C. Backman, N. Broadbent, and I. Joelsson. Oulu, Finland: Nordic Council for Arctic Medical Research, 1988, pp. 495–497.

Boyce, Thomas W., *et al.* "Social and Cultural Factors in Pregnancy Complications Among Navajo Women." *American Journal of Epidemiology* 124 (1986):pp. 242–253.

Canadian Broadcasting Corporation. 1987. "Doctoring the Family." Transcript of a broadcast on IDEAS.

Finerman, Ruthbeth D. "A Matter of Life and Death: Health Care Change in an Andean Community." *Soc. Sci. Med.* 18 (1984):pp. 329–334.

Fumoleau, Rene. *As Long as This Land Shall Last.* Toronto: McLelland and Stewart Ltd., 1974.

Gagnon, Joanne. 1987. Selected unpublished papers on the experience of the maternity program at the Hudson Bay Hospital Centre.

Graham-Cumming, G. "Prenatal care and infant mortality among Canadian Indians." *The Canadian Nurse*, September 1967, pp. 29–31.

Grant Higgins, Patricia, *et al.* "Labour and delivery in North America: A comparison between the native American and white cultures." *Nursing Times*, 16 September 1981, pp. 4–10.

_____. "Pueblo women of New Mexico: their background, culture and childbearing practices." *Topics in Clinical Nursing* 4 (1981):69–78.

Health and Welfare Canada. Medical Services Branch, NWT Region. *Report on Health Conditions in the N.W.T. 1961-1985*. Ottawa: Government of Canada, 1985.

Health and Welfare Canada. "Midwives—professionals or pariahs?" *Health Promotion*, Spring 1987, pp. 14–15.

Kaufert, Patricia A., Gilbert, P., O'Neil, J.D., Brown, R., Brown, P., Postl, B., Moffatt, M., Binns, B., and Harris, L.. "Obstetric Care in the Keewatin: Changes in the Place of Birth 1971-1985". In *Circumpolar Health 87*. Edited by H. Linderholm, C. Backman, N. Broadbent, and I. Joelsson. Oulu, Finland: Nordic Council for Arctic Medical Research, 1988, pp. 481–484.

Kenner, Bridget. "Midwifery in Nicaragua," *Nursing Times*, 18 February 1987, pp. 60–61.

Malloch, (Lesley) Paulette. *Dene Government Past and Future.* Yellowknife, NWT: Western Constitutional Forum, 1984.

McMaster University, Department of Obstetrics and Gynaecology. *Family Centred Maternity Care.* Hamilton: McMaster University.

Milligan, B. Carol. "Nursing Care and Beliefs of Expectant Navajo Women," *American Indian Quarterly,* Summer 1984, pp. 199–210.

Morrison, H.I., *et al.* "Infant Mortality on Canadian Indian Reserves 1976–1983", *Canadian Journal of Public Health,* July/August 1986, pp. 269–273.

Murdock, Alan I. "Factors Associated With High-Risk Pregnancies in Canadian Inuit," *Canadian Medical Association Journal.* 3 February 1979, pp. 291–294.

O'Neil, John. "The Politics of Health in the Fourth World: A Northern Canadian Example," *Human Organization.* 45 (Summer 1986).

O'Neil, John, Kaufert, P.A., Brown, P., Voisey, E., Moffat, M.M., Postl, B., Brown, R., and Binns, B. "Inuit Concerns About Obstetric Policy in the Keewatin Region, NWT". In *Circumpolar Health 87.* Edited by H. Linderholm, C. Backman, N.Broadbent, and I. Joelsson. Oulu, Finland: Nordic Council for Arctic Medical Research, 1988, pp. 485-489.

Parker, Tricia. "Born in Burma," *Nursing Times,* January 1987.

Pascoe, Marilinda. "Midwifery Work Exchange Project in Nicaragua," *Journal of Nurse-Midwifery,* March/April 1987, pp. 101–110.

Pedersen, Duncan, and Coloma, Carlos. "Traditional Medicine in Ecuador: The Structure of the Non-Formal Health Systems,"*Soc. Sci. Med.* 17 (1983):1249–1255.

Ross, Michael G. "Health Impact of Nurse Midwifery Program," *Nursing Research* 30 (November/December 1981).

Round, Barbara. *Midwifery Discussion Paper.* Yellowknife, N.W.T.: Northwest Territories, Department of Health, 1987.

Sargent, Carolyn. "The Implications of Role Expectations for Birth Assistance Among Bariba Women," *Soc. Sci. Med.,* 16 (1982):1483–1489.

Spady, D.W., *et al. Between Two Worlds: The report of the Northwest Territories perinatal and infant mortality and morbidity study.* Edmonton: Boreal Institute for Northern Studies, University of Alberta, 1982.

Young, T. Kue. "The Canadian North and the Third World: Is The Analogy Appropriate?," *Canadian Journal of Public Health,* July/August 1983, pp. 239–241.

PCBs in Inuit Women's Breastmilk

JoAnn Lowell

From a study carried out by Professor Albert Nantel, Director of Québec Toxicology at Laval University, on levels of polychlorinated biphenyls (PCBs) in breastmilk from Québec women, it was found that nursing Inuit mothers have PCB levels that are five to ten times greater than those found in women from southern Québec cities. Compared to a "tolerable" PCB intake of 1 microgram per kilogram of body weight per day, the Inuit women exhibited average levels that were three times this amount, up to a maximum level of 14.7 micrograms.

It is almost certain that these high levels are a result of the traditional diet of the Inuit which consists of fish, and land and sea mammals. PCBs are fat-soluble and accumulate in the fatty tissue of organisms that absorb or consume them. As fish are devoured by seals, walruses, and whales, the PCB levels are magnified tenfold with each movement up the food chain. A separate nutritional survey of the Inuit diet on Broughton Island in the Northwest Territories confirmed that sizeable amounts of PCBs are found in sea mammals.

The affected Inuit women from Professor Nantel's research live off the north-east tip of Hudson Bay, south from Baffin Island. For them, it is a "Catch-22" situation. Breast-feeding, which decreased in the 1970s has been encouraged again to help combat the outbreaks of infection among Inuit children (by production of antibodies in breastmilk). However, the PCBs in the milk have a cumulative effect that can be toxic to the infants' immature immune systems after six months of nursing, increasing their susceptibility to infections. As well, not only can most mothers not afford to stop breast-feeding but the traditional diet is also a deeply rooted and fundamental part of their culture.

Professor Nantel is currently working on a second study to monitor individual women's PCB levels, infants' immunity systems, and breast-feeding periods in order to give individual counsel. He warns that breast-feeding should not be abandoned and that the risks must be balanced with the benefits.

As the sea mammal contamination is an extension of a global pollution, it is a savage irony that the traditional way of life of the Inuit—with its ecological wisdom—has been desecrated and possibly altered forever.

Rights of Passage in the North: From Evacuation to the Birth of a Culture

Betty Anne Daviss-Putt

INTRODUCTION

A Story About How Far a Woman Will Go

It did border on the absurd. Here was Joyce, a young Inuk, sensibly brought up with a good understanding of community and what is reasonable, yet she was uprooting herself from Labrador for the pregnancy and birth. She presented herself with her husband on my Ontario doorstep, asking for a homebirth—in a community that was not her home.

The birth was at night—simple, sweet, uncomplicated. I couldn't help but think that all three hours of it would have been less stressful if she had been at her own home in Labrador. Joyce spoke to her mother immediately after the birth, the phone in one hand, a wet newborn clutched in the other, tears streaming down her face.

"This is wrong," I thought. Joyce has a close relationship with her mother and had really wanted her at the birth. Yet her mother had never been out of her settlement and did not have the wherewithal to transplant body and soul from Labrador to Appleton, Ontario.

If Joyce had attempted a homebirth in her Labrador settlement, she might have found an elder who would attend. But fear would have discouraged them. Fear founded not on the risk of complications as much as on the creation of an enemy in a position of authority—the nurse in the nursing station or the doctor in the nearest major health centre—whose services they might need later for other health care purposes. Ironically, the nurse may not have minded, as many nurses are starting to be sympathetic to the wishes of the women wanting to remain in

91

their settlements. But homebirths, although they may provide the ultimate in the "normal" environment, aren't the "norm" any more. Even when a mother feels strongly that the best outcome for the birth would be in her own sanctuary, how can she have a homebirth without social support? Social support is often a prerequisite for a good birth experience.

As an alternative, Joyce might have intentionally misled the nurse about her dates, a strategy now used by women to plan "accidental" births in the settlement. The real question is: Why did Joyce not, as her sister had done, take the accepted, all-expense-paid route to the Goose Bay hospital? Well, that just wasn't where she could imagine herself having her baby.

This is a story about a people who are trying to stop cultural annihilation by finding new power in old traditions. It is about enabling individuals and communities to accept or reject changes being imposed by a perceived authority. It is one chapter in the saga of traditional societies adopting the exported medical logic of modern civilization without being prepared to accept the consequences. It is the story of how Joyce and her people are using the childbirth issue to realize their coming of age.

Within about 30 years, the Inuit went from a nomadic life-style and birth in isolation, confined to family, to birth in a settlement at a nursing station, to birth under the control of physicians in hospitals in southern Canadian cities.

Some southern women in southern Canadian cities feel overwhelmed with alternatives in childbirth. Yet, some who have special needs recognize that even where midwives, doctors, and a variety of birth settings are offered, protocols place restrictions on choices. Meanwhile, for the Inuit, debates over choices have never been possible because choices have never really been available. Before northern women had access to hospitals they had no choice but to give birth without modern assistance. Now they have the mandate of using the southern medical system whether they want it or not.

The following pages will cover: traditional pregnancy and childbirth in the North; how and why it has changed; what the results are; and what directions might be taken in the future.

Traditional Pregnancy and Childbirth

Rituals and traditions concerning the "correct" way of doing things varied from region to region in northern Canada, but, throughout, common threads can be found. From 1985 to 1989 the author conducted interviews with elders and women representing regions from the Northwest Territories to Labrador. The following is a synopsis of the wealth of knowledge received. The reader should understand, however, that the print form does not do justice to the attitudes and enlightenment of the Inuit.

Before settlements were established, women of the North were dependent on available members of their nomadic family to assist at the births of their children; sometimes it was an older daughter or another relative, but usually it was the husband. Then, as settlements began to be established, when there was enough of a community of women to draw on, midwifery began to be more developed. Certain women, who were considered more experienced and capable, were turned to for their help. Younger women would attend births and learn from the elders. It was considered a great honour to be one of the younger women selected to fill the role. The older women provided pregnant women with advice on how to have a normal labour, and on how to keep their babies healthy. Birth was connected to the family, community, nature, and the land.

Learning about Menstruation and Birth
Sometimes the facts of life were passed on to daughters through the mother, but often, the mother would ask another mother or a grandmother to tell her daughter. Some stated that it seemed too intimate a ritual not to have someone else do the explaining; often women said their mothers were just too shy. Sometimes the woman who told a young woman about life cycles was the same person who later attended her birth.

Among the traditional ways of dealing with blood flow was the use of *aqayaq* [algae] as a sanitary napkin. To relieve cramps, and sometimes to bring on a period, heated sand was applied to the abdomen.

Pre-natal Care
The young pregnant woman was taught to be active, not lazy. Rather than lying around in the morning, and even before taking any bannock or tea, she was to get up and go outside. She was not to be pampered, but made to work hard so that the baby would have good fortitude and be strong of character. The woman (and sometimes her husband) was not allowed to loiter in doorways or she could be in danger of having a long labour. She (and in some places, her husband) could not leave the tent or igloo bottom-end first—that could predispose her to having a breech baby.

In some areas, midwives gained enough expertise to feel the baby's position and turn it from a breech to the preferable "head first" presentation.

Raw meat was considered good food for the pregnant mother and baby. One woman said that where she lived duck was avoided because it was thought that the baby might come out with a head that was shaped like a beak. Certain plants were used in teas. One of these appears to be in the same family as the red raspberry, a plant used by women universally for strengthening the uterus and easing labour.

The Birth
Births took place in tents or igloos; however, should a woman be accompanying men on the hunt, she would simply stop wherever she was to have the baby. She would not think of a "good location" as one where "better" help was available, but as one where she would feel comfortable. One woman talks about a frozen lake as being an especially exhilarating location, an environment in which she did best, as long as she had her *ulu* [knife] to cut the cord.

Midwives considered their knowledge important and women heeded their advice. The positions taken for labour varied from region to region, and the "right position" seemed to be important. One midwife felt that it was very important that the mother's birth position be symmetrical, (i.e., if she was kneeling, her knees should be placed evenly apart, not one extended farther forward or back). This precaution would ensure that the baby would come out in a good position. Large blocks of snow or wood were used by some to lean on when in a kneeling position. Others grasped two poles stuck in the ground. Others had someone stand behind to support them. Some lay down on their backs, but that seems to have been rare.

In prolonged labours, some thought that in the end it would be better to deliver on the back. The misfortune of having a long labour could be alleviated by holding the woman from behind and supporting her on each side.

In the memory of the elders, the births were usually quicker than they are today. Fast labours meant that the baby would be quick, not lazy throughout life. One elder who was accustomed to homebirths told me that her chief irritation in the hospital was over how much attention was paid to clocks and watches. She considered it an effective attempt to slow down her labour. One way to speed up a slow labour was to have someone run out of the igloo or tent very quickly, go around the shelter once or twice, and return.

Some believed that a baby knew its name before its parents did and that it would come out when called. Thus, everyone in the room would sit around thinking about what the name might be and shout out the different possibilities until the right one came along, at which time the baby would emerge.

If the baby did not come out after several days, the *symphysis pubis* could be cut. One woman also describes a procedure in which a nail was flattened with a hammer until it was very thin, and then used to make a slice above the pubic bone—a hole for the baby to come out. When I gasped and asked whether it was then sewn up, she said, "Of course...we wouldn't leave it open!" She was very matter-of-fact about this traditional Caesarean.

Comfort measures were not emphasized. Some women remember how cold it was. Others say that it could get quite warm in the igloos with seal oil lamps. Animal skins were laid over twigs bound together to create a warm floor. Massage is not a topic with which women seem familiar. Since most talk about giving birth with their coats on, my assumption is that massage wasn't done because no one would think to expose any area that didn't need to be. Sometimes a flat piece of wood wrapped in cloth was placed on the lower back for pressure.

I've not done well in finding out about the presence of children at births. But, I do know that many Inuit find it funny that southern women express concern that children will be afraid of the blood at a birth. Animal remains outside and at house entrances make blood an everyday part of a child's life in the North.

The Baby

In some areas it was thought that if the woman pushed hard, she would have a boy. On more than one occasion, if a boy was born, the midwife would reach down and cup his penis in her hands so it wouldn't go away. If this was not done it was feared that the baby would turn into a girl. No comment.

The umbilical cord was tied with caribou sinew. Whoever cut the cord became a very special person in the child's life. A male child would give that person his first catch when he became a hunter. A female child would give the person the first thing that she sewed or the first seal bladder that she extracted.

Babies were given fresh meat immediately after birth to make sure that they would have a taste for it and to make them strong. Babies were, and still are, breast-fed. The notion that supplements are better than mother's milk did not influence northern communities as extensively as it did the southern Indian bands. It was considered important for the mother to know when the baby was going to urinate so she could take the baby out from her hood. Diapers were not used.

The Placenta

To help expel a difficult placenta, a wad of grass was put at the back of the mother's mouth. The force of her vomiting at one end would dislodge and expel the placenta at the other. Sometimes the placenta was buried and rocks placed on top. There was a fear that if the dogs got it they would acquire an interest in human meat.

Postpartum

The elders do not recall the prevalence of postpartum haemorrhage that exists today. One reason suggested for this is that with the introduction of cooked meat and refined western food, the Vitamin C in raw meat, necessary to assimilate the iron in the body, is no longer a major part of the diet. Teas and prayer were used to handle haemorrhaging. One woman describes a prayer that was being conducted out loud for a woman who was going into shock as a result of a haemorrhage: "The mother heard our prayers and started to say them with us and she started to regain consciousness."

The Spiritual Aspects of the Birth

The act of birth is without question a spiritual experience. Inuit women would never assume they were bringing a child into the world alone, without a guiding spirit. Yet, since the spiritual aspect of a birth is not always able to be expressed in words, or learned without experiencing it, it is one aspect of Inuit birth knowledge that cannot simply be "taught" or passed on.

A few midwives today remember working with shamans. One very old woman in Spence Bay recalled that the shaman stood outside while she was inside with the woman. The history of fear associated with the shamans, the condemnation of their practice in Christian churches, and the fading of memories makes it difficult to find out about them.

How and Why Obstetric Care Changed in the North

Because the entrance of a human being into the world is such a significant event, birth in any society becomes burdened with issues of power and control. In traditional cultures the birth process is an integral part of the social and spiritual order. In modern societies, perinatal, maternal, and infant mortality are often quoted by public health administrators as parameters for judging community health standards. Who is in charge and who tries to take charge are political and emotional questions dependent on how communities evolve.

In the North, the change, within a few decades, to an obstetric system which evacuates virtually all pregnant women from their settlements, weeks before their due date, has not been without opposition. The rationale behind the shift has been described as an effort by the medical community and government to lower perinatal, infant mortality and infant morbidity rates, and the discovery by obstetricians of the need for more rigorous definition of what constitutes risk in childbirth. Yet reliable scientific data to support this rationale has been hard to obtain. The epidemiology (scientific patterns) in retrospect has been questionable or unavailable.

Other perspectives are required to understand how a transition which denies the fundamental beliefs and principles of Inuit could be made so easily and rapidly. The transition can be understood partially in terms of global changes in health and obstetric care. Clinical practice and acute care still wield great control in spite of efforts of health promotion groups in the World Health Organization (WHO) and Health and Welfare Canada to move toward a preventative, self care, and community approach to health. There has been a world-wide shift from childbirth as a female-centred act to a male-controlled one. The control of obstetric and general health care in the North is another example of the extension of white colonialism that exists in the North and developing countries. The struggle to institute the profession of midwifery is being reopened in Canada and other countries. In short, what is occurring in Canada's North is not without precedent elsewhere in the world. The difference lies not so much in the changes themselves but in the speed, completeness, and power with which they are enforced in the North.

Annual reports on health in the Northwest Territories state that 65.9 per cent of Inuit births occurred outside hospitals and nursing stations in 1965; the number had fallen to 14 per cent by 1969,[1] and continued to drop to almost zero in the following decade. The federal Medical Services Branch could not remove the licences of the Inuit elders who practised midwifery because no one had ever given them any in the first place. Ottawa had never trained the elders or had jurisdiction over their practices. However, the introduction of nursing station births and the increasingly frequent hospital confinements gradually drew the women away from Inuit birth settings, Inuit care-givers as primary practitioners, the Inuit language as the primary language to describe the progress of the birth, and the Inuit community as the social structure to provide normal Inuit relationships. It is ironic, sad, and embarrassing that Inuit have lost control over issues concerning their health in a country which is considered a leader in health promotion.

Joyce may not have studied the philosophy of health care, but she knows on an instinctive level and from her elders that birth is a normal process. She has seen firsthand the change in obstetrics in her lifetime and knows that something is lacking in the new medical approach.

Birth as the Domain of Women

In other cultures, especially matriarchal societies, birth is historically seen as a function of women, to be attended only by women. Even within the North American tradition, men did not enter into the birthing process until recently. Inuit culture, however, has traditionally been conducive to allowing males to be at births; in a nomadic society sometimes the only adult around to catch the baby (other than the mother) was the father. One of the most articulate and experienced midwives still living is a man from the James Bay area.

It's hard to tell whether the coming of the white man simply increased the need for someone else to be in charge, or increased concerns about following some assumptions about etiquette. A woman in Spence Bay, describing one of the first births that she attended when she moved to the settlement, explains that the first person who was called was the Bay manager—a man, of course, and a symbol of responsibility and authority. Was he called because they thought that he thought that he should be called, because important people should be at such an event, or because they genuinely thought that he knew what to do better than the community people?

It is important to put into perspective the seemingly acquiescent mentality of Inuit women allowing their births to be carried out by men. Rites of passage seemed still to be woman-controlled and woman-centred with the male being used as a helper rather than as someone whom power was relinquished. Meanwhile, I often wonder whether or not the ease with which evacuation was implemented had something to do with the fact that birth is a female act. Had it been the men who were told that their hunting grounds would now be changed to a small game reserve or the Winnipeg Zoo, the reaction might have been more immediate than it was for the change of birthing place for women.

For Joyce, exposing herself to a man other than her husband at an intimate event (not to mention other people she wouldn't know) made her anxious and afraid that she wouldn't open enough to allow the baby to come out.

Canadian Political Structures and Northern Health Care Perspectives

"The medicalization of child birth in the North is one dimension of the extension of southern power into northern Canada and the relationship between illness and colonialism."[2] One could put this another way: a woman's birth experience is a "microcosm of the politics of Inuit relationships with Western medical institutions and the larger Canadian society."[3]

The Northern Health Research Unit of the Department of Community Health Sciences at the University of Manitoba has conducted research on this issue. They explain how personal feelings of alienation during confinement in southern hospitals reflect the macro-political struggle against the system of internal colonialism that has characterized northern Canada:

> Inuit sought explanations for illness and misfortune in terms of the individual's relationship with his physical, social and spiritual environment. These explanations were both sociological and historical in the sense that misfortune brought about a critical examination of the social order. The healer's role was to facilitate this examination and assist in the construction of new social understandings. The ideology that validated the healer's role and activities emerged through community consensus rather than being imposed to support the interests of the dominant elite. With the arrival of missionaries and fur traders in most parts of the Canadian Arctic in the 1940s and 50s, illness and health emerged as commodities which could be traded for the spiritual and economic loyalties of the Inuit. [4]

An example of the coerciveness with which this could be done is provided in the history of Labrador, where Joyce comes from. It has been said that the Moravians selectively withheld medical assistance when members of the surrounding Inuit communities where slow to convert.[5]

As in other colonized parts of the world, whether there was coercion or not, a sense of obligation was felt toward those who treated illness and provided food, clothing, and supplies. There was also an element of belief, whether confused, dictated, or genuine, that God was providing a better way. Whatever the motivation for change, the white assistance altered the standard of living and, along with it, the spiritual, social, and moral direction of the Inuit. Although the white man's religion had its own series of codes to follow, illness and well-being were allowed to be a more secular affair.

Drs Pat Kaufert and John O'Neil comment on this shift away from moral and spiritual responsibility for health and disease, boldly stating that, "Less attention was paid to the maintenance of Inuit personal codes for social behaviour" as a means to achieve well-being:

> Formal western medicine was introduced in the Canadian North in the 1950s when physicians began to accompany the various ships supplying the missions and trading posts scattered across the Arctic coast. (Brett, 1969). The standard response to infectious disease epidemics such as tuberculosis was to remove infected individuals from their communities and relocate them to southern hospitals and sanatoria for extended periods of time. Other options such as encouraging the population to redistribute itself into smaller traditional groups were

sometimes proposed by field staff, but were rejected by southern authorities (Lee, 1975; Graham-Cumming, 1969). By separating survivors from their families and dependents, the health care system exacerbated the social damage already incurred as a result of these epidemics of infectious disease and the accompanying high levels of mortality. (Hodgson, 1982)[6]

Thus, say Kaufert and O'Neil, the government took control of medical care with implicit authority to disrupt the traditional family and social organization in the name of improved health. Sickness no longer presented a time during which one reflected with the traditional healer on how to increase one's harmony with nature and society. It was now a threat to life and the social order.

The stage was set for turning birth—traditionally a social, cultural, and spiritual act—into a medical act. The Inuit rituals of what and how to eat during pregnancy are reflections of the larger belief system that birth is an integral part of life and illness. Childbirth is not intellectually considered a disease even outside traditional societies. Yet, the acuteness of the event allows medicine to acquire a feeling of ownership over it; and, once birth is categorized as dangerous, it is difficult for the government to assume that any body, other than the medical one, could possibly deal with the awesome responsibility involved. Parallel to that sentiment is the low self-esteem of Inuit resulting from colonial attitudes about other aspects of health care. One Inuit politician stated that in other areas of business, art, and education, the Inuit feel that they can take over. But the mystique of medical knowledge and technique is a difficult hurdle.

Joyce recognized the expertise of the white colonial medical system, but wasn't prepared to trust it or her ability to function in it. As a child she had accidentally been sent by plane to a hospital for an ear operation. Either from barriers of language or lack of assertiveness, neither she nor her mother were able to communicate that it was her brother—not her—who should have been sent for the operation.

The Northern Approach Set in the
Context of Development of Midwifery in Canada
The nurse-midwives of the Northwest Territories have always been a curious enigma in our country, in that Canada is the only developed nation in the WHO that fails to officially recognize midwifery. "Each of the provinces of Canada has legislation which gives monopoly over childbirth to physicians. The Medical Services Branch is a federal government agency and outside provincial jurisdiction. Even so, the use of midwives went unchallenged by the medical profession, only because of the special conditions of the North. There was no change in the official attitudes of the profession towards midwifery."[7]

Of special interest in considering the future of the North is the research and commentary done by the Task Force on the Implementation of Midwifery in Ontario on various countries that have midwifery as an integral part of the health care system. The Netherlands and Denmark, where midwifery is a profession with its own college, distinct from the nursing and medical professions, are both viewed as countries with systems to emulate. The United States is considered "undesirable". Much of the criticism there is directed at the creation of the practitioner called the "nurse-midwife" and at failure of the legislation to recognize or regulate the midwives that are not nurse-midwives under a separate statutory regime.[8]

The Historical Details of How the Transition Took Place
There are various reasons why evacuation of pregnant women became a northern routine. The following are the details of the transition of Inuit homebirths in the North to those in hospitals in the South.

It is in vain that one searches for a definitive policy statement from the Medical Services Branch directing the evacuation of all women out of the North for their births. The history of evacuation has been an evolution of practice rather than the result of an official written directive. The following steps engineered the process.

1. The first step was the transfer of births out of the local setting and into the nursing station:
Through their training, professional ties, and ideology, the nurse-midwives (predominantly British) brought governmental and medical institutions into the communities. The nursing station was government territory and the nurse a government employee. As such, she held a position in a hierarchy which included physicians and administrators working in northern health care and which stretched from the nursing stations to Ottawa. Nurses had to accept and implement directives from higher up the system rather than respond to the demands of the community in which they were working.[9]

Drs Kaufert and O'Neil explain that nurses were expected to adopt a public health perspective which relied on personal knowledge of individuals and families. This knowledge was often constructed historically, with labels of "good" and "bad" based on assessments of personal hygiene, morality, and industriousness. They further suggest that, in not understanding Inuit culture, nurses tended to devalue women's roles and functions. Nurses had a high turnover rate, making it difficult for relationships to develop or for nurses to develop broader perspectives.[10]

I have noticed that when one interviews white people involved in the transition to the nursing station, there is a sentiment that it made sense because it was less crowded and cleaner. When one interviews Inuit, it is apparent that they do not view those factors as real problems. Besides, speaking the white man's logic of avoiding pathogens, the nursing station is the place to avoid, since it generally treats disease, and no doubt where all the sick members of the community and their germs congregate.

2. The next step was out of the nursing station and into the hospital:
The criterion for deciding eligibility for birth in a nursing station in the 1970s was a relatively informal assessment of the likelihood that birth complications might develop. With slight variations, the following statement was included in each of the annual reports from 1969 to 1977 (italics added): "We have continued the policy that sees all primigravida and grand multiparae (fifth or subsequent infants) evacuated to a hospital for delivery as are all complicated pregnancies or anticipated complications. Provided no complications ensued at the birth of the first infant or *if all else is well*, second, third or fourth babies are delivered at the nursing stations.[11]

The criteria for evacuation were not officially changed throughout the 1970s. A gradual and steady decline in the number of nursing-station births that occurred throughout this period was rather the result of a subjective and more strict interpretation of what was deemed "well". "By the early 1980s, official policy was against any births taking place in the nursing stations."[12] Kaufert and O'Neil point out that better communication systems and transportation allowed the nurse to have more contact and, subsequently, more reliance on outside forces. The midwives had only the women and community support to keep births in the community.

The degree of compliance by the women to leave the settlements varied depending on each woman's personality and the nature of the community. It appears that the appeal was stronger in some areas than others. Whereas some women felt that they needed to comply to keep good relations with the nurse, a number of women have told me they thought that not taking the plane would constitute a criminal act. They thought they would be arrested if they refused to go.

There is a legitimate fear on the part of the physicians and nurses who deal with emergencies in isolated settings. This, coupled with the fear of liability and damage to reputation and relationships should complications arise, is an imposing threat that encourages evacuation.

It's a tight-rope walk to please a community of Inuit who don't like evacuation but who have begun to expect a certain quality of health care. The question among white medical practitioners is, "Will Inuit be able to return to their traditional attitudes of acceptance even when something goes wrong?" Some white practitioners have expressed the fear that southern lawyers are going to start emerging to defend the Inuit against white mistakes made in the settlements. Furthermore, health care providers often feel that Inuit hold them responsible, not only for implementing, but for creating the policies, while the health care givers may not necessarily agree with them themselves. There has been an attitude on the part of non-Inuit that Inuit are not capable of taking responsibility because they have not taken enough initiatives until now to learn on their own. Unfortunately, colonial ideas die hard and confuse assumptions about who is being oppressed. One such example mentioned by Kaufert and O'Neil is indicative of this problem:

Clearly the struggle by Inuit for control over childbirth and the struggle for midwifery in Canada have much in common. We suggest that until northern nurses (midwives) and Inuit see themselves as victims of the same institutional and historical process, the trend toward medicalization of childbirth, and health in general, will continue to occur.[13]

Fortunately, conferences like the Northern Obstetrics Conference in Churchill, Manitoba in 1986 are now sensitizing nurses and administrators alike to the needs of the community, to the uniqueness of Inuit culture, and to the broader issues of midwifery in Canada. In some communities, the nurses can become the champions and allies of the rights of patients to make their own choices about the place and attendants at birth.

The Results of Evacuation

As the health care system in North America is almost totally oriented toward disease management, there is a strong tendency to look at birth not as a series of normal processes but as a series of risks. The pregnant woman is often treated as a person guilty of risk factors until proven innocent instead of the other way around. What's more, our system tends to focus only on medical or clinical factors and, periodically, epidemiological factors, as risks. The personal, cultural, political, and economic factors are not often recognized as factors posing serious threats.

Decisions about evacuation are made in a highly emotional and political milieu in which there is a battle over which party will control birth. Proponents of keeping birth in the settlements accuse those who favour evacuation of using clinical reasoning at the expense of personal, cultural, and spiritual factors. The proponents of evacuation accuse those who want to stay in the settlements of not being aware of the clinical risks.

Ironically, both sides accuse each other of not using scientific logic, and probably both are right. The medical practitioner often presents his/her case as if it is scientific evidence when it is, in fact, only clinical, based on case studies. The elders present the changes that they have seen, such as increased haemorrhage and a greater number of stillborn babies as compared with the old days, as evidence that something isn't being done correctly today. The elders' historical evidence shouldn't be seen as any more or less scientific than the physicians' clinical experience. At the same time, the elders shouldn't attribute present-day obstetric problems to clinical factors or to medical practitioners, since many problems are a result of life-style and environmental changes. Likewise, the medical profession should not feel obligated to take full responsibility for pregnancy and birth, since many pre-natal influences are beyond the practitioner's control. Often these are more favourably dealt with if they are understood not to be in the physician's jurisdiction.

Sometimes political philosophy is the real rationale used to shape decisions whereas both parties are under the illusion that the information presented is based on scientific rationale.

Joyce was told by a physician that if she had her baby at home it might die. Some medical practitioners are a little more subtle than that: "What will happen if the baby doesn't breathe?" or "The baby might get hypoxic." Such statements usually achieve the desired effect. First, the lay person assumes that the physician's facts are scientifically based, when, in fact, the evidence is not even clinically conclusive, let alone statistically valid. Very few doctors have even seen homebirths, don't know how babies are resuscitated at home, and somehow assume that they can't be. Resuscitation equipment is standard at homebirths today. The next assumption is that, if the baby didn't make it at home, it would in the hospital. Bereavement associations are filled with parents who assumed that modern medicine could work miracles on babies that simply were not able to live.

When the baby scare didn't work, the physician tried postpartum haemorrhage. He told Joyce that she might bleed to death. Again, the assumption was that midwives or the nursing station staff wouldn't be capable of giving intravenous solutions, the treatment used most commonly in hospitals for haemorrhage. This is a genuine concern and one not to be taken lightly should the rare event of a ruptured uterus occur. However, the use of oxytocin to artificially induce or augment labour is often what causes the ruptured uterus. It is seldom used, if at all, in outpost centres. When extensive research is done, it might show that a mother is less likely to die from a postpartum haemorrhage than from an accident on a prophylactic plane ride in or out of her settlement.

Joyce's fear of the hospital was based on "stories" of intervention. She had her own misconceptions, comparable to the doctor's hearsay fears of homebirth. In the end, Joyce made a decision based on her own personal and cultural values, hearsay case studies, and good scientific logic based on her study of the literature on the safety of homebirths. She used no economic logic whatsoever. She had to pay me and pay to get to me.

Clinical Results of Evacuation

The clinical scenario which everyone fears when births take place in the settlements is graphic and real: the mother's uterus ruptures and she bleeds to death on the Medevac plane. When pregnant women are transferred to hospitals in Iqaluit or Yellowknife, they have access to operative procedures. They also have the benefit of an experienced surgeon and medical staff who can, at least, attempt the repair of a ruptured uterus and can competently perform a Caesarean. These operations would be severely compromised if attempted at a nursing station.

When, however, women are transferred to a place like Churchill, there is little extra in the way of technology compared to the nursing station, since Caesarean sections are not available there. The benefit of moving to a hospital like Churchill would be access to the blood bank and medical staff. None the less, it is less traumatic to cross-match the woman's blood and send it ahead of time to the nursing station than to send the mother to Churchill. Experienced northern health practitioners, such as Dr Brian Postl, also caution the assumption that one will always have better qualified people in a hospital. A qualified midwife's experience might be superior to that of a general practitioner. Many physicians in the North are there to get experience shortly after medical school. They have been trained in hospitals where specialists were available to handle difficult cases, and where allowing births to take their natural course was not necessarily considered a priority. The question here is, why suffer the trauma of transfer if the place to which one is being transferred has little more than the nursing station, except, perhaps, the mystique of being a hospital?

The fear of death from haemorrhage can be juxtaposed with the fear of the hospital: the woman is anxious to get back home and the doctor suggests that, since she's a few days overdue, he can help her along by rupturing the membranes. The procedure to initiate labour doesn't work, and so, concerned that she might have ruptured membranes longer than 24 hours, at which time risk of infection goes up and a Caesarean is considered appropriate, he gives her pitocin to put her into labour. This works so well that she finds the contractions a little too intense, and, if she is in Winnipeg or Montreal, she wonders if there is something for the pain. She gets an epidural, a king of anaesthetics, that numbs her from the waist down, but then she cannot get into a vertical position when it comes to pushing out the baby (if that would have been allowed) and needs forceps and an episiotomy for delivery. All of this puts her at greater risk for postpartum haemorrhage. Or, she has a Caesarean, which is assumed to save her baby, but results in more respiratory distress than if the baby had come vaginally. Fortunately, this scenario occurs much less frequently in northern hospitals, such as in Iqaluit and Churchill, than in southern ones. (Maybe there are some advantages to using Churchill over the tertiary-care settings.)

The personal trauma of evacuation can also be manifested in clinical symptoms. For example, high stress levels can aggravate diabetes and toxaemia, two of the most dangerous conditions related to pregnancy, especially in the last two months when women are already suffering the stress of anticipating and experiencing evacuation. (This is discussed in more detail below).

Another possible result of evacuation is a change in exercise and nutrition. Women complain of being in a strange environment with strange food. It's also possible that they are not eating well because of lack of appetite or, that in the new environment, some women might be eating better than they would in their own community. Opportunity for exercise is usually decreased in a city location where natural activities such as hunting and fishing are not routine. Reports from Povungnituk suggest that women who were evacuated tended to increase smoking and gain easier access to drugs and alcohol.

Epidemiological Results of Evacuation
A good panorama of Inuit birth epidemiology is offered by Drs Lessard and Kinloch:

There are over 18,000 Inuit in the Northwest Territories. As a group they have the highest birth rate, the lowest cesarean section rate, and one of the highest perinatal death rates in Canada....Our experience is consistent with that documented in earlier reviews, which concluded that Inuit women tend to have efficient uterine action to endure labour well and to rarely have dystocia (difficult labour that impedes progress).[14]

If a woman in the North stays in her settlement to have her birth, whether she is at home or in the nursing station, what is essentially being provided in terms of facilities, is a homebirth. It is, therefore, important to understand that the safety of homebirths, a closing book until a few years ago, has reopened with an increasingly better understanding of epidemiology. Everyone from the Ontario task force to the international epidemiologists, such as those at Oxford and WHO, have rallied to undo misconceptions of the past and openly state the case for the safety of homebirths.[15] Meanwhile, the Northern Obstetrics Conference exposed faulty epidemiologic logic that contributes to assumptions that evacuation is "safer". Faulty scientific rationale on which to base such a move means that childbirth in the settlements is being considered once again.

Personal and Cultural Results of Evacuation

1) Implications for the Mother
Originally, evacuation was done seasonally, when the ice broke up in spring, and before the ice froze over in late summer. Now, women are transported to southern hospitals for periods ranging from two weeks to two months prior to delivery. In some areas, hostels are provided where pregnant Inuit women can find support from each other. In other areas, women are billeted with families. These families may be Inuit with similar foods and life-styles as the women, or they may be white. All accounts suggest that when the women are away from home they complain of loneliness, boredom, anxiety, fear, and lack of control and direction. Studies indicate that support reduces levels of stress and anxiety.[16] Levels of maternal anxiety have been associated with higher levels of pain and an increased need for analgesia by the woman during childbirth. Stress contributes to abnormalities during pregnancy, worse birth outcomes, and premature labour.[17]

Midwives working in hospitals around the world often find that mothers in labour in hospitals are anxious about their children left at home ten to 20 minutes from them. Not only are Inuit separated over a longer distance, but they are also separated during the most stressful part of their pregnancy, as well as during the labour and birth, with little or no chance of returning home. To be separated from one's husband at the time of delivery would not be tolerated today in the South. This is especially true with the general acceptance of the husband's presence at the birth. Inuit women are not only separated from husbands, but sometimes from toddlers who are still nursing at the time the mother has to leave the settlement for delivery of the next baby.

Perhaps the greatest personal risk posed by evacuation is the woman's loss of control over her own experience. Childbirth is easily viewed as an unknown, fearful experience. Added to that is the forced evacuation to unknown surroundings with unfamiliar practitioners wielding unknown, invasive instruments. This may establish a feeling of violation and subsequent denial of the experience. My greatest fear as a midwife is that women's interests and feelings of responsibility for their own health care is being co-opted. One young woman told me that the nurse was in charge of the pregnancy.

One of the dangerous results of sending everyone out for what is still considered, culturally, to be a normal process is that those cases that may really be at risk are not seen in the proper perspective. Teenagers, too fearful to leave, who have had poor nutrition and other life-style problems, or grand multiparae who have had problems with haemorrhage in the past, may be among those least likely to be compliant. The seriousness of their situation is clouded by their justified distrust that all pregnant women need to be sent out. They may not be convinced that in their situation it may really be true.

2) Implications for the Family

While anxieties are created in the woman about to deliver, other anxieties are created back home with the children missing their mothers and not always getting the attention they need. More stress is placed on fathers and extended families. There has been increasing focus on the possibility that concern over health of the pregnant woman has created health and social problems for other members of the family. The Keewatin research, the Povungnituk testimonies, and my own research all present evidence that women feel that behavioural changes in family members can have long-lasting effects on the unity of the family. Transcripts of meetings done in the Keewatin give a good account of such family problems. Young children develop problems such as bed-wetting or violent behaviour, problems which may be exacerbated when the mother returns with a new sibling, and teenage daughters get into trouble without their mothers' supervision; rifts between mothers and daughters can last for a long time afterwards.[18] Paediatric literature implicates stress as a precipitating factor in a number of childhood illnesses.[19]

Women worry about changing patterns affecting their relationships with their husbands and marriage. The Keewatin research states that husbands who are not accustomed to taking care of the children find child care and housekeeping difficult. Sometimes they have to take the very young children with them on the hunt or into the machine shop.[20] The extended family sometimes comes to the aid of the husband, but care of children in the extended family can be more formal, less intimate, and less attentive.[21]

106

In the Northwest Territories, the mother is often the bread-winner. Without her income, there is severe family financial strain. If the man does work, he might lose his job if he has to stay home to take care of sick children. Job security in the Northwest Territories, where there are only so many jobs available and unemployment so high, is a very important issue.[22]

People in Povungnituk talk about the concern that men were losing their understanding of the birthing process before their maternity centre was established. The studies in Keewatin came to the conclusion that families now endure childbirth instead of enjoying it. I would add that they now tolerate it instead of orchestrating it.

3) Community and Cultural Implications

Annie Okalik laughed hysterically at me when we first met. To think that I could be any kind of midwife having had only two children myself! In the North, as in any traditional society, a midwife is evaluated not just on the amount of knowledge and years of experience, but on the number of babies that she, herself, has had. This notion would have first been challenged when single nurses came to the settlements.

There is concern at the loss of traditional Inuit knowledge and competence. The older women can't tell the younger women "what it will be like" any more, because they don't know the intentions of the hospital staff.

The relationships that bonded people together are being broken. The pride of assisting at a birth, of telling birth stories, of sharing pregnancy and childbirth knowledge are an integral part of a woman's life done in her own unique way. Kaufert and O'Neil go so far as to say that this kind of activity is a woman's prerogative. They point out that when one's role is taken away there is a question of one's worth. Relationships are developed during the birthing process. The lesson of receiving help when in need, and having the pleasure of returning it when the neighbour or sister had her baby, used to emphasize the values of generosity and mutual interdependence that were vital to Inuit personal and cultural survival. Who wants to take the reward of his first hunt to a doctor in Montreal? Thus one can see that the normal roles played by children, young women and men, husbands, grandmothers, grandfathers, and midwives are changing.

The southern experience suggests that it takes just one generation of women forced to hand over control of their birth to create an entire generation which believes that relinquishing almost all responsibility for the process is normal. However, although young women in the South now complacently hand over control of their birth to someone else, Inuit women are not as far removed from their ancestral wisdom about birth.

None of the Inuit women interviewed to date by this author has expressed a preference for hospital birth. All who had both home and hospital experiences contrasted the artificial methods in the hospital to the ease and naturalness of "letting things happen" in the settlement.

The literature on the Povungnituk Maternity and the Northern Health Research Unit confirms this prevailing distaste for the medical approach. Usually the natural way is called the "Inuit" way whereas the medical approach is the "unnatural" or "white man's" way, an interesting commentary on the state of northern/southern affairs. Criticisms are directed at the artificial speeding up and slowing down of the labour, at the forced position on the back, at the impersonal nature of the treatment, and at the the feeling of being on an assembly line.

Political Results of Evacuation

To the nurse in the nursing station, evacuation means that she will not be held liable for anything that goes wrong, a very real threat should she deliver a baby in the settlement. Nurse-midwives who challenge the system and try to fill community wishes by doing births in the settlements are generally under surveillance and at risk of losing their jobs.

For the Inuit, there is concern that evacuation adds another shackle of dependency to white colonialism. They worry that even knowledge of a basic human function has been robbed from Inuit understanding. They also recognize that the increased dependency on hospitals is contributing to an overall deterioration in the quality of primary care services at the community level.

To a people so tied to community and land, the feeling of belonging dates back to where one started, where one is born. If you're born in Igloolik and move to Iqaluit and spend most of your life there, you're still from Igloolik. Some fear that land claims will not be honoured by the federal government for those born outside of the Northwest Territories. On a more profound level, however, the Northern Health Research Unit identified concern over the integrity of an individual born so far from home, outside Nunavut ("Our Land"); there seems to be a risk, not just of having Inuit rights denied, but of losing Inuit identity.

The constructive political result of evacuation has been a mobilization of forces in active resistance against it. Political parties have taken platforms on it. The Inuit Women's Association called in midwives from various backgrounds to form a panel at its annual general meeting in Igloolik in 1985, and there have been resolutions drawn up on evacuation at every annual meeting since. With an increase in the number of women represented in other Inuit organizations, and the restructuring of community health committees to reflect the emerging politicization of health as a women's issue, health and health care are now part of the move toward self-determination and cultural renewal:

> It is not surprising that child birth has emerged as a symbol for these efforts. In the broader societal context, public efforts to de-medicalize the birth process are in the vanguard of an historical and ideological shift towards greater public accountability and responsibility and less professional control over health resources and decision-making. In this context, midwifery has become a symbol for a more consumer-oriented health care system....It is not only the nurse-midwife but the traditional Inuit midwife whom many would like to see return.[23]

Economic Results of Evacuation

These have not been systematically tackled yet, but some question the expense of every pregnant woman being flown out, billeted, and hospitalized. According to the Povungnituk figures, a savings of about $100,000 per year on transportation alone was expected. Money for evacuation has not been transferred to the new Northwest Territories Department of Health. It remains an Ottawa responsibility.

The sapping of family resources is a big issue with the father missing hunting and working, and the mother's income gone. Sometimes the families try to unite at their own expense at the time of the birth.

Another economic consideration for the future will be liability insurance should births return to the settlements.

The Future

> Self-development is a fundamental part of the health promotion process....It is impossible to produce health among the powerless unless they are given tools, authority, budget and income.[24]

Although this may sound like a directive written specifically for the North, it was one given by the International Conference on Health Promotion to health ministers the world over.

The birth challenge is just one of many health issues in the North, including epidemics of alcoholism, family violence, and substance abuse, that require community initiatives. Time will tell whether the recent transfer of health jurisdiction from the Medical Services Branch (a symbol of white colonialism) to the Government of the Northwest Territories will result in necessary changes. Significant change will require that people from both the South and the North employ alternative models of health care.

Research

It is of obvious concern that future decisions be made by the communities. Participatory research is essential for any credible undertaking in the North. Research is now under way at many levels. The Inuit Women's Association and the Native Women's Association are undertaking projects to gather and retain the material on traditional births that is scattered and in danger of extinction. While this information is valuable from historical and clinical standpoints, it is also important to determine which of the traditional practices are compatible with current care.

In each community the involvement of the younger women in gathering the stories and information from the elders has been considered crucial. Both Lesley Paulette and I have noticed that much of the information we are gathering is new to the women we are using as translators, even when they are the very daughters of the elders being interviewed.

The Northern Health Research Unit has undertaken several projects in the Keewatin: a retrospective review of obstetric records for the Keewatin from 1979-1986; a prospective study of the impact of evacuation on women and their families; and a study of the ethnography of childbirth in Inuit culture.[25] It also looks forward to examining the statistics not just of pre-settlement but of pre-contact days before whites brought a refined food diet to the North, and when Inuit spent more time on the land. Also on the horizon is the possible investigation of increased risk of delivery en route and the simple risk of plane travel, which Postl speculates may exceed maternal deaths in nursing stations. He also suggests increased risks of hospital births be studied.

The analysis of obstetric risk and normalcy is not complete and may never be. Many are waiting patiently, hoping that the studies done by groups such as the Northern Health Research Unit will be conclusive on what steps should be taken for obstetrics in the North. There are a number of challenges that suggest that those decisions may never be definitive and will vary in interpretation from individual to individual and from community to community.

Future Alternative Initiatives: The Case of Povungnituk
Debates are now under way in many regions for a birthing centre approach or for a return to the nursing station plan with midwives. The Keewatin area is the most advanced in terms of research into the problem, but Povungnituk in Northern Québec is farthest ahead in doing something about it. The experience there is an example of how one community chose to take responsibility for themselves and provide care with a blend of old and new methods. They caution, however, that their experience should not necessarily be directly copied by other communities, since each community is unique and needs to develop its own system.

Why Povungnituk?
The Innuulisivik Maternity officially opened in Povungnituk in September 1986. How was Povungnituk able to bring birth back to the settlement when no other northern community so far has been able to resist what seemed like an inevitable tide—complete evacuation of all pregnant women?

Community leaders suggest that Povungnituk has a history of self-determination and that its people don't let things "get by...we ask questions."[26] It was in Povungnituk that one of the first co-operatives was established, a store run by Inuit, tackling the formidable competition of the Hudson's Bay Company. Povungnituk was also one of the three communities that refused to sign the James Bay and Northern Québec Agreement, to "sell for beads the heritage that is rightly ours."[27] It took a strong community to keep births in their settlements and accept the clinical risks involved in being eight hours away from a hospital that has facilities for surgery and anaesthesia.

From the beginning, there was public protest and lobbying over the obstetric evacuation issue. Povungnituk radio shows, in the early 1980s, discussed the problems of women being flown out. Two women were sent from a developing women's group in Povungnituk to the Inuit Women's Association meeting in Igloolik in 1985, where the first resolutions were made about reclaiming childbirth.

When it appeared that a hospital was to be established in Povungnituk, the POV Native Women's Association decided to propose the incorporation of a maternity practice aimed at meeting the specific demands of the population within its jurisdiction. The community was fortunate to have a sympathetic doctor, Jean François Proulx, who hoped that the *qablunnaaq* would be able to hand over what they knew to Inuit and then leave the community. The director of the hospital board, who was not in favour of midwives working in "his" hospital, resigned and was replaced by a woman elected by the community, Aani Tulugak. This was an overwhelming task for a young woman to take on, with the intimidation that facing medical professionals presents, but she was encouraged to stay and remain firm to her vision. As well, Andre Corriveau arrived at this time. A doctor in community medicine and trained in administration, he recognized that the midwives who work in the system would need their autonomy, just like nurses, doctors, dentists, and pharmacists in the hospital, and, as such, gave midwives their own portfolio on the hospital board.

Aani and a Swiss-trained midwife, Johanne Gagnon, visited all the local villages, held public meetings, and carried out public surveys and questionnaires in an effort to determine the needs and expectations of the population, to compare the risks of having births in the North with those in the South, to establish resource people and networks, and to determine criteria for the selection of local midwives. It should be remembered that Povungnituk is in the province of Québec. The federal Medical Services Branch withdrew its control and allowed the provincial government to take over the health jurisdiction in the Hudson Bay area long before the territorial government took jurisdiction over its health care from Ottawa.

Objective
The community involvement is reflected in the Innuulisivik Maternity's philosophy and objectives. These include: bringing birth back to the North as a healthy, normal part of life rather than a medical condition; returning the primary responsibility for health to people themselves; revitalizing common knowledge about birthing and rekindling involvement in the birth process; minimizing unnecessary evacuations out of the community; improving pre-natal and post-natal health education; fostering autonomy of women in self-health care; and training local women in midwifery.[28]

The perinatal committee of the centre assures that decisions are based on community concerns and judgements. Made up of two doctors, two midwives, and two midwives-in-training, it provides a place where each case can be discussed and decisions made, such as whether or not to send a woman to a southern hospital or to keep her in the settlement. Considerations reflect Inuit concerns and statistics rather than southern ones. For example, pregnant teens are considered higher risk than the norm by southern standards, but in Povungnituk they are considered at higher risk if sent to hospitals as opposed to delivering in Povungnituk.

When the physicians of Québec categorically denied the necessity to create a new profession of midwifery, the Povungnituk maternity sent a letter to the government encouraging it to maintain its plans anyway. The Government of Québec made its announcement to implement midwifery in the very week that the physicians made their public stand (May 1989). Povungnituk had learned and boldly stated that, to a woman who is under stress of anticipated evacuation, who chain-smokes, is getting overweight, or who is toxic, you don't make exhortations to stop smoking, stop eating so much, and force her to leave her home to have her baby.

Future Alternative Relations

When the prospect of returning births to the settlements presented itself as one means to regain personal and community self-determination, the women of the North sought the alliance of groups in the South, especially practising midwives. Inuit women are learning that danger lies not in contact with other societies and communities; it is in the attitude with which the political and cultural groups relate to each other. Southerners need to learn to empower and enable without being tempted to control. Inuit need to trust themselves to take responsibility.

IN SUMMARY

Circumstances and the federal Medical Services Branch offered Inuit a system based primarily on clinical logic which they assumed was superior to the Inuit treatment of birth. The Inuit almost wholeheartedly accepted it. For the future it appears that the wisest move would be to offer an informed choice to women and provide evacuation for those who want or need it. "Available" is quite different from "forced" evacuation.

In the new public health, it is considered important to help people discover what they already know about health and illness and have it recognized and legitimized. From there, care must be taken not to develop programs that negate those findings and their natural development. And, care must be taken not to develop programs by simply exchanging one expertise (medical) for another (community development).

Questions to be asked regarding the future of northern childbirth are: Will Inuit be able to develop the important skill of choosing the best every side has to offer? Will the "civilized" modern obstetric system be able to reconsider priorities that appreciate the Inuit perception of birth in conjunction with its own? Could it be that Inuit, rather than regressing to an inferior maternity system compared to the rest of civilization, are providing us with an example of how to develop self care in our own communities of the future?

Postscript

Joyce and her husband, Jonathan, have asked me whether or not I would consider coming to do her next delivery in her Labrador settlement. Clinically, epidemiologically, personally, and culturally, that would be fine. Since I wouldn't even want to begin to tackle the bad political logic that it would represent, Labrador will have to change its policies or Joyce will have to have another birth in Ontario.

Acknowledgement

Elders who offered information on the traditional aspects of birth: Minnie Alakarialak from Resolute Bay; Mabel Angolalik from Cambridge Bay; Leetia Tookai; Annie Napayok from Whale Cove; Nipisha Lyall from Spence Bay; Enik Powuk from Eskimo Point; Lucy Amarualik from Povungnituk; Annie Okalik from Pangnirtung; other elders and women that I have met over the years through the Inuit Women's Association and through travel.

Notes

1. P.A. Kaufert, P. Gilbert, J.D. O'Neil, R. Brown, P. Brown, B. Postl, M. Moffatt, B. Binns, and L. Harris, "Obstetric Care in the Keewatin: changes in the place of birth 1971–1985", *Circumpolar Health 87*, edited by H. Linderholm, C. Backman, N. Broadbent, and I. Joelsson (Oulu, Finland: Nordic Council on Arctic Medical Research, 1988), pp. 481–484.

2. John O'Neil, Patricia A. Kaufert, "The Politics of Obstetric Care: The Inuit Experience", *Births and Power: social change and the politics of reproduction*, edited by W. Penn Handwerker (Westview Press, 1990).

3. Ibid., p. 3.

4. Ibid., pp. 6–7.

5. Ibid., p. 7.

6. Ibid., pp. 7,9.

7. Ibid., pp. 17–18.

8. Government of Ontario. *Report of the Task Force on the Implementation of Midwifery in Ontario* (Toronto: Task Force on Implementation of Midwifery, 1987), pp. 39–54.

9. Supra 2., p. 13.

10. Ibid. p. 14

11. Ibid., p. 16.

12. Ibid., p. 16.

13. John D. O'Neil, "The Politics of Health in the Fourth World: A Northern Canadian Example", *Human Organization* 215 (summer, 1986): pp. 119–128.

14. Pierre Lessard and David Kinloch, "Northern obstetrics: a 5-year review of delivery among Inuit women", *Canadian Medical Association Journal* 137 (December 1987): pp. 1017–1021.

15. Lewis E. Mehl, *et al.*, "Outcomes of Elective Home Births: A Series of 1,146 Cases", *The Journal of Reproductive Medicine* 19 (November 1977): pp. 281–290.

16. Marshall Klaus, *et al.*, "Effects of Social Support during Parturition on Maternal and Infant Morbidity", *British Medical Journal*, 293 (September 1986):pp. 585–592.

17. Patricia Kaufert, John O'Neil, Brian Postl, *The Impact of Obstetric Evacuation Policy on Inuit Women and Their Families in the Keewatin Region, N.W.T.* (Winnipeg, Manitoba: University of Manitoba), p. 4.

18. J.D. O'Neil, P.A. Kaufert, P. Brown, E. Voisey, M.M. Moffatt, B. Postl, R.Brown, and B. Binns, "Inuit Concerns About Obstetric Policy in the Keewatin Region, N.W.T.", *Circumpolar Health 87*, Edited by H. Linderholm, C. Backman, N. Broadbent, and I. Joelsson. (Oulu, Finland: Nordic Council on Arctic Medical Research, 1988), pp. 485–489.

19. Supra 17., p. 4.

20. Supra 18., pp. 4–8.

21. Supra 18., pp. 4–8.

22. Supra 18., pp. 4–8.

23. Supra 19., p. 5.

24. Strengthening Communities: Enabling Individuals and Organizations to Improve Their Health, Review of Main Issues. A group paper presented at the International Conference on Health Promotion, Ottawa, 1986.

25. Supra 19., pp. 7–12.

26. Interview with Harry Tulugak, 22 March 1989.

27. Ibid.

28. Hand-out on the philosophy and objectives of the Innuulisivik Maternity, Povungnituk, 1986.

Marie Kilunik (Dogs Barking)

Marie Kilunik Apaulak Krako
Conversation with JoAnn Lowell
Translated by Lizzie Ippiak

I met Marie Kilunik Aupalak Krako in December of 1987 when I was interviewing Inuit ladies about their childbirthing experiences in Rankin Inlet and Chesterfield Inlet in the Northwest Territories. Lizzie Ippiak translated for me and as Marie's stories of life in the past unfolded, Lizzie often forgot to translate as she, too, got caught up in the action. The young children gathered around the kitchen table and listened intently; for many of them this was the first time they had heard their grandmother speak of these events. It occurred to me that all one has to do is ask, the stories are there and will gladly be shared. This is Marie's heritage to share...

I am 84 years old. I was born in a tent in Repulse Bay in July of 1904. My dad was a hunter, and in the winter we stayed on the land to hunt, and in the summer we went out to the sea. We walked from camp to camp, and in the winter and spring we used skis. In the fall my parents would wait for the snow, then gather it, and build it over the tent for winter. They used patches of snow to cover holes inside and outside, and they made a window covered with ice or seal intestine. The bottom was carved out to make a sunken floor, and we had a raised family bed covered with furs. It was heated and lit with whale oil—there was no wood. There was a separate igloo entrance to trap the cold, and over the winter the families were connected by snow passage ways between our igloos. In the summer, we cut and dried the fish for winter and in the fall, the two most important things were to make sure we had enough warm clothing and food stored from the year for the coming winter. Sometimes our winter storage was attacked by a polar bear or foxes. For clothing, the autumn caribou skin is best because each hair is hollow and fills with air, trapping heat. In the summer the layers are shed to cool off.

I remember it was summertime and raining. I never liked to cook in the tent, so I was outside cooking walrus meat when a polar bear walked toward me. I dropped the pot of cooked meat and crawled inside the tent on my hands and knees. Inside, my son, my grandson, and my daughter-in-law asked, "What's wrong?" I said, "There's a polar bear." They whipped open the tent and ran outside. The polar bear was startled and ran away to the ocean and into the water. They followed and shot and killed the polar bear, and we ate him for dinner. My husband loved polar bear meat.

My father and my uncle were shamans, and they were both good and wise. They would use chanting ways on a sick person and the sick person would start to heal right away. I would watch my father, but my parents told me not to. He would float up and suddenly disappear and he would shoot outside. My father would travel to another troubled camp by flying there so he could check up on them—then he was back in minutes. My father didn't want me to have a shaman power. He said my temper was too big and unpredictable and would make me dangerous enough to kill someone with my thoughts.

My mother would let me go out early for a little while before coming back to make breakfast. She said my children will be born earlier with short labours because of this.

I was married when I was 12 or 13 years old, before I had even menstruated. There was no ceremony. In the old days, the parents would choose a daughter-in-law and the son came and got her. At first I didn't like him but I came to love him. For the first two years we slept together but never touched each other—I was very scared the "first time". My second husband and I were married by a Catholic priest—I was baptized and married in the church on the same day. I have had ten children. I had two kids with my first marriage—my first son was named after my first husband. My third pregnancy was from the white doctor. He came up after my husband died and I was nurse to him. He flirted with me but I didn't want to go with him. I had seven kids with my second marriage. Only three of my kids are alive now—the three youngest.

My first child was born in a tent somewhere between here and Rankin Inlet, and I was all alone. In my first pregnancy my mother told me what to do and what not to do. From hearing that, I knew how, and I had all ten by myself. I was not scared, just tired of waiting for babies to be born. My fourth child was born in the springtime. My other baby was on my back and I was going to go out with my husband on the land. I bore that child outside near the sled. Quickly my husband made a wind-block out of snow on either side and caribou skin underneath. The other baby was on my back crying. The dogs were barking at my feet trying to eat the new baby. I had to push them away. I had a piece of broken glass to cut the cord, not a knife because it would be dangerous for infection.

Whoever was available for a birth, my mother or my mother-in-law, would come when I went into labour and bring a piece of broken glass, some thread, and a needle. I am scared to cut others.

When a child is born it is the parents or in-laws who name the child. The spirit of a relative or best friend, or relative who has just died will be born again in the new baby, so we name the new baby by their name, and then call out that name when the mother is birthing. So when Lizzie had her son, her mother had died and so we called out the name of her mother, Saimanaq, and that became his name.

Once the baby is born there is no ceremony, we are all just happy, and we go on with regular everyday life. My son Leo was born in the fall, in October, when we were travelling between camps. My mother-in-law fixed up a tent. She put up a pole and placed a tent over it and she got the bed ready and the tea ready, and I just got my leggings off and the baby was born. I didn't like people around when I was labouring; I preferred to be alone. I would kneel on my knees to give birth. There were furs on the floor and also bunched up into a circle were big pieces of fur which I could grab during a contraction.

In the old days I thought I was going through a rough time. That was before the white man came, but now it's worse for young girls because of the white man's ways. I worry a lot that girls go South into hospitals to have their babies. In the hospital I felt so homesick I didn't know what to do when I was away from home for so long. The first time I went to the hospital is when they took my eye out. I cried all the way to Churchill. I was worried about my husband and kids. I think the women should have their babies in their home in their own beds. But I keep quiet because maybe something could be wrong with the baby. Maybe doctors know better than I—but not the men doctors who never had children. When doctors say, "don't push," that's wrong, because that's when the baby is slowing down.

I believe that during Lizzie's labour (36 hours) the sex of the baby changed from a boy to a girl. Because a little girl had to labour along with her mom in order to help be born. My parents and in-laws told me that when a baby girl is born after a long labour the mother would take the umbilical cord between her fingers and put it into her mouth and suck in, and while the baby's spirit is alive she would make the penis come back out to make the baby go from a girl to a boy again.

Marie asked that night if I would name my first-born son after her. She asked if I would name him Kilunik which means "dogs barking". She said it is good luck, because when the polar bear would come to their village, the dogs would bark in warning and save the people from an attack. I made a promise with Marie that I would name my first-born son, Kilunik, after her. I have since had a daughter in March 1989. A week before she was born I remembered this evening with Marie and I told my partner about my promise and we both agreed that we wanted a son of ours to have Marie's name. In the future I look forward to having a son one day who will bear her name and the stories of Marie Kilunik Apaulak Krako shall carry forward with him.

Chapter III

VIOLENCE, WOMEN, AND THE COMMUNITY

Man Carrying Reluctant Wife by Pudlo Pudlat

Band-aid Solutions for Family Violence

Susan Sammons

In 1982, a sub-committee of the Baffin Women's Association was formed to deal with the issues of family violence and spousal assault. Composed of local women, this sub-committee became the Baffin Regional Agvvik Society in 1985. The need for a home for battered women in the Baffin Region was identified early in the society's history, but much work and lobbying was needed for the shelter to become a reality.

In March 1987, after receiving an operating budget from the Northwest Territories Department of Social Services, Nutaraq's Place first opened its doors, in a building owned by the GNWT Housing Corporation. The house is named after Leah Nutaraq, an Iqaluit woman who spent much of her life involved in issues concerning the family. To date, it is the only transition house in the eastern Arctic.

Soon after the house became operational, it became apparent that, beyond providing a safe and secure home for women and their children, many more resources would be needed to help remedy family violence problems in Baffin communities. It also became evident that the house was understaffed and under-funded, thus eliminating all but minimal services. Some of the gaps in services which were identified included: a children's program for residents at the house, an advocacy worker available to explain court and legal procedures, counselling for batterers, and a public education program.

It was soon noted that many of the house residents' children had either been witness to, or victims of, family violence themselves, and that much work was required to break the cycle of violence. Observations of many situations in which the children, as well as the mother, had been battered showed that parent–child bonding had been damaged when the mother had been unable to prevent the abuse.

From discussions with batterers, there is substantial evidence to suggest that batterers grow up in homes where violence is present, whether they encounter it as victims of violence themselves, or as witnesses to their fathers beating their mothers. In this atmosphere, children learn that violence is an acceptable and effective way to win arguments. They learn that physical power can be misused against weaker people with impunity. Without programs geared specifically to children from violent homes, the probability of the cycle repeating itself through subsequent generations is substantially increased.

For victims of violence to make use of the courts and the legal system itself, it is imperative that they be aware of these structures and how they operate. The majority of residents at Nutaraq's Place have little knowledge of court procedures, or the justice system in general. Owing to the small population of northern communities, there is competition for available legal services. As a result, lawyers and court workers are placed in a conflict situation, as they represent the batterers who have peace bonds against them and also represent them in court when necessary.

Due to this conflict situation, it is difficult for victims to find legal support if called upon as witnesses. Many female first- and second-time offenders are themselves victims of family violence and spousal assault. If women are to avail themselves of the legal options available to them, and if future conflicts with the law are to be prevented, this gap in services must be addressed.

Many of the women residents at our house eventually decide to return home. This decision is governed by several circumstances. For some, family pressures by parents and in-laws are too much to bear since the batterer may be the sole hunter in the family, and often the woman is perceived as selfish, and the source of other peoples' suffering if he is incarcerated.

An acute housing shortage in northern communities adds more pressure to this situation. There are few options available to women who do not want to return home. In Iqaluit, the largest Baffin community, the waiting list for public housing is two years long. It is often impossible for victims to move in with relatives, who may be under-housed themselves. Placing an additional woman and her children in a two-bedroom house already occupied by ten people can lead to the development of another potentially violent situation. Although government employment provides housing, this usually applies only to positions requiring education or skills at a level far above that commonly possessed by transition house residents. It is the lack of employment and the reliance on welfare which compels most women to return home.

More often than not, the women return to exactly the same situation from which they departed. In the meantime, the batterer has not received counselling for his violent behaviour since his wife and children left, a fact which poses the risk of more violence in the future.

At present, a volunteer group of concerned professionals, victims, and clergy are in the process of setting up a program for batterers which will be run on a volunteer basis (due to the lack of funding).

Public awareness concerning family violence is low, and substantial amounts of money need to be spent on bilingual public education programs. It is imperative that materials and media presentations be produced in Inuktitut as well as English. This has frequently been overlooked in the past, with the message not being understood by the community at large.

The family violence problem in northern communities is a difficult and complex issue. We all know it happens, but solving it will be a long-term undertaking. Unless adequate funding and services are allocated to address gaps in services, the probability of the cycle continuing into the next generation is almost certain.

Tawow Society Reaches Out to Families in Need

M. Agnes Sutherland, s.g.m.

In March 1970, Bishop Paul Piché gave me, as Director of Religious Education, the mandate to co-ordinate the religion programs and assist catechists and parents in the schools and missions of the Mackenzie–Fort Smith Diocese.

My office at the old mission soon became too small and crowded to provide all the services and activities under this mandate. As such, in July, I was offered the possibility of reopening the boarded-up St Ann's Hospital and employing staff to keep up with the growing needs. St Ann's was an old, three-floor wooden building. The halls were narrow, the ceiling low, the lighting poor, the rooms small, and the rounded floor squeaky. It smelled old and stale and the wind drafted from top to bottom. But, as everyone said, "It had a very special atmosphere and character."

St Ann's Yesterday

St Ann's Hospital, built in 1914 by the Oblate Brothers, was a marvel of the time. It served, until 1952, as the first centralized hospital for parts of northern Alberta and Saskatchewan, and the western Arctic.

It was a landmark in Fort Smith, and was also one of the most uniting relics in a community of people of varied colours, languages, ages, and denominations. It held many sentimental, psychological, and historical values and memories. It was a haven of healing, of life-giving, and even of final farewells. It represented an era when medical services and medications were yet rather primitive, but it also represented the best of the times, when miracles were made and lives saved and soothed.

As a final witness of these memories, people by the dozens silently expressed their sentiments in 1981, when this old monument burnt to the ground. They desperately grabbed whatever they could: boards, doors, door knobs, two-by-fours, crucifixes, pictures, windows, and more. They stood for hours in the cold, circling the huge fire, hot streams of tears rolling down their faces, too sad to express words and emotions.

It was fortunate for us that a new Fort Smith Health Centre had opened up two years earlier, in 1979, and we had by the time of the fire moved out of the old St Ann's Hospital building into the new centre.

St Ann's in the 1970s and 1980s

Within days of our moving into St Ann's in 1970, the third floor was sealed off and plastic sheets put up to cover the drafty windows and extra entrances. A feminine and artistic touch also quickly brought the old building to life to the delight of the old-timers, the young, and passers-by—not to mention the catechists and missionaries. It hadn't taken long before we were ready for business.

A month after we were settled in, a frightened, beaten, and bruised mother knocked at our door. She had been locked out of her own home, and for three days and nights had survived, swollen and feverish, without water or food, hiding with her dog beneath a bushy tree. We later learned that the worried batterer had searched desperately for her around and out of town while she was secretly sheltered with us. It seemed that everyone in town knew of her disappearance and was looking for her, except, of course, us. But, "Ignorance is bliss"—this incident was our only and most effective advertising for what is now called the first shelter in the Northwest Territories for battered women.

Gradually, children popped in after school for curiosity's sake, then to watch TV, play games, or just to chat or borrow the washroom. Most needed a home away from home while mothers were at work or when there was too much drinking or arguing on the weekends or in the evenings.

As well, transients and the homeless, hungry and cold, often stopped in and, after a bowl of hot soup and a sandwich, asked to remain as overnight guests, especially in the winter months when they could hardly survive sleeping in the nearby bush, in cold trucks, or under makeshift shelters.

But the majority of our clients came because they were victims of family violence or related problems. Children, mothers, families, alcoholics, transients, immigrants, students, teens, homeless men, and senior citizens kept the tradition of knocking at our door at all hours of the day or night. They came in all kinds of crisis situations or simply for a bit of emergency assistance and caring. Many came for a time away, for quiet and peace, or just to talk or cry.

Some arrived alone and others with the RCMP, a social worker, a friend, a relative, or a member of Uncle Gabe's Friendship Centre or Thebacha College. Many arrived with their young children even before they were physically battered, and all felt assured that they could come and be accepted.

Many who came had lived their lives for years with their health seriously affected, their self-esteem destroyed, their faces permanently disfigured, and their bones broken and rebroken. They lived among their friends and family—hiding their injuries, their shame, their pain, or they lived completely isolated from any human contact.

On at least one occasion we were caught with a crisis of our own. When a mother of five disappeared to go on a binge, leaving her five children with us, I became an instant mother, which was an experience, especially for me, as one of the children was only a week-old infant. The older siblings also added their bit of spice as they adjusted to such a tiny, precious baby. Often when I was out of sight they could not resist taking the baby out of the crib into the play corner or on the floor, believing that it was a toy or doll.

Fortunately, many concerned mothers dropped in with baby clothing, pampers, and other necessities; offered emergency baby-sitting services; and gave helpful instructions on preparing the baby's bottle and formula, and on changing diapers. We survived none the worse for the excitement, worries, and caring for the youngsters.

The First Shelter in the N.W.T. for Battered Women

In the 16 years I was involved with this informal crisis centre, I frequently witnessed people who were discouraged, abused, and emotionally distraught and desperate for a safe place to escape from a threatening situation and for a place to rebuild their lives. Although alcohol and drugs were, and still are, often blamed and given as the excuse for so much of the violence, I also believe that immaturity, possessiveness, jealousy, and various forms of insecurity are major factors for many of the tragedies. Alcohol, of course, adds just the right ingredient to trigger the explosion; often just at the wrong time and to the wrong person. Weak men flatter and abuse weaker women as their only way to deal with contradictions and ruffled feathers, and to exert power and control.

One evening, a young mother and her six-year-old daughter asked for overnight shelter because her new apartment would not be ready for a few days. I asked no questions and took it for granted that she was new in town, perhaps as a new student at Thebacha College. Later in the evening, when the youngster was comfortably tucked in bed, the mother joined me in the TV room. She talked about her plans to end her common-law relationship, and then I realized she was another battered woman. We chatted until the small hours of the morning. I warned her and impressed upon her the risks and dangers of returning home alone to inform her partner that she was leaving and to pick up her belongings. The RCMP or a Social Services staff member would be happy to go with her. It was indeed a difficult decision to end such a painful relationship at this particular time when both wife and husband were so emotionally upset.

She seemed to realize that it could be very dangerous situation, but did decide to go back alone the next morning after taking her daughter to school. By 11 a.m. she had been shot to death. This was a shocking experience for me and for the community; my only consolation being that the mother and daughter did find shelter that last night and that the little one was spared not only her life but perhaps the awful nightmare of witnessing the brutal death of her mother.

At four one cold, blizzarding morning, the door bell rang endlessly. As I opened it, a young mother collapsed at my feet, and a second later her young husband rushed toward us. I expected to be shot then and there, but he had no weapon. He had come purposely to inform me that she had consumed an assortment of pills. How we succeeded in getting her in the car and to the hospital for emergency treatment on time, I don't really know.

Then, there were the three little girls just colouring pictures, seemingly innocent, chatting and playing with their dolls. Suddenly, one quietly came into the office where I was typing and whispered, "Sister, what can I do when my sister (nine years old) wakes me up at four o'clock in the morning to tell me she wants to kill herself because she can't stand Mom and Dad fighting any more?"

Needless to say, I stopped typing in a hurry. As a teacher and a principal, I had often been aware and involved with families and children in crisis situations, and this was one such case. Even 20 years earlier, I had realized again and again how difficult it was to reach out and find help for such emergencies. We are fortunate today that so much more has been achieved in making it possible to find all sorts of resources, qualified people and agencies, and even financial assistance for the suffering and helpless in our society. Love and caring are most essential, but it also takes practical actions to remedy and solve problems.

There were the teens, some who arrived drugged, confused, restless, and sometimes aggressive. I must admit that I was often frightened, but with God's help and strength, managed to gather sufficient courage and inspiration to at least momentarily take care of them until more professional and experienced social workers took over.

There were also intriguing and amusing incidents. Apparently, the old building had become known as a ghost town where all the spirits of the many deceased patients wandered about. We moved in, oblivious to all these fears and superstitions, but soon became aware that some folks were very worried and concerned about our safety and well-being. Some folks dropped in simply to enquire about or to caution us of the possible dangers. It became routine to expect our guests to show signs of fear and anxiety at least by the second evening and whisper very cautiously: "Are there any ghosts in this house? Do they ever harm you?" I shared my feelings by admitting that I considered it an honour to live and work in the same home where so many of their friends and relatives had spent their last hours and felt assured that their spirits of love, caring, and blessings were more powerful and were to our advantage rather than an obstacle to harm us in any way. Probably sensing my peace, they soon became reassured and finally showed no further signs of unrest or fear.

One teen, who today is a famous singer and guitarist, developed his talent by spending hours playing on the old piano and singing. As we were sipping a cup of coffee one afternoon, he asked, "Sister, do you believe in spirits?" I suspected why he asked such a question, so I responded, "Yes, but probably not in the same way as you do." He picked up on my response immediately. "Well, when I die I'm coming right back to revenge on you, Sister...and to scare you to death." Grinning from ear to ear, I added, "That's okay, for I'll know where you've landed." He wrinkled his forehead and thought for a second, then laughed out loud. That was the end of his search for ghosts in the old hospital, but he did continue to play the old piano and sing "to his heart's content".

The little ones were the most charming and loveable. In spite of the fact that most had left home with mothers under much pressure and under painful circumstances, they soon were taking over the huge hallways where they could ride their bikes, big cars, and wagons. Above all, though, they loved the playroom—a child's paradise with so many attractive and amusing toys: cars and trucks, a playhouse, a stove and fridge, and much more made possible by the generosity of concerned people from the community.

One little fellow in particular, little Mark, was very special. His mother was very depressed, and he spent most of his time in my office, cutting out designs, colouring, and chatting away endlessly. Mark was not a Catholic but was quick to notice the religious symbols around the centre. He enjoyed coming with me to the cafeteria for his meals and was soon intrigued with the size and novelty of the cafeteria setting and, above all, with the unfamiliar expressions: Father So and So, Sister So and So, and Brother So and So. Finally, after a few days, little Mark decided that he might just as well join the confraternity and began calling himself Brother Mark. He even got to work and printed a name sign for his bedroom door—in grade-one-style printing. Brother Mark's name still remained on that particular door in the old hospital until it burned down. I never had the courage to remove it. Mark and his mom were only in the North a short while, but I have never forgotten the charming little fellow and the many, many more just like him. It has often been the most heartbreaking of my experiences dealing with families in crisis and witnessing the pain, suffering, and fear expressed by the innocent children and teens whose parents fight and destroy each other.

These clients were only a few of the many who needed a helping hand in time of emergency. The centre had become a place where all were accepted, and it continued to grow even after it moved, in 1979, to the new Fort Smith Health Centre, with its newer and more modern facilities. It was not until 1984, however, that a new transition house was built by the Tawow ("welcome" in Cree) Society whose members had been struggling long and hard to make such a goal a reality.

The Tawow Society was formed in June 1984 by a group of dedicated citizens concerned with the high rate of assaultive crimes in the community and, in particular, with the high incidence of spousal assault. Spousal assault had surfaced as a grass roots issue around this time and had "brought everything out into the open: battering, sexual and emotional abuse, child abuse, and the close connection of alcohol to family violence." Gradually there developed more public-education, health, and awareness programs; more open discussion; and more preventive services and projects such as workshops, conferences, surveys. As well, the need for setting up shelters became apparent. St Ann's crisis centre itself was just not appropriate for the numbers arriving for help, especially given the economic realities.

The Tawow Society applied for funding for a research project to assess the needs and resources available to victims of family violence in Fort Smith and to establish a data base to support project development. Sutherland House was established from this project.

Sutherland House

Sutherland House was officially opened 8 December 1987, but had actually been in operation since January 1987. It accepts all victims of spousal assault, whether the abuse comes from mental, emotional, physical, or sexual sources. It is a six-bedroom facility accommodating as many as 12 women and their children for periods of up to six weeks at a time. It is staffed 24 hours a day by very concerned and efficient women in the community. Its funding is covered by the Mackenzie–Fort Smith Diocese, the territorial Department of Social Services, and the Department of Secretary of State of Canada. Donations have also been received from the Fort Smith Town Hall and concerned citizens.

The Spousal Assault Task Force

In 1985, Dennis Patterson, then the territorial minister responsible for the Status of Women, published the report of the Task Force on Spousal Assault. The task force consisted of a team of seven women from a variety of communities and represented a cross-section of northern cultural backgrounds. It was chaired by John Bayly, a lawyer from Yellowknife.

The Spousal Assault Task Force Report was dedicated to the memory of women like Dorothy, Roberta, and Agnes, for whom its recommendations and public awareness programs came too late. It revealed for the first time that spousal assault in the Northwest Territories is a social problem of grave proportions. It is affecting the hearts of families and communities but especially individuals who live in constant anxiety, and in danger of permanent injury and even death.

It reported on the effectiveness of government agency responses and on the nature, extent, and seriousness of the problem of family violence in northern communities. After visiting more than 30 communities, it listed 104 recommendations concerning new measures which might be undertaken to deal with the problem of battered spouses, including the urgent need for safe shelters. It also initiated a three-year plan of action for the Government of the Northwest Territories. Its chairperson stated, "We uncovered much but we believe far more escaped our notice and was not brought to our attention." The report was presented to the territorial assembly, and the need for safe shelters was gradually taken as a very serious and urgent problem.

Reports from across Canada record that there is a definite increase in the numbers of shelters and safe homes. In 1987, there were 230 shelters as compared with 71 in 1979. In the Northwest Territories, there are three shelters for long- and short-term clients: Nutaraq's Place in Iqaluit, Sutherland House in Fort Smith, and McTeer House in Yellowknife. As well, there are several safe homes: Hay River Safe House and the Women's Coalition Group; Jerimicka Family Home in Lac La Marte; Geddes Family in Fort Providence; Fort Simpson Support Group; Baker Lake Hospice; Spence Bay Shelter; Inuvik Safe Home; Pond Inlet; Tuktoyaktuk Home; and Coppermine Awareness Centre. There are also more in the development stages, with the main purpose of providing security, a breathing space, and a time for women to make serious decisions and receive counselling with support and understanding. Families, friends, and neighbours continue to offer their homes and whatever they can do as they had done before.

The Next Step
In my contacts with northern women, either at the crisis centre, the Religious Education Centre, or through my research and interviews, several women have expressed how they have been abused again and again.

> "...the white man brought our people booze, bingos, gambling, TV, parties, venereal diseases and all kinds of evils but they did not teach our men how to abuse us. Even in the bush, in the tents we suffered and were controlled but, of course, liquor only made it a lot worse."

We have yet to meet anyone who solved problems with alcohol and drugs. In fact, jealousies and tempers automatically become more explosive, and a whole series of new problems escalate and intensify the old ones a hundredfold and more.

Elimination of wife beating depends not only on eliminating sexual inequality but also altering the system of violence which affects so much of our society and is not limited to any particular group. Family violence crosses all socioeconomic, cultural, ethnic, and religious backgrounds. Yet, to accept assault of anyone as natural is to justify violence as a means of solving conflict. Wife assault is usually tolerated more than any other kind of violence. Bystanders are known to be more willing to interfere in fights between men and strangers than between couples. Cultural and social norms which legitimate the use of force between family members and hold that the marriage licence is equally a "hitting licence" are, unfortunately, not just a matter of folk culture.

Family violence touches the deepest values, attitudes, and sanctity of the family as a whole. Violence has a tremendously destructive influence on the entire family. It causes great pain in both the battered and the batterer, not to mention the offspring. It creates distrust in love, restlessness, pressures at work and at home, financial pressures, and increases drinking. It destroys self-esteem and good family routine and relationships. Usually the batterers are men, but this role is sometimes reversed. Men, too, are entitled to support, understanding, and human resources. Unless we get to the root of the problem and tackle it honestly and fairly for all concerned, we risk creating new divisions, new power struggles and controls. The whole community and our nation must strive to solve this age-old cycle of unacceptable behaviour patterns in a truly Christian way where there is sincere give-and-take and equality in justice and love, rather than dependence on the courts and the penal system. We must whole-heartedly strive for prevention as a superior and ideal solution.

Physical punishment begins in infancy with slaps to correct and teach. Mommy and Daddy are the first, usually the only ones, to hit an infant throughout childhood. The child, therefore, learns that those who love him or her most are also those who hit and spank: "Spare the rod and spoil the child." Physical punishment is used to train and teach about dangerous things to be avoided. It also establishes the moral rightness of hitting family members.

Finally, the unintended consequence is the lesson learned early in life—that when something is really important it justifies the use of physical force. Should we then be surprised that when the same form of dealing with frustrations and contradictions is used by parents, the greatest and most wonderful in the eyes of a child, it provides a lasting and vivid role model for family relationships?

The task force specifically requested in its recommendations that churches play an active role in stimulating discussions about the moral and spiritual values which are affected by spousal assault in their parishes and the wider community.

According to Bishop Sperry, the Anglican Bishop of the Arctic Diocese, his "church is solidly behind the efforts of assaulted women to assert their rights as human beings." Bishop Sperry believes that a wife who takes steps to eliminate psychological and physical abuse from her family may very well be leading the way to a more Christian home, especially if the violent husband seeks help himself. He continues, "The dignity of womanhood must be accepted in our society. There is still residual thinking, even in our homes, that Mom is Dad's property. That thinking must be changed" (September 1986 Spousal Assault Network Newsletter, Yellowknife).

In 1984 in Iqaluit, the Anglican Synod discussed family violence and spousal assault and passed a motion expressing its concerns and condemning family violence. Now it's on every agenda of every major conference under the heading of "social concerns". Spousal assault is a sin against humanity. Bishop Sperry has asked his congregation to be more militant, to get together and act, to be outspoken about the harm that spousal assault causes in their communities. Aside from the fact that most churchgoers are women and that some church vocabulary, rituals, and male decisions tend to emphasize a second-class nature of women, it is only right and just that the majority of women expect more active involvement from their churches and Christian members. It is not sufficient for us to be pro-life and in favour of Christian marriages unless there is a continuous support system and spiritual nourishment and growth for the whole family. We must not only pride ourselves as peace-thinkers but brand ourselves as peacemakers.

The paradox of why the haven where most people look for love, gentleness, and fulfilment can be one of the most violent and secretive spots in our society is at times overwhelming. However, we must not get so enveloped in pessimism and a sense of hopelessness that we overlook the reality and blessings of our country and people, where we have every reason to believe that there are far more healthy and happy families in our midst. They are the backbone, the stabilizers, the role models that our society really need, and they are the glory of our nation. Like so many of you, I am sure, I can testify that a happy and violence-free home is possible. I never once saw the least sign of violence or abuse between my parents, and they even found ways and means to restore peace and harmony among their over-active siblings who always had so many reasons to argue, scream, name-call, and even at times come to blows. They always managed to cool off tempers without physical force. The eleventh commandment in our home was that meal times were sacred and were never open for settling scores. These were special moments for sharing good news, bragging, telling stories, joking and teasing, and they were fun times making us feel good to be together.

Family life, and all it is and stands for, has always been of prime importance to Canadians. In fact, do we not hear again and again immigrants of all lands proclaiming loud and clear that they chose to leave their own homeland and all that entails to start a new life here, raising their families in freedom and choice and giving them the very best in life? What better place can they choose to live? Not only the best in education, material benefits, and leisure, but above all, the opportunity to mature, enjoy, and live in a violence-free world on the streets and in their homes.

Although I no longer have access to a building or an area where I can continue to accommodate the homeless and the poorest of the poor, I continue to be in touch with them and respond to their simple needs in various ways. I forever remain grateful for the years I was fortunate enough to be able to share my home with them. They taught me a lot and shared their simple life-style in many ways.

I am also forever grateful to the sisters and the ladies of the town who were always ready and willing to give a helping hand in time of emergencies or replace me when my other duties and responsibilities called me away from the centre: Sisters Rosalie Cherlet, Denise Emond, Rosanne Hebert Yvette Nadeau, Olga Vigoureux and Lucienne Hebert; and mothers and concerned women of the community—Anita Dube, Jeanne Dube, Sylvia Haslam, and Anne Hutchinson.

SURVIVAL and *HELP*: Two Plays About Taking Action on Spousal Assault

Jokeypak Killiktee and Malchi Arreak
Performed by Tununiq Theatre

S *URVIVAL* and *HELP* were developed by the actors, with help and advice from elders and Alice Panipakoocho, Pond Inlet's social worker. The plays were presented in Inuktitut only. They were first performed in Pond Inlet by Tununiq Theatre in November 1987, and then toured Baffin Island.

The project was initiated and sponsored by the Northwest Territories Department of Culture and Communications, with additional funding from the Women's Secretariat.

For information regarding the right to perform these plays, please contact Tununiq Theatre, Pond Inlet, Baffin Island, N.W.T.

SURVIVAL

Cast

Alice . . . . .39 years old, the wife
Thomas . . . . 44 years old, the husband
Martha . . . . the social worker
Lydia . . . . the daughter
Taqiapik . . . . the elder

Technician . . . . David Qamaniq
Director . . . . Jan Selman
Administrator. . . . . Ellen Hamilton
Spousal Assault Counsellor on Tour . . . . Aiju Peter

SCENE 1

(The scene begins in the living room which is lit with a lamp. Alice asks Lydia to try on a sweater. Lydia gets it all wrong and they share a laugh. Alice sighs.)

Alice: Before I got married I was really happy. Then my husband started beating me up. My husband treats me like I'm nothing, like I'm not human. I want to tell someone but I'm too scared.

Lydia: Be brave, why don't you tell someone about him? You will get help.

Alice: I'm afraid to.

(The outside door is heard opening and Lydia quickly goes out to the bedroom. Thomas comes stumbling in and knocks the lamp over. Darkness...)

Alice: What are you doing now?

Thomas: What are you going to do if I tell you? You're nothing. You're worthless.

(Thomas hits her and Alice screams and cries out.)

Alice: Don't do that!

(She screams. Lights...)

136

SCENE 2

(The next day Thomas is getting up from the couch where he slept. He gets a glass of water, drinks it down, then pours another glass and goes to the table where his wife is sitting.)

Thomas: Did you make me mad? Is that why you have a black eye?

(Alice doesn't answer. She covers her face with her hands. He looks at her for a few seconds then walks to the bathroom. There is silence. Thomas comes back, puts his work clothes on, then leaves. Lydia, the daughter, comes out from the bedroom and sees her mother crying. She goes to the table and sits down across from her mother.)

Lydia: Mother! Mother!

Alice: What?

Lydia: Tell someone about him.

Alice: I'm afraid of him.

Lydia: Shall I tell on him myself?

Alice: No. If you tell on him he's going to kill me.

(Lydia gets ready to go to school, then leaves. Alice gets up, she cleans the house. After she finishes, she puts make-up on.)

Alice: I wonder how much make-up I've used to cover my bruises.

(The husband comes in for his coffee break and sits down.)

Thomas: Alice! Give me some tea.

(She brings him a cup of tea then moves away and sits. There is silence, then, after awhile, she speaks.)

Alice: I need some money.

Thomas: What are you going to buy?

Alice: The children don't have anything to eat. We need some food.

Thomas: If I didn't have a job, where would you get money? I'm the only one who supports you. Don't get things that are useless.

(Thomas gives Alice some money then leaves. Alice picks up her purse and goes to get some groceries.)

SCENE 3

(The next day Alice is sweeping. Thomas is sitting on the couch listening to the radio. Alice then does the dishes. Taqiapik, the old man from the church, comes in and sits down at the kitchen table. Thomas turns the radio off and joins him.)

Thomas: Is it getting colder out?

Taqiapik: Yeah, it'll be like this for awhile.

Thomas: There's tea if you want some.

Taqiapik: Yeah, okay, thanks.

Thomas: Alice, bring us some tea.

(Alice brings the tea over. Thomas, nervous, makes small talk.)

Thomas: Last night I went seal hunting.

Taqiapik: You didn't get one, did you?

Thomas: No.

Taqiapik: What happened to your eye?

Alice: (Laughing it off) I bumped into something.

Taqiapik: Would you please sit down beside your husband.

(Alice sits down beside her husband.)

Taqiapik: I hear rumours that you two have problems. What kind of problems do you have?

Thomas: None that I know of.

Taqiapik: Alice, what about you?

(Frightened, Alice looks at her husband then looks at Taqiapik.)

Alice: I can't think of anything either.

Thomas: Maybe someone made things up?

(Silence)

Thomas: You can't believe people these days.

(Silence)

138

Taqiapik: I came here to help you. (Pause) Since you don't have any problems, there's nothing I can say. (Pause) My skidoo ski broke today so I have to go work on it before it's too late, because I want to go seal hunting in the morning.

(He leaves. Alice moves to a chair in the living-room. They sit, not looking at one another. Then Thomas crosses to her.)

Thomas: Have you been talking about me behind my back? Women! Their tongues are too loose. Did you criticize me in front of other people?

(Alice starts to cry.)

Alice: I never said anything. Maybe people saw my bruises when I went to the store.

(Thomas grabs Alice and starts to pull her hair. She breaks free and grabs a baseball bat and yells.)

Alice: I'm going to kill you. I will! I'm really going to kill you!

(Thomas grabs the bat, pulls it from her, hits her on the head and knocks her out. He goes to her.)

Thomas: I think I killed her.

(The lights go out.)

SCENE 4

(The next day Martha, the social worker, comes to see Alice who is sitting on the couch. Martha introduces herself and asks if she can come in. She sits.)

Martha: I'm Martha, the social worker. I'm here to talk to you. Your daughter phoned me last night. She told me you were beaten up. I'm here to help you. How is your head?

Alice: It's a lot better than last night.

Martha: Was he drunk when he beat you?

Alice: No, he wasn't drunk. He also beats me up when he's drunk.

Martha: He almost killed you.

(Alice doesn't answer.)

Martha: He might really kill you next time.

(Alice answers quietly.)

Alice: Yes.

Martha: Why did he beat you?

Alice: There was a person here last night. He was concerned about us and asked us if we had any problems. We both said we had no problems. The person just left. Maybe he didn't know what else to do. Thomas thought I told on him, so he beat me up.

Martha: How long has he been beating you up?

Alice: For many years.

Martha: What reason does he give for beating you up?

Alice: I don't know what I do to make him hurt me.

Martha: There is no reason good enough for a man to beat his wife. If a man assaults his wife he can be sent to court. Do you understand?

Alice: Yes, I understand.

Martha: Do you know that we can help you?

Alice: Yes, but I'm afraid to tell on my husband.

Martha: If you are afraid of your husband we can help you go to another settlement with your kids.

Alice: But I don't have the education to get a job. I wouldn't be able to support my kids.

Martha: We can give you money for food and also for a place to stay.

Alice: What if my husband follows me? I don't want to leave my family.

Martha: If you don't want to leave your husband you need to have some protection.

Alice: How can I be protected?

Martha: Is there somewhere you can go if there is a problem?

Alice: I could go to my older sister's.

Martha: Would you mind if I speak to your sister, tell her your situation, and ask if you can go there when there is trouble?

Alice: Yes, you can speak to her.

Martha: It is good that you will try to keep safe, but I want you to think very hard about whether to stay living with Thomas. I know that it is not easy, but you must think about yourself and your children's future.

Alice: Even though I don't love Thomas any more, I don't want to give up on him. But I will think about my decision. I will talk with an Elder about my problem.

Martha: I'm going now. We'll talk again soon.

(Martha touches her and the lights dim.)

SCENE 5

(The next day Taqiapik comes to see Alice and Thomas. Alice is in the kitchen. Thomas is sleeping on the couch. Alice wakes Thomas.)

Alice: Thomas! Thomas! Wake up, someone's here to see you.

(Thomas gets up and sits with Taqiapik. Alice brings tea and joins them.)

Taqiapik: Why didn't you people tell me you had a problem?

Alice: I was afraid of my husband.

Taqiapik: Thomas, why did you lie to me?

Thomas: I didn't have the guts to tell you.

Taqiapik: I love you both and I don't want you to hurt each other's feelings. Right now I want you both to tell the truth about your problems.

Thomas: I started to cheat on Alice and I'd get mad at the other girl but I'd always turn to Alice and start beating her up and I couldn't stop. Up to now I still beat her up.

Taqiapik: Alice, what problems do you have?

Alice: He seems to beat me for no reason and I get confused.

Taqiapik: Violence is the worst thing in marriage. If you don't talk about your problems they just get bigger and bigger. Spousal assault is a common problem; you're not the only ones who have this problem. Tell each other the truth, for instance, "I slept with another man, will you please forgive me." It won't be easy at first but you'll both be happier afterwards. Forgive each other. Don't keep any secrets and don't blame each other. You will have a lot happier marriage.

Thomas: I'm really sorry about what I've done to Alice. If only I hadn't gone out with another women it wouldn't have happened. What am I to do now?

Alice: Even though you say you'll change, I know you're not going to. You'll start beating me up again. I don't believe you when you say that. You're just lying.

Taqiapik: Battering can be harmful to life, and it also breaks your mind. People who hurt each other physically have to try very hard to work things out.

Thomas: I don't want to split up with Alice.

(Before Thomas finishes Alice cuts him off.)

Alice: Thomas! I want to split up with you. I'm very tired of being beaten up.

(Alice turns to Taqiapik.)

Alice: I want to split up with this man. He always lies.

Taqiapik: Alice! You should take time and try to think about this. You should think about your children.

Alice: I've been thinking for a very long time about being beaten and I have made up my mind to leave Thomas. If I leave him I believe the children will be happier.

Taqiapik: Has anyone talked with you about these problems before?

Alice: Yes. Thomas always says he'll stop but after awhile he starts beating me up again.

Taqiapik: Yes. I think the best thing for you to do is split up. Life is worth a lot.

THE END

HELP

Cast

Julie . . . . 22 years old
Dave . . . . 24 years old
Verna . . . . .the friend
Saaqatiaq . . . . Dave's father
Kiviuaq . . . . Dave's mother

Technician . . . . David Qamaniq
Director . . . . Jan Selman
Administrator. . . . . Ellen Hamilton
Spousal Assault Counsellor on Tour . . . . Aiju Peter

SCENE 1 — "TROUBLES"

(Julie is making supper and listening to the radio. Verna walks in.)

Verna: Mmm, that smells good! What is it?

Julie: Caribou stew with vegetables. Want to stay for some? (Offers a taste) How do you like it?

Verna: Very much—you should become a part-time cook.

Julie: I wouldn't mind, but my child is still too small and Dave wouldn't like me staying away.

(Dave walks in and slumps down. The baby cries.)

Dave: Can't you shut that baby up?

(Julie rushes to the bedroom.)

Dave: Stop her crying—give her a bottle.

Verna: Have patience, Julie is working hard too.

(Dave turns the radio off.)

Dave: Who asked you? Why don't you shut up—you're just making me angry.

(Julie comes out after the baby is quiet.)

Dave: Julie! Did you make supper yet?

Julie: Yes! It's done.

(Dave goes to the kitchen table. Julie ladles out a bowl and gives it to Dave.)

Dave: Yuk, what have you done with this stew? It's terrible.

Julie: You're always complaining.

Dave: Shut up! You're driving me crazy!

Julie: That's it! I'm not going to cook for you ever again!

(Dave drags Julie and pushes her, then grabs her and drags her offstage.)

SCENE 2 — "HELP"
(Julie starts crying out, Verna goes to the door.)

Verna: Ah! What are you doing to her?

(She goes to centre stage, cries are heard. She goes to the phone and fumbles with it. She calls Dave's parents.)

Verna: Saaqatiaq! Please come over right now. Dave is beating his wife! Hurry!

(Half crying, Verna goes to the door.)

Verna: Dave! Stop it! (She shouts) Dave! Stop it right now! (She doesn't know what to do.)

(Saaqatiaq and Kiviuq rush in.)

Saaqatiaq: Where are they? (Verna points to the bedroom door. Saaqatiaq goes in and an argument can be heard.)

Kiviuq: (Goes to front of stage.) These days our lives are different. The younger generation hardly ever listens to us. How are we going to cope with all the changes? (Pause) We parents should not only *look* at our children's way of life, we should take action. We should help our children when they are in trouble.

(Music. The elders bring the couple out and sit them on the couch as if to counsel them. After a few moments they leave. The lights dim on Julie and Dave, miserable.)

SCENE 3 — "RECONCILIATION"
(The next day, Julie is on the couch. Dave is drinking tea in the kitchen, deciding how to break the ice. Finally, he goes to her.)

144

Dave: I'm sorry honey. I love you. I'm sorry I hurt you.

(Julie doesn't speak.)

Dave: Please forgive me. I'll never do it again.

Julie: I thought you told me the truth. You said you'd never hit me again. Why did you hit me?

Dave: I didn't know what I was doing. I'm really sorry.

Julie: When you drink you always get mad for no reason.

Dave: It's not your fault I hit you. It's just that it's so hard to get a job. Sometimes I wonder if I'll ever get a well-paying one.

Julie: I know you didn't want to hurt me. Why don't we talk about what's on your mind?

Dave: I don't want to hurt you. I love you and my son too much. I don't want you to leave me.

Julie: I love you too. But when you beat me we are so far away from each other. I don't want to break up either.

(Dave and Julie hug each other. Music. Lights dim)

SCENE 4 — "FRIENDS"
(The next day Julie and Verna are talking at the kitchen table. Julie sounds very hopeful.)

Julie: Dave is much better now. He said that he'll never beat me up again. He has changed a lot.

Verna: Right! He's said that before. I wonder if he's telling the truth? I read somewhere that when someone beats his wife he'll probably do it again. What will you do if he does?

(Julie avoids Verna's gaze. She goes and gets the unfolded laundry.)

Julie: I have no idea.

Verna: You can do different things. You can separate for a while or you can go to court and get a divorce. The RCMP can issue a peace bond for a length of time or you can go to Social Services. They can help you move to another settlement or you can get counselling. Do you understand all this?

Julie: Yes. I'm going to have to find out more about these things.

(Verna stops Julie's folding to get her attention.)

Verna: I'm saying these things because you're my friend. No one has the right to beat you up—you need to know all this.

Julie: Right. I don't think Dave is going to beat me up again.

SCENE 5 — "DRUNK"
(Dave walks in drunk. He acts very cool toward Verna.)

Dave: Hi love! Is supper on?

Julie: Oh no! I forgot—I'll start it right now.

Verna: I'll help you, it'll be a lot quicker.

Dave: Don't bother, Julie can do it by herself. Why are you here, anyway?

(Verna can tell Dave is barely controlling himself. She doesn't answer.)

Dave: (Slight increase in tone.) So you've got no answer. You feed Julie these crazy ideas. Get out of here, Verna.

Julie: No! She's my friend, she can stay if she wants to. I thought you were going to leave her alone!

Dave: Why are you on her side? All she does is try to split us up.

Julie: No! It's not like that. She's only trying to help.

Dave: Do whatever you want. You'd rather be with her than me. Fine—I'm going out.

Julie: Dave, Dave! Don't you want dinner? Wait!

Dave: Forget it!

Julie: That son of a bitch is drunk again.

(Dave stops, shocked to hear such words from Julie. He returns and literally growls at Julie. Verna runs out to get Dave's parents.)

Dave: Is that what she's teaching you? To hate me? (Pause) Answer me!

Julie: No! You think that but it's not true!

146

Dave: Shut up! If you don't, I'm going to shut you up!

Julie: I don't care! Do what you want!

(Dave, goaded beyond his limit, hits her! Saaqatiaq and Kiviuq appear quickly and Dave is stopped.)

SCENE 6 — "TALKING"
(Elders get Dave and Julie together.)

Saaqatiaq: Why did you beat her?

Dave: She always tries to make me mad.

Saaqatiaq: Julie, do you try and get him mad?

Julie: No. But when he swears at me I get mad.

Saaqatiaq: Sit down!

(They sit.)

Saaqatiaq: Is the only reason that you hit her because she makes you mad?

Dave: Verna tries to make us split up—that's why I was mad.

Saaqatiaq: Julie, does Verna try to split you up?

Julie: No, she wasn't trying to split us up—she was telling me what I could do if he beat me up again.

Kiviuq: David, if you didn't beat your wife, no one would be talking about you. But you have to know that Verna was talking to Julie only because she loves her and wants to help. If you're good to your wife she will love you too. (Pause) Because your husband has a short temper, don't talk to him when he is mad. Wait till he's cooled down—then you can talk to him.

Julie: I understand.

Kiviuq: Dave, does anything else make you angry?

Dave: I can't find a job. Everything builds up inside me and I can't find the words to talk about it.

Saaqatiaq: These days are hard, but you can't give up. You are still young and there are many different things you can do—you can train for a job you like or you can learn to carve. Some people say they can't carve but I don't believe that—

147

anybody who is seriously willing to do something can learn. So if there is something you'd like to do, do it without being lazy. Laziness doesn't help anybody. And don't forget you are Inuk. Inuit have always survived by helping one another—nobody will turn a relative down. We have survived this cold Arctic using only the things that we made. There are more problems to look at these days, but if you try to avoid these problems it's easier now to survive—so don't be lazy.

(They sit in silence for awhile.)

Kiviuq: You should talk with your wife about these things. If you talk you won't get mad at her so easily. You'll be good friends. She's a small girl, not strong—she feels pain like you do. Think about how you would feel being beaten like that. (Pause) You shouldn't beat your wife or her love for you will die.

(Silence. Dave thinks about what has been said.)

Saaqatiaq: Yes. We've always been told that men shouldn't beat their wives. No matter how bad things are, no matter what problems you have between you, you should not beat your wife. You must learn to control your temper. You should talk things out together.

Saaqatiaq: You two should talk these things over.

(The elders leave. Julie crosses to Verna.)

Julie: Come again tomorrow.

(Verna leaves. Silence)

Julie: Dave, I don't want to break up with you. I want to help you with your problems.

Dave: Me too.

Julie: I know when you get troubled you hold it inside until you explode. If we could just talk about things more, then we wouldn't get so mad.

Dave: I'll try Julie. I've never been much of a talker though.

Julie: But if we talk about what's bothering us instead of getting mad, we'll get along better.

Dave: I'll try, I'll really try, honey. It'll take both of us to work it out.

Julie: I've finally realized that when you're not happy I should try to help you.

Dave: When I get mad I should not go drinking. Instead, I should talk to you because I love you and I don't want to split up with you.

Julie: We'll think about the baby—we don't want him to see us fight.

Dave: I'm happy they came to talk to us—I know it's going to help us.

Julie: I hope so.

SCENE 7 — "HOPE"
(Julie is knitting, Verna arrives. She has a cake. Julie serves cake and tea.)

Verna: How are you doing now, Julie?

Julie: Things are much better now. We talk more. Dave is trying to teach himself to let off anger in other ways and to relax more.

Verna: Does he still hit you?

Julie: No, he's come close, but he hasn't done it. He has been controlling himself. It will be a long process, but I think that we are going to make it and stay together. (They smile.) Thank you for helping.

(Music. Lights.)

(Curtain call)

(The actors sing an Ajajaa about being happy to have survived the winter.)

THE END

Violence Toward Women and Children

Janet Mancini Billson

The Traditional Patterns: "You're not allowed to do that..."

In traditional Inuit culture, although male and female roles were complementary and mutually respected, the male was defined as the major "provider" and "boss". Many say there were hardly any problems between married couples. Kudloo recalls: "Only once in a long while the wife cheated on the husband. Nowadays, it's happening more and more. There never used to be those kinds of problems. Everybody got along, working with each other. For some of them, the problem is alcohol or drugs; but for some of them, when they get too much on their minds because their kids are up to something bad, they start worrying and they start fighting."

Two hundred years ago, if husband and wife did not get along, they could break up; the man could take another wife—more than one in certain circumstances. The unhappy wife could simply announce that she was finished with her husband, even 100 years ago, but for her the penalty was high, as Leah points out: "She could say that, but she would be left alone—shunned or abandoned, but she wouldn't survive alone because she wouldn't know how to hunt. It would be hard, very hard for her to get another husband." Thus, the importance of the male's provider role cemented the wife into her marriage, happy or not. However, if the other members of the small camp heard that her husband was hurting her, she was accorded some protection. Sara explains: "The elders or the others who were concerned would go to the husband right away and tell him, 'If you don't stop that, if you don't wake up and realize what kind of mistake you're making, okay, take a hike.' It was never shunning or rejection, but if he kept doing that, they would tell him, 'It's not nice to hit your wife, she's your wife, you're not allowed to do that, it's not our nature, if you can't control yourself, let us help. If you don't want that, forget it, and take a hike.'" The man would be forced to make the choice of changing his behaviour or leaving the camp. A man whose wife was wronging him would receive the same protection. As Leah explains: "If the woman was doing something wrong, the elders would come to the woman and say, 'You're not being a good wife.' And if the woman was being beaten or neglected by her husband, the elders would come forward and help her."

Loss of Balance in Settlements: "Seems like he was threatened..."

When Inuit families moved to the settlements, females seemed to adapt more easily to the new life. Today they are more likely than men to complete their high school educations, to obtain and hold jobs—and less likely to develop problems with alcohol, drugs, and crime. Now the roles in a wage-employment, consumer economy are reversed, and the women, especially the younger women, are more likely to be the major providers for their families. This may constitute the central, underlying reason for the alarming rates of spousal assault[1] that plague northern communities: men feel threatened by their loss of status and identity, by the increased power and status of the women—to restore their sense of a balance of power, men hit the women.

Although some men may argue that it was traditionally acceptable for a man to hit his wife, and maintain that they can still do so if she fails to obey, Daisy counters that argument: "We say traditional, but was it traditional? If you look back at our culture, assault wasn't traditional. There wasn't a lot of wife beating out on the land, because there weren't all the social pressures. Maybe the wife beatings became more prevalent as the social pressures increased. Then we accepted it. I can beat on her, she's my property. And she's supposed to obey."

One elder, Martha says: "I don't really know why men beat up their wives now, but in the old days men used to go hunting every day if it was good weather. If the weather was bad for a few days and they had to stay home, I noticed that they became irritable and angry, and more men are staying home nowadays, and some even babysit, and maybe it makes them feel weak. Maybe they get angry." She adds that she was raised to know that if a man is angry with you or if he hits you, "As a woman you don't hit back or talk back because you know the man is stronger than you." She does not remember many incidents of spousal assault in any case, "because we were told not to do things like that." The elderly women agree that for all these reasons violence between couples was rare in an earlier era; but they hear about it "a lot in this generation."

Abuse is one way a man can exert power when he perceives his woman as the dominant one, as Rachel, a separated housing officer, relates: "It was the case in my relationship. I was working and he was not, and I think that's another reason the relationship didn't work out. Seemed like he was threatened about anything." A high school teacher agrees: "This idea of women having a right to speak, or young people questioning adults, is not an indigenous idea, but it is important. What they're learning through the media and the school, and what they're discovering, is that they do have some power. They're testing it out. This is probably causing disruptions in the homes, spousal assault, and all that. But the women aren't taking that lying down. Before, they would sort of hush it up, they would be ashamed of it because sometimes it would be sort of an incest situation and they did not want to shame their own families. Or the boyfriend might threaten a girl and say, 'If you don't listen to me I'm going to beat you up,' and she gets the black eyes and all that. But now they're taking the matter to the police, and the men are being charged with physical violence, and they're being taken out of the town. They're daring to come forth, although a lot is still hushed up, I think." Still, it is the woman who is more likely to be forced to "leave the camp", symbolically at least, because if she seeks divorce in order to stop the offending behaviour, she risks stigma, shunning, and criticism.

Rates of Spousal Assault: "A lot we don't see..."

The rates of spousal assault vary from community to community, depending on its size, relative economic prosperity, and the availability of alcohol. The larger "wet" communities with high levels of unemployment suffer from higher rates of spousal assault. Smaller, tighter communities, especially those that are "dry" (prohibit the sale and/or consumption of alcohol) are less likely to have severe problems in this area.

Employment is not an antidote to assault since many cases involve employed males. Nor is being an officially "dry" town, as a nurse explains the impact of illicitly imported alcohol: "The rates of spousal assault go in spurts, related to how much alcohol is in town. If someone gets a shipment in, we may see two or three people in a weekend, and then we won't see anyone for another month. So that's a hard statistic to give." Still, in "wet" towns, women and men are much more likely to cite drinking as the major cause of spousal assault.

Assault is often an invisible problem because many women will not discuss it even with their families or friends. Another nurse estimates that, "there's a lot that goes on that we don't see...probably we see 25 per cent of what is actually happening." Even though most cases do not require medical treatment, she believes spousal assault is a big problem: "It's something that the whole community is going to have to deal with. It seems that the women come and they want help at the moment, but then, it's a cycle, they just go back. So, I think it's going to have to come from the community, to have a support group, and they're trying."

Most women consider spousal assault a top priority and a major issue for women. According to one RCMP constable, his small community is relatively quiet: "Break-ins and drunks. Very few family problems. Disturbing the peace. Those are the main calls. There's not very much violence, family-wise, that we get called out to. Like in Iqaluit, they usually get more family violence calls. Here we get very few, especially these two years I've been here; we used to get more. It seems like it's getting better, or maybe somebody else is hearing about it other than us. Like the mental health committee is getting involved in spousal assault. We get a few calls, but only involving younger families. I don't think the women really have a problem. If you look at the majority, maybe a few get beat up by their husbands. If I said there was lots going on in town, I'm sure I would be wrong.

Even if they don't complain about it, you would see women with a bruise or a black eye. But we don't see that that often, maybe once in a blue moon. That's why I said there's hardly any. We're lucky here that we don't really have that problem."

Even in towns where people suspect that spousal assault rates are high, they seldom hear anyone talk about it. To a large extent, the problem is an invisible one, surfacing only in the occasional call for police, nursing, or counselling help, or in the unexplained bruises. As one woman comments: "I don't hear too much about that. It's something that I think is very private. It's happened to a couple of friends of mine but it's something that they just don't want to talk about. Yet, I know it's happened because I hear rumours, and I see the black eyes and the bruises."

In the teen group, assault is not as prevalent as pregnancy: "There's a lot of girls that are pregnant and their kids go into adoption. So there are some short-term relationships going on there, but they end."

The Causes of Spousal Assault: "When a guy gets mad..."

A) The Male–Female Power Differential
Sheer strength is a source of power for men and is perceived as being a significant reason that men assault their partners. In combination with suppressed emotions, alcohol, and anger, it creates an ominous force. A 54-year-old weaver says that: "When a guy gets mad, and if the man thinks that he is stronger than her, then he easily beats her. When the man thinks that he is the boss of the house, he is kind of mean to his people. When the married couples don't really understand each other and don't really talk about their feelings, then they will end up fighting."

B) Drunkenness and Drug Abuse
Often the power imbalance—and the violence—is aggravated by abuse of alcohol or drugs. Local RCMP in one community estimated that, "probably about 80 per cent" of spousal assaults involve alcohol use, usually by the man, but often by the woman as well. Inuit women talk freely about the power issue and about the invasion of alcohol into their lives.

One woman, who is married with two children and has a relatively traditional life-style, thinks spousal assault is the most pressing problem facing her community: "I think I would list that as a first priority, because I don't want it to happen at all." She blames drugs and alcohol for the loss of control, and believes that all too often both partners are drinking when violence occurs: "I think it's both the couple living together. They take drugs and alcohol, and they start to fight and they separate, and then they get back together again. I think that's the biggest problem why they don't want to get married." This confirms estimates by counsellors and RCMP that spousal assault is more likely to erupt among younger couples who are living together, but are not yet married. As indicated in the section on staying single, many women delay or avoid a legal commitment because there has been a history of abuse in the relationship.

"Alcohol was never invented by Inuit people, and when an Inuit man drinks, he is easily able to drink his senses away, and then when he doesn't know what he's doing he is able to beat up his wife," Geela hypothesizes.

C) Disagreement and Jealousy

Others insist that disagreement is the central cause of assault; alcohol is usually, but not always, present. A normally compliant woman may find herself the victim of spousal assault if she speaks up or disagrees. "For instance, if I was married to this guy, and all that time I was saying yes to him, even if I didn't want to obey him, and then I got tired of it and I started saying no to these things, and he got so used to me saying yes to everything and finally I said no, then he would beat me up. That's what happens," says Julie. Some women argue that even if they were to "obey" their men consistently, they would still get beaten.

Jealousy is frequently cited by Inuit women as an important factor in spousal assault. Violence is triggered for some couples by the man's suspicion that his woman is having an affair. In the words of elder Rosie: "There are different reasons why men hit their wives. Maybe they're jealous or the woman cheated on him. If they had a problem and they didn't talk to anyone, it's all bottled up inside and they get angry and they take it out on the wife."

Rhoda, who works for the Hudson's Bay Company, laments her former husband's jealousy: "I don't know why men hit their women, but I know how it feels because it has happened to me. With my husband, the thing that used to make him abuse me was that he thought I was with somebody else. Jealousy. He wasn't drinking when he hit me—he has never touched a drop." What made him jealous? "My visits—to anywhere!—he would question them. Whatever I did seemed to be a threat to him. Very jealous." The double standard, common in western culture, pertains to the Inuit as well. It is far more acceptable for a man to have an affair and to expect his woman to accept it than the reverse. Often, it is the man who is the first to cheat. The woman feels angry and wronged, and if she confronts her man may receive blows instead of an apology. Annie expresses her fear of commitment: "That was one of the reasons why I never wanted to get married too soon in my life, because that could be a problem when you're young, growing up together. You get depressed with each other for a while, or he gets jealous, then that could be a problem." She will wait for someone who will not, for any reason, be "mean" to her.

D) Lack of Communication

Compared with Inuit women, Inuit men are seen as not being in touch with their feelings, or open about them; so instead of communicating with the women in their lives, they strike out in a release of frustration and tension. It is not surprising that many more women than men approach social service agencies and mental health committees. "Most Inuit men, when they have a problem, they don't talk to anybody. They don't admit it. Women are open."

Lucie is grateful that her boyfriend is not like that: "My boyfriend doesn't hide anything. He never did. He's really open. I don't think he would hide any feelings. But guys who hide their feelings usually beat up their girlfriends. If they're shy to express their feelings, and if something happens and then he starts beating her and goes to jail for that, then they start blaming the girl because she did this and she did that, which I don't like." In this type of situation, the feelings come out anyway, but in a way that hurts the woman. What would she do if her boyfriend changed, stopped being so open, started drinking, and beat her? "Try to talk to him. Not in a hurry, but show him that you really love him and try telling him step by step what your feelings for him are and what you're seeing in him—the change. One day at a time, or whatever it takes, if you want to keep that love." She would let him know that she sees a change she doesn't like, "not in a very straight-forward way, but in a long way." If he persisted in hitting her, she would not know what to do. "I've never been hit before."

The Inuit woman's greater openness is defined as a strength, not as a weakness, as it is for men. A woman in her late 30s, who is trying to establish a support group for assault victims, believes that men are stronger physically, but women are stronger emotionally: "I talk to a lot of women my age, and I think women are very strong. If we went through something really bad, we're more open to talk to somebody, but men, most of them just keep it to themselves." A health assistant agrees: "The mental health committee, and the health committee, are mostly women, so in community things, they're more involved, although there are usually a few token men, and they don't usually add a lot. They [men] don't usually have a lot to offer, although they are more likely to go to the bigger communities for regional board meetings."

Problems in Dealing with Violence: "It's going underground..."

A) The Complexities of Reporting and Police Intervention

One of the most paradoxical issues surrounding spousal assault is the pattern of reporting and laying charges. Many women are reluctant to report assaults because of national RCMP policy. As a constable explains: "If we are presented with any evidence of assault, we have to lay charges, and that's it. The woman will be subpoenaed to court. She can say she's not going to talk or give evidence. If she's subpoenaed, and put on the stand where she stands mute, at that point the Crown has to make a decision of whether to deal with her for not giving evidence—if she's given a written statement prior to her appearance—or just let it die. So, spousal assault is prevalent, but it's becoming hidden. In this community, it's going underground on us. I don't think there's anything we can do about it, as law enforcement officers, because the women are scared. Originally they used to come to us for help, and we used to go down to defuse it, and we could show discretion on the scene. If the woman didn't want to lay charges, we'd say fine. And we'd go down and defuse it the next time. But that wasn't solving anything either. We would walk in, defuse the situation, walk out, the husband wouldn't be charged, and wouldn't have to pay any kind of penalty for it. It was just as easy for him to walk in and beat her up the next time.

"Before, it would be really frustrating. A woman would come in at 3 o'clock in the morning and say her husband had beaten her up; so you take the statement and everything, you make up the file, you lay the charges, and you've done a fair amount of work and then, two days later, she comes in and says, 'Oh, we're in love again and I want to drop the charges.' That was happening constantly. That's where the bad reputation started—'Oh, the police won't do anything about it.' Because the police were getting so used to it, they would say, 'Fine, you come back in three or four days and if you still want to lay charges, we'll do it,' or, 'Fine, you come back in two days, but you have to swear the information yourself, lay the charges yourself.' In Canada, usually the charges are all laid by the police, you don't lay your own charges, because all the offences are offences against the person and offences against the Crown, against everybody. That gave us some bad press. I think that's where this policy came from."

These frustrations are echoed by another constable. "Probably one of the most frustrating parts of the job is spousal assault. A lot of times the woman was pressured to say, 'Well, I don't want to lay charges.' Or she was scared to lay charges. So the force just decided, okay, if the evidence is there, from the wife or from independent witnesses, we will lay charges. That's a national policy. It's a good idea in that once the evidence is before us, everyone realizes that the charges will be laid, and the wife can go home and say, 'Gee, you know, what can I do? They won't listen to me, they won't drop the charges.' So maybe it takes the heat off her. But, by the same token, I think we don't get as many calls about spousal assault because the women say, 'Well, if I go to the police tonight and say that hubby beat me, I know that three or four months from now I will be going to court, and I'm going to get up there and say to the judge that I don't want to say anything, and the judge is going to say, too bad, you have to tell me what happened.' So I think that there will be fewer spousal assaults reported, or the increase will be less than it would have been. So, I'm of two minds. My personal opinion is that the policy is a bit too strict. There should be a little bit of leniency. But I understand the rationale behind it, and I agree with the basic concept of it. There should be an out though. Right now, the force is very firm with it—that is the policy and you will stick to it."

Because of this complex situation, women are now, perhaps, just as likely to go to social services or the mental health committee—or not appeal for help at all—as they are to go to the RCMP for protection and justice. An example of this dilemma is a woman who was trying to complete an advanced degree in the South. According to police: "She is right in the middle of a situation right now. A year ago we were going to charge him with spousal assault. She begged us, that since they were going to the South for her schooling, to let her get her life straightened out; all it would take to get them back on track was to get him out of this environment. And we went along with it. We thought, if we charge him, we're going to disrupt this whole family. She's going to be down in nursing school, he's going to be up here, we're going to have to drag her up here for the trial, everything was going to be disrupted. Within four weeks he was charged again. They returned to the North, and she has asked the police for a peace bond."

B) Shelters and Safe Houses

Another typical mechanism, utilized by many contemporary societies for providing support and protection of battered women, is the community-based shelter. In small, northern communities, however, shelters may not be an ideal answer to the problem of spousal assault: "I think we would have to build more than a couple of shelters because it wouldn't take long for a guy to find out which one his wife was in in a settlement of 250 to 1000 people, or maybe the person running the shelter would phone him." Flying a victim to one of the larger communities, like Iqaluit or Yellowknife, is fraught with problems. First, it removes the woman from her usual support network of family and friends; second, it may remove her children from school; third, it removes her from the ability to earn a livelihood, if she is working; and fourth, it makes it even more difficult for the woman to effect a reconciliation with her partner (with professional assistance), if that is the course of action she chooses to take.

Even safe houses (existing homes in an underground, informal network) may not be effective in a tiny community. Beyond the problems of logistics and privacy, there are other concerns from a police point of view: "Sometimes shelters and safe houses are being used to protect the guy from being charged, to try to defuse the situation themselves, and to get the woman out without police involvement. Some of the comments filtering back are, 'They haven't got the woman's problem solved,' 'They're not really trying to solve it,' or 'They're trying to keep the guy's butt out of court.' When that's the case then we're not going to support it at all. I would support the system if they've got the woman's interest at heart: get her out of that house so he can't beat on her; give her a safe place where she can sit down and get her head straight and decide, 'Yes, I'm not going to put up with that any more'; call the police in; and go the charge route. But if they're just going to have it to drag the woman out so the police don't find out, and then throw her back into that relationship, it isn't going to solve anything."

One solution to the shelter problem in small communities may be to be open about the shelter's location, inform the husband that his wife is there (with her permission), and set a time when he can come to visit her. This method is used in some of the provinces where rules of visitation include that the man must be sober, and he must understand that the police will be called immediately if he makes or threatens any disturbance. This provides a cooling-off period, ensures both parties are sober, and offers a controlled environment for discussion and decision making. Locks on the doors and peep holes provide control over access. In cases of severe assault or use of weapons, the police can be involved.

Whatever the pros and cons of shelters and safe houses, at the present time, RCMP internal policy does not readily mesh with their use: "If you're running the safe house, and you notify me and say, 'Mary is down here, she just got a severe beating, I'm notifying you so if the husband shows up, you can come and get him,' then I'm obligated to talk to her, and pick him up. Spousal assault is a crime! If you notify me only when the husband is acting belligerently or trying to break the door down, it might be too late. That wouldn't work up here, because most of these guys are drunk when it's occurring. You can't talk any common sense to them anyway. They're stubborn, there's tunnel vision."

New Versions of Traditional Responses: "Straighten it out..."

In general, reporting the problems of spousal assault to the police or placing women and children in shelters also fly in the face of traditional Inuit values and mechanisms for resolving male–female conflict. As Sara cautions: "Most of the older people in this community are definitely of the opinion that the community and the family should take care of their own problems. If a man is beating up his wife, the police should stay out, social services should stay out, because originally and traditionally there weren't those services to intervene. The parents would step in and say 'If you're married you have to live together, and you've got to straighten it out.'"

A) Spousal Assault Committees

Some communities have attempted to create spousal assault committees similar to the youth justice committees or the mental health committees, which consist of respected men and women, including elders, who will hear cases and help resolve them. Meetings are held to co-ordinate the activities of the spousal assault committees with those of local police and counsellors.

B) Alternative Measures

Alternative measures, such as community service or restitution, commonly used in cases of juvenile delinquency, for example, are considered by many to be a far more productive response to spousal assault. The problem is, however, that the RCMP have no right to participate in alternative measures programs and are bound by their national policy mandating arrest and prosecution for reported spouse assaulters: "We have no right as police officers, unless it's written into the legislation like it is for young offenders—alternative measures, that's law. That option is there. We identify it, we bring it to the prosecutor's attention, as an agent for the attorney general. Then a decision whether it goes to criminal court or alternative measures is made. That decision isn't made by the police officer. It's identified by the police officer that it should be an option, but it isn't our right. It would have to be legislated, similarly, that spousal assault could be dealt with in the community. A lot of elders give signals that that's the way they would like it again, and we just tell them, 'If it's not reported to us and the beatings are still going on, it's not being resolved traditionally out there. These women are still getting beaten. You have the opportunity as parents to step in, you're not resolving it.'"

C) Support Groups

Another attempt at resolving male–female conflicts in the community is the creation of support groups. One woman is trying to establish a support group of former victims and perpetrators (male and female) who are also respected members of their community. She says that it cannot have anything to do with the legal or police functions. It can be an informal network only. Another woman works on a one-to-one basis with assault victims: "It's not very good; I wish there wasn't any spousal assault, because it's bad. I wouldn't want anybody to go through it. I've been through it, and that's why I try to help other women whose husbands or boyfriends beat them."

In some communities, support groups for men who assault are being set up: "These batterers are seeking help. They want help. They don't want to hurt their wives any more, or their girlfriends. I think that's a very positive move on both parts, the women and the men."

Other Domestic Violence Problems: "Scared of the kids..."

The mental health committee in any community can delineate the problems facing its people. In some, spousal assault and lack of parental ability to discipline their children rank high on the list of complaints. Another problem, which reflects both these complaints, is assault by teenage sons against their parents (usually, but not always, the mother). This is a very disturbing problem that flies in the face of many traditional Inuit values: "The worst cases are the mothers who come to us to talk because they get scared of the kids. They [the kids] don't listen to the parents or they get abusive to them. It seems to be happening more and more with the teenagers."

Conversely, some young people go to the committees because "their parents don't care about them; they don't understand or treat their kids seriously." They try to help these families. "Sometimes it's very hard."

Children as Victims: "They're caught..."

As far as intentional physical assault against children goes, it is perceived as being a rare occurrence. Naturally, child abuse is a hidden problem everywhere, as is incest, but there is general agreement that Inuit children are not likely to be on the receiving end of parental blows. If a man is out of control, he is more likely to hit his wife than to hit his children. This fits in with our observations of Inuit families: children are nurtured, treated with great affection, and given relatively broad freedoms.

RCMP do not lay many charges of child abuse, and nurses interviewed do not report many cases, although, as everywhere, some exist. One constable observes: "I'm sure that at the nursing station, they see these kids day in and day out, and we'd be notified forthwith if there was any evidence of child abuse, and we would act in the same way. It's a criminal act and we would go after it."

Like children everywhere, Inuit children who grow up in a violent home are also victims, although they are not apt to be the direct targets of physical assault. Geela reflects on the feelings of many Inuit women when she talks about the impact of family violence: "The thing that really hurts me today is when children are involved in that relationship and they see fights. It's one of the concerns I have with the couples who have children, and they're exposed to these violent things that are happening. It was happening to my kids when they were really young, and it had some influence, especially on my boy. The girls don't seem to have that much affect, but my boy, I don't know what it is. The only thing I try to do is understand him. I think he has anger." The anger might be toward the assaultive father or toward the arguing parents. In any case: "Sometimes, if he's in school, and if he gets bothered by someone, he lets his anger out easily. I don't know what it is, but it's quite hard. I see it in other kids. I see it where it isn't tried to be corrected, where the parents just keep doing it. That's where it hurts me the most—with the children. They're caught." The children see and feel the anger between their parents and are afraid. They hold the fear and their own anger inside, until it comes out later, perhaps in school where they get in trouble for an outburst. Of course, research indicates that girls are also deeply affected by growing up in violent homes since they tend, more than others, to seek mates who will perpetuate abuse in their lives. Even for those who were young when their parents separated, the trauma leaves an indelible impression.

Incest: "Never traditionally accepted..."

Incest and sexual assault also exist in Inuit communities, both traditionally and in modern times. According to an RCMP officer: "Complaints do surface on occasion. I don't think we'll go a whole year without one surfacing again. I don't think they're all being reported to us. Especially father–daughter. Most people adhere to the tradition of adoption. You go into any family unit, the people kids are calling Mommy and Daddy aren't Mommy and Daddy. They're aunts and uncles, whatever. It's the father and the younger female, maybe between eight and 12 years old. We just finished one case in Supreme Court last February. The man was 66 years old, the girl is now 14, but four years ago it was brought to our attention, and the assaults had occurred the two years prior to that. I hear two points of view in town. A lot of them will say it's traditionally accepted, and then there are Inuit who say 'b.s.', it was never traditionally accepted. People did it and got away with it, because the law didn't step in and charge them. So they knew it was going on, but it wasn't accepted. At the hearing of the case in Supreme Court, the court- house was just stuffed with people, and there were a lot of people who really couldn't understand why the court was taking the attitude that it's unacceptable."

Assault and Liberation: "Talking about women's rights..."

Of concern to Inuit feminists is the fact that some men and women believe that women's liberation has perhaps gone too far in attempting to rebalance male–female relationships. As a minister cautions: "I think a lot of people have started to realize...especially now with the Charter of Rights, they start talking about women's rights. I have seen, especially girls, start to change a lot. Especially in the North. The women and the girls seem to have over-reacted. Even the little things that they can solve, they usually go to the RCMP, or they go to social workers. Even though they could solve their problems before, they used to solve them among themselves. When it happens now, it seems that a lot of people end up with a criminal record. That's the way I see it. For example, last year, a man was ready to go out hunting; he asked his wife to make bannock for him, because he would be going out for a couple of days, and they have to take bannock, but she wanted to go to the bingo games, so her husband pushed her a little bit. 'The bingo games are not really important, I want to bring the bannock with me.' The woman was mad and she reported it to the RCMP and went to court for this. They called it spousal assault. It's not that. The woman tried to put him in jail, but the judge was really understanding and realized that it wasn't that serious, so they dropped the charges. That's just an example. They never did that kind of thing before." Many who support the rights of women to equal opportunity and respect add that they are worried that many women take "women's lib too seriously." That is, in their search for independence and equality, they may unwittingly also work against the norm of sharing. It is a fine balance, to be sure.

Notes

1. The terms "spousal assault" and "wife battering" seem particularly problematic for Inuit women, since so many have chosen not to marry. Family violence might be construed to mean violence only in a couple living together. In the absence of more appropriate terms, spousal assault is used here to mean any assault between male and female partners who are in an intimate relationship, married or not, living together or not. "Heteroviolence" is more accurate, but seems unnecessarily technical.

A Beaten Woman

A woman is beaten. She has a black eye, the left side of her chin and her left arm are a mass of green–yellow bruises. She has a cut on her forehead from where she hit the counter. Her forearm is scorched from the wood stove.

Her husband has left the house. She went to see a counsellor a few weeks ago, after the last beating, and she knows she should call now. They talk and a decision is made to call the RCMP and have charges laid. This is done. They are very nice to her; they take her to the nursing station, bring her tea; they take some pictures of the bruises and the cut.

The RCMP tell her that her husband has been picked up and will be charged, but they will have to let him go in about an hour. They suggest she and her two kids stay somewhere else. There is no shelter or transition home. She calls her sister, who reluctantly takes her in. The sister lives in a two-bedroom house and has three children of her own. They all squeeze in for the night.

The next day she goes to see the counsellor. He tells her she did the right thing. He also tells her that she is eligible for social assistance and housing. According to the mandate of Social Services and the Housing Corporation this is true, but the fact is that there is no extra housing in town. Many homes already contain two, sometimes three, families. She has to continue to stay with her sister and her sister's husband and kids.

Three weeks have passed and life is very stressful. Everyone is quiet around her. Those who aren't quiet, lecture her. Her sister's husband thinks she has betrayed her husband and is destroying a family. The bank office has been to talk to her and told her she should not appear in court. It will only mean the end of her family. Her sister is finding it difficult to be supportive with all the outside pressures, the crowded house, and her brother-in-law phoning and banging on the door.

A month has passed and the preliminary trial date has arrived. A plane lands, and a judge, a clerk, a Crown prosecutor, a court worker, and defence attorney get off and turn the community centre into a court room.

Her husband is talking to his lawyer. She asks the court worker when her lawyer will arrive. She is told that she doesn't need a lawyer because the Crown, who represents the country, will help her tell her story. A man approaches her and introduces himself as the Crown. He asks if she is okay and did she make and sign this statement. "Yes, yes," she says, and he leaves.

Her husband pleads not guilty, and a new court date is set. The new date is six weeks away. This is good, the court worker tells her; it's usually a much longer wait. She cannot figure what is so good about living in a two-bedroom house with three adults and five children for six weeks and be lectured by half the town for ruining her family.

The six weeks pass. The court date arrives, the plane arrives and she goes to the community centre to ask the man who represents the country what will happen. He isn't there. She sits in the corner and waits. A woman comes to her and introduces herself as the Crown. She asks her how she is, and if she is ready to tell her story. She says she is ready. She asks the Crown what will happen. The Crown assures her that with the pictures the RCMP have and the medical report they will convict her husband of assault.

The Crown doesn't tell her that he will likely get a $200 or $250 fine and be released on the condition that he keep the peace. She doesn't ask where she is living or if she knows that she is entitled to apply for sole possession of the home, and that she can get a lawyer through legal aid to help her. The court worker would tell her, except the court worker, who landed with the plane, has 14 other people to speak to as well. The counsellor would tell her, except that he is an alcohol counsellor and he has only had a one-day seminar on family violence. He doesn't know that justice would help her get her house back.

She tells her story. She cries a lot. She is nervous and upset and hasn't had much sleep for weeks. The judge says that her husband hit her without permission and fines him $200 and tells him he can't hit her for a year. Then they tell her she can go.

She leaves the court alone because no one wants to be associated with a woman who breaks up a perfectly good family. She returns to her sister's house and has tea. Her sister asks her if she will be going home now. She says she has no choice. It was awful being hit and screamed at by one person, but by a town, it's much worse. And her husband doesn't work and hasn't for six months and so he won't be able to pay his fine. If he doesn't, he'll go to jail and then everyone will be even more upset with her.

She hasn't anywhere else to go. Once she went to Yellowknife for medical treatment, but she hasn't been anywhere else. Yellowknife is a city and she doesn't think she can adjust to that, nor does she know how she would get there. And she always hears that there is very little housing and that a two-bedroom apartment would cost her $1500 a month.

She packs her things and takes the kids and goes home. He cannot pay the fine, but she can. She did it once before when he was charged for driving his truck while drunk. She pulls out her sewing basket and some beads and starts to decorate the moccasins she has made. She will have to make a lot of moccasins to earn $200. But she has two months—she can do it—she's done it before.

Chapter IV

WOMEN IN THE WORKPLACE

Woman Sewing Skin by Eli Weetaluktuk

Dene Women and Work

Phoebe Nahanni

Introduction: The Concept of Work

Among the many facets of life in the Canadian North, none affects the lives of women more than the concept of "work". One has only to examine the many changes in the socio-economic conditions of the North in the past two decades to realize how "work" has changed the lives of northern women. Discussion in this paper will be directed at the concepts of work for northern women in general and Dene women in particular.

For many Dene women in contemporary society, "work" has three meanings: a) work in the "bush", where the way of life is based on hunting, fishing, trapping, and gathering; b) domestic work in the household setting; and c) work outside the home, commonly known as "having a job".

The quality and goals conceptually inherent in these types of work are not complementary in terms of ideology, time, and Dene women. While I do not intend to provide a detailed analysis of this complicated situation, broad distinctions in the three meanings of "work" from the northern perspective cannot be ignored.

Perspectives on the quality and goals of each of the three meanings of "work", and their relationship with each other, will be discussed within the framework of the two economies: formal and informal. The formal economy is the commercial economy as it operates in the industrialized world. The informal economy operates on the community and household levels and is often characterized by subsistence and small-scale bartering (Ross and Usher 1986). Information for this paper was drawn from secondary sources on the northern economy, descriptive information from newspapers, correspondence with community people, and my personal experiences.

TABLE 1

Types of "Work" in the Dene Setting

	"Bush"	Household in the Community	Industrial and Formal Economy
Time	• seasonal • flexible	• determined by clock • some flexibility • dependent on service hours	• determined by clock • time means money
Benefits	• whole family • sharing of resources	• some families • some sharing dependent on available services and commodities	• individual • provides income and employment as well as experience in wage economy
Ideology	• egalitarianism • sharing	• division of labour • some sharing	• capitalistic

The term "work" is defined as a human activity; a physical or mental exertion directed to some purpose or end. It is obvious from this definition that we all work. Why then, in contemporary society, are some human activities to which this definition would apply not called "work"? "Work", as it is known today happens when a person provides labour in exchange for money. Work of this kind happens in the "workplace". When a person works in the "workplace", that person is employed. Employment is a very important factor in determining socio-economic well-being.

Where employment is concerned, with respect to aboriginal peoples of Canada, two matters can be stated. Prior to 1981, employment statistics on native people were sporadic or non-existent; however, since the 1981 Census, there have been enough statistics on aboriginal peoples to conclude that 40 per cent of native women over the age of 15 were considered part of the labour force (either working or, if unemployed, actively looking for work). The Census also reflected that 16.5 per cent of this labour force was unemployed; those who were employed had an average income of $6,063; and approximately 60 per cent of those employed were in the clerical/sales services. What are all those other women doing who are not reflected in these numbers?(White 1985:14–18)

A recent debate and research sponsored by the Royal Commission on the Economic Union and Development Prospects for Canada (1981) concluded that northern Canada was, and is, experiencing a severe condition of underdevelopment. Two immediate measures were proposed to ameliorate this serious situation. It was recommended, first, that non-renewable resource extraction and first-stage

170

processing take place, and, second that the gap in wages between natives and non-natives be reduced through government-enhanced, education training programs (Whittington 1985:2).

Three prevailing arguments were advanced to counter the conclusions based on conventional economic analysis. First, conventional economic analysis fails to account for the significance of the traditional economy of the aboriginal people. Second, the dominant framework of the northern economy is intended to benefit the non-natives who are short-term residents and who are highly educated. Third, the development of the traditional economy, and the structural accommodation between native and western economies, will determine the course of northern development and not necessarily mobility, education, and the need for jobs in the non-renewable sector (Whittington 1985:3).

Currently, there are no consistent data available to quantify the traditional economy and, thus, to determine the kind of work that women and men do. A true economic picture cannot be provided in charts or figures. It was noted earlier that northern women, in general, have had to adjust to the socio-economic changes in northern Canada. The acceleration of changes in the last 20 years forces northern people, not only to make the necessary adjustments, but also to assert their rights to survival as a people. As for the women, it is assumed that most Dene women have always acted in the interest of protecting the family.

The three situations in which women find themselves are the "bush" environment, the household environment in the community, and the environment of the "workplace" when having a job outside the home. In real life, the assessment might not be as clear-cut, but for the purpose of understanding the concept of "work", I propose two questions. (1) Assuming the Dene women make deliberate distinctions between goals and benefits of the environments in which they find themselves, does the distinction assist or facilitate their choice of future direction? (2) What are the major conflicts or barriers that impede their choice?

The Region: Northern Canada

The northern Canada that I am referring to is the Northwest Territories, which has been divided by the legislative assembly into districts and regions. The Dene live in the communities found in the Mackenzie District or Denendeh. This district is further divided into three regions: Inuvik Region, Fort Smith Region, and Yellowknife Region.

In 1985, the estimated population of the Northwest Territories was 51,021 (24,245 females and 26,776 males). The composition is roughly as follows: 17 per cent Dene, 6 per cent Métis, 30 per cent Inuit, and 42 per cent non-indigenous (Outcrop 1986; Whittington 1985:54). The Dene live in 32 communities in Denendeh and compose the majority in 27 of those communities.

TABLE 2

Structure of the Formal and Informal Economic Sectors in Northern Canada

Formal Economy Industrial	Informal Economy Non-industrial

• in relation to Canada and the world
• internal economic relations
• government
• corporate
• small business
	• "bush"
	• household
	• traditional
	    - domestic
	            - commodity exchange
	
	    - household
	          - cult of domesticity
	          - small-scale barter

Linkages
• wage economy
• welfare economy
• commodity exchange and small-scale bartering

Northern Economy

The uniqueness of the northern economy is characterized not only by the existence of a dual economy—the formal economy and the informal economy—but also by the way in which they are linked in the northern communities (Whittington 1985; Ross and Usher 1986). Let us examine how aspects of these economies directly relate to the concerns of Dene women and work (Table 2).

The formal economy in the North today is the economy that was introduced into the North by government and industry. The process began incrementally from the beginning of the fur trade and with much more force in the last 20 years. Economic progress in the domain of conventional economics is easily measured. For example, in 1987, the economic activities measured in the Northwest Territories included those of fishing (domestic and commercial), hunting and trapping, marine mammal harvesting, forestry, agriculture, non-renewable resources and energy development, service industries (government and private), and income employment (government and private). The Department of Economic Development reported in 1987 that the highest production rate in non-renewable resources for 1986 was mining; in renewable resources, tourism. Public administration, community, business, and personnel services provided 46 per cent of the employment sector (Outcrop 1987:58). This has been the case since 1981. Government is the largest industry, followed by mining and tourism (Whittington 1985:34).

The northern informal economy is community-based and still predominates in Dene communities in northwestern Canada. These communities are characterized by their small population, by the great distances between them, and by the presence of government and industry. The majority of the Dene inhabitants are

172

engaged in hunting, fishing, and trapping. Community populations range from 65 to 1000. Usually present in the community are a church or two; a community hall; a school or two; the RCMP; the Hudson's Bay Company (The Bay) store; private entrepreneurs (variety increases with the size of the community); an airstrip or airport; nursing station or hospital; and government offices that include administration, forestry, parks, post office, and public works. Houses are generally small, except for those owned by government and private entrepreneurs. Most homes will have a clothes-line, a snowmobile parked in front, sled dogs tied on posts nearby, and outhouses placed not too far away. Some will have smoke houses and a frame for stretching moose or caribou hides. The majority of these homes have neither indoor plumbing nor electricity. Roads are usually made of gravel.

Government and industry generate employment for wages and make the formal economy function on a small scale in the community. However, the informal economy (traditional pursuits), characterized by hunting, fishing, and trapping activities (i.e., subsistence and bartering), predominates in the majority of the northern communities. Few families depend solely on either the informal or the formal economy.

The link between the formal and informal economies is through wage employment. Dene who decide to work for wages generally do so to augment their income earned from hunting, fishing, and trapping. They will work for wages to make enough money to purchase items important for their land-based life-style— items such as snowmobiles, tools, motors for boats, canoes, and paddles. Working for wages means that the Dene will be able to continue to hunt, fish, and trap.

Ross and Usher (1986) and Whittington (1985) identify a third economic sector—the welfare economy. They appear to agree that the welfare system is just another source of income to be tapped in time of need or in the off-season when people are unable to hunt, fish, or trap. The irreconcilable difference is that the time spent in the wage economy undermines the time that could be used in the traditional economy. The welfare economy supports the two.

Women's Workplace: The "Bush"

Prior to the 1940s, the traditional Dene society was organized into family units consisting of collectives of up to 20 people. These family units were scattered throughout the land. Their economy was based primarily on hunting, fishing, trapping, and gathering. They were nomadic, not in the sense that they wandered aimlessly, scratching out an existence, but their travels were planned in migratory cycles according to the season. Some families travelled within well-defined areas where they had established several seasonal campsites. Travels beyond these well-defined areas were determined by supply and conservation of the accessible resources.

Recent historical research speculates that matriarchal tendencies existed among the Dene in earlier times. However, since the turn of the 20th century, bilateral arrangements have existed among the Dene, in which women and men share the tasks. This implies that these tasks were defined. Many elders say that life was equally difficult for women and men. One had to know "how to work" to be of assistance to the family and, most of all, to be able to survive in the harsh boreal climate.

Dene women learned "how to work" from older female relatives. The quality of their work was contingent on their awareness of several categories of knowledge: the family background; cultural matters, such as customs, norms, and conventions; childbearing and nurturing; and aspects of the physical and biological environment which enabled them to provide for their families by hunting, fishing, trapping, and preparing the harvest for domestic use. For Dene women, work began at an early age. Often, young girls were given small pails to get water or some wiring to prepare the rabbit snare. By the time they reached puberty, they knew how to relate to different members of the family, how to make a fire, how to hunt small game and fish, and how to recognize seasonal changes.

The ideology of the bush environment included a sense of place and family, stability through knowing the customs, egalitarianism, co-operation, controlling one's use of the resources, and self-sufficiency. The overall benefits included the continued replenishment of resources, stability and predictability within the family, and knowledge by observing the physical and biological environment. In the context of life in the bush, time was viewed as a valuable opportunity.

Women's Workplace: The Household in the Settlement

The gradual move to the communities began in the 1940s. Many Dene say that the church and compulsory education for their children accelerated this move, so that by the 1960s most families were settled in permanent homes. The 1940s marked the breakdown of the family and the anguish of many mothers and fathers. At first, parents continued their seasonal rounds while their children were at convent schools, and then reunited with their children in the settlements in the summer months. Imagine their anguish over the changes in their children. They were not learning "how to work" as their parents had—from the family and the bush environment. Instead they were learning different behaviours and skills that opposed the continuation of their customs and languages. Their children were learning skills to prepare them for the industrial economy: boys to become heavy equipment operators and girls to become nurses and secretaries. Skills learned for the bush environment gained no recognition in formal education.

In the context of settlement life, tanning hides became archaic in light of the leather goods that could be purchased from the local stores. The dedication the women had put into the art of making moccasins, parkas, and so on was overshadowed by the abundance and simplicity of clothing available in the local stores and mail order catalogues. Settlement life facilitated the accumulation of goods. Now the Dene could not easily pick up their goods and travel. To remain in the settlements, the Dene had to work for money—money that would enable them to buy food and clothing at the local stores. When work was not available, they could apply for welfare.

The move from the "bush" way of life to the settlement way of life required some fundamental adjustments in thinking and behaviour. But first, it was necessary to recognize that adjustments needed to take place. For the elderly and parents this was difficult. Since the 1940s they had witnessed the erosion of the family and their customs. And without the language, parents and grandparents were unable to transfer critical knowledge of the Dene way of life.

The next generation of Dene were learning in a school environment from a stiff desk. They learned a new meaning of time: time became a concept of linear and compartmentalized segments divided into minutes and hours rather than into night and day, and seasonal changes. There was confusion over moral behaviour. Rather than learning from their family, Dene children were learning good and bad behaviour from strangers. Thus it was generally instilled in their innocent minds that a good person went to church and a bad person did not. Memorizing institutional rules was far more valuable than experiencing and learning the characteristics of the weather and seasons, they were told.

In the end, everyone was confused. The Dene children returned to their parents often more confused than their parents. Grandmothers and mothers had to bear the anguish as they patiently watched their children struggle with this confusion.

In addition to the anxieties brought on by the loss of control over what their children learned, parents had to get on with providing for their families. To stay in the communities, income had to be earned for food and clothing to be bought from the stores. Adjusting to this new situation began with men finding seasonal jobs for wages while women stayed home to look after home and children. Not only had the ideology of household maintenance crept into Dene society, but how women and men were to relate to each other. No longer were women and men on an equal footing. Women depended on their husbands to earn the means for obtaining food and clothing. Earning money raised the prestige of men over women. The meaning of time and its importance to the wage economy overshadowed the value of time as it was understood in the bush environment. Women's domestic work increased but was no longer considered important work.

Work in the "bush" household is not the same as work in the community household. Household work became housework in the settlements. In the context of the "bush", women and men could balance their responsibilities in maintaining the home with the practice of going out on the land and bringing their children along with them. For women, work in the bush was, and is, physically difficult, but there were always other members of the family to help. There was a sense of order and predictability in the way people related to one another.

Housework in the community was comparatively difficult in that women often found themselves alone in the nuclear-family setting. In most cases, they were provided with government-built homes which were often not big enough for the large Dene families. This meant that these large families were either crowded together or divided among houses which were not located close to each other. Where was the glory of living in the community for women? What benefits did they enjoy? There was no glory in being isolated and overburdened with housework which was not recognized as important work in the wage economy. And yet, men were able to "go to work" because their women supported them by keeping their clothes clean and pressed, and meals prepared. On the other hand, life in the community was easier for some women. But the price they had to pay was to postpone, if not give up, the ideology of the bush environment. They had to submit to the ideology of the wage economy and the "cult of domesticity". They had to become competitive consumers and share the prestige, if, and when, the men were successful wage earners.

Some women have continued to take the time to make traditional clothing such as moccasins, mukluks, and mitts for their family. Most women sew for the enjoyment. Now even the occasional moccasin sewer sews because a few dollars can be earned from the final product. If their husbands are successful hunters, and the women are in a position to prepare the hides as they always did in the bush environment, they will have the material to make traditional clothing to sell to the local arts and crafts outlet or directly to tourists. Another type of work that women do on a voluntary basis is to care for the elderly, but even this is becoming a burden because of the social pressures felt by women, such as those caused by alcohol and drug abuse.

So far, I have attempted to describe the meaning of work in the context of the bush and the community environment. To my knowledge, no attempt has ever been made to establish the value of women's work in either of these two environments. What is attempted here is to provide some interpretation of the predicaments faced by Dene women as they experience the transition from the bush to the community and how they fare in the changing conditions of their socio-economic circumstances.

Women's Workplace: "Having a Job" Outside the Home

Work for pay outside the home is a recent phenomenon bought about by the introduction of the industrial or wage economy. Women who work outside the home generally do so for someone other than their family and in exchange for money. In the past, Dene women worked outside the home to earn income to pay the bills; to maintain their husband's credit at The Bay for tools, clothing and food; or to have extra cash for personal needs. Now, Dene women either work, or are seeking ways to become self-employed and balance these aspirations with family responsibilities.

In a small settlement, regular jobs are limited, and most are seasonal in nature. The regular jobs include those available at local enterprises, such as casual labour at The Bay, or support and cleaning staff in government offices, hotels, nursing stations, and schools. The seasonal jobs originating in or close to the settlement include some tourism, certain kinds of public works, recreation, forestry, and parks. When there are no jobs to be had in the communities, there are always bush camps to which the Dene can turn. However, not all Dene have this option nor are they in a position to depend solely on the traditional economy.

Wage Employment Opportunities for Dene Women

Where women were concerned, government and industry were slow to respond in terms of policy and programs. The needs of women were not apparent to either government or industry prior to 1975, the International Year of Women. Government felt no public pressure until then, although it had been urged earlier, to respond to the needs of women in general. In northern Canada, Dene and Métis women did not formally organize until 1977–78 when the Native Women's Association of the N.W.T. was formed to voice their concerns.

In 1985, the Government of the Northwest Territories, in response to public pressure and the United Nations assessment of the achievements of the Decade of Women (1975–85), stated its policy on equality between women and men and, in addition, prepared the *Five Year Action Plan on Equality of Women.* This is an impressive plan of action on paper, and it is hoped that it will be carried out successfully (Government of the Northwest Territories 1985).

To determine what employment interests and goals women had in industry, and what problems and obstacles they faced if they wanted this type of employment, Lynda Lange (1984) conducted a three-year survey of the employment of native women at the Norman Wells Oilfield Expansion and Pipeline Project. She interviewed women from the communities of Fort Norman, Fort Franklin, Fort Simpson, and Wrigley. Four observations are significant in clarifying the preferences of the women employed: 68 per cent would like full-time jobs; 68 per cent stated a definite preference for other than office work; good social environment at work is important; and 65 per cent did not consider it a problem to do a job considered "men's work".

From the number of obstacles and problems identified in the study, four are mentioned below.

(1) Employment seemed to be closely related to the level of schooling completed, whereas employment in the home community seemed to be related to the training courses taken. Existing jobs in the community that needed filling will create whatever training is necessary to fill them. Training courses tend not to create jobs.

(2) Application forms appear to be a major barrier. Seventy-five per cent said they were interested in the employment but few filled out application forms.

(3) Lack of child care was seen as a serious impediment. Almost 50 per cent who were interested in the jobs said they did not apply because they could not find child care services. Most prefer the care of relatives or friends in the community. Approximately 50 per cent of the women who held these jobs were working mothers, and the majority were single mothers.

(4) Being native was felt to be a more important factor than being female. Prejudices with respect to race and sex prevailed. Twenty-five per cent of those who answered said this affected them most. Male chauvinism was reflected in non-native employers rather than members of their own communities.

177

The Future

What is important in the world of "work", for the present and future, is for women to recognize that part of the answer is to distinguish the goals of the "bush" way of life from the community way of life, and those required and attainable in "having a job". In the first instance, women are doing what they have been taught to do and are able to pass on their skills to their children; in the second situation, women are part of a consumer society, consuming products that are not necessarily designed for the northern environment; and, in the third circumstance, women are selling their labour and valuable time in exchange for money.

I suggest that problems arise when women fail to recognize that the goals of these three types of work do not necessarily complement each other. It is difficult. I do not believe it is any easier now to recognize the stress that comes from moving from an independent and sharing milieu to a totally dependent and competitive situation. Women, through their community and territorial organizations, are now attempting to seize the problem created by the dichotomies in goals.

Education and the way curricula are designed and taught is a concern to women. Community women must find ways to make sure that their culture, customs, and languages are included in the formal education of their children and must find ways to apply them in the world of "work". Education should not be designed solely for meeting the needs of the industrial economy.

In reality, many women have made their choices to remain in the communities where their elders, children, and families live, and will take advantage of government employment programs when they become available. In the past five years, women have been encouraged to take advantage of training programs offered by industry and government. To those women who accept this route, I suggest they recognize that government programs are intended to make it easy for them to change from their previous working condition (without pay) into another working condition (with pay). This fact can only make them more aware of the important role they have in educating themselves and their children about the values of their culture in comparison with what they are forced to do now through wage employment. I have met many women who find the responsibilities unbearable at times. Often, nostalgically, they would recall the virtues of the "bush" way of life and wonder how on earth they made the choice to leave it.

I think most northern women today have similar thoughts. And perhaps it is time that we all think about our goals and the goals of the three types of "work" mentioned. After all, technology has been signalling the demise of many jobs done by workers, and there is every indication in the Canadian economy that the way work is now perceived needs reviewing. Dene women, or other women joining the work force in the future, have to realize that the concept and perception of work is constantly changing. Thus, how work is being viewed has to be assessed according to the prevailing circumstances.

References

Canadian Council on Social Development. *Overview* 6 (Autumn 1988).

Government of Canada. *Census 1986*. Ottawa: Supply and Services Canada, 1986, pp. 92–123.

Government of the Northwest Territories. *Five Year Action Plan on Equality for Women*. Yellowknife: Women's Secretariat, 1985.

Lange, Lynda. *Employment of native women at the Norman Wells expansion and pipeline project: goals and problems*. Unpublished paper, 1984.

Mackenzie, Barbara. *History of the Native Women's Association of the N.W.T. and Resource Manual*. Yellowknife: Canarctic Graphics Ltd., 1984.

Menicoche, Lorayne. Personal correspondence, 1988.

Outcrop Ltd. *NWT Databook 1986-87*. Yellowknife: Outcrop Ltd. Northern Publisher, 1986.

Ross, David P., and Usher, Peter J. *From the Roots Up. Economic Development as if Community Mattered*. Croton-on-Hudson, N.Y.: Bootstrap Press, 1986.

White, Pamela M. *Native Women: A Statistical Overview*. Ottawa: Minister of Supply and Services Canada, September 1985.

Whittington, Michael S. (Co-ordinator). *The North*. Toronto: University of Toronto Press, in co-operation with the Royal Commission on the Economic Union and Development Prospects for Canada and the Canadian Government Publishing Centre, Supply and Services, 1985.

Nindal Kwanindur [1]

Barb Adam-MacLellan

When I decided to write an article about women and literacy in the Yukon Territory, I did so with some trepidation. I am hardly an expert on literacy, nor am I a writer of any experience. I was unsure where my questions would lead me, what issues would arise, and to what extent these issues would relate specifically to Yukon women. With respect to native women and literacy, I discovered it is impossible to write about native women as a separate entity apart from the community in which they live. In a closely knit community, the life of each person not only affects one's own family members but the community as a whole. Native women and men share a common educational history, and to write about women alone would leave an incomplete picture. In this article I hope to address some special concerns of women, but the greater part will relate to the entire native community. [2]

Literacy by itself has no relevance. It is a means to an end, the end being the ability to see oneself within the context of society as a whole. It is a foundation from which a person understands and evaluates current issues that affect one's life. It is a platform from which one can question authority and discriminate between rhetoric and justice, and it gives an individual the self-confidence necessary to lobby for, and demand, equality in a multicultural society. Literacy is a political issue; anything less is merely an academic exercise.

The problem of illiteracy does not confine itself to the native community, yet, for the most part, it is a native issue in the Yukon.

Illiteracy, in some Yukon communities, is extreme and estimated to be as high as 80 per cent. [3] Adult illiteracy among native people is often rooted in the earlier years of public education. Cultural incontinuity and a long history of non-involvement in the public education system has contributed to high rates of illiteracy among Yukon Indians. [4]

The Educational Process and Illiteracy: The Past

The attitudes of native people toward white "educational experiences" today have been shaped by the past and current alienation of Indian people from educational practices. Indian children's experiences in mission schools have had a profound negative influence on Yukon Indians, and, to this day, its scars are felt by many who were forced to spend the formative years of their life cut off from their families, communities, and culture.

According to a documentary entitled, *The Mission Syndrome*, produced by NEDDA,[5] early missionaries destroyed the family unit, which was the foundation of Yukon Indian culture. Taking children away to schools for years at a time resulted in a profound estrangement of young people from their families, and an equally profound alienation of the young from their culture, mother tongue, and the skills associated with a traditional life-style.

For many native people, the school environment was devoid of any genuine human interaction. The intimacy and tenderness of family life was replaced by an unfamiliar sterile environment, controlled by a set of rules that were stringently adhered to in order to avoid a strapping.[6] Many waited and hoped that the day they turned 16 would come quickly. One woman with whom I spoke said that the rigidity of institutional life turned her, temporarily, into a juvenile delinquent.

Those who were directly affected by mission school life have passed their associations and bitter memories of that time onto their children. These memories often manifest themselves in an unwillingness to partake in present-day educational experiences that are organized by the white system.

According to a report entitled, *Possible Causes of Low Academic Achievement Among Yukon Indians*, "The alienation of Indian people is a direct consequence, and an adaptation to, a long history of attempts by the dominant culture, both in the school system and elsewhere, to deny the dignity and worth of Indian culture through implicit and explicit policies of forced assimilation."[7]

The Educational Process and Illiteracy: The Present

Despite the educational history of native people, there is much evidence indicating that Yukon Indians are not only motivated to learn, but continue to make painful compromises in order to acquire an education. In response to educational interests, Yukon Indians have recently started to take more control over their children's education,[8] and are prepared to develop their own alternative education system if Indian needs are not met.

The cultural and economic adaptations that native people have made are quite astounding, even to the point of adopting a foreign religion, culture, and language. Perhaps this was literacy for self-defence in the face of a white population that was becoming a majority in Indian territory. But today the rewards of education are more tangible as native people seek self-government.

Louise Profeit-LeBlanc, native adviser, says:

Today education is necessary for survival. It is what we need to be self-determining, just as hunting and fishing were once traditional skills that were necessary for survival.

Many native people who have gone through the education process agree that, as the process of self-government takes shape, education will be dealt with as an integral part of the economic, social, and political development of Indian people. Those at the forefront of the process of self-government recognize that the loss of a traditional life-style and the roles associated with that life-style have motivated many to acquire or upgrade literacy skills. Many feel that this is absolutely necessary in order to make a complete transition from the present situation to a more self-determined social, political, and economic life.

Mary Jane Jim of the Council for Yukon Indians, commented upon this:

> The white system is not going to wait for us to catch up; we have to hurry up and acquire these skills in order to keep abreast of social and economic development. Literacy is a very realistic skill requirement and, in this day and age, it is something we can't ignore.

There is an increasing push to have Yukon Indians service their own people. Community health workers, social workers, drug and alcohol counsellors, and band employees are under pressure to upgrade their literacy skills, and, for some, to become computer-literate as well. Advanced literacy skills are required to write proposals for funding, to administer funds, to lobby government agencies, and to review numerous government studies.

The acquisition of literacy skills is important for the entire native community. Literacy may help bridge the gap between a traditional and modern native life-style, and hasten the process of political and economic development. It is only recently that books have found a place in native culture. The print media has become especially important as native people attempt to preserve the legends and wisdom of the elders before they are gone. Basic literacy skills, on a personal level, help individuals to understand everyday concerns like employment applications, government and community notices, banking forms, application forms, and telephone directories.

For women in particular, literacy skills will help them to obtain information and services about human and civil rights, fair employment practices, health services, social welfare, and Canadian law.

The importance of education is accepted by many native people; however, for a great number of the Indian population, education is not necessarily a priority issue. While some argue that education is an integral part of the overall development of native people, others maintain that, on a personal level, other social problems must be dealt with first.

According to Bobbie Smith, Director of the Women's Directorate, there exists a priority of concerns for native women:

Education is not necessarily a priority for those women dealing with problems of self-esteem and substance abuse, or for those who are victims of assault. These women are involved in a struggle that takes one day at time.

The Other Side of the Educational Process

The negative attitude of Indian people toward "white education" is promoted by the fact that the educational system continues today to alienate native people from the culture into which they were born.

Sandra Ward of the Yukon Indian Women's Association explains:

> ...public schools separate us from our culture in many ways. We are alienated for our values and beliefs in the school community unless we fit into an 'accepted pattern of life' or 'way of thinking'. Many native values and beliefs are very different from this 'pattern' so, consequently, many of us either go through the school system suffering from an inferiority complex or drop out and retreat to our families where we are better understood and accepted.

In a territory where education is compulsory, free, and accessible, it may seem difficult to explain the high rate of illiteracy as a failure of the education system. In the Yukon, however, the education system reflects the aspirations, values, and culture of the dominant Canadian society. The system, not unlike its past, is premised on white, middle class, urban, and culturally ethnocentric values and attitudes, with little regard paid to the rich history and cultural traditions of Yukon Indians. For example, some native students lose interest and drop out of school because they are unable to see their interests, culture, or history reflected in the school curriculum.

In a brief on education of Yukon Indians, presented by the Yukon Native Brotherhood in the early 1970s, it states:

> You give them an education that makes them neither 'white men' nor Indian for they cannot survive or find jobs in the white man's world. When they come back to us they do not know how to make a living in the village and so are an extra mouth to feed for their family rather than any help to them.

As past experiences demonstrate, the attempt to educate Indian people using a non-native educational model has disconnected many from their culture and has unsuccessfully attempted to integrate them into new socio-economic spheres where they are unable to be fully integrated.

Eleanor Millard, co-ordinator of Project Wordpower, a Whitehorse-based literacy project, believes that the native people who have achieved a university-level education are over-challenged, undertrained, and sometimes employed in the wrong field:

> Because they are often in high-profile positions, they are expected by employers to have academic and professional interests and abilities beyond the norm for their peers.

Within the native community itself, education that is not born out of the perceived need by the entire community can distance elders from youth and men from women, and can threaten the very fabric of society. Many elders feel that the traditional wisdom and cultural heritage they could share with youth currently has no place in existing educational settings. The Yukon Native Brotherhood states:

> Emphasis on non-Indian values for success in school with a rejection of the Indian's values, has made many pupils feel superior to and more knowledgeable than their elders and family with the result that there is a loss of respect for traditions and the elder's wisdom. Your system has bred an indifference in the attitude of Indian parents on seeing their children going the white man's way.

Literacy Programs Today

There are two types of programs available for those people interested in upgrading or acquiring literacy skills. First, the Department of Education, through Yukon College, runs an academic development program in Whitehorse and in the communities. In the Whitehorse program, a Level I literacy class, two levels of upgrading, and a college preparation course are offered. In the rural community learning centres, two levels of upgrading are available and, where possible, attempts are made by the instructors to accommodate literacy-level students. To date, the Level I literacy class is not offered, and there are few college preparation courses in the rural learning centres.

The second type of literacy program is offered in the Yukon through the Yukon Literacy Council. The most visible program, Project Wordpower, is located in Whitehorse. It provides free, private tutoring services for adults wishing to improve their literacy skills. As well, a second pilot project was set up in Haines Junction at the beginning of 1988. The learners involved in this program are a diverse group, and according to Eleanor Millard, "don't represent the percentage of native people in the community."

Students are involved in both types of programs for different reasons, but one of the major motivating factors in the rural college courses is the training allowance. As Louise Profeit-LeBlanc suggests:

The money draws the people out. They are getting paid to become literate; if it weren't for the money, many students wouldn't be there.

In some of the more remote communities, upgrading classes fulfil a social need.

In Old Crow, during the cold winter months, there is not much activity within the community. The classes are an opportunity for people to get together and visit.[9]

For many potential literacy students, the classroom is a setting which has too many negative memories; past failure and racism makes formal learning not only culturally alien but an untenable prospect in itself. The number of Indian students currently enrolled in any type of literacy class or program accounts for a very small percentage of the total number of non-reading Indians.

There are many reasons why participation in these programs is so low; the primary reason appears to be the lack of community ownership by native people. The literacy classes available today have not been initiated by native people; consequently, they are poorly supported. Indian people do not feel these programs are their own.

For the most part, existing literacy and educational classes are white, middle class structures, organized and implemented by these white, middle class people for Indian people. While the majority of potential students are native, the tutors are almost entirely white, educated women between 25 and 45 years of age. It is unfortunate that even the more flexible local literacy group in the Yukon is almost entirely a white, middle class movement that reflects a set of values unfamiliar to many native people.

It is also to be expected that, like the education system in the North, the literacy programs organized by the dominant culture will have only limited success, for they fail to take into account the necessity of involving Indian people themselves, who must determine that literacy is an issue and be responsible for identifying their own priorities. The full support and confidence of the people will come when individual communities feel that they are in control of educational programs. Existing literacy groups can facilitate the development of new programs by supporting native-controlled, local initiatives.

The other barriers to the development of successful literacy programs are integrally related to the larger problem of a lack of Indian control. They include:
a) the lack of grass roots literacy projects in the rural communities;
b) failure to accommodate the cultural needs of native people;
c) a lack of understanding of the dynamics of community life; and
d) a lack of cultural continuity between the teaching and learning styles of native people and those of white people.

It is believed that grass roots projects, which are often run by volunteer organizations, can provide exciting and creative alternatives to learning, and can respond with more flexibility to the needs of individual students, especially the needs of working women with children. To date, Whitehorse is the only community that has a well-established literacy program. While the need for literacy projects is very real in Whitehorse, there is an even greater need in the rural communities, where the rates of illiteracy are the highest. It is unfortunate that in the rural communities there is no established literacy program available through the college or the Yukon Literacy Council.

The failure to accommodate the cultural needs of native people and lack of understanding of the dynamics of community life precludes any real success.

Mary Jane Jim explains:

...if somebody in the community gets a moose, people won't show up at the class because they'll be helping to butcher and distribute it throughout the village. Literacy classes must be flexible enough to adjust to this type of activity in the community.

There is a lack of cultural continuity between the teaching and learning styles. While many attempts are being made to provide culturally appropriate material, especially content that is relevant to the needs and lives of women, the existing literacy programs still reflect the aspirations and expectations of a white, middle class society. As a result, the approach, content, and style of instruction is often foreign to native culture.

Women and Literacy

Over 60 per cent of the students enrolled in all of the classes are native women, most of whom are young mothers between 20 and 30 years of age. A number of the women are mothers, supporting children with the training allowance provided when enrolled in an educational class.

For many native women, the desire to become educated is closely linked to their children. This is not isolated to minority groups only, but is a global trend; women seek education as a way of improving the quality of their lives and the lives of their children.

Many of the younger native women are handed a lot of responsibility when they have children. They respond very positively to that challenge. Many of them are students in the community learning centres or in upgrading classes in Whitehorse and, as well, carry on with their domestic responsibilities.[10]

For many women entering literacy classes in the rural communities, there is a lack of adequate, affordable day care. Outside Whitehorse, only two communities have day care facilities and neither of these accepts babies.[11]

As Bobbie Smith indicates, many native women prefer to leave their children with extended family members, but sometimes there are anxieties over the ability of the care-givers to make a long-term commitment.

The inflexibility of the training allowances, on which so many rely, creates further problems. In most communities, the training allowance is available to full-time students only. This further compounds the financial hardships faced by families in the community. It also requires a mother not only to find full-time day care but, also, to juggle family and community responsibilities, and continue to do schoolwork.

Community obligations can often take up a significant portion of a woman's time. According to many of the women with whom I spoke, women are frequently the driving force behind community life. This is not new—many native communities traditionally are matriarchal. Native women have an active role to play in village life and divide their time among caring for families, elders, and community volunteer work.

Hazel Fekete, co-ordinator of Academic Development for Yukon College, says: "There is a tremendous pull between schoolwork and family life; you can't decide not to be a parent. If something gives way, it is usually the educational classes."

Apart from the financial difficulties native women face, there are also other serious complications. Women's involvement in education can pose a threat to the unity of family life. A woman's desire to improve her situation and that of her family can be viewed as a threat by a partner who has lost his traditional role in society.

For many native men, change has hurled them into a void, without a place in either the traditional or modern culture. The loss of a traditional life-style and high unemployment in rural communities has left many men without a significant role to play in village life.

The improvements sought by women are sometimes perceived as a threat by men who are feeling unsure of their role in the community.

One woman with whom I spoke talked about the physical abuse some women experienced when they pursued educational opportunities, and this was in families where there had been no history of previous abuse.

In Linda MacLeod's report on battered women in Canada, including northern women, her research indicated that, "Where the woman is dominant in terms of decision-making power or earning power, or where the woman is perceived to be superior in some other way, violence is often used by the man to shift the balance of power.[12]

The support of the family and community is as important today as it was in the past, and is vital to the survival of the literacy projects. Failure to grant equal partnership to all community members will only alienate individuals and threaten group security.

The Future of the Literacy Program

The purpose of literacy is to give people increased control over their lives and access to opportunities that would otherwise be denied them. As Ms LeBlanc states:

> Literacy is a freeing experience; it gives a person the freedom of choice. It is also an empowering experience. It gives people the skills to articulate their needs and concerns. As people become educated,

their pool of knowledge empowers the rest of their community. This is a traditional trait; elders pass on their wisdom and knowledge for the betterment of the whole community.

When literacy and education do not empower for equal opportunity and against discrimination, people quickly become bitter and disillusioned.

If there is agreement that existing literacy programs are not living up to their potential, a new look at literacy programs must be taken. In doing this, there must be substantial involvement by Indian people, as well as the involvement and co-operation of the private sector, government and non-governmental organizations, and community-based groups. It is critical that the general population be informed of the wastage of human potential as a result of illiteracy. It is not only essential, but practical, to first deal with literacy concerns at the earliest possible time—in elementary school.

There are many superior northern educators whose approach to learning has been creative and flexible in attempting to meet the needs of a variety of students; however, if success is to occur, policy changes at upper levels of government must be made to reflect the interests the programs are designed to serve. It is vital that the students be located at the centre of the plans and decisions pertaining to the programs. The other components of a successful program are an openness to innovative ideas and experimentation, and even more fundamental is the need to have decentralized programs so that communities feel the programs are their own, or that they can make them so.

Notes

1. This is a Southern Tuchone phrase and its literal English translation is, "I'm going to tell you something—pass my thoughts on to you." This appropriately reflects my view about literacy. I chose this title to convey my sense of what literacy is. Literacy is more than just reading; it is communicating who you are and having the ability to articulate your needs on your own terms, making your own voice heard by others. It is about empowerment. See: Kity Smith, "Nindal Kwanindur (I'm Going to Tell you a Story)", Julie Cruikshank (ed.), (Whitehorse: Council for Yukon Indians and Government of Yukon, 1982).

2. I have spoken with many people, yet it was beyond the scope of this article to canvass all those for whom literacy is an issue. The opinions expressed are my own except where expressly stated.

3. There are no current statistics which reveal the rate of illiteracy in the Yukon. According to the 1981 Census, 14 per cent of the population had less then a grade nine education. This percentage does not take into account those people who have achieved this grade but still test at a much lower literacy level. (Grade nine is the level accepted as the minimum amount of schooling necessary to function in a developed, industrialized country.) Insufficient statistics are a major handicap in planning for future literacy programs in the Yukon. A comprehensive survey should be undertaken in order to determine the extent to which literacy is a problem.

4. In the Yukon Territory, native people are in the minority, making up approximately 30 per cent of the total population. However, when combined with a highly educated public service and business population, native people account for a significant proportion of those who are functionally illiterate.

5. NEDDA is a half-hour TV program on CBC North. The word Nedda means "your eye".

6. Dr Richard King, a teacher at the school in Carcross, once said that children are treated as a good stock farm might treat their animals. They were deloused, shorn, fed, clothed, and cared for when sick, but loving relationships were non-existent.

7. P.D. Trapnell, *Possible Causes of Low Academic Achievement Among Yukon Indians: A Brief Literature Review* (Vancouver: A.D. Consultants), p. 68.

8. In the land claims negotiations with the federal and territorial governments, the Council for Yukon Indians is negotiating provisions that will provide bands with greater control in areas such as education, health, and housing.

9. Taken from my interview with Louise Profeit-LeBlanc.

10. Taken from my interview with Eleanor Millard.

11. Provision of support services goes hand-in-hand with literacy programming. This is especially important for women in northern communities who need child care services and flexible training allowances.

12. Linda MacLeod, *Battered But Not Beaten: Preventing Wife Battering in Canada* (Ottawa:Canadian Advisory Council on the Status of Women, June 1987), pp. 38–39.

"Flexible Is an Understatement"

Debby Dobson

Every day I go to work in an office building, like a lot of other people in Canada do. I sit at a desk, I use a phone and a computer, I attend and chair meetings.

The difference a northern setting makes in doing all of these ordinary tasks lies in the distances people must come to attend the meetings or workshops, and in the distances I must travel to tell people about new programs. Because we are a small department serving a comparatively small population, there is only one of me, whereas in southern Canada there would be a whole division of people. As a result, I've learned to work on my own and to adapt, adapt, adapt—to say I must be flexible is an understatement.

I have just returned to work after being on maternity leave. I received 17 weeks' leave at 93 per cent pay, but only after two months of sorting out the paperwork documenting my absence.

With all other kinds of leave, you sign one piece of paper, provide a little bit of documentation, and you've got your time without even having left your desk. Not maternity leave—and you don't dare complain because many people think you're lucky you get anything. You're either incredibly pregnant or hauling around a newborn infant as you get one piece of paper signed in one place to give to someone else in another place where they eventually lose it. Then you have to start all over again. I kept saying to myself, "Men wouldn't have to put up with this hassle." Sometimes I wonder if people remember how they got here. Where do they think they really came from?

I know I feel differently about work now that I have a daughter. I don't want to be away from home as much. To keep in touch with my "field" though, it is necessary to spend a lot of time travelling; but there is no provision made to cover the cost of long-distance telephone calls at night to your child or care-giver, to see how things are going. The hours you spend travelling, or just sitting in a motel room watching television or doing extra work to keep busy, all the time wondering how things are at home, are never counted as overtime or tacked on to vacation leave. Although my job classification is currently being reviewed, I am still being paid less than the men (and another woman who won a grievance based on pay discrepancy) who are doing the same work. It's one of those situations where you can't say outright that it's because you are a woman; but it sure feels like it.

I'm trying to organize a day care at my workplace so that my daughter and I can both be in the same place during the day while I work. I didn't have any trouble finding other women in the building to help me. Most of the men also agreed that it would be nice. But there are others, like male politicians, who say the idea is too expensive, and argue that if the government gives funding for a day care in one place, then everyone will want it.

I think it would be easier if the traditional [native] attitude to child care permeated the "modern" offices of the North. There are always kids around at native gatherings, and there is always someone to help look after them.

In many ways though, it's no easier for native women. A student in one of the programs I was supervising had to quit because her mother, who didn't want her in school, said she wouldn't baby-sit for her any more. In that same class, another female student quit because the male student who was charged with sexually assaulting her was allowed to stay in the same class while waiting for the court party [circuit court] to arrive.

It's not impossible for women to work and raise kids at the same time. For most of us, it's a necessity. However, I have been questioning some of the assumptions about work. Why is it, for example, that work has to be done between 8:30 a.m. and 5:00 p.m., when flex-time can give you some leeway to adjust to family demands? And, why not allow women to take their babies with them on trips? Travelling with your child is not impossible, even though it involves more hassle, more baggage, and finding sitters. At least, when I did it, I got to feed my daughter her supper and tuck her in at night for the seven days we were away from home.

If this day care at-work project happens, my daughter will have a better understanding of me and what I do. When she grows up I know she'll be able to take care of herself; I hope it will be easier for her than it's been for me. I hope I pass on to her that family is important and that work is good and fulfilling—not just necessary.

Nursing in the North: Challenge and Isolation

Brenda Canitz

They all just sat there. No one could believe what had happened. The tiny, blueing body just lay there, absolutely motionless, with all the tubes and signs of assault from resuscitation. The baby had died. It shouldn't have died. The nurse must have missed something. She should have done more. As the nurse sat there looking at its tiny, innocent, wax-like shape, she could feel the emptiness inside her grow. She was past feeling tired. The loneliness she had ignored for such a long time was now everywhere. The power and energy of the frustration were gone. She was empty. And as she sat there grasping for something, anything to hang on to, she could feel herself slipping away. She began to cry.[1]

Providing health care in an isolated northern community is a challenging and rewarding experience. But for the nurses who provide the care, there is within the glory and power of this position, unhappiness accompanied by personal and professional losses. Nurses are often alone in this demanding job. During the time they are in the North, they give their lives to the job, for the people have many needs, and the work never ends. The support and care required in the communities they serve, and the constant demands of the bureaucratic structure, leave little time and energy for the nurse herself. For these and many other reasons, nurses' careers in the North are short; and when they leave the North, they take with them strong memories, and sometimes emotional and/or physical scars.

The nurses of the North are a small, often unrecognized group of professionals within the Canadian health care system. They are a major influence on the health and lives of native and northern populations. For decades, nurses have provided 24-hour comprehensive health care under the auspices of the federal and territorial governments. This care is provided within the milieu of a different culture, in small and remote northern communities, with little on-site back-up or assistance from other health care workers. The nurses work within the limitations of a harsh environment; personal and professional isolation; and unpredictable, often unreliable, modes of transportation and communication. They are the backbone of the northern health care system.

The health of Canada's native population has historically been in crisis. Throughout the last century, there have been many changes and advances in technology affecting northern health care; however, as measured by standard health indicators such as infant mortality and life expectancy, native populations still maintain a lower level of health compared with the overall Canadian population. For all persons living in isolated settlements there are limitations in the health resources available to them. Specialized services, such as optometry, dentistry, and physiotherapy are provided by short-stay, fly-in teams, once or twice a year. Individuals who require extensive treatment or hospitalization are separated from their families, friends, culture, and food, and are sent to an austere, regimented, foreign environment—the southern hospital.

The quality of health care services available to native and northern populations, and, subsequently, the level of health realized by these populations, are functions of how well nurses are able to adjust and cope in their isolated nursing stations.

The following are reflections on nursing in the North and the health care system generally. Hopefully, this will provide insight into the complex nature of this health care profession. This article will address several key issues which are important to nursing in the North: stress and burnout, power and control, isolation and loneliness, gender, and cultural awareness. To provide a historical picture, the first section will be a brief review of early health care in the North.

Early Health Care

Traditionally, health care for native people was provided by a variety of traditional health care personnel such as medicine men/women, shamans, midwives, bone setters, and herbalists. These traditional health care workers were active in all areas of daily living and were leaders in areas of hunting, crafts, and culture. They were integral members of their communities who acted as the "thinkers" of the group.

This traditional health care has since been pushed aside by the introduction of the southern health care system. The European zeal for fur and whale products in the early 1900s drove explorers and traders further into the isolation of the North, bringing them in contact with the small, nomadic groups of native peoples. Europeans used their basic medical supplies to treat many of the minor injuries and ailments of natives that visited the post. After the explorers and fur traders, the northern natives were exposed to yet another conqueror, the missionaries. The missionaries approached the natives with the same salesmanship and zeal as the fur traders; but instead of furs they collected "saved souls"—and the competition was fierce.[2] The missionaries also used their primitive medical supplies to offer health care in their roles as spiritual leaders and educators.

In the mid-20th century, native populations suffered a large number of deaths caused by massive epidemics and widespread starvation. The federal government attempted to intervene in this appalling situation by initiating several "help" programs in the North:[3] food was shipped to many northern areas; health care services were increased; residential schools were established for all children; and health survey expeditions toured the North each summer, testing for tuberculosis and other medical conditions. Many people were sent to southern hospitals for extended treatment without really knowing what was wrong or where they were going. Many never returned. Families that were once nomadic began spending more time around settlement areas to be able to take part in social and health programs.

These changes, plus the advancement of southern scientific technology, have pushed native people from traditional medicines and shamanism to cosmopolitan health care.[4] Traditional beliefs that illness developed from societal factors were replaced by the European belief that illness is caused by individual characteristics.

Through much of this transition native people were nothing more than innocent bystanders, treated paternalistically by the colonizing agents. Throughout this process, native people who were stripped of their independence and autonomy began to doubt themselves. They lost faith in their own knowledge and skills, and, more and more, turned over responsibilities to the "conquerors".

Consequently, more native people began spending longer periods of time around the trading posts, the community needs increased, and government began to initiate health services. They began by instructing local people in the basics of first aid and minor illnesses. The native population grew even more dependent on these services. In response to the heightened demand, nurses were recruited to work in the northern areas.

Nursing in the North

The First Nurses
In the 1920s and 1930s larger communities in the North received institutional health care in the form of nursing stations. These early stations were set up in existing buildings within the communities. These "shacks"—usually small, dark, and poorly equipped—often served as both the clinics and the living quarters for the nurses.

The choice of the nurse as the primary health care professional in the North is an interesting one. Nurses were sent North for a variety of reasons. Nurses had the most comprehensive education of all the health care professionals, and were, consequently, well equipped to deal with a broad range of health care needs, from asepsis, acute care, and public, maternal, and child health to basic health education. As well, few doctors would accept the challenge of living and working in the North.[5]

Nurses in the North were an independent group, chosen for their clinical expertise, sense of adventure, and self-sufficient attitudes. Virtually all were young, female, and single. They were usually contracted for one-year periods, during which time they had little contact with the outside world other than the odd plane and sporadic calls on the radio phone.

Within the communities, the relationship between the nurses and native people was one of power and control. Nurses represented the government, and carried out many of its paternalistic policies. For the Inuit, this relationship was often described as *ilira* (a respect tinged with fear), a term used to describe an extraordinary power whose behaviour is seen as volatile and unpredictable.[6]

Religious attitudes carried over from the days of the missionaries still governed the approach of these early health care workers. Many nurses were Sisters of various religious orders who had come to "save" these "diseased savages" and their souls. With little or no regard for the realities of survival on the land, they preached strict religious morals condemning the traditional native practices of polygamy, infanticide, and voluntary suicide by those that were old, weak, or diseased.

The nurses were isolated within the community. In their positions of power and influence, they felt independent and separate from the native people they served. They participated very little in the activities of the native community. Moreover, native people perceived the nurses' personal situations—adult women living without men or families—as very peculiar. Since there were very few non-natives in town, and the nurses were usually the only single, non-native women, their social activities were limited.

The nurses' approach to health care was a reflection of the government's attitude toward natives and northern development. The nurses isolated themselves within their work, seldom consulting with the community, or developing cultural awareness and sensitivity. They were often righteous and intolerant of native behaviour and beliefs. As a result, they knew little about native perceptions of health and illness, and rarely asked for a native perspective on treating certain illnesses or problems. The nurses were frustrated with the primitive, seemingly irresponsible, ways of Inuit, and they chose to "rescue them" by changing their ways. They found the native nutritional and hygienic habits intolerable. The non-native professionals monopolized the caring and healing aspects of life, seldom utilizing the expertise of the local shamans or midwives. An elder once recalled:

The nurse told me whenever one of my children was sick, or when I thought a child might get sick, I was to bring it to the nursing station right away. She would take the child and return it to me when it was better. I never know what she does.

In all fairness, with this paternalistic approach there was dedication and genuine caring. They did what they thought was best—alone, working long hours against incredible odds. Most of their patients couldn't speak English, and in the absence of a translator, nurses had to rely on their ears, eyes, and fingertips to pinpoint the disease and treat it within the restrictions of the resources of the nursing stations. Most of the medical supplies were received annually on the supply barge, and many were damaged or destroyed in the process. Epidemics of infectious diseases were still common, the native people had little built-up natural resistance, and immunization was yet unknown. Emergency evacuations were practically unheard of; as a nurse in the North, you did what you could with what you had, and that was that.

Today's Health Care

The rapid transition of the native culture and the northern health care system has continued in the second half of this century. Although the federal government has maintained primary responsibility for native care, the past few years have seen a transfer of responsibility for some health care needs of native people to the territorial government.

In the 1950s and 1960s, most communities in the North received their first bona fide nursing stations. These immense structures overshadowed most of the matchbox shacks of the communities—their very presence was a powerful control. And with the new structures came more and more nurses equipped with better educations and technology and also having the independent and adventurous spirit of their predecessors.

Today, health care in the North is still largely provided by nurses. There are a few communities which have resident doctors on a consulting basis, but, for the most part, the responsibility and accountability of health care rests with the nurses. There are visits from a general practitioner every one to two months, and specialty clinics such as dental, opthamological, and ear–nose–throat arrive in a community, set up their portable clinics, provide assembly-line care, and do what they can in a couple of days before setting off for the next community.

Nurses in isolated posts function as several health care professionals. Their day-to-day care is similar to that provided anywhere else in Canada by a general practitioner. The nurses deal with colds, pregnancy, and chest pains, in addition to employee physicals, marital problems, and depression. They also assume responsibility for pre- and post-natal clinics, immunizations, and elderly home visits. They are the resident dentist—applying temporary fillings or pulling teeth that just can't wait for the next dentist's visit. At night, a nurse must mysteriously transform herself into an entire emergency department—to single-handedly suture, bandage, resuscitate, and console both the patients and their families. Northern nurses are X-ray technicians and radiologists; they are laboratory technicians and pathologists, as they draw blood, collect urine and take swabs to pin-point and identify disease; and they may often be public health inspectors responsible for public services in the community.

197

With advances in technology, transportation, and communication, the direction and control of most of the nursing stations are centralized in Yellowknife, Iqaluit, Whitehorse, and Ottawa. This attempt to streamline the system and cut costs has resulted in major policy changes within the Medical Services Branch of Health and Welfare Canada. In-patient care is now limited within the nursing stations. Pregnant women and patients with illnesses requiring any length of acute health care are flown to regional hospitals. Families are, therefore, separated for long periods of time, with very little communication. As well, funds which could allow families to travel to visit with their families in far-off hospitals are limited. The strong social support of family and friends is lost.[7]

The mandate of Health and Welfare Canada is preventative health care, but in the North, demands for acute care and emergency services have always been high and are rising, and as the population rises, the complement of nurses fails to rise accordingly. As a result, acute care takes priority by its very immediacy, and other forms of health care are not given adequate attention. This is demonstrated in rising infant mortality rates and an increase in suicides and accidents. To fulfil the ever-increasing needs, the nurses devote personal time to develop and deliver health education and promotion.

There are differing opinions of what the role of the nursing station should be in the community. Administrators tend to believe that nursing stations should operate according to a standard, rather restricted, set of guidelines. In contrast, many nurses view the nursing station as an integral part of the community which should respond realistically to the demands placed upon it. The communities feel they are entitled to health care similar to the rest of Canada, and they believe the nursing station should provide these services.

Many articles have been written about the transition of nursing in the Canadian North from the early 1920s to the present day. One is struck by how little the issues have changed in the last 50 to 60 years. Most of the nurses are still single women, who stay in these high stress, high turnover positions for very short periods of time. The nurses tell of the challenge and responsibilities of the job; the lack of personnel and resources; and of the loneliness inherent in this unique position.[8]

Critical Issues in Northern Nursing
The five key issues for northern nursing are stress, power and control, isolation, gender, and cross-cultural identification.

Stress and Burnout
It had only taken five or six attempts to get Pierre on the phone. He agreed the history and the preliminary laboratory work didn't look good. The febrile, lethargic young boy would need to go to Yellowknife for treatment. If her diagnosis were true, this would be the sixth case of meningitis in four months. The nurse knew Pierre and the pilot had just returned from a traumatic Medevac, and had had little rest. She made sandwiches and a thermos of hot chocolate to send along.

All of a sudden the emergency bell rang furiously. There at the door was Aaron with his 15-year-old son seizuring in his arms. They quickly moved him to the clinic room stretcher. The nurse put in an airway and started to slowly give the IV valium. As she watched the seizure slowly dissipate there was a flicker in the lights and then darkness. She waited for the emergency generator to come on, but there was nothing. She waited a minute longer to assure the seizure had stopped. The father stayed with the young man as she grabbed the flashlight to find her way to the furnace room to kick-start the generator. As she walked along the dark hall she heard the plane pass overhead—relief at last. She just hoped they could squeeze the two stretchers on or she'd be up another night....As she waved goodbye to the plane and crawled back in the truck on the tarmac she felt the fatigue sweep over her as the adrenaline rush wore off. She hadn't slept through the night in two weeks and the clinic had been busy. She felt wiped, over-extended, and burnt out. Sometimes she just didn't have the energy to do anything— even caring or listening were becoming a chore. She wondered if the adrenaline would ever fail her and not show up...

Health professionals rate amongst the highest of all occupations in terms of stress and subsequent burnout.[9] Much of this stress has been attributed to the strong emotional reactions associated with working closely with patients.[10]

Burnout is a syndrome of emotional exhaustion and cynicism that frequently occurs when workers are involved in human services, education, and personnel work.[11] Burnout is caused by excessive or constant stress or negative conditions with which the individual has not been able to cope or adapt.

Generally, nursing is a highly stressful occupation.[12] The constant, interpersonal nature of nurses' work and the ever-present morbidity and mortality, combined with the subservient position of nursing within the health care system, where nurses have many responsibilities but little authority, form a complex source of stress.

Working as a nurse in remote locations increases the already high stress level generally associated with nursing.[13] The stress and the burnout consist of the complex interplay of several factors associated with northern nursing:

1)There is decreased support personally and professionally.[14] Social support is a major intervening factor in alleviating and coping with stress and burnout.[15]

2)Limited resources result in additional stresses in terms of having to "make do" with available health care supplies and with a lack of institutional and recreational resources.[16]

3) Working alone in a nursing station involves a drastic role change with little administrative or professional support. Beginning nurse-practitioners undergo an adjustment period which averages about six months. During this time and often throughout their employment, many practitioners report frustration and anxiety stemming from ambiguous job descriptions and lack of administrative support in their clinical setting.[17]

4) Nurses in isolated posts refer to the stress and worry of living and working in a harsh environment. Weather conditions control recreational activities; services such as electricity, water, and sewage (which are often lacking or insufficient); and access to additional emergency health care services through medical evacuations.[18]

Power and Control

"We need another nurse, Annie. I haven't slept more than three hours in a row for over a week. Both of us are exhausted. I'm afraid I'll miss something or make a mistake...", the nurse pleaded over the scratchy phone line.

"I've told you, Brenda, there is nothing I can do; there is no one to come. You'll just have to make do."

"Annie, I've been 'making do' ever since I started working here. I have three kids in croupettes and many more coming in daily—clinics go until six or seven o'clock at night and then we still have all those in-patients and calls throughout the night..."

"You should Medevac them out to Yellowknife if they need care. You know that is the policy. Nurses are not to provide long-term acute care. If you choose not to adhere to that policy there is nothing I can do."

"Annie, be realistic. These kids need three to six hours in a croupette to loosen things up and they are well on the road to recovery. After that they do quite well at home with a sheet and some steam. Why should we submit them to the trauma of a Medevac to Yellowknife, where they poke and prod them for everything under the sun? They are gone for a minimum of two weeks, separated from their mother and the rest of the family."

"Now Brenda, I know you are upset. I'm sure you have worked very hard. Just close the nursing station for the afternoon and deal with only the emergencies. Catch up on your sleep. You'll feel better after that..."

"Annie, what are you talking about—we're in the middle of a pneumonia epidemic! Every child wheezing and gasping for breath is an emergency to the parents and to me. This isn't a hospital in a big city—this is a nursing station and Francis and I are it!!! You've been up here—I can't believe you'd say that. It's ridiculous. I understand there is no one; but that is due to no recruitment and poor planning.

No wonder everyone leaves—the entire responsibility for health care falls on the nurse and there is no support or back-up. I'm writing 'lack of personnel' on every chart and if anything happens, Annie —it's coming right back to you! I have to go —20 people are waiting to be seen."

"Try and get some rest Brenda, you'll..."
CLICK!

Although nurses constitute the largest group of health care workers in Canada, isolated-post nurses comprise only a small group, and are, subsequently, powerless.

The virtually solo practice of being on call 24 hours a day, seven days a week, leaves the nurses with very little control and feeling relatively powerless to work as they choose. The writings of individual nurses note the uncertainty and lack of control in their daily lives.[19] This powerlessness, however, is transformed somewhat when the role of the nurse in the community is examined. Even though they feel relatively powerless to work as they prefer, they do wield a certain amount of power, merely because of their non-native status and their monopoly over health care in the community. They decide who is "sick" or is not, and develop the many programs and philosophies for each individual station.

Nurses in the North are, first and foremost, nurses, and with that they carry the expectations, limitations, and stereotypes of their profession. The subservience of nurses is due to the historical domination of men in the health care system and society.[20] The attributes of a "good nurse" closely mirror the male image of the "model" woman—quiet, caring, and giving. While these submissive, compassionate traits may comfort the ill, they perpetuate the position of powerlessness for women, and nurses in particular, who are confronted with organizational hierarchies dominated by men in the role of physician and administrator. Any power nurses have is "given" to them by physicians and institutional administrators.

The concept of control is an integral part of any study of power. Who controls the power? How is the power distributed? There are many factors that may contribute to how much control individuals feel they have in their lives. Nurses in the North function within the larger bureaucratic structure of Health and Welfare Canada.[21] Additionally, nurses function within the larger health care system that is directed by, and organized around, the medical profession.[22] Most decisions are not made locally, and the "institutions" of government bureaucracy and the medical profession serve as decision-making bodies which can appear as mechanisms of control.[23] At a local level, the needs and demands of the people in a community serve as a powerful and compelling force. When people are sick or in need, human nature propels us to help in whatever way we can. Locally, people see the nurse as a powerful figure who controls what and how health care will be delivered.[24]

The nursing station is seen as a "community building", even though the nurses live in the station. Their homes may become a hub of activity as visitors drop by for many reasons—to have a shower, borrow something, ask for assistance, or merely pass the time. Visiting government officials, health care personnel, and support staff often stay at the nursing station for lack of any other place to go. Many of these visitors expect the nurse to cook and clean for them but, in return, do very little for their room and board. "Visitors" place an amazing strain on station nurses and consume more of their precious private time.

Due to the construction and arrangement of the buildings, nurses can never get away from the activities of the nursing station. For example, the emergency night bell can be heard in every room so that even when an individual nurse is not on call, her sleep or personal rest time is disturbed. Most nursing stations request that a family member remain to assist patients while they are in the nursing station—not only to provide assistance to the patient, but to ensure that the patient is not left alone while the nurse divides her time between other necessary duties. These individuals must often share the personal facilities of the nurses.

Nursing support staff (reception, housekeeping, and maintenance) are often part-time and work only during the week. The administrative work normally done by the receptionist is assumed by the nurse. Nurses are left with the responsibility of cooking meals for the patients and the attendant family members. On weekends, nurses are responsible for cleaning and minor maintenance, including snow shovelling and ensuring that the furnace and sewage systems are functioning.

The "expanded role" of nurses is limited only to isolated communities where physicians refuse to practice. When physicians choose to work in an area, the scope of nursing is limited. In contrast, when staffing is in short supply and resources are strained, nurses are told, "Do whatever you can." Again, this is a function of a larger, systemic hierarchy, which is controlled and directed by physicians. Official policy stipulates that all nursing activities are to be carried out under the supervision of a licensed physician, even though the physician may be hundreds of miles away and have little knowledge of the needs or activities of the nursing station. Despite this, zone and regional medical officers are concerned about nurses "stepping into the domain of medicine". There are many memos to remind nurses of the limitations of their roles.

Beset by such ambiguities, nurses are often forced to "play games" to get things done.[25] This means cajoling physicians and administrators—or even manipulating the information passed on to them—in order to get what they need. Owing to the isolation of their situation, nurses control much of the information essential to diagnosis and treatment. The administration is so cumbersome, and often insensitive to the individual needs of the worker, that nurses twist communication to get what they need—allowing a staff member to take an unauthorized day off in return for extra hours (for which they are not paid overtime); or buying paint for the clinic rooms and calling it a case of juice to circumvent months of waiting and the paperwork required just to get maintenance supplies.

Once a patient leaves the nursing station and goes to the referring hospital, the nurse loses all influence or direction she may have had locally with the patient's care. Many doctors do not consult the nursing station when planning the treatment or discharge of patients, despite the fact that many treatments or follow-up procedures are limited in isolated areas.

Even though the community may not be an "institution" of control, community opinions are a major influence for the nurses. Local decisions and demands directly affect both the nurse's work and the functioning of the nursing station. She is faced daily with individual and community requests, but has little authority to meet the demands of either. She is usually the intermediary between the community and the bureaucrats whose opinions often differ.

Far from strengthening her credibility, the nurse's enforced role as go-between makes her position at the local level fragile. Although most communities have no influence over health care issues, some do have recourse on a political level. This rather negative type of control automatically pits the nurse and the community in opposition to each other.

In other instances, however, the nurse is subject to administrative constraints in taking an active part in community-initiated health care projects. One community wanted to learn more about the running of a nursing station, so they requested a pilot project be approved by the federal government, in keeping with its decentralization policy. This request was supported by local government and nursing personnel.

The response was a quick and emphatic "no"; and various bureaucrats outside the community moved to immediately defuse the momentum of the request. Local nursing station personnel were admonished for their encouragement of the project. High-ranking health care bureaucrats made visits to the community to assure the residents that the government was doing all it could to provide "top of the line" health care. A multitude of letters were received from various bureaucratic levels outlining the difficulties and dangers of running a health care system when "you didn't know what you were doing." The momentum died. Local people again felt they were incapable of deciding what their health care needs were and how they could best be met.

Isolation and Loneliness

She went out for a walk, hoping that she might see someone who would ask her in for tea. It was a cold, windy night, and the streets were bare except for a few kids playing street hockey. She returned to the nursing station and just sat on the footstool staring out into the luminescent darkness of the northern light.

She felt lonely—that certain emptiness that seems to linger. Everyone had been friendly and helpful, but there was no one she could really talk to. There was no one who really knew her, or understood her well enough that she could let down her happy, knowledgeable

facade. There was no one she could discuss the traumas and tribula-
tions of her job with—everything was confidential, and news travelled
fast in a small town.

It was like she had left herself behind—she was always "the
nurse"; never Brenda. She just wanted to be herself and not always
explaining, helping, and caring. She wanted to talk about familiar
things, hear and see familiar faces, go to a movie, eat in a restaurant,
get a hug....That was not to be. She had left all that behind. She was
here in the Arctic in a nursing station and that was that.

Research on remote settlements has noted several factors important and
unique to isolated-post living.[26] The life-style of the North is stressful due to
climate, cultural differences, long travel distances, and lack of resources. As with
lack of control, lonely people report a common feeling of personal powerlessness,
which may be conducive to being less productive at work.

One of the primary issues people associate with isolation is the concept of
loneliness. "Loneliness" is that sense of being without family, friends, or some
form of social support.[27] This is the perception of the individual, as perceived
support may vary from one individual to another in the same situation. Loneliness
is associated with poor adjustment to stress. It has been noted that the less lonely
one is, the less detrimental the effects of stress are. Furthermore, loneliness can be
associated with poor adjustment to stress as the individual is isolated from persons
who provide social support.

In addition to personal isolation, there is professional isolation experienced
by living in an isolated northern community.[28] Resources typically available in
urban settings are extremely distant. There is virtually no continuing education,
and resource books are usually limited and out of date. There is limited opportunity
to discuss individual cases, and workshops are limited, with few nurses able to
attend. Due to the demands and limited resources of the job, there is no opportunity
for self-study or research within the nursing station.

There are many occupational hazards of this profession that are directly
connected to the isolation in which nurses live. They are vulnerable to physical
violence and, due to the diversity of their work and means of transportation, they
are often vulnerable to injury.

Gender

"Boy that nurse in _____ really needs to get out—what a battle axe!
All we wanted was a cup of tea and she got all heated up and told us
she had other things to do than entertain travelling clinics. I don't
know what she was doing—there were only about three people in the
waiting room..."

***

"Brenda, now really, these people won't be in your way—just put them in the spare room. You don't have to go to any special trouble. I'm sure they would be happy to eat whatever you're preparing for yourself."

***

"So, here is your little boudoir—which room is yours?"

***

"I think these are the best looking nurses we've seen yet today, don't you, Ted?"

***

"Don't worry dear—I'll write it all out and send it up to you on an order sheet."

As for most women, issues of gender for northern nurses are present in all aspects of their lives. Typically, women have less leeway than men in society in terms of power, status, and income; and living in an isolated community accentuates this social phenomenon. The disadvantages of remote communities are particularly harder on women than on men.[29]

For northern nurses many of the issues of gender are magnified by the lack of personal privacy and the intensity of the professional responsibilities. Gender issues generally fall under two main categories—private and public.

Private Issues

Being a single woman in the isolation of the North can mean many things, not all of them good. Most people are very supportive and respectful, but not all. Many men (single and otherwise) hint directly or indirectly at the pent-up sexual desires of nurses, and some even go so far as to offer their "humble services". When that fails, the woman is deemed incapable; or is considered to be the villain (bitch), child (deary), or merely non-existent. It all seems somewhat ironic because often what is needed the most is a hug, that simple, friendly human contact which is the hardest thing to find.

Another serious issue for women in the North is the reality of violence. Most nursing stations do not have a comprehensive security system, and the constant threat of intrusion or violence leaves each and every nurse feeling isolated.

Public Issues

Public issues of gender are merely extensions of the private issues of gender. The lack of power and status for nurses is largely dependent on the fact that the majority of nurses are women.

Nursing is traditionally a female profession; but in the North, their role is expanded—carrying out activities that are usually allocated to medicine and men.[30] Since the higher echelons of health care departments are dominated by men, departmental policies and practice reflect their lack of sensitivity to women and the issues that affect them. Housing is often limited to shared quarters within or attached to the nursing station—private family dwellings, when they are available, are automatically allocated to physicians. These difficulties, and the erratic and demanding work situation inherent in the system, makes it virtually impossible for women with children to obtain jobs in the North. They require 24-hour child care which few northern communities have available.

Hiring practices for nurses are very different. Most isolation-post nursing positions are specifically restricted to single people (usually women) without dependents; however, most non-natives who come North to work, like teachers, public servants, and the RCMP, are married. The agencies hiring these groups prefer family units due to the need for increased support of the individual members and stability in the northern work force.[31] This doesn't apply to the nursing profession.

Cultural Awareness

The old man had a bad heart, and now he was drum dancing. Where did he get the energy to dance like that with a heart rate of 36? The nurse watched as he re-enacted a hunt with such intensity and precision, never missing a beat. She watched the faces of those around him as they looked on with pride at an old man dancing like that.... They had said he was a "good shaman", yet she had never seen him practice.

She thought back to the many discussions she had had with the old man and his family, about what a pacemaker could do for his heart, how it would be inserted, and what it would look like. He still refused to have it.

The old man said his time had come. He had had a good life and he was ready to pass his soul on to the next generation. He wanted to spend his last days, however many there were, with his family in the familiarity of his community. He did not want to be shuffled around by southern bureaucratic hospitals and their space-age technology. She could not argue with him.

Through her day-dream she heard someone call her name. She looked up to see a crowd gathered around his crumpled body on the floor. 'No', she thought, 'not now, I'm not ready for you to die, I've never really said good-bye'....She gave a few quick breaths—no pulse—compressions—a breath...a couple more and there was a gurgle in his throat. He opened his eyes and smiled. 'Hi!'

She visited him more often over the next few weeks. All could feel his time was drawing near. Through their many discussions, the nurse and the old shaman were able to say goodbye, and she could join him and his family in accepting life's ultimate end as a natural progression.

That came several weeks later; only this time he was alone. His time had come.

To be effective as a health care provider in a cross-cultural situation, nurses must acquire knowledge about that culture. Before nurses are able to provide culturally sensitive and supportive care they must be aware of their own cultural values and practices. This means resisting the inherent ethnocentrism—the philosophy that the beliefs and practices of one's own culture are best for all—to avoid cross-cultural communication breakdown. How the nurse feels about herself within a different culture, and how she feels about native people in general, will greatly influence the relationship that develops in her role as a health care provider. Implementing culturally sensitive programs and co-operating with local informal health care personnel takes additional time and effort.

Unfortunately, time is one of the many things nurses don't have. The realities of culture shock, professional reality shock, lack of sleep, overwhelming frustration, and lack of support cause many nurses to remain within the protection of their professional status and their nursing station. This isolation further alienates the nurse from experiencing northern culture and practices and developing open and accepting attitudes toward them.

To truly assist the community in obtaining a high level of health care, the nurses must look beyond the nursing station and the immediate clinical needs that turn up at the door. Nurses need to acquire the attitude of a consultant. As consultants, nurses are there to act on the needs of the people, medical or otherwise, as voiced by the people. They are there to assist people and give them the information they require to achieve their goals. Nurses must offer support, whether by implementing a community-based counselling program or pursuing local control of health services. Nurses must work with the community, whether it is a protest against low-level flights or the affirmation of native philosophy.

If improvement in the health of native Canadians is to be achieved, attention must be focused on socio-economic issues. After decades, even centuries of suppression, control, and dependence, the spirit and essence of native cultures are in a fragile state. People of these cultures are subsequently in a state of limbo. Many have lost their language and their cultural identity, and many have lost their land base; consequently, their links with nature have been weakened. As a result they are not as self-reliant.

Specifically, nurses need to focus on the many social and political issues affecting native people. Most of the health care issues affecting native people today can be traced to the inequities and imbalances in the basic necessities of life—inadequate diet, housing, or clean water; and the historical disregard and oppression of these cultural groups.

Outcomes

She sat bolt upright in bed—the emergency bell; she must get up. As she swung her legs over the edge of the bed and searched with her toes for her slippers, she sensed something was wrong. She immediately felt anxious—her bedroom was different; something was happening. As she blinked to orient herself, the nurse realized she was in her parents' house. She was at home. She listened again, just in case there was a bell or someone calling for help. Nothing came. It was the same dream...hearing a doorbell, a telephone, a child crying in the night, and never being able to find them. She hadn't had the dream for a month or two, although it had been eight months since she worked in the nursing station; in the beginning, it recurred at least once a week. For a nurse, it was a horrible feeling—knowing someone needed you, but being unable to reach them. You knew there was no one else who could help in emergencies, and you often worried you would sleep through the bell or not hear the telephone.

Many aspects of nursing in the North were difficult, and she carried with her heavy memories of fatigue, loneliness, and tragedy. But through it all, she remembered the joy of seeing a patient recover, recalling the fun of winter camping with families, and the many touches and "thank yous" that had carried her through the tough days. It was all behind her now; she had left the North. Or had she?

Health care in the North is largely dependent on the nurses who provide the care. The success of their work rests upon the individual and, in many cases, highly personal factors—who they are, how they perceive their job and their position within the community, and their approach to native people. The job is multi-faceted, and, at one time or another, most nurses assume varied roles.

The dynamics of the northern health care system, and their effects on the nurses who work within that system, can be both positive and negative. Many northern communities have some of the most comprehensive, accessible, and high-quality health care available in the world. Since health care needs in the North are varied, and must be met using limited resources, the environment provides an excellent opportunity for nurses to fully utilize their education and past experiences without the restrictions present in the South.[32]

On the negative side, northern health care costs have remained high; and over the past 50 years, only minor improvement has been noted in the traditional measures of health status—infant mortality and life expectancy—for the native population.[33] Many nurses who come to the North for the first time have little experience in the various aspects of care given; and limited resources and personnel do not provide adequate time for orientation or ongoing in-service education. As a result, the new nurse is often left to "figure things out for herself."

This is an insensitive and often dangerous practice, leading to a disjointed health care program with few innovations. The turnover rate for nurses practising in the North is high. There are perpetual shortages of health care personnel, and positions are often left unstaffed for long periods of time. Neither the health care system nor its personnel can be tailored to the special beliefs or needs of the native population; consequently, little use is made of the native healers and midwives who could assume some of the burden.

The fact that most nurses are single women maintains a subtle, but effective, form of isolation and control. They are alone, with little social support and with little opportunity to separate themselves from the government's health care apparatus and their professional posts. They go for long periods of time with little relaxation or sleep, yet continue to function with the intensity and compassion inherent in life-and-death situations. This leaves them vulnerable to the stress and strains of their work.

Nurses leaving their positions in the North often take many long-term problems with them. Many jump every time the phone or doorbell rings. It takes time for the habits born of "being ready just in case" to gradually disappear. Those who may have been victims of physical and/or sexual violence take even deeper scars with them when they leave the North. Considering that most nurses are already tired, stressed, and working with limited support and extended responsibilities, these attacks can be the final blow to an already fragile psyche.

If she is lucky, a nurse leaves the northern health care system before becoming convinced that it can't function without her. She leaves while she still has skills that are marketable in other areas of health care. She makes a career change while still possessing the capability to work with others in a non-supervisory role. She gets out while she still has the clarity of vision to look beyond race and social class to see the person who is sick and needs help.

Native health care remains in crisis. The current system is failing. Working at the grass roots level of the health care system, nurses are in the best position to improve the health status of native people by co-operating with them on socio-economic and health care issues. It is the only way we will improve a currently dismal situation.

To accomplish this, the direction of the health care programs must come from the local level. Programs must represent native needs and native solutions. Equally important to all of this, we must become concerned for the well-being of health care workers—for it is the nurses of the North who can help pull the system forward to meet the future needs of native and northern people.

Notes

1. The introductory anecdotes of each section in this article are taken from personal experience and diary entries at the nursing stations in the Northwest Territories.

2. See Kenneth Coates, *Canada's Colonies: A History of the Yukon and Northwest Territories* (Toronto: Lorimer and Co. Publishers, 1985).

3. See Coates, 1985, and H. Roche Robertson, *Health Care in Canada, A Commentary* (Toronto: Southam Murray Publishers, 1973).

4. See H. Brian Brett, "A Synopsis of Northern Medical History", *Canadian Medical Association Journal* 10 (1969):pp. 521–525, and John D. O'Neil, "Health Care in a Canadian Arctic Village: Continuities and Change", in D.Coburn *et al. (ed.), Health and Canadian Society* (Toronto: Fitzhenry and Whiteside, 1981):pp. 123–142.

5. See W.J. Copeman, "The Underserviced Area Program of the Ministry of Health", *Canadian Family Physician* 33 (1987): pp. 1683–1687, and G. Graham-Cumming, "Northern Health Services", *Canadian Medical Association Journal*, 100 (September 1969):pp. 526–531.

6. See Jean Briggs, *Never in Anger: Portrait of an Eskimo Family* (Cambridge, Mass.: *Harvard University Press, 1970);* Hugh Brody, *The People's Land: Eskimos and Whites in the Eastern Arctic* (Middlesex, England: Penguin Books, 1975); and O'Neil, 1981.

7. See Editor. "Northern Health Care", *Northline, Newsletter of the Association of Canadian Universities for Northern Studies*, 4(2) (1948):pp. 1–4.

8. The articles I would direct your attention to include: Bridgitta Arnoti's article, "Yukon Medicine: The Vital Role of Public Health Nurses", *Canadian Medical Association Journal*, 15 February 1984, pp. 492–496. Arnoti tells of the vital role nurses play in the Yukon health care system. See Corinne Hodgson's *A Preliminary Report on Nurses in Northern Manitoba and the Keewatin District, Northwest Territories,* an unpublished manuscript done for the Department of Anthropology, McMaster University, Hamilton (1979). In her report, Hodgson examines the interpersonal problems faced by white nurses when dispensing care to a native population. In Peter A. Sarsfield's 1984 serial article, "Arctic Diary" in *The Medical Post*, he captures the milieu of northern health care. Also Arlene Jorgenson's *Working in a Remote or Northern Post in Canada,* which was submitted to Occupational Environments and Health Surveillance, Red River College, Winnipeg, Manitoba (1985) is worth noting. Jorgenson outlines the occupational hazards unique to nursing in the North.

9. See Barnett, __, "Burnout Experienced by Recent Pharmacy Graduates of Mercer University", *American Journal of Hospital Pharmacy,* 43 (1986):pp. 2780–2784, and Christina Maslach and Susan Jackson, "Burnout in Health Professions", in G. Saunders and J. Suls, (eds.) *Social Psychology of Health and Illness* (Hillsdale, N.Y.: Lawrence Erlbaum, 1982).

10. See Hans Selye, *The Stress of Life* (New York: McGraw-Hill, 1976).

11. See Maslach and Jackson, 1982.

12. See Pamela Gray-Toft and James G. Anderson, "Stress among Hospital Nursing Staff: Its Causes and Effects", *Social Science and Medicine* 15A: pp. 639–647, Rosemary Scully, "Stress in the Nurse", *American Journal of Nursing* 80 (May 1980):pp. 912–918.

13. See Maureen Flannery, "Simple Living and Hard Choices", *The Hastings Center Report* (August 1982):pp. 9–12, and Peter A. Sarsfield, "Arctic Diary" series, *The Medical Post*, 1984.

14. See Laura Jamieson, "Rural Health—Better Service, Bigger Demands", *Health Care* 23 (1981):pp. 14–19, and Terri Ormiston, "Nurses at Work", *The Australian Nurses Journal* 12(9) (1983):pp. 22–23.

15. See Kathleen Ell, "Social Networks, Social Support, and Health Status: A Review", *Social Service Review*, March 1984, pp. 133–149, and Emily E.M. Smythe, "Who's Going to Take Care of the Nurses?" in Janet Muff (ed.), *Socialization, Sexism and Stereotyping: Women's Issues in Nursing* (Toronto:C.V. Mosby, 1982): pp. 337–350.

16. See Flannery, 1982, and H.M. Sampath, "Migration and Mental Health of Non-Eskimos in the Eastern Arctic", unpublished report prepared for the Department of Sociology and Anthropology, Memorial University of Newfoundland, n.d.

17. See Janet Lukas, "Factors in Nurse Practitioner Role Adjustment", *Nurse Practitioner*, 7(3) (1982):pp. 22–50, Jerry L. Weston, "Ambiguities Limited the Role of Nurse Practitioners and Physician Assistants", *American Journal of Public Health*, 74(1) (1984):pp. 6–7, and Lorna J. Williams, "'Ideal Nurse' and 'Real Nurse'", *The Australian Nurses Journal*, 7(9) (1978):pp. 44–46.

18. See Jean Baker, "Medevac!", *Up Here*, March/April 1988, pp. 53–55, Betty Lee, *Litiapik* (Toronto: McLelland and Stewart Ltd., 1975), and Sarsfield, 1984.

19. See Donald Brown, "Nursing in Canoe Narrows", *Canadian Nurse*, 71(9) (September 1975):pp. 38–39, Brenda Canitz *et al.*, "The North...The People, The Places, The Job", contributing author, *Canadian Nurse*, 80(1) (1984):pp. 24–29, and Lee, 1975.

20. See Carol Brown, "Women Workers in the Health Service Industry", in Elizabeth Fee (ed.), *Women and Health: The Politics of Sex in Medicine*, (Farmingdale, N.Y.: Baywood Publishing Inc., 1982: pp. 105–115, and Janet Muff, "Why Doesn't a Smart Girl Like You Go to Medical School?", in Janet Muff (ed.), *Socialization, Sexism and Stereotyping: Women's Issues in Nursing* (Toronto: C.V. Mosby, 1982): pp. 234–247.

21. See Harriet E. Ferrari, (1974) "Role and Activities of the Outpost Nurse in Northern Canada", *Symposium on Circumpolar Health—Yellowknife, NWT*.

22. See Mary L. Bennett, "The Rural Family Practitioner: The Quest for Role Identity" *Journal of Advanced Nursing*, 9 (1984):pp.145–155, Judy Coburn, "I See and I am Silent: A Short History of Nursing in Ontario", in David Coburn (ed.), *Health and Canadian Society*, (Markham, Ontario: Fitzhenry and Whiteside, 1987):pp. 441–462, Charlotte Gray, "Nurse Practitioners: Stepping into the Doctor's Domain?", *Canadian Medical Association Journal*, 128 (1 June 1983):pp. 1305–1309; and E.C. Hallman and D. Westlund, "Canadian Nurse Practitioners Battle Underutilization", *Nurse Practitioner*, 10(6) (1983).

23. See Flannery, 1982; and M. Tellis-Nayak and V. Tellis-Nayak, "Games That Professionals Play: The Social Psychology of Physician–Nurse Interaction" *Social Science and Medicine*,18(12) (1984):pp. 1063–1069.

24. See O'Neil, 1981; and John D. O'Neil and Peter A. Sarsfield, *The Gjoa Haven Gambit: An Inuit Community's Attempt to Exercise Responsibility in Local Health Services*, unpublished manuscript, n.d.

25. See Patricia A. Prescott, "Physician–Nurse Relationships", *Annals of Internal Medicine*,103 (1985):pp. 127–133, and Tellis-Nayak and Tellis-Nayak, 1984.

26. See James Burke and S. Eugene Barnes, "Behaviouristic Factors of Isolated Communities", *Ekistics* 278, September/October, 1979, pp. 301–304; and Sampath,N.D., and John S. Willis, "Disease and death in Canada's North", *Medical Services Journal of Canada*, 19 (1963):pp.747–768, and D.A. Russell, L.A. Peplau, and C.E. Cutrona, "The Revised UCLA Loneliness Scale: Concurrent and Discriminant Validity Evidence", *Journal of Personality and Social Psychology*, 39 (1980):pp. 772–480.

27. See S. Norwicki, and M.F. Duke, "The Effect of Locus of Control on Peer Relationships Across Age Groups", *Journal of Genetic Psychology*,43 (1975):pp. 275–280, and S. Norwicki, and M.F. Duke, "A locus of control scale for college as well as non-college adults", *Journal of Personality Assessment*, 38 (1974):pp. 136–137.

28. See Jennifer Evans, and Ruth Cooperstock, *Psychosocial Impacts of Resource Development on Women*. Unpublished manuscript prepared for Addiction Research Foundation (1982); Kathleen Jamieson and Arlene McLaren, *Roughing it in the Bush*. Unpublished manuscript prepared for Environmental and Social Affairs, Petro-Canada Resources, Calgary Alberta (1983); Miriam Wall,

"Women and Development in Northwestern Ontario", *Alternatives* 14(1) (1987):pp.14–17; and Gregg S. Wilkinson, "Isolation and Psychological Disorder", *Psychological Reports* 36 (1975):pp.631–634.

29. See Burke and Barnes; 1979, Evans and Cooperstock, 1982; Jamieson and McLaren, 1983; Rex Lucas, *Minetown, Milltown, Railtown* (Toronto: University of Toronto Press, 1971); and Ira Robinson, *New Industrial Towns on Canada's Resource Frontier* (Chicago: University of Chicago Press, 1962).

30. See Bonnie Bullough, "Barriers to the Nurse Practitioner Movement: Problems of Women in a Women's Field", *International Journal of Health Services* 5 (1975): pp. 225–233, Marilyn Edumunds, "Do Nurse Practitioners Still Practise Nursing?", *Nurse Practitioner* 9(5) (1984): pp. 47–51; Eva Gamarnikow, "Sexual Division of Labour: The Case of Nursing", in Annette Kuhn, and Ann-Marie Wolpe (eds.), *Feminism and Materialism: Women and Modes of Production* (London: Routledge and Kegan Paul Publishers, 1978): pp.97–123, and Gray, 1983.

31. See Evans and Cooperstock, 1982, and Sampath, n.d..

32. See T. Kue Young, "The Canadian North and the Third World: Is the Analogy Appropriate?", *Canadian Journal of Public Health* 74 (1983): pp. 239–241.

33. See Government of Canada, *Report on Health Conditions in the NWT* (Yellowknife: Medical Services Branch, Health and Welfare, 1986), and Young, 1983.

Summary of Arts and Crafts: Women and Their Work

Prepared by Kate Irving
Written by Lynn Fogwill and Cheryl Fennell for the
N.W.T. Advisory Council on the Status of Women

Introduction

In 1988, the Northwest Territories Advisory Council on the Status of Women commissioned an independent research project to investigate and analyse arts and crafts activities in the Northwest Territories as they involve and affect women. The council wanted to improve the status of women working in arts and crafts. The researchers were hired to determine the current situation of these women, to find out what changes were desired, and to make recommendations.

The authors started from the premise that women are vital to the arts and crafts industry. They produce exquisite work: wearable art such as mukluks, *kamiks* [boots], *amautiks* [hooded parkas], and slippers; ivory and soapstone carvings; beautifully decorated parkas and baskets; ancient decorating art in porcupine quill and moosehair tufting; gorgeous weavings and applique wall-hangings; and charming creations such as the Spence Bay packing animals.

They produce their crafts in their homes, together in sewing groups, or in industrial sewing centres. They sell their work for money to put food on the table and clothes on their children. They take pride in their crafts and pleasure in the finished products.

The authors based their findings and recommendations primarily on what these women told them. The women were treated as the most important source of ideas and opinions on the problems and opportunities associated with arts and crafts. The key element of the research process was a series of personal interviews with women producers, women who own or work in craft-shops, and key women in the economic and political life of Northwest Territories communities. These interviews were conducted in Iqaluit, Rankin Inlet, Spence Bay, Inuvik, Fort Norman, Fort Simpson, and Fort Liard. In addition, telephone interviews were conducted with women in Baker Lake, Cambridge Bay, Holman Island, Aklavik, Tuktoyaktuk, Gjoa Haven, Fort McPherson, Coppermine, Fort Providence, Rae–Edzo, Fort Franklin, Eskimo Point, Jean Marie River, Pangnirtung, Arctic Bay, Cape Dorset, Broughton Island, and Yellowknife. Supplementary consultations were done with current and former craft-shop managers, personnel from the Government of the Northwest Territories Department of Economic Development, staff from the co-ops and The Bay, private retailers, adult educators, members of women's organizations, and local politicians. Previous research reports on arts and crafts were also reviewed.

This article summarizes the findings and recommendations. The full report and copies of the summary report in English and Inuktitut are available from the Women's Secretariat in Yellowknife.

The Findings

The project findings focus on the women working in the arts and crafts industry, rather than on the industry itself. Comments on the industry are, therefore, limited to specific aspects which affect the working lives of the women involved.

In 1987, formal arts and crafts sales accounted for $22 million. Informal, door-to-door, and "in-kind" transactions probably accounted for much more. Approximately 20 per cent were sold in the Northwest Territories with the rest going to southern Canada and overseas. Data for the entire territory were not available, but it is interesting to note that income generated by arts and crafts in the Baffin region alone was $9.7 million in 1986; this represents 11 per cent of the region's total income.

The researchers found that women are the key to a vital and flourishing cottage industry in arts and crafts in the Northwest Territories. It is primarily their industry, and yet they have very little input, let alone control, over the directives and decisions which affect them.

If women are to continue to produce the crafts and artwork synonymous with the North, and if they are to continue to generate significant income in their communities, they must be provided with the opportunities and support to assume ownership and control.

The findings and recommendations in the report are based on an assessment of what must happen to enable women to take charge of their craft work; not on what is needed to make the craft industry healthier. Women are the key to a healthier craft industry, and they are capable of taking it into their own hands.

The findings are discussed under three headings: the status of women in the arts and crafts industry; the role of government in the arts and crafts industry; and the preservation of traditional northern crafts.

214

1. The Status of Women in the Arts and Crafts Industry

Women are the foundation of the arts and crafts industry and the key to its vitality. Their role is underestimated, unrecognized, and undervalued. They have not been included in the policy development and decision making that affects them. They tend to be "invisible"—the production of crafts is seen as an extension of their traditional role in the household. Recent studies have focused on marketing, quality control, and new products, rather than on the situation and needs of the producers and the reality of a "cottage industry".

> *We aren't bodies to be counted in an office from nine to five.* (Baker Lake)

> *The government doesn't care for ideas about what we want to do for our community....They don't care unless the ladies are producing....They want to operate the ladies like sewing machines.* (Spence Bay)

Northern craftswomen are at a critical juncture. They have come too far into the modern world to ignore the reality of the formal market-place. At the same time, crafts are more than a source of income; they are a critical link to the women's past, traditions, and culture. Many women in the eastern Arctic saw their first "money" when they made clothing for white people coming North in the 1950s. The sewing centres and craft shops established by governments served as gathering places for women to work and to support each other. Recent closings have left many women dislocated. They want something re-established, but on their own terms, not those of outsiders.

> *My idea is for a council of women to do it together, with government helping with start-up money.* (Rankin Inlet)

Very few women depend on the sale of crafts as their only source of income, but these sales can be significant and critical to the survival of their families. Typically, they are combined with transfer payments, wages, and subsistence activities. Deductions for craft income are made from social assistance cheques, and much income is probably kept "informal" and "hidden" because of this. This serves as a disincentive and lowers the status of the producer; women often accept low prices because of this or because they need the money immediately.

There are "industry-related" problems, and there are problems that stem from the fact that women work a double or triple day. The former include availability and the cost of raw materials and tools, inadequate marketing, and low prices. The latter refer to the situation of most women producers who are caring for children and/or grandchildren, running a household, and managing seasonal hunting or fishing activities as well as producing crafts.

Women lack the self-confidence and skills needed to make the "system" work for them. They know what the problems are and have ideas for solutions, but they need assistance in developing business skills in the areas of pricing, marketing, bookkeeping, ordering, running a retail operation, and other activities.

The government wanted native women to take over a sewing centre but none of the women would do it because they didn't have enough education. They were afraid of losing money. (Inuvik)

We need some wonderful workshops for women to realize the value of what they do. (Iqaluit)

Women are tired of studies that never have their recommendations implemented. However, they were pleased that this particular study was conducted by women about women, and they were pleased that their opinions were being treated as important.

There is money from Economic Development to study the problem, but there is no money for the policy to work. (Inuvik)

2. The Role of Government in the Arts and Crafts Industry
There is a lack of clarity, a lack of vision, and a lack of government policy. The social and cultural aspects of the arts and crafts industry are not recognized as important. There are regional strategies being devised and plans to develop a policy being considered; however, these focus solely on the economic aspects and do not directly involve the women producers.

There is a lack of co-ordination and co-operation among the several government departments involved. Some initiatives are being taken, but they are in isolation.

Privatization of the craft shops in the last three years has had, at best, a mixed benefit. At worst, it has caused severe economic and social dislocation. All of the "privatization" efforts studied have resulted in the closing of the craft shops involved, with one exception. That exception, Fort Simpson, is not making money, and the owners still do not have legal title. Opinions on the benefits of privatization were mixed, but most of the women producers were unhappy with both the method and the results.

After the craft shop closed, I was hungry for something all the time and kept wondering what I was going to do; but I had no place to go. (Spence Bay)

3. Preservation of Traditional Northern Crafts

There is a distinct possibility that in only a few years the craft industry could die out because not enough young women are learning the skills required to produce quality arts and crafts.

Older and middle-aged women want to teach their artistry and skill but are unable to interest young women or children. Young women have a greater number of options today and don't learn from elders as they used to. Children rarely see or appreciate the finished work that their mothers and grandmothers produce. Craftwork is associated with low pay, exploitation, and a past way of life.

The Recommendations

The report's recommendations are based on the premise that although the required programs and funding mechanisms are in place, they have not been available because the women have tended to be "invisible" to the decision makers. These recommendations are based on the same three categories as the findings. They are simply listed here. Rationales for each are based on the findings and appear in the full report.

1. There must be a territorial policy on arts and crafts, developed by the Government of the Northwest Territories in consultation with women producers and their organizations.

2. The Government of the Northwest Territories must establish an ongoing mechanism to effect co-operation and co-ordination among departments with an interest in arts and crafts. An interdepartmental co-ordination committee, co-chaired by the Department of Economic Development and the Women's Secretariat, is suggested.

3. The privatization of craft shops should be re-evaluated. The problems of the craft shops should be separated from the discussion on privatization. Privatization should be assessed as one of several economic models in the context of finding the most effective and appropriate role for government.

4. The Government of the Northwest Territories should investigate options to allow flexibility in social assistance in relation to craft income.

5. The Northwest Territories Advisory Council on the Status of Women should advocate and support efforts to empower women producers so that they may take control of their work. This involves education and training combined with opportunities to network.

6. The Government of the Northwest Territories should fund regional workshops for women in arts and crafts. They should use experiential learning methods to enable women to gain the self-confidence and skills they need.

7. The Government of the Northwest Territories should provide ongoing, appropriate training programs using a co-ordinated approach among departments. Courses should be short, intense, have built-in follow-up, be delivered locally, involve consultation with the women producers, include child care arrangements, and make use of distance-education tools.

8. The Government of the Northwest Territories should actively support new and existing women's craft co-operatives and organizations, particularly through start-up funding and organizational development support.

9. There should be a special advocate for women working in the arts and crafts industry, located in the Women's Secretariat.

10. The Government of the Northwest Territories should assess the participation of women in existing grant programs, and take steps to ensure that the participation rate mirrors their involvement in the industry.

11. The Government of the Northwest Territories, in co-operation with the Dene Cultural Institute, the Inuit Cultural Institute, the Native Women's Association, and the Inuit Women's Association, should map out an immediate program for visually documenting all aspects of traditional craft productions.

12. The Government of the Northwest Territories should develop a curriculum and special projects to give children positive exposure to arts and crafts in the schools. This should reflect the links with traditional culture and the potential for community-based jobs.

13. The Government of the Northwest Territories should investigate the potential for an "apprenticeship" program for young women wishing to train with elders. Funding support for the young women and the elders should be included.

Chapter V

RETHINKING POWER AND POLITICS

Woman with Bird Image by Pudlo Pudlat

Women and Politics—A Talk with Three Greenlandic Women

Marianne Lykke Thomsen

Henriette Rasmussen from Qasigiannguit, is 37 years old, a journalist and teacher by profession. Henriette has been involved in politics for the past few years, and was co-founder of the now-dissolved alternative women's group, *Kilut*. Since 1983 she has been the representative of the left wing party, *Inuit Ataqatigiit*, in the Nuuk Municipal Council, and since 1984 has served as an elected member of the *Landsting* (parliament), and chairperson of its Finance Committee.

Lise Lennert from Maniitsoq, is 39 years old, and has taught in primary school for many years. She has been active in the Greenland Women's Association, *Arnat Peqatigiit Kattuffiat* since 1979, serving as a member of the board of directors, then vice-president and, later, president. Lise is a member of the *Siumut* party. She was appointed chairperson of the Home Rule Equality Committee by the *Landsting* in 1986.

Mariane Petersen, 50, is also from Maniitsoq. She is a certified interpreter, but for the past six years has been working as a curator at the Greenland National Museum. From 1979 to 1983 she served as an elected member of the Nuuk Municipal Council for the *Siumut* party.

***

MLT: How would you characterize the situation in Greenland with regard to women and leadership?

HR: Even though in my mind this is not a typical question for Inuit, I can say that we have always had women leaders in Greenland. However, they are not very visible, owing to the fact that our social structure is quite discriminatory toward them. They should be accepted more as our leaders, but our capitalistic and competitive society does not encourage us to do so. Leaders are those personalities toward whom we all show respect and devotion. A politician is not necessarily a leader.

MLT: So, what you are talking about is formal versus informal leadership—the leadership of the system as opposed to leadership inherent in the society?

HR: Yes, if these would only overlap. They rarely do, for women at least. Women leaders will never be assertive; yet, to assert oneself is not necessarily negative. In fact, we should be more assertive more often. We don't acknowledge the powers which we possess nearly enough.

LL: This is because it is not considered feminine to tell society that one is capable and committed as a woman. We have many women leaders who are extremely powerful, at the family level. If they were not around, our society would suffer from even more social disasters.

HR: In our generation, women who are talented and willing to fight for their rights are not considered feminine to men. The men look down on us if we bring forward our points of view and discuss our problems among them. Of course, I find that to be their problem more than ours. It is an era in history that has to quietly disappear. It is difficult for those men, who find it hard to accept us, to work themselves away from this situation. This may also account for the fact that few women are willing to take the lead. It can certainly be feminine, though, to fight, and I think women should go for it more often.

LL: A lot of women do not, or dare not, get up front. In the Nordic countries there is a focus on getting as many women leaders as possible into the public and private sectors as a way of attempting to attain a just society. We will never achieve a society of justice and harmony ourselves if we do not get more women leaders in the labour market. To my knowledge, this is a discussion that Greenlandic women have never had.

Equality Status within the Society

MLT: Have you managed to get an equality committee established?

LL: Yes. While I was chairperson for the Greenland Women's Association, I worked on getting an equality committee established under the Home Rule Government. In 1980, I attended the United Nations International Women's Conference in Copenhagen. Following the conference, I began looking into how I could utilize my experience for the benefit of my country, and for women in particular. Setting up an equality committee is what I came up with. In 1985, the *Landsting* passed a bill concerning the establishment of the Equality Committee, and the first appointed committee started working in September 1986. However, a governmental crisis, calling for an election, put the committee work on hold until the *Landsting* Autumn Gathering in 1987. A new committee was appointed at the gathering and constituted in November of that year. [1]

HR: The discussions initiated by the Equality Committee, and the issues raised, have to date been very good and to the point. Two examples include the problems connected to the upbringing of our children; and, more recently, as discussed at the conference in Sisimiut, getting more women candidates elected at the next election.[2] I would, however, expect the Equality Committee to be much more outspoken in the media, thus making sure that it will not become one of those committees working for itself. This is imperative in order to succeed in implementing the present goal—men and women accepted as being equally responsible for society and its future development.

MLT: I understand that the committee is in need of resources.

LL: We have a part-time counsellor from Home Rule at our disposal, but as the chairperson, I have to do the work along with my full-time job as a teacher. This is often when all the offices are closed, leaving me limited time to do the job—running cases, feeding the media, doing the field-work for day care and preschool programs, and working at the educational institutions.

Moreover, the progress of the committee is complicated because the members live in communities scattered along the coast and because some members, at times, fail to show commitment and drive. Nevertheless, one has to realize that if we all sit down, like in other committees under the Home Rule, and wait for the chairperson to carry the workload, we will not get very far. Everyone agrees on this, but no one does anything to change the situation.

Three or four times, office heads and directors in the Home Rule Government administration have asked me: "What is it that you want? The other committees work this way. Why are you putting forward special demands?" It should be noted though, that, in general, it is not the administration causing major problems. The problem is getting enough time to do the most important part—the field-work, the consciousness-raising, and the educational work, to prevent people from commenting, "Such a luxury problem. We do not want that."

MLT: It sounds like you are dealing with problems that require some attention, now that the Equality Committee is already in place and secured by legislation.

HR: That is true. We have to work on removing these obstacles, ensuring the committee better facilities and working conditions.

MP: The politicians have to be made aware by the committee members, and by women in general, that if they did not just set up the committee to shut the women up, then they have to show some initiative and give the necessary financial and personnel support. I do not think the bill, as such, contains anything. For example, I have not yet seen or heard of any real support from the politicians for the committee's work.

HR: I do not believe the intention was to make the women shut up. Rather it is the lack of awareness about how one creates equality between men and women. People in general, as in the *Landsting*, are extremely ignorant about what exactly should be done. A dialogue on this is definitely needed.

LL: Society gives us equal rights and opportunities. The question of equal importance or equal value is not as tangible. In theory, boys and girls have equal access to education, and at this time, there are more girls getting high school degrees than boys. When it comes to continuing education, however, that is when the girls drop out, and the boys are the ones who are more likely to finish. This whole process has not been explored. The issue is also very emotional because interference means encroachment on individual freedom. There will be an outcry if we try to decide on the futures of the young girls' lives in terms of children and education.

HR: I think the girls would benefit if we, as women, would talk to them about these matters.

MP: Not only the girls—society needs our input. Many times I have wanted to comment on this, but did not dare for fear of the consequences.

MLT: How about financial equality? I am aware that, in principle, men and women get equal pay.

HR: The question of equality is not only a matter of sex. The personal income levels within Greenlandic society are as different as they are in India—a very hierarchical society! As women politicians, it is our responsibility to promote equality between men and women, precisely by working toward equal distribution of property values and responsibilities for all citizens. If we get a chance to change the value-system of the present society, the financial aspects of equality will be one of our priorities.

LL: This is why we would like to see more women participate in the decision-making process. To achieve this goal, we need to identify the barriers experienced by women in these forums. One of our initial projects was to send out question-naires to the 27 elected women politicians in the municipal councils and the *Landsting*. Unfortunately, we got a small response, and we are now trying to simplify the questionnaire and enlarge our target group to include more women with an interest in politics. In this way, we hope to collect some valuable information for our future work.

HR: I think that women have to make a choice. We cannot expect to be good mothers and good housewives if we also want to be good politicians, unless we insist that our husbands and sons take over more of the housework and reverse the roles a bit. My husband for one, has accepted some responsibility for our home and children, but only in this way have I been able to participate in politics. However, this has to be our own choice and initiative as women. We cannot afford to wait for our husbands to let us participate.

MP: One has to learn to make priorities. For me it was never a problem, being a single mother with three children. The children learned early on to help with the different tasks, but clearly, this is not always the case.

LL: Or, we could urge society to provide assistance to those choosing to become politicians. As well, I think that the consciousness-raising that we are talking about here is linked to greater access to education. Making more and more people aware of the necessity to share tasks is going on, but it is a slow process.

Women and Politics

MLT: The Equality Committee is not the only forum in which work is done to increase the number of women in decision-making bodies. Initiatives in this direction are also occasionally taken in the various women's groups and organiza-tions such as *Kilut* and *Arnat Peqatigiit*.[2]

LL: *Papiit* is another body formed after the first "unofficial, cross-party," inter-arctic women's conference, arranged by the Knud Rasmussen Folk High School, in Sisimiut in 1984. At this conference the women from Nuuk, as the majority, were asked to support women politicians and to start a women's magazine. The name *Papiit*, meaning tail feathers, was inspired by the dove of peace, the worldwide symbol for women's work for peace and philosophy of life in general. The bird symbolizes the elected woman politician and the tail feathers symbolize women's support for her.

However, a specific idea about the support needed was very difficult to get. At a conference in 1987, which was a continuation of the women's conference in 1984, we decided that individual participants returning to their home communities would be responsible for forming initiative groups to replace *Papiit*. Inspired by the title of the conference, *Arnat Kalaallit Nipaat*—The Voice of Greenlandic Women—the groups are now called the voice of women from this or that community. For example, *Nuummi Arnat Nipaat* is The Voice of the Nuuk Women. The participants at the conference came from nine different communities, and we sincerely hope they can all get groups together. Hopefully the idea will spread, even to those communities that were not represented.

In addition to the *Nipaat* groups, a group was also formed to examine the basis for establishing an umbrella organization to include the various women's groups and organizations, and their different areas of interest. We hope it will be provided for in future budgets.

HR: As chairperson of the Finance Committee, I have asked that an annual grant be given to the *Arnat Peqatigiit* which will be distributed to all women's organizations and groups in the future. The unwritten law of contributing only to *Arnat Peqatigiit* goes back to the time when they were the only group. It is time that this changed.

MLT: It is my impression that Greenlandic women, in general, agree that more women should enter the political arena. There are still only a few women politicians—why is this?

LL: One of the problems is that Greenlandic women got their eligibility and the vote handed to them. Our mothers and grandmothers did not have to fight to reach this point. Many of these women, however, have worked in different kinds of organizations, not necessarily women's organizations, where they have really shown their strength. Yet the leap from there to becoming politicians in a municipal or provincial setting was too great. They felt they had to sacrifice their families too much for this. We are still in the process of learning. I believe the interest is there, but when women within the political parties are asked to run for office, they still prefer substituting for the men. Consequently, only every fifth candidate is a woman. I think that our decision in principle from the conference in Sisimiut will be hard to put into effect. There we demanded that 50 per cent of the candidates for election in the next two years be women. It is important to motivate women to run for office by encouraging them to get prepared to work with the Home Rule and municipal administrations. Men are not going to leave their seats voluntarily.

MP: It is not a proper goal just to demand that in two years' time, or at the next election, such and such a percentage of the candidates be women. We need to discuss the problems thoroughly, and prepare and present our material so that more people are inclined to vote for women. We have to demonstrate our capability at the professional level.

HR: We may have to wait many years for the development we wish to see—a 50–50 representation. In any event, though, we will not give up easily. The key is to keep on trying, and in *Inuit Ataqatigiit*, for example, we have, with some success, stressed the importance of feminine values.

LL: One of our reasons for wanting female participation in the political process is that women look at things differently than men. We would like to enrich the political process—make changes in the present situation in which society functions exclusively on the premises of men. We know very well that, in order to develop a society in harmony, we must work together. Nevertheless, the situation is very bad concerning women and politics. The kind of power that men have does not particularly appeal to women. Yet, if we want to be part of the game, we have to accept the existing structures until there are enough of us with the same convictions and commitments to break down and rebuild a more flexible system. Until then, the women already in politics will have to work alone and with large areas of responsibility. We are aware of this, so we instinctively volunteer our support and, at the same time, try to make more women confident with and interested in participating.

Right now we have come to a standstill where we have no common goal to fight for, other than saying that there are not enough women in politics. This is not specific enough. From what we experienced with the *Arnat Suleqatigiit*, women have to have something common to work toward.[3] This became evident once the crisis centre was established. Once it was established, women's interests started fading away.

MLT: What about the well known *ad hoc* group phenomenon?

HR: Each of us has our support groups. What we have to do, though, is find some very specific cases that we can work on politically until they are completed.

The members of *Kilut* chose to dissolve their group which had been working with battered women and anti-violence campaigns. We found that some of the work we were doing overlapped with our political work in *Inuit Ataqatigiit*, and that other groups gradually took over these areas of concern. The *Arnat Suleqatigiit*, for example, was more or less born out of the work that *Kilut* had previously undertaken.

LL: We must not give up easily. We have to get together as one and start from there.

MP: I belong to the group of people that Lise says gives up too easily. Three elections within three years and nothing has happened. I don't want to take the trouble of running again. The women totally failed to support their sisters at the last election to the *Landsting*. Why? I have analysed the situation to find a reason, and the only answer I can think of is that we, the women, who were not elected into office are just not good enough.

HR: I still believe we can do it. We have to prove this to both women and men. I know that we are as competent as the men in these matters, but it is not enough that the women candidates are as good as the men. For a woman to alter the very conservative attitudes of the constituents in order to get elected, she simply has to make a greater effort than is required from the men. In this respect, changes within Greenlandic society are very slow. We treat each other badly here in Greenland. We have been through some elections where we worked hard. Mariane knows, because we have been in the same election campaign. We put all our strength together then, and yet, only two women were elected to the *Landsting*. Women do not vote for women, and the constituents don't listen to the women either. *Inuit Ataqatigiit* has for some time had a policy that has made the members aware of this situation. The women within the party want women elected to offices. I got in because the women within *Inuit Ataqatigiit* have been very actively involved in the political work and, therefore, are quite influential.

MP: In addition to what Henriette said about finding common ground and debating the problems that we share, we can only be successful if we help each other first. We have a small population in Greenland, yet I have always felt sorry that we are so divided. Instead of working together on common problems, people are forming separate groups. This way we will never get together. This is reinforced by the fact that Greenland is split into various political parties. Even within families people are divided. We must learn that no matter how many groups or parties the individuals within a family may belong to, we must talk to one another. We have not yet come this far.

HR: If we hope to contribute to any major changes in our society and to alter society's view of women as equally competent political leaders and an important resource, we must not give up. We must educate ourselves and encourage our young girls to get an education and to participate in the work on equal terms with us. It is important that we engage in politics. It is the only way we can attain any influence. It is an obligation as well as an opportunity that we must not let pass by.

LL: I find it very depressing that we cannot find women ten or more years younger than ourselves to continue the struggle. I do not know the reason why, but we have to think of new strategies to make them interested. Greenlandic society is still very young; the Home Rule Government is barely ten years old. Yet, it is hard to accept that things are so slow. We cannot afford to waste women's resources. Think of all those years when the three of us were working and how often our work was unacknowledged.

HR: Our society is not acceptable as it is. I keep searching for our cultural heritage in every step we take politically. The standards and values that we are applying in our society have failed. Yet, nobody considers the values of our cultural heritage—they have no immediate monetary value.

Self-Criticism

MLT: I have noticed that all of you show a great deal of self-criticism.

HR: I find it very positive that we are able to criticize ourselves and concentrate on dealing with our own values and problems. That is important progress in itself. Ten years ago we criticized the men, because of their total ignorance and male chauvinism. This was when we got into discussions about upbringing. We realized that we actually had a lot to say concerning the upbringing of our children; we could admit that this was where many mistakes were made. The boys are brought up to become "masters" with power—the girls are never brought up this way. We realized that our efforts should be directed toward this particular situation.

We have had a women's day, a children's day, and a men's day, with different activities at the *Aasivik* gatherings.[4] On the men's day last year, the men were once again encouraged to open up, because we realized that many of our problems, including assault on women, venereal diseases, and alcohol, often happen because of the men's tendency to be reserved. Greenlandic society is no different from other societies. Men rarely talk about their feelings and inner conflicts, which then degenerate into assaulting us. The women in many cases become so suppressed that they have no energy to even keep the family together.

MP: The men are certainly criticized by the women. To answer your question, however, we must analyse our problems and ourselves to be able to get ahead in this world. We have to become fully aware of the things we do wrong and how we can improve ourselves. A male friend of mine recently gave a very gratifying evaluation of women, saying that we are the ones that should be credited for keeping society from falling apart, by tending to our jobs, our children, and our homes.

LL: One of the things we can be happy about as women is the change in attitude over the past 20 years by men toward the role of being a father. Men are taking more interest in the upbringing of our children. This can also be utilized tactically when approaching male politicians. They need to be praised for their efforts, and we need them to become fully involved in the discussions about our methods of bringing up our children.

Raising Our Children

MLT: In many of the social conditions that we have touched upon, you have focused on matters concerning the upbringing of your chidren.

LL: Following the major political issues, such as the introduction of the Home Rule Government and withdrawal from the EEC, the members of *Papiit* thought it was time to start looking at the family situation. How do we want to bring up our children here in Greenland? How much influence should we let the European (Danish) model have upon the upbringing of our children? And how can we protect our own cultural heritage which we do not want to lose? We tried to encourage debate around these questions, but found that they were far too broad and complex to comprehend.

HR: If only we could bring up our boys to accept the girls as equal to them! It is said that African women tend to spoil their husbands. We do the same thing here in Greenland sometimes. We have discussed this problem and have become aware of the consequences it has, and how it is in conflict with modern value systems and male–female living arrangements. The boys who are being spoiled run into serious problems when they grow up and suddenly discover that they cannot treat women as subordinates. No one should expect women to accept this today, although there are still many who do. It takes generations of work and awareness to solve this. What we can do is to work with boys and girls on this, have the schools and teachers work on it, and make sure it is included in the objectives of day care and preschool programs. Boys and girls must be brought up on equal terms.

LL: There are many in our mothers' generation bringing their grandchildren up differently. They have their favourite child—*qujagisarqarneq*. This is very unfortunate, since every child should be welcome in a family. We have our differences, fair enough, but it is sad to see children in a family being treated differently because one individual is named after somebody special, or when some women favour girls, and others boys—*arnannguarneq* or *angutinnguarneq*. This whole situation has never been debated officially. I think our generation has a different view on these things; we ought to discuss it even though it may hurt some people.

Education, Reproduction, and Health

MLT: Are there any other taboos affecting women and their position in society?

HR: It is important that we open up and remove the taboo around sexual relations here in Greenland. Many women have huge problems with their abdomens, owing to the fact that we wear clothes in accordance with fashion rather than the arctic climate, but mainly because of the many incidents of venereal disease which often cause spontaneous abortions and other serious complications.

It is also not acceptable to have multiple sexual relations. As a member of the National Health Board, I feel that we ought to make an even greater effort to combat sexually transmitted diseases threatening our society. In order to succeed in this, however, we all have to make an effort. This is another area in which we need to educate each other as well as our children.

Ignorance of contraceptives is another related problem. Too many Greenlandic women have their babies at a young age. The young teenagers in school know far too little about sex. At the same time, it is a very emotionally charged issue. It is difficult to talk about, and to set limits for young people as to when it is reasonable for them to have babies. In my opinion, the young women should complete a reasonable level of education before they start having babies.

MP: I agree that young people are having children too early. Besides the problems it causes for the individual, society is severely affected by the subsequent problems of not being able to provide proper child care facilities and housing, and in dealing with the huge number of school drop-outs. One would become extremely unpopular saying this in public. It is beyond my comprehension why young people keep doing this.

HR: *Qaa - allatta*! Let us write and start a discussion on this in the media! I have wanted to do so for a long time.

LL: It has become very accepted, almost "in", to become a grandmother at a young age—before turning 40! However, ultimately, it is the young mother who has sole responsibility for the child. She often ends up getting a poor start on her adult life, she has poor living conditions, and she has a position way down at the bottom of the hierarchy.

HR: There is nothing wrong with having children, but the young girls should be made fully aware that if they wish to live a good and dignified life, and have their freedom as women, education is the key word. Becoming mothers too early can weaken their position in society. The young girls disregarded our work on abortion when it was a major issue in the media. We emphasized that abortion should be seen as an option to be considered under special circumstances. We simply did not get hold of them when they were adolescents.

LL: We have to learn to administer our freedom better. Consciousness-raising has to begin within the family. It is not solely the responsibility of the schools and institutions. This is why it is so important that men be included in the discussions about upbringing and education.

Generation Gap

MLT: Is there a gap between the generations?

HR: At the *Aasivik* gatherings, which are the best cultural alternative to our present society, there is a strong solidarity between the generations. This is also true within the families. However, a gap still exists between the generations, caused by social problems such as poor housing. Especially in the towns, children, adolescents, adults, and old people have very few possibilities to get together, even though they would like to do so. Our homes are too small. The pubs are practically the only place where people can gather in great numbers! As yet, we do not have any public indoor places in which all generations can assemble, and, because of this, generations easily become separated.

MP: To answer this question, you have to divide society into villages and towns. There are tremendous differences in the relationships between generations in the smaller communities as compared with larger communities. Nuuk should be seen completely isolated from the rest of the country in this regard. The generation gap is hard to measure. In some places the gap is very wide, reinforced by the political party split within the families. In other places there is none.

Media Attention to Women's Issues

MLT: The women's magazine *Kilut* has not yet been replaced. Do women's activities get any attention from other media, such as radio, TV, or newspapers?

HR: For some years, the *Kilut* group published a magazine in which many women expressed their thoughts through poetry and open letters. It was very positive, and I think we should continue to print women's magazines and newsletters to express our opinions, visions, and innermost wishes. Journalists don't mind if we bring articles to them, but it still depends on the journalist's background whether it will be printed or not.

MLT: What you are saying is that we have to pay attention to the fact that the media can be manipulative and undemocratic?

HR: The media is clearly coloured by the interests of male journalists. Journalists do not by themselves examine women's situations. For example, they won't examine the need for, or conditions of, crisis centres. There may be some coverage when we have conferences like the *Arnat Kalaallit Nipaat*, but then only as tiny features on TV or radio.

MP: This came out during the last conference. From my experience, absolutely no journalists payed any attention to us. Not once did they voluntarily ask us what was going on. Everything had to be delivered to them on a silver plate by the women participating in the conference.

MLT: There are quite a few women journalists by now, though.

MP: That is right, and we are continuously wondering why they are not active or interested in these matters.

LL: I had great expectations of journalists being interested in the conference. We notified them ahead of time to make sure they would attend. Yet, the interest from the press was so little. We practically had to force two journalists, who happened to be present by accident, to give us some coverage. They had completed their work on a hunters' conference which had just ended in the same location. *Atuagagdliutit* had promised us a woman journalist, but she didn't show up, and the other country-wide newspaper did not, at that time, have any Greenlandic-speaking journalists to send.

   I am thoroughly disappointed with the media after having so many experiences like that. Press releases and debates about legalized abortion, the initiatives with the fur workshops, and the joint protests by women's groups and midwives against suspension of subsidized milk to pregnant women and women with babies were never printed, although we kept reminding them. It seems as if a repressing mechanism automatically starts every time these issues appear—the material coming from the women's groups is considered second-rate.

Notes

1. The Equality Committee consists of a chairperson and six members appointed by the *Landsting*. Five members are nominated by the following organizations: *Kanukoka*–the Association of Municipalities in Greenland; *Arnat Peqatigiit (Kattuffiat)*; SIK—the Labour Union; the Greenland Employers' Organization; and, finally, one member is proposed jointly by the *Kilut, Arnat Suleqatigiit* and *Aalisartut Piniartullu Nuliaasa Aappaasalu Peqatigiit*—the Fishermens' and Hunters' Wives' Association.

2. Currently there are three country-wide women's organizations in Greenland besides the newly established *Nipaat* (Women's Voice) working groups. The most recent one is the *Aalisartut Piniartullu Nuliaasa Aappaasalu Peqatigiit*. It was formed in Nuuk in 1982, and was constituted as a country-wide organization in October 1987 in support of hunting and fishing as a livelihood.

3. *Arnat Suleqatigiit* are groups of women mainly engaged on a voluntary basis in the establishment and operation of crisis centres for women and children. They started as one small working group in Nuuk in 1981, and are now almost country-wide, having established crisis centres in many larger communities.

4. *Aasivik* is the name of the annual summer gatherings, an old tradition of the Greenland Inuit revived as a grass roots movement in 1976 by a group of young radical Greenlanders. It is seen as a means of fighting pressure from the Danish colonial attitude toward Greenland.

Visions of Women: Partners for Change

Kataujuk Society and
N.W.T. Advisory Council on the Status of Women

This is an excerpt taken from a report of a workshop sponsored by Kataujuk Society and the N.W.T. Advisory Council on the Status of Women, held in Rankin Inlet, 25–29 March 1988. It was provided by Jennifer Rigby of the Government of the Northwest Territories Women's Secretariat.

Introduction

During the 1987–88 year, the Northwest Territories Advisory Council on the Status of Women initiated a major conference for women of the Northwest Territories. A planning committee composed of the Advisory Council, the Women's Secretariat, the N.W.T. Native Women's Association, the Inuit Women's Association, the Immigrant Women's Association, the Association Culturelle Franco-Tenoise, the Métis Association, the Dene Cultural Institute, the Yellowknife YWCA, and individual committed women began the process of designing the workshop. After several meetings, this committee decided to focus the conference around the personal and community skills necessary for women to take leadership roles in their own communities. Furthermore, the committee insisted that the conference workshops be experiential in nature, rather than lecture-style, so that learning would be on a more profoundly integrated level for the participants.

The Kataujuk Society of Rankin Inlet sponsored this conference for 48 women from 22 communities. The workshops were designed collectively by the sponsoring agency, the planning committee, and the workshop facilitators. The participants were selected by each sponsoring organization. This selection process was left to the individual organizations, although the planning committee decided to give priority to the selection of women already active in their community who needed additional skills in order to assume leadership roles.

A commitment was also made ensuring that 25 per cent of the participants were women between 17 and 24 years of age. Prospective participants were informed of the workshops and each wrote a letter outlining her reasons for wishing to attend.

Workshop Objectives

The planning committee felt a mutual concern about the problems and barriers northern women face both in establishing control over their own lives and in directing the course of their communities' development. The rapid transition from one economic–cultural base to another has had a devastating effect for most northerners.

The resulting confusion and societal collapse have proven to be extra onerous burdens for women who also face the inequities inherent in being female. Unemployment rates, education levels, income levels, and statistics on family violence confirm the fact that northern women have few of the opportunities necessary to direct the "systems" which control their lives. They are, however, often on the receiving end of alcohol treatment, safe-home assistance, and other remedial social programs.

The workshop organizers decided to start giving women an opportunity to learn the skills, insights, and information necessary to impact on their environment from a position of power rather than from one of confused reaction. As a result, it was decided that the workshop would focus on personal insight and confidence-building, while at the same time building a sense of commonality among the women by introducing collective problem-solving and social awareness activities. The planning committee realized that this sense of personal confidence and mutuality among the women would be heightened by the participation of women of different ages and cultural backgrounds.

The agenda was planned to be largely experimental in format so that these women would have an opportunity to explore the issues in their lives and begin the process of individual and collective problem solving.

***

Evaluations were done individually and by the whole group. The responses are highlighted here.

Question #1: I came to this workshop because..."
Many women responded that they came in order to learn more about themselves and their community. Many were curious to attend a wholly female conference and learn from other women.

Question #2: "I learned..."

Most participants reported that they learned more about themselves and learned some techniques for coping with the stress and problems in their lives. They reported an increased awareness of the problems they shared with other women of other ages and cultures. Many said that they felt more assertive and realized the importance of caring for themselves. One participant wrote that she learned "that when women come together they are very strong and can make things happen."

Question #3: "And I learned..."

Participants responded to this sentence completion saying that they learned more about communicating (both listening and self-expression) and overcoming shyness. Others responded that they had learned more about how to organize in their community. One respondent reported that she learned, "That by putting myself first and getting to know who I am and living again myself, that I can learn to love others and say no, so that I can get their respect and some time to myself..."!

Question #4: "I felt..."

Many participants reported that the workshop gave them a feeling of relief and buoyancy in the discovery that they were not alone in their problems and challenges. Others wrote about their feelings of renewed pride and confidence in themselves. Some responded that they felt an admiration for the women they'd met and were coming home with a sense of inspiration regarding the power of women to overcome societal problems. Many wrote about how they had learned about the variety of feelings women experience. One woman's response read, "I felt a sense of relief and now I feel good." Another woman said she felt "good about myself in solving personal problems; to co-operate, to be part of anything that I want to do, to be able to achieve anything."

Question #5: "Some things I especially liked were.."

Most of the participants reported that they liked all the experiential activities that gave them an opportunity to "tell their stories" and feel accepted for who they were. Almost all the participants said they especially appreciated the opportunity to express feelings and experiences they had kept "locked" inside. As one woman said, "I especially liked when we would talk or relax and think back to five years old, and being able to say that I am sensational, beautiful, peaceful, and thankful." Questionnaires mentioned over and over the value of having younger and older women together for this workshop. The young people and elders themselves pinpointed this as a highlight. One young woman responded that she especially liked "the elders and having them share their wisdom with me." An elder reported that she especially enjoyed learning "how we could be more helpful to the young people in our communities, we can encourage them to lead better lives."

Question #6: "I realize that women in my community..."

Many of the women felt that women in their communities needed the benefits of a similar workshop experience in order to realize their own potential and power. As one woman summed up, "They are afraid and scared due to the fact that they feel they have no value." Other participants pinpointed issues that were predominant in their friends' lives at home. Issues such as lack of affordable day care, wife-beating, and isolation were mentioned. However, the majority of participants expressed a desire to work more closely with women in their community in order to change their collective lot in life. Many hoped that similar workshops could be held in their home town. As one participant stated, "I realize that women in my community need this kind of workshop to realize what we can achieve—to be ourselves in home, job, community, and the whole nation."

Question #7: "I wish we..."

Almost all the participants responded that they wished this type of workshop could happen more frequently. Many asked that a similar workshop be held in their community or region. Others hoped that the participants of this particular workshop would get together twice a year. Several women wished that the sessions were longer. The following are a selection of comments: "I wish we could keep in contact with each other and be lifelong friends, and meet like this again"; "I wish we had more sessions like this for other women to learn as I have from these past few days." One elder wrote that she wished "women (were) more united and helped each other not only in their own community. I want women groups to get together from different communities." Another elder said she now believed "that women's groups throughout Canada should help one another by way of consultation."

Question #8: "A decision I have made for myself..."

Most participants reported having made decisions regarding their own mental and physical health. They decided to make more time for themselves and become more assertive in daily life. Many also made decisions to organize support or community development groups. Several wanted to bring their new-found self-awareness and strength to the aid of their friends. As one woman said, "A decision I have made for myself is to take the initiative to start a support group on my own and to practise my new skills starting today, hour by hour." Another woman said that she had decided "to be myself and not what others want me to be." In general, the response to this question reflected the increased amount of control women felt over their lives. One elder summed things up neatly with her statement, "I do not give much credit for the things I am capable of doing myself, now I understand that I can be helpful to others, and I also understand now that I have to give some credit to myself, for there are things I am very capable of doing!"

Post-Conference Evaluation

Approximately one-third of the workshop participants were contacted ten weeks after the close of the conference to ascertain the long-term effects of the workshop on their lives. All those contacted reported that the outstanding memory of the conference was the feeling of relief and commonality inherent in the discovery that they weren't alone in their private struggles and dreams. The majority mentioned that, until this workshop, they hadn't realized how other women often felt stressed, overburdened, and fearful. Nor had they realized that other women wished, like they, to take more control of their lives and begin to work toward their dreams. The effect of this realization and the skills they learned at the workshop had various tangible results in their daily lives. The following is a collection of the comments made by the women who were contacted:

- "It was good to learn the step-by-step way to feel better about myself."

- "I didn't think the things that happened to me could happen to others. I felt very close to the other women."

- "I am less stressed now and worry less. It helped my relationship with my boyfriend."

- "I can understand things in my family and community better."

- "When I got home I noted that I felt happier."

- "My mother and I are closer now. She talks to me more and we talk about when we were children."

- "Our women's group would like to have a workshop like that one in our community."

- "When I got home some men asked if they could have a workshop like that."

Many of the women reported on the workshop to their local and regional women's groups. A few discussed the workshop on the local radio station. There was a general consensus that a similar workshop should be held at the community level. And, since the workshop, a similar gathering has been requested by the Spence Bay Women's Group. Several women reported that they were now working (both paid and volunteer) in the areas of concern that they had pinpointed at the conference, (e.g., organizing community events and adult education programs). A few stated that the improved status of their own home life and personal and mental health was making it possible for them to reach out to work on community issues.

Summary

The educational, financial, and social reality for women of the Northwest Territories is extremely harsh. The statistical information alone paints a picture of inadequate finances, illiteracy (the highest level in Canada), high unemployment, and a variety of health problems. While government programs are necessary, it is essential that women learn how to organize themselves collectively in order to turn the tide of societal disintegration. A prerequisite for this spirit of collectivism is a personal sense of well-being and a feeling of commonality with other women. The Rankin Inlet conference, and its resulting impact, is an example of the amount of personal and communal power freed up when women have an opportunity to understand and appreciate their own uniqueness and similarities. It is also a lesson in terms of education and social change. That is, when an individual's needs are met holistically (emotionally, physically, socially, and intellectually) they begin to take a pro-active role in educating themselves and changing their community.

Inuit Women in Greenland and Canada: Awareness and Involvement in Political Development

Marianne Lykke Thomsen

Political Awareness and Women's Representation

Owing to its longer history of contact with the western world, Greenland is, in many ways, more advanced than the Canadian North. The most notable differences are those related to Greenland's industrial development, political institutions, and social and educational facilities.

Although full political rights were introduced for men in 1908, it was not until 40 years later that enfranchisement for women was achieved. However, women were not able to take advantage of this opportunity. The male-dominated traditions inherent in the system continued to create obstacles long after the introduction of universal suffrage. It has been suggested, as well, that women did not gain strength and awareness from having to fight for these political rights. Moreover, most women were not prepared to sacrifice their families to engage in political activity.

In the 1950s and 1960s, a reorganization of Greenland society was undertaken in an attempt to achieve a degree of compatibility with Danish society. A large portion of the population was relocated to central locations to facilitate industrial development and, in particular, the fishing industry. This led indirectly to a greater awareness of ethnic identity among Greenlanders, culminating in the achievement of Home Rule in 1979. At the same time, the paternalistic, assimilationist approach to development limited women's roles to that of a migrant labour reserve for the fishing industry.

The movement of Greenland society toward greater autonomy has encouraged the participation of women. Although women have played an integral part in the achievement of self-governing status, their contribution to the establishment and operation of Home Rule has been largely unacknowledged and unwelcomed. For example, the last decade has seen only a nominal increase in the number of women representatives in political and administrative positions within Home Rule; today, just two of the 27 members of the *Landsting* (parliament) are women.[1]

Generally, it would appear that Danish paternalism still pervades the operational structures and attitudes of the Home Rule government. Thus, women in Greenland must now address paternalism in their own structures, in addition to the discrimination inherent in the Danish authority.

Women's involvement in formal political activity was further hampered by the development of party politics in Greenland. Party politics has affected (and, to some extent, undermined) the unity among the active and outspoken minority of women. The cohesiveness of this small group had already been severely strained by age differences among its members and by conflict concerning the group's orientation. Despite this, one cannot overlook the fact that party politics have given women an opportunity to participate in political organizations.[2]

In northern Canada, contact between Inuit and government has been more recent. Public administration in northern Canada, as in Greenland, has been shaped by the administration of an "intruding society". The political voice of the Canadian Inuit exists, for the most part, within private national and regional organizations. However, native representation within the Government of the Northwest Territories and with the Kativik Regional Government—"the regional administration entity" of the Inuit of northern Québec—is steadily increasing. The orientation of individuals toward national political parties has emerged in a limited way with Inuit representation in the Senate and Parliament of the Canadian federal government. To some extent, Inuit participation in this public government system necessitates the adoption of political partisanship.

As was the case in Greenland, formal leadership went first to Inuit men, with Inuit women continuing to hold a minority position within decision-making bodies.[3] The limited representation of Inuit women impeded their ability to address women's concerns in political arenas.

The impact of the modernization process in northern Canada has led to frustration within the existing system and has encouraged the desire for self-government. Inuit have felt alienated from government decisions which directly affect their lives. Inuit women, like their Greenland counterparts, have been politically active in the issues of self-determination, particularly at the grass roots level, where women have strength as political activists and lobbyists. However, such activities have often been overshadowed by political activities undertaken at the national and regional levels.

Despite these barriers, Inuit women are becoming involved in regional and national politics, but, as in Greenland, there is an emphasis on ethnic identity and struggles with "external" parties, such as the federal, provincial, and territorial governments.

The relatively recent process of federal–territorial devolution in Canada may allow women's participation to be more enriched and meaningful. It may be possible to avoid the problems of Greenland, where "consensus-building" had already been redefined and applied in such a way that the decision-making process became less democratic.

Women have experienced some benefits from a changing attitude within government; for example, compensatory initiatives, like the decentralization process and the establishment of measures to integrate women into decision-making and administrative positions, have been initiated.[4]

The general integration of women into processes leading toward self-government has most recently been illustrated by women's involvement in the Atii management training program.[5] The few Inuit women who hold leadership positions within Inuit organizations and the territorial government have demonstrated their ability and competence, and continue to provide positive role models for aspiring women candidates.

Recruitment and Access to Political Positions in Greenland

In Greenland, most local councils have one or two women members. Midwives or maternity assistants have traditionally been represented at local levels. Beyond this, women have primarily held positions on what are considered to be "less strategic", service-oriented committees and boards concerned with education, health, and housing.

Women active in Greenland politics have questioned why their direct involvement in political decision making tends to remain at virtually the same level. Some of the factors which appear to have contributed to this lack of movement are:

a) patterns and attitudes associated with the upbringing of children;
b) limited resources and infrastructure to deal with the geographical vastness; and
c) a limited number of role models for women.

The patterns of upbringing shape stereotypical role models that are sexually discriminatory. Girls are not encouraged to be outspoken and assertive; boys are not encouraged to share the responsibilities of maintaining the household. This, however, is gradually changing.

With limited infrastructure and resources, it is difficult to mobilize and communicate with women at the national level. Thus, while many women have some familiarity with organizational structures, it is not easy to develop the larger networks needed to unite women.

Even though the number of qualified women candidates has increased, those willing to run for office are too few to make a marked impact or to create an awareness about women's abilities and commitment. Many women involved in politics prefer to keep a low profile rather than take a lead position.

There are several factors which seem to account for the low number of women political candidates. First, almost any involvement is a pioneering experience. For those women who take up the challenge, considerable self-confidence is a prerequisite. In addition, as the structure of Greenland society becomes more complex, those with formal education, or familiarity with the system, are in great demand in other areas. Therefore, although the number of women with the necessary educational background has increased, it is still not sufficient to meet the demand.

In general, educated women are too busy learning and applying skills within the workplace to become involved in politics, and they appear committed to making changes and seeking reform through their professions rather than political office.

Another deterrent faced by women is the forced mobility that often comes with political life. This discourages many women with small children—who otherwise possess the required skills— from becoming political candidates.

The political parties tend to hand-pick or promote certain individuals for political office. Although this is not unique to Greenland, it is a practice more visible in a relatively small society, and one that left women little opportunity to improve their representation. Unless strongly promoted by the party in question, a candidate may find it very difficult to break through tradition-bound voting habits.

The governing party, *Siumut*, has acknowledged that the average Greenlander has played only a limited role in the Home Rule process until now; the government has been run almost entirely by a small elite. As a remedial measure, the party recently accepted a proposal from women members to hold a women's seminar. This resulted from a decision at the party's annual general meeting to get *Siumut* women into political positions, since there are no women representing the party in either the *Landsting* or *Landsstyre* (Government).

The other coalition party, *Inuit Ataqatigiit*, has followed a decision-in-principle to have equal representation of men and women both on the party's executive committee and as candidates in municipal and national elections. In comparison with *Siumut, Inuit Ataqatigiit* is a small party, so its active promotion of women has had little impact on the composition of the *Landsting*. None the less, the positive effect can be seen in recent election campaigns which have clearly supported the concerns of women's organizations and individual women in the media.

Without question, an extraordinary lobbying effort is required to move beyond the rhetoric of election campaigns. To serve this purpose, *ad hoc* support groups composed of women of different generations and political orientation have been formed. These *Arnat Nipaat* (Women's Voice) groups are meant to encourage and support aspiring women candidates, to teach women to become more specific in their political activities, and to encompass within the political agenda, issues relating to economic, commercial, and environmental conditions.

In Greenland, little attention is paid to the political, economic, and social dynamics of the relationship between the sexes. In 1985, the *Landsting* voted to establish an "equality committee", first proposed in 1982 by *Arnat Peqatigiit Kattuffiat*, the national women's organization, and supported by other women's groups. According to committee members and other women politicians, the mandate of the committee has been limited to identifying the barriers women experience in entering the political process; however, the women involved are determined to make this a platform for the further integration of women into politics. It remains to be seen whether the needed recognition and support of women's contributions, along with improvements in working conditions for women, will be adequately addressed by the committee.

The closest Canadian equivalent to the Equality Committee is the Canadian Advisory Council on the Status of Women, which has Inuit representation. As an "external" body, with little specific orientation toward Inuit society, it does not have any direct impact on the composition of Inuit organizations.

Education and Employment Opportunities

Education and employment are closely related. Education is a crucial element in the recruitment process for employment opportunities. Both in Greenland and Canada, access to education is, in theory, equal; however, there are systemic barriers unique to women which are not always adequately recognized or redressed.

For the growing number of educated women in Greenland, the range of opportunities in education and training has improved considerably since the establishment of Home Rule. Although emphasis has been placed on providing education for youth, adult education and upgrading programs have also been made available.

Much effort has been devoted to having Greenlanders assume positions currently held by Danes. Hence, those who manage to finish their education are almost certain to get a job within their field of interest—provided they stay in the larger communities. In smaller settlements, employment opportunities are few; some short-term projects have been established for men and elderly women, and several low-budget projects, such as education programs for young women, are in place.

Young women are encouraged to continue their education in the larger centres, although this often means that they will never return to live in their home communities. The scarcity of semi-professional and professional positions in the home communities is a critical situation which the Home Rule government has not, as yet, been able or willing to change.

Day care is an essential component of education. It can be the determining factor in a woman's ability to obtain an education. The traditional practice of providing child care through the extended family is less common today; therefore, day care facilities with trained educators are required. Although these centres have become established in Greenland, applicants must still wait for a vacancy before considering educational or training opportunities. Even where these facilities are functioning satisfactorily, the drop-out rate for women is high. In part, this is attributable to the other pressures facing single mothers and young women in general.

There is an inherent dichotomy related to the patterns of upbringing and the high priority accorded education. Women want the opportunity to work, since their income is often essential to the viability of the household. Yet, in the philosophy of upbringing, men are still treated as the sole bread-winners. To remedy this dilemma, the sharing of family tasks is strongly being promoted with some success. Also, efforts are under way to eliminate sexual stereotyping and to ensure that boys and girls are brought up on equal terms.

In addition to the lack of adequate day care facilities and the need to promote and acknowledge the importance of sharing family tasks, there remains the problem of geographical remoteness between the mother and the family. This is a matter which must be addressed if there is to be any improvement in women's access and opportunities in education, employment, and political affairs.

To a degree, these circumstances resemble the situation in Canada. If one has an education and is willing to settle in a larger community, the opportunities are there. However, education is not as readily available in Canada as it is in Greenland. The resettlement of Inuit into larger centres has not been as profound in northern Canada, the result being limitations on the types of services and facilities provided in Inuit communities. For example, Canadian Inuit must travel far from home, to a different environment and culture, to obtain a post-secondary education. Many Inuit are thereby discouraged from ever starting, or else drop out along the way. Again, there is the problem of access to quality day care. Single mothers who choose to pursue higher learning or training programs must choose between leaving the children with other family members or uprooting the entire family unit.

Although training facilities of various kinds are gradually expanding, they fail to meet the needs created by modernization and development. Women want to take advantage of the opportunities created by government—often at the insistence of Inuit organizations—but not all are ready to cope with the adjustments that accompany such change. For example, men are not yet expected to share the responsibility of maintaining the family. This is partially due to the notion that "freedom" is required for subsistence activities, and the general welfare of the community; however, this may not always be a relevant excuse in modern Inuit society.

At one level, women are encouraged to continue their education by the number of individuals of their own culture and sex returning to the communities to assume the limited, well-paid jobs. At another level, they are affected by the dichotomy between a career and their families. The conflict these women face is no doubt generated by the weight of tradition and pressure to adapt to the respected and valued role of the mother as the primary nurturer and maintainer of the family.[6]

By being aware of the dangers related to accelerated cultural change, elders can maintain some control over younger generations. For women, this often means a strong emphasis on, and promotion of, traditional roles. In some instances, this may be an inhibiting factor to a young woman's involvement in other spheres, including education and training. The difference in viewpoint can create a gap between generations. Unfortunately, some younger women do not get involved in forums with older women because they feel uncomfortable with some of the judgements and moral beliefs expressed. The participation of younger women becomes an ongoing negotiation over resources and the division of activities, not only between Inuit men and women, but between different generations of women, in an attempt to come to a mutual understanding of differing strategies in life.[7]

In many places, local employment opportunities are still scarce or are of a short-term, make-work nature—designed elsewhere, but nevertheless depended upon by the locals. The Government of the Northwest Territories' *Five Year Action Plan on Equality for Women*, combined with other measures such as the decentralization process and affirmative action programs, may improve the provision of services and employment facilities in the communities. The prospect of securing self-government may encourage more people to obtain an education, in the hope that further decentralization will create and transfer more training opportunities and semi-professional and professional jobs to the local communities. Women play an active role as volunteers in efforts aimed at improving the conditions of Inuit society. Nevertheless, their participation in decision making seems to conform to the predetermined division of labour. As a result, planning and management emphasize male occupations, with the task of maintaining the family resting with women. The majority of Inuit women are now employed within the service sector, providing little freedom, if any, for public service. Such participation requires a certain amount of mobility, given geographical distances and the dependency on administrative centres outside Inuit territory. Without the essential infrastructural support such as adequate day-care facilities, women remain in the local service sector.

Should the formal involvement of women increase, some volunteer activities could be recognized as paid positions, for the benefit of society generally, as well as for the women involved. Some initiatives undertaken by the Native Women's Association of the Northwest Territories such as the establishment of a training centre, provide good examples of potential development.[8]

Inuit Women's Groups and Organizations

The creation of alternative organizations is not a new phenomenon among Inuit women. Their motivation is derived from the failure of formal political forums to acknowledge or represent their concerns. At various organizational levels, women's groups have proved to be important vehicles for political education and involvement as well as a means of combatting feelings of isolation and powerlessness. In many situations, both in Canada and Greenland, women have been able to join forces to press for the improvement of conditions crucial to their communities.

The concerns raised by women often deal with basic requirements; however, these are not always recognized or given the attention that they deserve by formal political systems. In some cases, they are issues that have a more far-reaching and important effect on Inuit life than those which preoccupy political authorities.

Thus, women's organizations serve an important purpose by making women more visible, and by giving them an opportunity to be represented collectively in different forums.

In Greenland, local women's groups date back to 1948 with the founding of *Arnat Peqatigiit*, a housewives' league which was later to become a country-wide organization (*Kattuffiat*). With *Arnat Peqatigiit* as a platform, women began an active involvement in public affairs. They also became influential in commission work and policy and legal reform regarding health and social issues such as housing, public facilities, family law, and abortion. The most recent accomplishment of women's lobbying efforts was the establishment of the Equality Committee under Home Rule.

Since the late 1970s there has been a tendency to regroup due to clashes between ideologies, activities, and generations. For example, *Kilut*, emerged in opposition to the rather hierarchical structure of *Arnat Peqatigiit*. It's fairly conservative, Danish-oriented ideologies, and its passive image left the younger, politically active women to group together to form *Kilut*. Despite their differences, the two groups have worked together to reinforce women's participation in political processes, to arrange political seminars, and to communicate women's issues through the media.

Organizational differences have done little to prevent the development of a more flexible relationship and mutual respect in dealing with the Equality Committee and the proposed establishment of an umbrella organization to encompass all women's groups. The latter project will unite a variety of women's groups with divergent interests with the aim of ensuring equal access to funding and creating more solidarity among women. It is expected that this move will eventually provide the needed encouragement and support for women choosing to run for political office. The primary goal of all the groups involved is the attainment of better representation for women on decision-making bodies.

In Canada, independent women's groups have been in existence in a number of communities since the late 1950s.[9] The idea of establishing a national Inuit women's association developed more recently, in connection with constitutional negotiations on aboriginal rights. Inuit women found that there were too many differences between themselves and Indian women to allow the Native Women's Association to represent them at constitutional conferences. They preferred to have their ideas and concerns raised by the Inuit Committee on National Issues—which was formed to negotiate Inuit rights through the constitutional conferences—and expressed the opinion that an organization for Inuit women, complementary to the general Inuit organizations, would be valuable to all parties. The concept was endorsed by the Inuit Tapirisat of Canada, the national Inuit organization in Canada, and in 1981, *Pauktuutit*, the national Inuit women's association was established.[10]

Notwithstanding the fact that *Pauktuutit* is a fairly new organization, it has already acted upon a number of resolutions related directly or indirectly to self-government. Some of the resolutions have been specifically directed toward improving conditions for women, while others have been more general, pertaining to Inuit society as a whole.

Through *Pauktuutit* and some of the regional native women's associations with Inuit representation, women have been able to exert pressure at higher levels within government bureaucracies. The work of *Pauktuutit* has enabled Inuit women to participate on an equal footing with men in the promotion of a holistic approach to economic, social, cultural, and political development. This includes equal representation in the different levels of governmental and non-governmental structures.[11]

Pauktuutit has not as yet demonstrated a particularly strong profile in the larger issues facing Inuit as people. Rather, it focuses on fostering a willingness to incorporate women into decision-making roles and responsible positions within Inuit organizations and governments. Although it may be too early to make a reasonable evaluation, this strategy may not be adequate to make up for the uneven representation of women within other organizations.

The nomination and promotion of women candidates for political office has not been practised by Inuit women's organizations in Canada. In contrast, this has been the strategy adopted by women's organizations in several municipal and national elections in Greenland. The reluctance of Inuit women's organizations in northern Canada may be attributable, in part, to the fact that Inuit territory is under three different jurisdictions. Although the Native Women's Association of the Northwest Territories appeared to be moving in a direction similar to that of the Greenland women's organizations with the passage of a resolution calling for more active involvement in territorial and national politics, this position has since been modified.

Ethnicity and Feminism Hard to Combine?

Inuit women have always maintained that their organizations are primarily complementary, rather than conflictual, with men and Inuit political activities. It continues to be more crucial to Inuit women in both Greenland and Canada to secure the rights of Inuit as a people than to secure the rights of the women.

Generally, Inuit women have not applied feminist strategies as a means of securing representation and influence in Canada. They have, to some extent, distanced themselves from other women's groups to emphasise their ethnic identity and the solidarity of their society. In many instances, they have refused to work with the more radical Indian women, even when organizations have been set up to encompass both groups. However, there is danger in being too flexible and patient, as can be seen in the case of Greenland.

Greenlandic women, who were very patient and supportive during the initial preparations for the transfer of powers from Denmark to the Home Rule, were frustrated and disappointed to find themselves neglected by male politicians. Now that the Home Rule system is in place, it is still extremely difficult for women to be recognized as equal participants at all levels.

Women have had relatively little success in advancing their participation on decision-making bodies. The struggle to recruit women candidates and have them elected to political office continues. The attitude of male politicians toward women's participation, and tradition-bound voting habits, are the reasons often cited for this protracted struggle.

Inuit women in Canada may or may not experience a similar situation once land claims negotiations are completed and the green light is given to some form of self-government. At present, it is considered far more important to perform collectively as Inuit toward Euro-Canadian governments and administrations rather than reveal possible internal weaknesses. But, in fact, Inuit women are visible participants in this process.

Assistance and guidance from government programs directed toward native women may help prevent the situation from becoming as striking as that in Greenland.

The dilemma faced by women during the Home Rule negotiations, and which still causes problems for women today, was one identified in the mid-1970s by two Greenlandic women. They emphasized that consciousness-raising among Greenlanders with respect to ethnic identity and national feeling left little room for awareness about the relations between men and women. On the other hand, by being an important partner in the struggle for ethnic identity, the Greenlandic women's movement has had to take a wider perspective than most in the Western world. Thus, it has proved difficult for women to combine movements or to transfer methods and strategies.

Nevertheless, for many years, Greenlandic women have long maintained a working relationship with the formally established women's organizations in Denmark. In the past, some Greenlandic women have also been extensively involved in more radical initiatives; however, these ties have weakened since the introduction of Home Rule.

From the mid-1960s to mid-1970s, Greenlandic women received support in the form of leadership training and other programs from the Danish Women's Society. The society also provided information and support on the question of legal abortion which arose with the introduction of the Abortion Act in 1975. A subcommittee for Greenlandic women, formed in 1960, has assisted Inuit women living in Denmark. In addition, Greenlandic women have continued a formal relationship with Denmark through a representative on the Danish Equal Status Council, which was the source of inspiration for the Equality Committee in Greenland. Finally, the Greenlandic membership in the Nordic Council gives women the opportunity to join the Nordic Forum for Women.

At first glance, debate among Canadian Inuit women only indirectly addresses their relationship with feminist movements, as mentioned above. However, since Inuit women have their own national forum in *Pauktuutit*, the situation is changing. Women are more prepared and receptive to collaboration. Again, this can hardly be avoided given the fact that governments tend to direct their programs to native people as one category and to women as another. Furthermore, the sensitivity that Euro-Canadian women have displayed toward Inuit women striving to define their own situation indicates greater awareness and a desire to collaborate on equal terms.

Canadian Inuit women are involved in a number of projects, council work, and programs set up by government agencies and southern organizations, such as the Aboriginal Women's Program, the Advisory Council on the Status of Women, the Women's Secretariat, and the Northern Women's Program of the Canadian Research Institute for the Advancement of Women.

Whereas Inuit women in Canada can benefit, to some extent, from collaboration with other native and non-native women's organizations, Greenlandic women now feel somewhat isolated, because they are largely left out of the political processes; at the same time, their contacts with the outside world are sporadic.

Despite the fact that pan-arctic initiatives, such as the Inuit Circumpolar Conference Women's Commission, have proved thoroughly disappointing, the idea of future collaboration among Inuit women remains a desirable goal. It is recognized that, through this type of networking, the ideas and inventions necessary for integrating women into decision-making bodies can be communicated to the entire arctic community.

Need for Flexibility

Inuit women are demonstrating a willingness to participate at all levels of political development, but they face a number of difficulties, some of which have been illustrated above.

The roles of women are changing drastically, creating a gap between generations. Inuit women do not form a homogeneous group, but are divided according to age, experience, education, and party politics. Elderly women sometimes take a critical view of society, given their life-long experience, and even though the authority and respect that surrounds them is impressive and inspiring, it causes some problems and dilemmas for the younger women. The opportunities available in education and employment have begun to alter life-styles and to differentiate the roles of young women from those of the previous generation.

If women are to become more integrated into decision-making bodies, certain aspects of their valued traditional role may have to be "renegotiated". Women can be outspoken and assertive. Young women and men should be encouraged to share family responsibilities and they should play equal roles in society as a whole. Inuit women's organizations are already engaged in this process.

The barriers of tradition and public opinion are difficult to overcome. It is for this reason that the most active political figures are those women (and men) who have had greater exposure to a European or Euro-Canadian life-style. Their familiarity with other cultures seems to give them the necessary self-confidence to make individual choices with regard to the balance between political activity and family matters.

Many women do possess the skills and resources required of politicians. Yet, the political structures do not immediately attract women, because they fail to provide the flexibility that would allow women to be both good mothers, in the traditional sense, and good politicians.

In Greenland, women are expressing a strong desire to make the political system more flexible and humane, but they are well aware that such change can only be achieved through better representation. For this to happen, women themselves must change. For example, the attitude toward women candidates in general should be one of confidence and trust in their capabilities. It is crucial that women be prepared to vote for women. This directly reflects on the number of women who are willing to run for political office.

Notes

1. This was clearly illustrated by the refusal of their request for a seat on the Home Rule Commission in the 1970s. At that time, women did not have any elected members of the *Landstrad* (Provincial Council). See Kleivan, 1975.

2. See Kalaallit Nunaanni Arnat Peqatigiit Kattuffiat, 1983.

3. See Matthiason, 1976.

4. In the author's opinion, Inuit claims, related to collective rights as a distinct ethnic "group" with an emphasis on political consensus, would be more convincing to the Canadian authorities if women were better represented in the various political organizations and institutions run by Inuit. In any event, the public response to Inuit women in Canada seems greater than that in Greenland. In all likelihood, this response is related to the publicity surrounding Indian women's struggles against discrimination originating from the Indian Act. There are a few specific cases where Inuit women were also affected by these discriminatory provisions. See Thomson, 1983, and *Igalaaq*, 1982.

5. See Dufton, 1987.

6. See Cronk, 1987.

7. See Thomsen, 1988.

8. See Mackenzie, 1984, and Smellie, 1987.

9. See Matthiasson, 1976, and Morissette, 1983.

10. See *Igalaaq*, 1982.

11. See *Pauktuutit*, 1986.

References

Cronk, Faith. "The Northwest Territories Advisory Council on the Status of Women, Observations on Education and Research", in Adams, Peter W. *Education, Research Information Systems and the North.* Ottawa:ACUNS, 1987, pp. 31–32.

Igalaaq, March 1982, p. 4.

Dufton, Rebecca. "Atii is different from other training programs". *Nunavut*, November/December 1987:p. 4.

Kalaallit Nunaanni Arnat Pegaigiit. "Arnat Politikkilu/Kvinder og Politik". *Kalaallit Nunaanni Arnat Pegatigiit*, Nuuk 1983.

Kleivan, Inge. "Ukiut ingerlanerani arnap Kalaallit-nunaanni inissimanea taallatsiaqataarlugu.../Glimt af kvindens rolle i Gronland gennem tiderne", in *Tidskriftet Gronland* 8(9) (1975).

Mackenzie, Barbara. *History of the Native Women's Association of the N.W.T. and Resource Manual.* Yellowknife, N.W.T.:Canarctic Graphics Ltd., 1984.

Matthiasson, John S. "Northern Baffin Women in Three Cultural Periods". *The Western Canadian Journal of Anthropology* 6(3) (1976).

Morissette, Diane. *Native Women in Quebec: Resources and Associations.* Secretary of State, Quebec Regional Directorate, 1983.

Pauktuutit. *Pauktuutit Annual Report, 1985/86.* Ottawa.

Rasmussen, Henriette Lundby. "Den gronlandske kvindes stilling: Dansk Sociologiforenings Orsmode", in Dahl, Jens, et al. (eds.). *Sociologiske perspektiver i Gronlandsforskningen.* Kobenhavn, 1975.

Risager, Helene. "Gronland—vores store lillesoster", *Kvinden og Samfundet.* Kobenhavn, 1975.

Smellie, Janet. "Upgrading added to life skills' programs". *News/North*, 2 November 1987.

News/North, 9 November 1987.

Thomsen, Marianne. "The role of Inuit women with regard to development of self-government in the Canadian Arctic". *Folk* 30 (1988):pp. 85–110.

Thomson, Janet. "Igloolik women fight for their rights". *News/North*, 4 November 1983.

Hay River Women's Centre

Jodi Whyte

In May 1988, the Hay River Women's Centre, the only women's centre in the Northwest Territories, celebrated the end of Phase I, which took almost three years to complete.

Originally called the Women's Coalition, the centre was formed in 1985 by primarily white, southern, professional women. Noting their ethnic and economic background is not intended to detract from their accomplishments. On the contrary, it explains the centre's very existence. Like many of us, these women had witnessed the good that had come from other centres in the South and they sought to import the concept of sisterhood and action into the North.

In the fall of 1986, the centre, with its first grant from the Department of Secretary of State of Canada, opened a small resource centre operated by a half-time co-ordinator. The resource centre provided periodicals, books, film nights, guest speakers, and workshops aimed at improving women's image of themselves. At the same time, a group of women began to recognize the need for programming aimed at women who were experiencing violence. The Safe Home Network was established and became fully operational in the spring of 1987, providing accommodation, counselling, and a 24 hour crisis line.

Between January 1987 and the summer of 1988, the centre secured a shelter, the first second-stage house in the Northwest Territories with paid positions for an executive director, researchers, full-time shelter staff, and an administrative assistant. Fifteen women, trained to operate a crisis line, provided counselling for the victims of family violence and sexual assault, the depressed, the lonely, and the homeless.

As Phase I drew to its end, we celebrated, patted ourselves on the back, breathed deeply, and wondered what it meant. Was there only a Phase I? There is no doubt that, while we were pleased to see the thriving centre completed, we were anxious, almost fearful, about Phase II. We debated what lay ahead, but in fact we knew all along that while we were providing a much needed service through our programming and shelter, we had, in fact, turned our backs on the big picture: the cause of violence, and the role of women as care-givers, as forever-givers.

The maxim for the women's movement in North America had been, "The personal is the political." For those of us who had stepped into the love–hate, violence-filled world of the south Mackenzie, the personal had become everything. First we were victims, then helpers. As helpers we had re-experienced the fears, pains, and longings. Phase I for me meant acknowledging that I, as a helper, had forgotten that the problem was not "her" fear and "his" violence, it was *our* combined history.

We saw ourselves as providers of safety and friendship; our satisfaction with that role left us as contributors to a social services architectural perspective which imprisons the victims of violence in shelters. Our contribution to the historical oppression was not in the provision of shelter, but both in the taking of shelter and in presuming that our safety (physical, mental, and economic) was to be attributed to anything greater than luck. We, too, had taken safety in a world of self-help and endless transition. The real problem, the cause of violence, was not to be seen or heard or discussed.

It has taken the women's movement 20 years to move our society forward, to gain some acknowledgment of our right to work outside the home, to pursue dreams that are independent of the ones we hold for our families. This movement was made possible, in part, by the technological revolution. But here in the Northwest Territories, that revolution, and the evolution that accompanies it, is still just in the beginning stages. While I am cautious of technology, I also recognize that it has provided the little equality I have. It allows me to maintain a home and a job, to manage more efficiently, and to pursue activities outside those worlds as well. It lets me "nuke" my food, electronically clean my home, slice and dice my left-overs, and so on. Most importantly it has given me choices: the right to choose to work, and to have, or not to have, children. But I am an immigrant here. I bring with me the skill to earn, and thus the right to choose. For most, however, this is not true. This is what defines our Phase II, and also what aligns it with the women's movement as a whole. We all began, budding feminists everywhere, faced with the concrete and the personal—the violence, the oppression, the inequality, the dependence. But as educated women, as women who could access technology, who no longer belonged to a society of hunters and trappers, we could choose not to be biological breeders, and then choose whether or not we would be mothers, workers, students, or all of these.

If I were in Toronto, or Vancouver, or Halifax, I would know what Phase II would look like. It would be a world of lobbying and a careful root canal of the political system. My aim would be to change the economic infrastructure. But, I am not in any of those places, nor am I anywhere that for more than a split second here and there resembles them. In those few instances it is rational to talk about changing the economic system and power accessibility, but most often we must face the multi-levelled needs that exist here.

The complexity of defining Phase II is the result of our population, our isolation, the immaturity of our government, the mix of culture, the diversity of life-styles and languages, and so on. We must attempt a movement on several levels at once so that we may reach women at their level. While we recognize that there are a handful of educated, informed women in the North who want to participate in political action, we must also recognize that most women are still experiencing their personal battle in isolation, and do not yet see their struggles as part of an overall struggle. Consequently, it is essential that we, as a northern women's centre, deliver programming aimed at improving self-esteem and assertiveness, continue to aid women in their personal struggles, and, at the same time, lobby for family law reform, literacy training, and child care services.

It is a slow and often lonely process. To be successful as northern women we must account for the diversity among us. We must recognize that as women, regardless of our personal histories, we share a common world history.

At a conference held in Rankin Inlet in the spring of 1988, one woman expressed what she had come to realize about women in her community:

> Women in my community don't realize that change is needed to end the many difficulties facing them....They either don't know or don't realize change is coming. They will have to adjust to fit into the new way of thinking and acting. They have to realize that they are people, too.

For these women the change will seem to be happening at a remarkable pace. Conferences, such as the one in Rankin Inlet, will be the catalyst for these changes because they are a forum for an exchange of experiences and strengths. They must remain the main thrust of change for northern women if they are to control the pace and choose the direction for their new history.

Our role is partly defined by our needs as women to be involved in the broader issues at stake in improving the status of women. We must also play a supporting role to the needs and desires of others. Phase II for the Hay River Women's Centre then, means graduating from counsellor to advocate, from local advocate to lobbyist, from writing letters to the editor to writing alternate policy for the government.

If we want to accomplish what we have set out to do in Phase II, we must broaden the scope and depth of our activities in the Northwest Territories and elsewhere. To this end, we have chosen to become more active in federal women's organizations such as the National Action Committee, in complementing the work of our local Advisory Council, and we will redirect some of our efforts away from health-related boards and committees to become more involved in economic and education boards.

It was said vaguely in 1985 that the mandate of the centre would be to improve the status of women. To this end, a resource centre was founded, workshops given, a report issued, and a newsletter sent to members. Phase II calls for concrete action aimed at attaining equal rights for women in the North. The resource centre, the crisis line, shelter, second stage house, volunteer training, and workshops remain. The newsletter has been expanded to provide information about issues facing all women, and is mailed to residents all over the Northwest Territories as well as organizations in Ontario, Alberta, and British Columbia. This will act as a link between us, and allow us to see trends developing in the North. From these trends we can call for, and participate collectively in, action. The centre can respond to the need for know-how skills when they are requested with programming that helps women to think through the political process.

Finally, the time has come for northern women to meet face-to-face, to unite with one another behind the cause of equality, and to plan for future action. Phase II officially began in March 1989, in Hay River, with a conference unofficially entitled, "Women and Political Action North of 60." Who came? Women who recognize that "they are people too."

Editor's Note: At the time of publication, the Hay River Women's Centre was facing the possibility of having to close its doors. The centre has been seriously affected by cutbacks to the Secretary of State Women's Program.

Mary Simon: Walking in Two Worlds But in One Spirit

Based on an Interview with Marianne Stenbaek

In Mary Simon's living room in Kuujjuaq, there hangs a poster from the Maniilaq Association in Kotzebue, Alaska. Underneath these various pictures of Inuit life on the poster, is the inscription, "I walk in two worlds, with one spirit". Probably no other phrase sums up Mary Simon's life and work as well as that one.

She leads a very modern and active life politicking with prime minsters and dignitaries, doing television shows, and generally being at home in all aspects of contemporary life. Yet, at the same time, she is equally at home in an Inuit camp—fishing, hunting, and cooking dinner over an open fire. Fully at home in the two worlds, but with one strong Inuit spirit.

Mary's Simon's life and work are characterized by genuine concern for the people she serves, and the desire to preserve the Inuit way of life for future generations. She embodies what a woman politician should be at her very best: a human, concerned with the individual, the old, and the young; and concerned with the environment and peace. She listens to people and remembers their concerns.

Mary Simon was born in 1946 in Kangiqsualujjaq, northern Québec. Her father was a white Canadian who made his living as a hunter and guide. Her mother taught her all the traditional skills of an Inuit household. Her childhood and adolescent years coincided with the years of enormous change in northern Québec, years that saw the Inuit community change from a traditional hunting society to a society in which both the federal and provincial governments had an increasingly greater role. This was a society where enormous changes took place, as one Inuk told me, "One day in our lives sees as much change as ten years in southern society".

Mary Simon's life reflects many of these changes, but in the most positive way possible. Her career has spanned many activities, which has given her a wide range of experience in economic, social, cultural, and environmental matters concerning Inuit and the Arctic. Her distinguished career includes: radio and television broadcaster with the CBC Northern Service, Secretary of the Board of the Northern Québec Inuit Association, Secretary-General of Kativik School Board, Vice-President and then President of Makivik Corporation, and Vice-Chairperson of Canada's Native Economic Development Program. Mary also played a prominent role in the constitutional talks between aboriginal peoples and federal and provincial governments.

For many years she has directly or indirectly been involved in the political life of Canadian native people. She has played an important role in land claims negotiations and in the discussions of arctic sovereignty; and she has been deeply involved in the economic and political development of northern Québec.

Her role on the international scene started in 1977 when the Inuit Circumpolar Conference (ICC) was founded in Barrow, Alaska. The ICC is the international organization which represents all the world's Inuit from Canada, Alaska, Greenland, and Siberia. It has had non-governmental organization status at the United Nation's since 1983. The objective of the ICC is to promote and safeguard the Inuit way of life, and to become a voice for Inuit rights both on the national and international levels. She has served on the Executive Council of the ICC and has been its Canadian vice-president. In August 1986, at the ICC Fourth General Assembly, she was elected its president, which was a great honour and an extremely unusual one within a male-oriented society. She is the first woman, and the first Canadian and Québecois to hold this very important position.[1]

During the last two years, Mary Simon has worked on preparing a comprehensive arctic policy for the Inuit in Alaska, Canada, and Greenland, which could become a blueprint for arctic development in many different spheres, such as education, culture, women's rights, resource management, environmental protection, scientific research, and communications. This work has the potential of shaping and changing the future of the Arctic, for Canada, Alaska, and Greenland, and possibly even the Siberian Arctic, as ICC represents all of these regions.

Mary Simon's family has been an enormous source of learning and of strength for her. As she herself once said in a previous interview when I asked about her parents' influence on her: "My parents have very strong characters. We were taught at a very early age that we had a responsibility to make sure we took care of ourselves and those that we loved, and it went beyond that, to help our people, ourselves as a people, and to make sure that the 'assimilation attitudes' of the governments were not going to overtake us. So there has always been a sense of responsibility in me toward not only myself as an individual, but also toward my people. That ties in with my own feeling that you have to be there in order to do it yourself."

Perhaps the greatest family influence on Mary was her grandmother, an elderly Inuk lady who taught Mary to sew, making her rip out everything that was not perfect. Mary got her need for perfection from her grandmother, and, more importantly, she also got her very strong sense of culture and of language from her. It was her grandmother who used to take Mary visiting in the communities, and who used to travel with her and her brothers and sisters in the summers to other camps along Ungava Bay so that Mary would know all the members of her large family. It was Mary's grandmother who, in the many long evening nights, spent hours telling Mary the legends and stories of her family and of her people. It was Mary's grandmother who kindled in her the strong love of the people, the culture, and the land.

These are some of the outward facts and influences of Mary Simon's life, but what is she like as a person? I have been very fortunate to have been a friend of Mary's for several years and have got to know her well. What strikes one the most about her is her kindness, her enormous sense of responsibility to the Inuit people and to other aboriginal peoples, her sense of self-discipline and self-sacrifice, and her good sense of humour. What has impressed me the most, is to see how she really cares about people—particularly about the elders, and about the children. She cares about the constituents who have elected her to office. She is very unlike the many politicians who, once elected, tend to forget who elected them and where they came from. Mary always remembers. She goes to great lengths to keep in touch with people, to share sorrows and joys with them, to go visiting, to remember their concerns. I suppose the other thing I have been very impressed with is that she really is a thoroughly modern woman. She is as at home shopping at the most fashionable boutiques as she is fishing on the ice. But whatever she does, whether it's dining at Rideau Hall, or making tea at a fishing camp, she always retains the sense of herself and an enormous sense of her "Inuitness". She really has succeeded in that almost impossible task of bridging the traditional way with the modern urban way without catastrophic consequences. She has made personal sacrifices—many of them—and she has had difficult times, but she really has succeeded in becoming that nebulous being, the modern Inuk, walking in two worlds, but in one spirit.

I interviewed her at her southern home in Pointe Claire, Québec prior to the ICC General Assembly in Sisimuit, Greenland, July 1989.

Marianne Stenbaek: What are your priorities as president of the ICC?

Mary Simon: First of all, there are a number of priorities that the executive council has established. At our council meeting, we went through the different resolutions and decisions that were made at the last General Assembly in Kotzebue, and discussed how we could implement some of the initiatives that had been undertaken by the delegates. To some extent those set some of the priorities that I have.

Also, I had my own priorities when I was running for election and those form a part of the overall ICC objectives. One priority which has always been consistent with my views is the development of a comprehensive arctic policy. I see a real need for this type of initiative coming from the ICC, and I have always emphasized the importance of coming out with a comprehensive statement that deals with the different elements of the Arctic that are often not necessarily seen in a comprehensive way. Many times various issues are seen in very segmented ways, but you have to look at those in a global sense, and I think that the creation of an arctic policy from the Inuit perspective will bring about that focus. There is a need to look at the issues in a global sense and how they interrelate with each other and how one affects the other. So that's one of my priorities—making sure that we develop a comprehensive arctic policy from the perspective of the Inuit in the three regions.

Marianne Stenbaek: Youth and children, as well as women, have always been a priority with you. What are some of things you would like to accomplish in this realm?

Mary Simon: Well, let's take the issue of women first. The most important thing is to find ways of involving more women, not only in the work-force, but in the development of our society. In terms of the involvement of women, there are certain initiatives that we can undertake that would bring forth a better focus on some of the main problems. For example, I would like to have someone work with me on the issue of youth and women. We would start working with some of the organizations that are directly involved with women and youth in the different regions to see how we can assist them in developing their own particular needs, and to include them in the work that we are doing. However, this is dependent on funding, and that is what I want people to understand. Many of the priorities or aspirations that I have as an individual running an organization like ICC are dependent on the amount of funds that we can raise in order to carry these out.

I would also like to hire someone that would work with me because I can't do all of this by myself. As you know, running an organization and also being responsible for specific projects is very time-consuming, and everyone suffers if you focus too much on one project.

Another thing is the involvement of youth and women in the ICC. That is an issue which I will address before the next General Assembly. The ICC Executive Council will be having a discussion on the representation of Inuit women at ICC's General Assembly. This was an issue at the last General Assembly, and the council has been requested by the delegates to look into the problem of representation.

Marianne Stenbaek: Are there other specific issues, for example, about women that you wish to address?

Mary Simon: Well, one thing that I would like is to have more women involved and better represented. But I think that what has to happen, not only with women but with the youth as well, is that they have to take on more responsibility. Accordingly, we must be available to provide support to these individuals. There are women's organizations dealing with women, and there are youth organizations dealing with youth, but the biggest complaint that ICC has had is that ICC does not involve these two groups in a satisfactory way. I don't think that ICC should be doing the work for them, but that we should be doing it *with* them. ICC has to be in existence for a long time and if there are certain organizations that are created to represent certain groups of people like women, youth, or elders, we have to involve those people within their organizations and work with them in their organizations.

Marianne Stenbaek: How do you feel, being a woman running the ICC? A lot of people wonder how women ever get votes in such a patriarchal society. Do you see it as a major step forward for Inuit women or have you not thought much about it?

Mary Simon: The first question, how do I feel about it? I feel great! I think it is great being a woman and being able to have this responsibility. I do not think it really matters whether you are female or male, if the commitment is there and you feel a sense of responsibility and you enjoy doing what you're doing, I think *that* is the important thing. Now, has it been difficult? Not with the ICC, but when you look at my career as a whole, when I first got involved in political development, and in elected positions for different organizations, it used to be difficult sometimes being a woman because the majority of people that I had to work with were men. Unfortunately, there has not been the same involvement of women as there has been by men in these fields. As a result, I have had to work mostly with men in my political career. There have been some trying times because I am a woman, but I have learned that if you believe in yourself, if you are willing to work hard, and you are willing to sometimes work harder than the people that are working around you, then at some point there is a breakthrough and you are able to stand up on your own and be recognized for what you have accomplished. I think that the magic to all of this, the determining factor in being able to break through that barrier, is believing in yourself, being able to work, and just going for it.

Marianne Stenbaek: Has it ever been an advantage to be a woman in this work? You know, sometimes a woman may have more intuitive understanding, a better understanding, a different approach?

Mary Simon: Well, I suppose there are different approaches. I definitely think that between women and men there are different approaches and that can be advantageous sometimes. It's hard for me to comment on whether it has been a good thing or a bad thing to be a woman. You know, it is difficult to say because it depends on the situation, but I've never dwelt on the fact that I was a women in my work. Other people have had problems with it, but I haven't had problems with it, and when other people do, I just say to myself that it is their problem and not mine. I just proceed the way I think I should proceed, and that is, if you believe in something and you want to make a change in something, you have to be involved and you have to believe in what you do. I go by what I am told by our constituents. When you are an elected person, you are working on issues that are affecting your constituency.

Mary Stenbaek: Do you like being president?

Mary Simon: I love it.

Mary Stenbaek: What do you hope to have accomplished by the time your first term runs out?

Mary Simon: Well, I would like to be sure that ICC is in a more financially sound situation where we do not have to spend six months out of the year negotiating funding agreements. Right now, that is what we do. We are fundraising and trying to get enough money together to do particular projects. If we could get certain commitments from sources that are able to give funding for longer periods of time, even if it is for only a two- or three-year period, then the few of us that are involved in the ICC, and there are few of us, could devote more time to the process rather than to fundraising. I would like to try and see that happen within the next three years, to make it more financially stable. I don't know if it is possible but it is one of the goals that I have.

The other thing is to continue to make sure that ICC is a credible organization—that it is there to effectively promote the interests and aspirations of the Inuit as a whole. We are an international organization dealing with issues of common interest through an international forum. And, in a way, that has a positive effect at the regional level. We are not working somewhere out in left field with people back home doing something else. I want to make sure that that link is kept with ICC and the people, at the community level—and that's something that we need to develop. It needs a lot of work.

Notes
1. Mary Simon was re-elected president of the Inuit Circumpolar Conference at the ICC Fifth General Assembly, 1989, in Sisimuit, Greenland.

The Spence Bay Women

Sarah Tokolik
Based on an interview with Angela Bernal

Our group started in the spring of 1985. Over the radio, it was asked that all the ladies meet in order that a women's group could be formed. The Secretary Manager of Spence Bay asked the women to come to his house one evening and told us to pick a vice-president and a president. We voted for whomever we wanted. We were not sure what we were supposed to be doing, he didn't tell us. All he said was to vote for officers. We knew every one in town, so we picked ones that would be strong and would talk out. There are eight of us. We've had two secretaries who have left, and we now have our third. Our president is an older woman, she's close to 75 or 80. The youngest woman is in her late 20s or early 30s.

We began by talking about the ladies in Spence Bay, and about the younger people who are not learning how to make traditional clothes or how to speak our language. Then we started sewing. We meet on Saturdays. We are all willing to help. When we have big problems though, all the community committees get together. There are many committees here—education, alcohol and drug, social services, health, and recreation. We all get together to discuss something that concerns the community.

Our group meets twice a month to talk about our concerns, and we invite other ladies, too, if they want to come and talk with us. For example, we have been talking about AIDS since we heard that it is a very dangerous problem. It can happen to anyone. We've heard a lot about it on TV, in Inuktitut.

We have also been talking about sending pregnant ladies to Yellowknife. They get sent out at least three weeks, or a month before they have the baby. Many of the older ladies came when we talked about midwives. We had the nurse with us as well. We wanted the nurse to hear what we had to say about sending the women out too early and the nurse answered us. The older ladies said they would have no problems delivering babies. Five or six older ladies said that they can deliver babies and they've delivered babies before. If women have problems, then it's okay if they are sent to Yellowknife, but if they're young and if they don't have any problems with the baby, the elders know for sure that they can deliver the baby themselves. The nurse said if they deliver the baby in their homes, and if all of a sudden they have trouble with the baby or the mother, it's our responsibility. It's better to send them out in case there are problems, in case the mother or baby is going to die. We don't want anyone to have big problems like that. I was getting really scared. It seemed like they were really trying to scare us.

They don't seem to want us to have the babies in the communities at all. Sometimes if the babies come out too early, they deliver them at the nursing station with no problem. Last year before Christmas, we had two of them delivered at the nursing station. One was scheduled to leave the next day, but she had the baby in the morning. She went home in a day. It must cost them a lot of money too—for air fare, and room and board.

One time we discussed the issue of many ladies having babies so young or getting abortions. We've been having abortions here in town, and we have had a couple of very young girls (12–13 years of age) who have babies. So we talked about this. The group would talk to the girls, and we would try to explain things and tell them they shouldn't have them while they are so young.

We invite anyone who would like to learn to make *kamiks* [boots], or who needs help in cutting caribou clothes, or duffle. It's usually the same group of ladies but we invite other women too. The ladies know that we meet every Saturday from one to four in the community hall, through the whole year except from July to September. The women bring their own materials and when they have skins, they bring their own.

We have some girls who come, not all the time, but they come all together once in a while. They start by learning to soften the caribou and sealskins. We can do the stretching outside, freeze the skins outside in the winter-time, freeze the caribou legs outside, and show them which way to cut the legs. We ask them to bring anything that they would like to learn, like caribou skins, or sealskins. That way they can learn to do their own clothing.

In the North you need those clothes. You'll freeze if you don't wear them. In December and January, people wear them. Right now we're mostly cleaning skins and sewing clothes, and we are also making dried fish.

I made a caribou parka for my son, Bruce. That's the first time I made a caribou parka. I couldn't believe it. I couldn't believe myself. I should have done it years before but I didn't. My mom wanted to do it; she thought I wouldn't do it as quickly, but I did. The ladies were really proud of me. I should have done that ten years ago. My mom, who's been sewing for a long time, wouldn't let me do it because she thought I was going to spoil it. I feel we shouldn't just leave it up to our mothers, we should do it ourselves, and teach our kids. If I show my daughter how to make *kamiks*, and if she spoils them, it's okay. Before they were afraid to spoil material or skins but even if she spoils it, but keeps trying, she'll learn. That's the only way she's going to learn.

We also just started, not too long ago, making waterproof *kamiks*. My mom kept telling me, "You're going to spoil it," but I really wanted to try it, so I did make a pair, and they turned out very well. They were waterproof. I wasn't trying hard enough I guess, because she kept telling me, "You're going to spoil it, you won't do it right." But I was really eager to do it and I did it very well.

You take the fur off the sealskin first. You have to dry it, then you have to chew it with your teeth, to make it really soft. I'm sewing it right now but I haven't finished it. I left it because I'm working on something else. You have to keep it frozen so it won't spoil.

I know many young girls are not learning anything at all about their culture, such as cleaning skins, or making clothes. But, I really enjoy doing that. We've been doing this and it's helping. I know its helping. I was the one who brought that up—learning to prepare skins exactly the same way as our grandparents did. My mother taught me to prepare skins this way so I taught them to do it the same way.

Women in Politics in the North: An Interview with Caroline Anawak

Karen Illnik

Women and Political Development

Caroline Anawak came to the North in May 1969. She originally settled in Rae–Edzo, after completing a development training program with the now-defunct Company of Young Canadians. Since that time, she has lived and worked throughout the Northwest Territories. She was interviewed at her home in Rankin Inlet where she lives with her husband and nine children.

KI: You have certainly known a lot of other women in the North that have been involved in politics. First of all, what set them apart from other women? What made them special? What kind of qualities did they bring to what they were doing? In particular, how did they break the traditional mould—the big dividing line between men and women which is very predominant in native cultures?

CA: I think that, for the most part, the women fall into two categories. Some women broke the mould by either choosing not to marry into their own culture, or going it alone and not marrying; or by separating from their husbands and eking out a life-style of their own. But in all cases, they were fighters, and they were able to articulate very clearly the problems that people have. They had vision, they had energy, and they were able to put forth the problems so that they were clear to people and government. I think those are the three areas and the three qualities that you'll find in most women who are leaders in the North.

KI: Could you describe the obstacles to women who want to get involved, or who are involved, in politics in the North?

CA: Oh, there are a number of things. First of all, I think that most of the time you are dealing with people who can't believe you're you. I think that attitude means that they can't believe that somebody can sit down, articulate clearly, and hang around long enough to have an impact on issues. I think the system in the North is used to people acting quite irregularly about something and then burning out. You have to be tireless in taking care of yourself, because no one else is going to.

As well, you are struggling with other factors. Economically, the prime consideration is trying to earn a living in the middle of all this other activity. You are struggling with your environment and climate, and balancing your family responsibilities with other commitments—how hard it is just to keep a family going and putting food on the table. You have a vision that forces you out of your house to do things because you believe in them so much. It's a high price to pay for being involved in politics, there are no two ways about it.

KI: What are the special strengths that women can bring to the political scene?

CA: Historically, I think women have suffered. They have held things together so often; in many cases, their menfolk have succumbed to pressures, so that they have had to do everything. Women have been put to the test so many times in their struggle for survival here—basic survival. They could call on these resources and the same strengths, and keep going in tough times when it looks like goals are about to be achieved. When it looks like the planning and the exercise of trying to get somewhere is going to take much longer, and others are giving up hope, usually you'll see women hang right in there. If struggling builds character, then, my God, we've all got character up here.

KI: For young women today, who are beginning perhaps, to be more politically aware, concerned about things that are going on in the North, and who want to get involved in the current issues, how different is it for them compared with your experiences when you arrived on the scene 20 years ago?

CA: To a certain extent, I think because some of these issues have been going on for so long, there is less homework in figuring out where things are at. I think that they don't necessarily have to struggle to show their interest, and I don't think they necessarily even have to have that same level of commitment. They just have to have a basic interest and a basic desire to help where it is needed.

I do think that there is a difference between those who have been around for a long time, and those who have come along in politics fairly recently. I'm not suggesting that their commitment is any less sincere, but I think that what the movement needs now are people who fully believe they can fight City Hall and win. You need people taking care of each other in the struggle. I think the need is just as strong now as ever. Because some of us have been out there a long, long time, every time a younger person shows an interest, we're delighted. Every time a younger person, regardless of age, burns with the same intensity, that is magic and that is special.

KI: How can a young person become involved? How do they break in?

CA: Well, we are trying our best through raising our own daughters, and by talking to kids in classes, even in elementary schools. We are trying to raise awareness that they can do something about issues that are important to them—that people can, and will, listen. We are encouraging young girls, especially, to take that step, to get involved, and to know that they have to arm themselves with an energy to get through those tough times. But we are now also seeing more of an interest in mutually supporting each other in the struggle.

KI: What should they do to prepare themselves? What routes should they take? What kinds of hats should they wear? What kind of education should they arm themselves with?

CA: I think the first thing is to tell people to stay in school. But, we must also tell them to ask questions—teach them how to ask the questions and how to stay with the question until you get your answers. Don't be put off by someone who cannot believe your intensity or your level of interest. Go for it. If you're angry, stay cool, we tell them. Cool, calculated anger enables you to very carefully look at the problem and articulate it. Hot anger is gone in a flash, and you really have worn out your welcome in the halls of government or wherever else you plan to make your case. Get out there. Talk with women. Start organizations. Read. Read newspapers. Listen to the territorial news. It is not boring—the issues are not somebody else's. So, we're saying, do your basic homework, and get together with people who are already involved in the same things. As young women, you should realize how special other women are, and do things just to show you know how special those other people are around you.

The women's movement can help women console each other in hard times, energize each other in tough times, and accomplish things in good times. It has to keep that foremost in its mind.

Future Politics
KI: What will be the biggest political issues in the near future?

CA: I think you will see land claims being an ongoing issue. We're really going to have to try and get it across to much of the leadership that there is a real danger as people place far too much hope on land claims making things better. It will be the individual communities or regional development corporations and what they do with the money, the power, the board recognition, the structure itself. They will make it work or not make it work. But we'll have to address the other issues that keep people strong.

We'll have to come up with an education system that really turns out winners, so that our kids are actually coming out with something in hand, because they are going to be competing more and more with people coming from the South, well-armed with educational diplomas, degrees, and certificates.

We're going to have to look at the native language issue, and somehow find a way to entrench it so that studying in their own language is not "optional" to the Inuit or Dene. This is particularly important in a system where you have to fight your way through an educational system for close to 12 years with those who do not understand or place the same emphasis on your language as your parents and grandparents have.

Also, I see a real need to strengthen our day care system so that people can access the training opportunities. If you cannot even get out the door in the morning, you cannot access these opportunities, despite press releases at the highest levels of this government about how there are aboriginal programs, permanent action programs, and training-for-management programs. I know if you are female and you cannot find a baby-sitter, you cannot get out the door. I feel so sad when I see young children pulled out of school to baby-sit in order that others in the family can hold a job just to feed the rest of the troops in the house. Yet, by necessity, someone has to be sacrificed to haul babies around on their back at the age of ten or 12. What are we proposing to do for those young, young women if we don't even get on with building a real day care system?

We should be building in the dollars for head-start programs, for adult literacy education, and for preventative health care. In the health care area alone, 85 per cent of the dollars are now directed toward treatment—that leaves less than 15 per cent toward preventative programs. We do not have the luxury here of a well-informed public that realizes that it is their own responsibility for their own good health. We do not have programs here that have worked in the South that have convinced people to become more involved in their own health and nutrition. We do not have programs that are available in every southern community on dental awareness, therapy, and dentistry. As a result, we have children walking around with no teeth in their head by the time they are 20; we have young people who wait in line for a year for glasses or for an eye check-up. This is totally unacceptable, and we have got to look at creating a health system that is both responsive and accessible. We don't have those things in the North. We don't have anything to fall back on. If you're losing your baby, it is a six-hour plane ride from Repulse Bay to the nearest hospital in Churchill, Manitoba. We don't have the ability to treat trauma within the first 40 minutes, in order to stabilize basic signs for a six-hour ride. Because of a lack of interpreters and lack of development of terminology in the Inuktitut language, we don't have the ability to explain to people some of the more complicated processes of treatment or the nature of the more serious diseases and their ramifications.

272

So, we're writing history up here in more ways than one by building in systems that fit people. We've got so far to go that all of these issues in the coming years will be first priority. If I was to identify one issue that will consume our time, it certainly has to be the economy. This issue begins with building an economy in the North, and not just maintaining our heavy dependence upon government. It necessitates looking at how to make things go forward in small communities, as well as on a regional basis; whether it is the wise plan of development corporations, or whether it is the small entrepreneurs in the small communities being funded and assisted to get into business, or whether it is on the territorial level with our leaders saying, "Where on earth is it we're going, and let's have a strategy to get there". I see lots of politicians, but very few statesmen who know how to sit down and come up with an economic blueprint.

What it calls for is vision, and I see lots of talkers but very few people with vision. And with vision I see that all this must come in "stage one" of political development for us to grow and develop. I see little of it at the territorial level or at the regional level, and that will be a major, major issue to turn our attention to in the next ten years.

KI: My final question is, are you as committed today as you were 20 years ago?

CA: Just as committed.

APPENDICES

Appendix I

This appendix provides a statistical overview of the Northwest Territories documenting, in chart form, data covering:
  a) population by ethnicity;
  b) population by gender and age;
  c) population and birth rate by ethnicity;
  d) live births by age of mother; and
  e) education by highest level achieved.

The statistical data used to formulate the charts were provided by the Women's Secretariat of the Government of the Northwest Territories from the following sources:

1981 Census (GNWT Bureau of Statistics)
1986 Census (GNWT Bureau of Statistics)
(ethnic breakdowns not yet available)
Report on Health Conditions in the NWT, 1986, Medical Services Branch
Various Statistics, Indian and Northern Affairs Canada, Yellowknife
Various Statistics, GNWT Department of Municipal and Community Affairs
Various Statistics, GNWT Women's Secretariat

The charts were prepared by Duncan Noble and Mary Crnkovich.

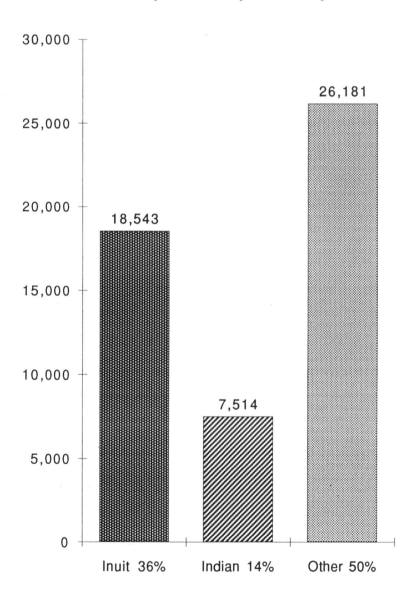

Population by Ethnicity

Inuit 36%	18,543
Indian 14%	7,514
Other 50%	26,181

Population by Gender and Age

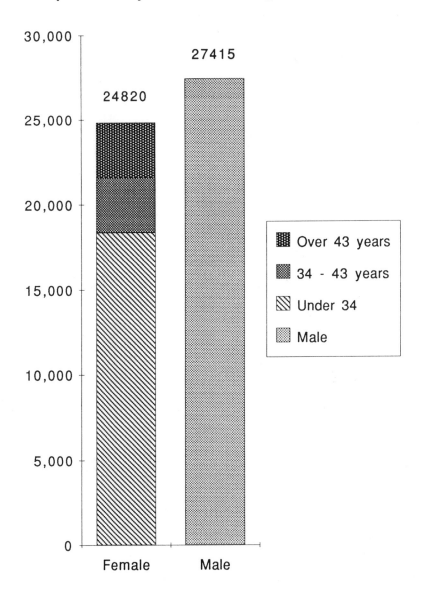

Population and Birth Rate by Ethnicity

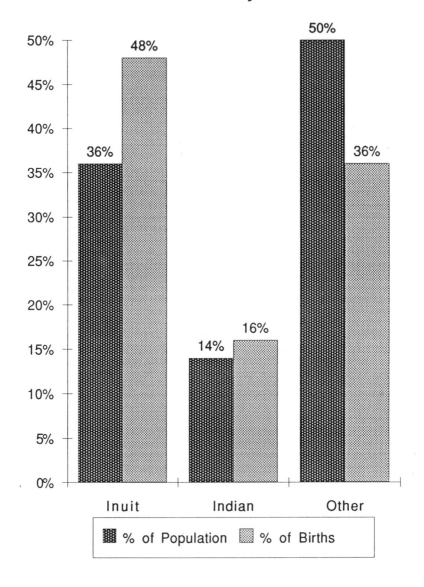

Live Births by Age of Mother

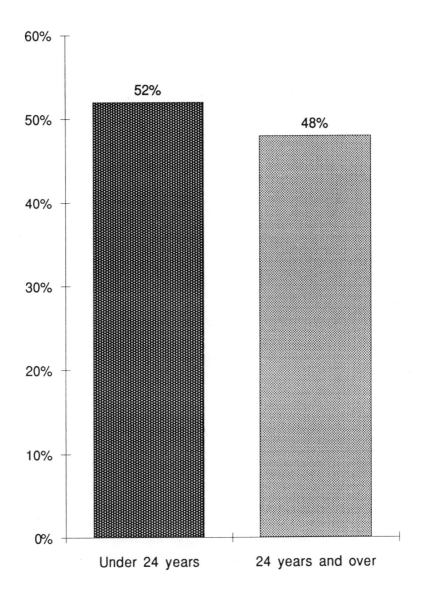

Education by Highest Level Achieved

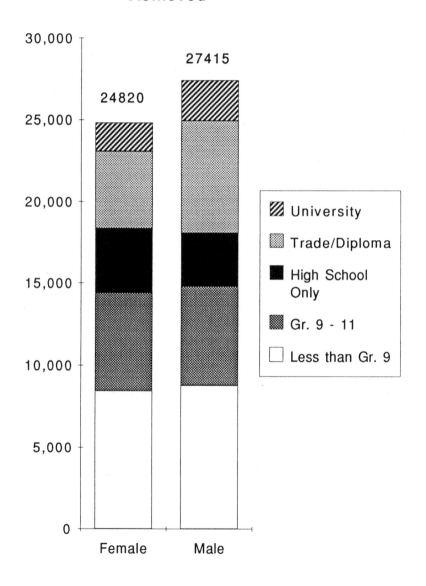

Appendix II

Notes on Contributors

Barbara Adam-MacLellan
Barbara lives with her husband, David, and two young children, Shari Lynn and Eric in Whitehorse, Yukon. Barbara was actively involved with the Yukon Literacy Council as a board member and instructor. She is now working in the home and divides her time between caring for four young children (her own and two others), and managing her extensive volunteer obligations. In her "spare time" she likes to write children's stories.

Caroline Anawak
Caroline is originally from Toronto, Ontario. She came to Rae–Edzo, Northwest Territories (N.W.T.) in May 1969, after completing community development training with the now-defunct Company of Young Canadians. She has lived and worked in various N.W.T. communities and has held many elected, appointed, and volunteer positions. She now lives in Rankin Inlet with her husband and nine children. Her main interests are psychology and law.

Angela Bernal
Angela travelled with her partner, Joseph, and their child, Sara, across the N.W.T. in the summer of 1988. During their journey Angela met and spoke with many women. The transcripts of the conversations shared are the basis of several stories contained in this book. Angela is an anthropologist who was born and raised in Bogota, Colombia. She has lived in Ottawa for two years. She describes her northern journey as a beautiful experience and an encounter between two very different cultures. She spoke with other mothers about their lives and their families in conditions very different from Colombia. She and her family, including their new-born son, Julian, are now living in Ottawa.

Janet Mancini Billson

Janet is a native of Ontario and was educated through high school in Vancouver, B.C. She received her Ph.D. from Brandeis University, Boston, and now lives in Providence, Rhode Island, where she is Professor of Sociology and Women's Studies at Rhode Island College; she also has a private practice facilitating support groups for women. For the past two years, Janet has devoted her time and energies to interviewing women from various cultural groups in Canada (Inuit, Blood, Iroquois, Mennonite, Chinese, Scottish, West Indian, French-Canadian, and Ukrainian) in preparation for a book on changing gender roles and special problems of women in the Canadian multicultural landscape.

Lynn Brooks

Lynn is a founding member and chairperson of the Society against Family Abuse, and a member of the Ministerial Advisory Committee on Spousal Assault. She has been, and continues to be, an active advocate of quality child care. She was a founding member of the N.W.T. Child Care Association and, in 1982, became Director of Children's Services for the YWCA. She co-ordinated the development of voluntary child care standards for the N.W.T. in 1983–84 and was the first territorial member of the Canadian Day Care Advocacy Association. She married Bob Brooks in 1985 and lives with him and her daughter, Maggie, and two foster daughters, Shelly and Annie, in Yellowknife. Her oldest daughter, Shannon, and granddaughter, Krystal, live in Calgary.

Brenda Canitz

Brenda was born and raised on a farm in southern Saskatchewan, and studied nursing at the University of Saskatchewan in Saskatoon. Most of her professional work has been in nursing stations in the Northwest Territories. At present, she is a graduate student in Behavioural Science and Community Health at the University of Toronto. Her general interest revolves around issues of rural and northern health care. She is currently working on research for a Master's thesis, entitled "A Study of Isolated Post Nursing".

Anne Crawford

Anne lives in Apex, N.W.T. along with a skidoo; a husband; a four-wheel drive truck; various brothers and sisters, in and out of law; neighbours; mobs of kids; and packs of dogs. Most insist they really are trying to help her build her house. In past years, she has lived in Yellowknife, where she was general counsel to the Métis Association of the N.W.T. and spent time working in the fields of land claims and constitutional development. She also ran a criminal legal-aid practice in Dogrib communities. More recently, in the eastern Arctic, she ran a law practice, was elected to the local education council, taught at Arctic College, and finally succumbed to the siren song of government by accepting her current position as Regional Superintendent of Justice for the Baffin Region.

284

Mary Crnkovich

Mary is a feminist researcher interested in women's issues, northern political development, and labour law. She now lives in Ottawa where she hopes to combine feminism with the practice of law; failing that, she has decided she would like to build houses for the rest of her life. Mary's life before *Gossip* included working with the Inuit Tapirisat of Canada, Nunavut Land Claims Project, and Tungavik Federation of Nunavut as a researcher and negotiator for the Nunavut land claim. She recently completed articles with Sack, Goldblatt, Mitchell, a Toronto firm specializing in union-side labour law.

Betty Ann Daviss-Putt

Betty Ann has been a practising midwife for 14 years and a consultant to the Inuit Women's Association since 1985. Her training and experience was initiated with the traditional midwives of Central America, and continued in the United States and in the Netherlands, where she completed an observer internship. She is on the board of the Midwives Alliance of North America and has recently formed Midwives Alliance for Traditional Exchange and Research. She is now in the process of writing a book on traditional midwives. Her article in this book is an abridgement of a chapter of this upcoming publication. She is now in private practice in the Ottawa–Hull region.

Debby Dobson

Debby was born in Moncton, New Brunswick in March 1953. She is a single parent with one daughter. She has been a Yellowknife resident for approximately ten years. She obtained a B.A. from Dalhousie University, Halifax; a B.Ed. from the University of Toronto, and a M.A. from the University of Sheffield in England. Her most persistent hobbies are writing short stories (one published in *Grain*) and humorous pieces for CBC radio in Yellowknife. Debby spent five years teaching English in Yellowknife and, for the past four years, has been the Secondary English Language Arts Consultant for the territorial government.

Helen Fallding

Helen grew up in southern Ontario and first escaped to the Yukon in 1980. Officially trained as a wildlife biologist, she is an activist at heart and has channelled her energies into battles for environmental, feminist, gay, and native rights. She is currently a land claims researcher with the Carcross/Tagish Indian band. Her latest volunteer project is developing non-native solidarity with the aboriginal rights movement and planning a Yukon Gay Pride Day. She notes that her partner, Lisa, keeps her "sane and warm on those long winter nights".

Toni Graeme

Toni is living in Victoria, B.C. She spent a decade in the North, from 1978 to 1988. She began in Whitehorse, Yukon, as a part-time waitress/part-time resource person for the Whitehorse Status of Women. In 1984, she became Executive Director of the Women's Secretariat of the Government of the Northwest Territories. When she left her position with the Women's Secretariat in 1988, she did not leave her interests and commitments in the North behind. She continues to volunteer with Project North and is the Chair of the Fundraising Committee of Project North's group in Victoria. She also writes a monthly article for *Nunatsiaq News* called "A Course of Action". In the last federal election, she was the campaign manager for NDP candidate, Peter Kusugak, in the federal riding of Nunatsiaq. In Victoria, Toni has her own business, *Tiara Promotions*. Her work involves fundraising, promoting, and organizing *anything and everything*. She specializes in dealing with artists, holistic health practitioners, and art gallery operators.

Alice Hill
Alice was born in the bush on the north shore of Great Bear Lake, close to Cameron Bay. She was raised in the traditional Dene culture until attending mission school at four years of age. Following her schooling in residential schools, she went to work at The Bay. Since that time, she has worked for the federal Department of Indian Affairs and Northern Development and the territorial government. After more than 15 years of working in government at both the territorial and federal levels, she joined the Native Women's Association of the N.W.T. in January 1988. As executive director, her primary mandate is to ensure that the association is meeting the needs of women at the community level and developing programs to deal with child sexual abuse, family violence, and substance abuse. Other activities include lobbying the territorial government to have native languages declared official languages of the territorial government and legislative assembly; and acting as liaison between the government and communities on the child sexual abuse project. This latter initiative requires extensive lobbying and communications with all levels of government; however, it is not something she regards as an endless struggle.

Karen Illnik
Karen has lived in the North since 1978. For seven of those years she has lived in the Keewatin region. She is married and has three children. They live in Arviat (Eskimo Point), N.W.T. Currently, Karen is a freelance writer for *Nunatsiaq News*. She is also the instructor–facilitator for the women's course at Arctic College, which is being conducted in Arviat.

Kate Irving
Kate came to the North in 1980. Her current position, as Acting Director of the Women's Secretariat of the GNWT, reflects her commitment to women's issues. In addition to this, she has been actively involved in the New Democratic Party at both the federal and territorial levels. She currently serves as a board member with Yellowknife Day Care.

JoAnn Lowell

JoAnn is an architect, urban planner, and researcher whose involvement with issues such as childbirth and child welfare began as a result of her Master's degree in architecture, which examines the place of birth and alternative birthing centres. She currently lives in Yellowknife with her partner, Wayne, and her young daughter, Aysia. She has several projects underway, including anthropological research, publication of her articles and artwork, and design of a house for a native family. In addition, JoAnn has been actively involved with a group of women planning a women's centre, coffeehouse, and bookstore in Yellowknife.

Marianne Lykke Thomsen

Currently, Marianne is completing her Master's thesis for the Institute for Eskimology, University of Copenhagen. Since 1983, she has visited Canada a number of times to conduct field studies on the conditions of Inuit women. In 1986 she spent a year in Canada studying at the Centre for Northern Studies and Research at McGill University. When not travelling, she lives in Nuuk, Greenland, where she is also completing follow-up studies on the political situation of Greenlandic women.

Suzanne Manomie

Suzanne was born in British Colombia and has lived throughout Canada. She graduated from the Anglican Women's Training College in Toronto and, after working for a year as the Director of Christian Education at a church in Vancouver, was hired as a secretary at St Luke's Hospital in Pangnirtung, which at the time was run by the church. Her husband, the famous carver, Enook Manomie, was a convalescent TB patient for several months in Pangnirtung. The couple fell in love and were married in July 1971. Over the years Suzanne and Enook have adopted six children by customary adoption. In addition to looking after her home and family, Suzanne has been doing some freelance writing while Enook divides his time between hunting and carving.

Phoebe Nahanni

Phoebe is a Slavey-speaking Dene woman from Fort Simpson, N.W.T. She was educated in the North, and completed her B.A. at the University of Western Ontario. She spent a number of years working with the Dene Nation and Dene–Métis Secretariat, primarily focusing on land claims issues and political development. Prior to this, she worked for the National Indian Brotherhood (Assembly of First Nations) as the research director and reference librarian. She has lived in Montreal for the past seven years with her husband and three children. She is currently completing her Master's degree in Geography from McGill University.

Lesley Paulette

Lesley is a childbirth resource consultant. She was the project co-ordinator for the Family Centred Maternity Care Project of the Native Women's Association of the NWT. She lives in Fitzgerald (close to Fort Smith, N.W.T.) where she is virtually unreachable by phone. Her article was provided by Alice Hill, Executive Director of the Association.

Maata Pudlat

Maata was born in a camp about four or five miles from Cape Dorset, N.W.T. Since 1982, she has worked as a classroom assistant at the local school. She has four children, ranging in age from three to 16. Whenever Maata gets the chance, she likes to spend her time out on the land pursuing her greatest pastime, fishing. In addition to having a good sense of humour, Maata says she likes to be very open and forward because she thinks it is important in telling her story.

Susan Sammons

Susan has taught in the eastern Arctic since 1977. She was Program Consultant to the Department of Education, GNWT, Keewatin Region, from 1985 to 1986. Following this, she served as Director of the Baffin Region Agvvik Society from 1986 to 1987, and as an instructor in Communications at Arctic College in Iqaluit, N.W.T., where she lives with her husband and one son Nanaiq. She holds Ph.D. and M.A. degrees in Linguistics from the University of Michigan, a B.A. in English/Political Science from the University of Winnipeg, and a Diploma in Education from McGill University.

Marianne Stenbaek

Marianne Stenbaek is the Director of the Centre for Northern Studies and Research at McGill University in Montreal and President of the Association of Canadian Universities for Northern Studies (ACUNS). She has worked closely with the Inuit Circumpolar Conference in developing its Arctic Policy and has spearheaded efforts to establish research links with universities in the Soviet Union and throughout the circumpolar world. She holds a Ph.D. in English Literature from the Université de Montreal and is a specialist in northern communications issues.

Agnes Sutherland

Sister Sutherland was born in Fort Chipewyan, Alberta, in 1926. After obtaining her Bachelor of Education from the University of Alberta and her Master's in Religious Education from Spokane, she trained as a Grey Nun in Alberta. She taught junior and senior high school in Fort McMurray, Alberta and Fort Smith, N.W.T., and was the principal of St John's Separate School, Fort McMurray. In 1984, she was awarded Citizen of the Year in Fort Smith in recognition of her contribution and commitment to providing safe shelters for abused women; appropriately, the first transition house was called Sutherland House. Her other volunteer projects include the Youth Fine Options Program; the Youth Justice

Program; teaching English to Polish immigrants; and serving as a board member of the Friendship Centre, Uncle Gabe's. She is currently completing interviews and research for two books on Bishop Paul Piché and the contribution of missionaries, especially women, to the people of the North in education, nursing, and social services.

Sarah Tokolik

Sarah was born in Spence Bay where she continues to live with her husband, Iola, and their children, Bruce, Sally, and Isabel. For many years Sarah has worked at the local school as a classroom assistant. She is actively involved in the community women's group. At the time of her interview she was struggling to ensure that her language and culture would be preserved in the school curriculum. At last word, Sarah had been successful in the debate surrounding language policy, and she is now teaching in Inuktitut to senior classes.

Mary Ellen Thomas

Mary Ellen came to Pangnirtung in 1978 to work as an adult educator after spending many years working on Indian reserves in northern Saskatchewan. In 1982, she moved to Iqaluit where she continued to work as an adult educator. Her first daughter was born in 1985, and a second in 1988. Mary Ellen is expecting a third child in June 1990. In the meantime, she has continued to do "the work I love" and is following her dreams. Unlike many who came North, she says she has not been in a "holding pattern". She has been living her life "to the fullest", exploring the possibilities and achieving new goals.

Jodi Whyte

Jodi is an independent consultant whose work focuses on family violence. She is the founder of the Hay River Women's Group and Women's Resource Centre, and is publisher of *Women's Press*, a monthly newspaper distributed throughout the N.W.T. In her "spare time", she serves as Vice-President of the N.W.T. National Action Committee (NAC) on the Status of Women, and is chair of the NAC's national educational and trust fund. She has lived in Hay River for the past ten years.

HQ 1453 G68 1990

Gossip : a spoken history
of women in the North

HQ 1453 G68 1990

Gossip : a spoken history
of women in the North

DATE DUE

NOV 0 1 1994			
OCT 2 1 1996			
OCT 1 6 1996			
MAR 2 1 2000			
MAR 2 3 2001			
JAN 1 5 2002			
FEB 1 3 2002			
APR 1 5 2004			
APR 2 2004			
APR 1 8 2006			
261-2500		Printed in USA	